TRAVELS OF BOLLYWOOD CINEMA

TRAVELS OF BOLLYWOOD CINEMA

From Bombay to LA

edited by

Anjali Gera Roy
Chua Beng Huat

OXFORD
UNIVERSITY PRESS

OXFORD
UNIVERSITY PRESS

Oxford University Press is a department of the University of Oxford.
It furthers the University's objective of excellence in research, scholarship,
and education by publishing worldwide. Oxford is a registered trademark of
Oxford University Press in the UK and in certain other countries

Published in India by
Oxford University Press
YMCA Library Building, 1 Jai Singh Road, New Delhi 110 001, India

© Oxford University Press 2012

The moral rights of the author have been asserted

First Edition published in 2012

ISBN-13: 978-0-19-807598-1
ISBN-10: 0-19-807598-7

Typeset in 10.5/13 Adobe Garamond Pro
by Excellent Laser Typesetters, Pitampura, Delhi 110 034
Printed in India at Artxel, New Delhi 110 020

Contents

Acknowledgements

This book is an outcome of a workshop on the same topic held at the Asia Research Institute (ARI), National University of Singapore (NUS) in February 2009. The majority of papers included in the volume were presented at the ARI Workshop. But additional papers were solicited to cover regions unrepresented in the workshop to make the volume as representative as possible.

We would like to thank the ARI for awarding us a generous grant for holding the workshop. In particular, we would like to thank Professor Lily Kong, the then director of ARI, who extended us her wholehearted support in this endeavour as in all others. We would also like to extend a very special thanks to Professor Edwin Thumboo who graciously agreed to open the workshop. We appreciate the contributions of members of the Cultural Studies Cluster, Charles Leary and Liew Kai Khiun, in particular, and of the faculty of the South Asian Studies Programme and the Department of English at NUS. We also need to convey our thanks to presenters who travelled from different parts of the world to present their papers at the workshop and to those who sent their papers later for the volume. Thanks are also due to Deepak Kumaran Menon for a special screening of his film *Chemman Chaalai* (The Gravel Road) and to the panelists at the panel discussion that included Deepak Kumaran Menon, Suhail Abbasi, Irene Nexica, Rajendra Gour, and Mohamad Ali. Finally, we acknowledge the support of the director of the National Library of Singapore for making room for the panel discussion and an exhibition on Indian cinema in the National Library at Esplanade.

But most of all we would like to thank the administrative staff at ARI who put themselves out to make sure that everything went perfectly.

Thanks Valerie for smiling through every major and minor disaster; Alison for staying back on your birthday to help out; Sharon for your gentle presence; and Henry for the all round support.

Finally, we would like to thank the anonymous reviewers and, in particular, the editorial team at Oxford University Press for helping and offering us unstinting assistance in completing this project.

The Bollywood Turn in South Asian Cinema

National, Transnational, or Global?

ANJALI GERA ROY AND CHUA BENG HUAT

Bollywood, Tollywood, Kollywood

Bollywood, a portmanteau of Bombay and Hollywood, coined by the English language media in India to define 'India's popular film industry based in Mumbai—a blend of Bombay (Mumbai was earlier known as Bombay) and Hollywood', has been almost universally adopted as a convenient label to refer to films produced by filmmakers from the Indian subcontinent, despite the industry's vociferous objections to the use of the term to describe a cinema that evolved independent of and is 'supremely' indifferent to the American popular film.[1] The shadow of Hollywood has undeniably loomed large over Bollywood as the original benchmark and competition since the silent era. But the name 'Bollywood' not only reinforces Hollywood's continuing dominance in the global cultural space, but also conceals the hegemonizing hold of Hindi commercial cinema, produced in Mumbai, over other production centres in Chennai, Kolkata, and Hyderabad which are as old, if not as big, as Mumbai. Film scholars have expressed their concern

over the indiscriminate use of the term that dissolves the differences
between art house and commercial; regional, national, and diasporic; the
National Film Development Corporation (NFDC) film and the *masala*[2]
film (Rajadhyaksha 2003; Prasad 2003). In the ultimate analysis, the fine
calibrations through which distinctions between different kinds of films
are made by film theorists and critics of cinema become redundant in
the perception of the consumers of these films, raising important questions about the conceptualization of national cinemas. The boundaries
between mainstream Hindi filmmakers, who according to Derek Bose,
'intelligently *design* films that are viable both locally and internationally',
and the diaspora films of Gurinder Chadha, Deepa Mehta, or Mira Nair,
'with an Indian soul in a foreign body' appear to be increasingly blurred
(Bose 2006: 13). If Bollywood can be viewed as 'a space unto itself,
a *pure* space so to say' (Ray 2001: 136–84), waiting to be appropriated from Australia and Japan to Ethiopia, even British director Danny
Boyle's Oscar winning *Slumdog Millionaire* (2009) could legitimately
qualify as a Bollywood film.

This book seeks to examine the historical and spatial flows of
Indian popular cinema from Bombay (Mumbai) and other production
centres in the Indian subcontinent to different spaces of consumption
for nearly a century, culminating in the Bollywood-inspired-Oscar-
winning film *Slumdog Millionaire*. Bollywood's crossovers in the new
millennium, while bringing in greater visibility in the global north, have
also raised anxieties about the appropriation of 'resistant' local cultures
by the global culture industry. Arguing that the global consumer's
enthusiastic 'discovery' of Bollywood's pleasures in the mid-1990s erases
nearly a century-long history of Indian cinematic travels to British
Malaya, Fiji, Guyana, Trinidad, Mauritius, East and South Africa with
the old diasporas, and with and without the new diasporas to the former
USSR, Middle East, the UK, the US, Canada, and Australia, this volume
brings together essays by new and established scholars in anthropology,
history, literary, cultural, media, communication, and film studies to
show that Indian cinema has always crossed borders and boundaries.
Through tracing its multidirectional flows before and in the present
global process, this book also seeks to unpack the relationship of the
global culture industry to nation states, global capitalist networks, and
transnational formations to rethink the nation as a category.

Origins and Travels of Bollywood Cinema

Historians of cinema have produced evidence to convincingly demonstrate that Hollywood did not ever pose a serious threat to the producers of Indian cinema in the domestic market (Chowdhry 2000; Bose 2006). Notwithstanding allegations of unoriginality, plagiarism, and technical rawness, new findings by Vijay Mishra, Manas Ray, Brian Larkin, and others also confirm that it was the disavowed Hindi masala film, which interrogated Hollywood's planetary dominance throughout the twentieth century and has emerged as a sole contender to Hollywood in its global reach in the new millennium (Mishra 2002; Ray 2001: 136–84; Larkin 1997: 46–62, 2002: 739–62). However, whether Bollywood will take over Hollywood in the future, as a euphoric Indian media, intoxicated by the box-office ratings of Bollywood blockbusters like *Singh is Kinng* (2008) and *Ghajini* (2009) or the critical acclaim of Bollywood-based films prophesies, is another question in view of its paltry 2 per cent global market share.[3] Almost a decade ago, Rajadhyaksha had sounded a sobering note by pointing out the problems of confusing Bollywood with Indian cinema and the dangers of indulging in the kind of cultural nationalism that implicates us in a global culture industry, which appropriates an ensemble of Indian popular cultural forms for Western voyeuristic pleasures (2003). Following Rajadhyaksha's cautionary reminder, the claims of Bollywood to being a global culture, despite its ubiquity since he published his essay, need to be assessed more rationally than through uncritical cheerleading. We need to deliberate on a number of questions such as: has Bollywood really invaded the global popular space as the Indian media claims or is it still locked up in South Asian ghettos in global cities? Derek Bose responds to those who dismiss Bollywood going global as being 'just a lot of hype and hope' by taking an objective look at the exciting possibilities of looking at the bigger picture of Bollywood emerging as a major global brand in the future, which has been confirmed by the branding of *Slumdog Millionaire* as Bolly-wood (2006). Similarly, Haseenah Ebrahim, in her ethnographic study of Bollywood's visibility in mainstream cinema halls in South Africa, produces data to prove that Bollywood has indeed moved from the ghetto to the mainstream (2008: 63–76). However, in New York City, as in other global cities, Bollywood films are screened only in a few dilapidated theatres in neighbourhoods with strong South Asian concentration and frequented by disparate diasporic groups from the subcontinent.

Where does Bollywood originate and in which directions does it flow? How do Bollywood's travels in the new global process differ from those of popular Hindi or Tamil films in the past? Do Bollywood's travels still follow the old trade and migration routes from South and South-east Asia across the Middle East to Africa, or does it circulate across new superhighways to Europe, North and South America, Canada, and Australia in addition to the new electronic media in a blink? Is Bollywood global, transnational, national, or regional? Finally, what is global culture, if there be any, how does it relate to the local, and can Bollywood be considered a culture of globalization? A distinction must be made between colonial productions and exchanges of the 1930s, international flows of the Raj Kapoor, M.G. Ramachandran, or Satyajit Ray films in the 1950s and 1960s, the Rajesh Khanna and Amitabh Bachchan starrers of the 1970s and 1980s, and the cultural economy of circulation in which the Karan Johar, Mani Ratnam, or Sanjay Leela Bhansali films have been travelling in the mediascapes produced after the mid-1990s.

How serious are the claims to Indian cinema's globalization? Does the presence of a few 'alternative' whites, usually academics, old hippies, or new converts to 'Asian Kool', signify the mainstreaming of Indian cinema? While Hindi films have always been a prime example of 'identification in disidentification', with Hindi films and filmstars conquering the hearts of even enemy dictators, the new forms of identification produced by Bollywood may be ascribed to cultural difference rather than cultural proximity. If a former Pakistani prime minister's serenading a Mumbai film star's pretty sister with an old Hindi film melody that raised many eyebrows in the 1980s is the function of proximity, a British-Australian pre-teen reciting the lyrics of '*Jind Mahi*' is the consequence of exoticization. While the 'Bollyliterate' honourable head of state was following established sub-continental courtship conventions, audiences of *Slumdog Millionaire*, 'whether lured by exoticism or curiosity', have been introduced to India within the stereotyped conventions of Hollywood.[4]

Limits of the National Cinema

Discussions of Indian cinema in the popular media and the academia emerging in the 1980s have been largely framed under the rubric of national cinema while problematizing notions of the national in engaging a cross-border text, and the growing interest, particularly in the South Asian diaspora, in its transnational or global flows. Formal studies of Indian cinema, which borrowed the frame of national cinema to elucidate a cultural artefact with subcontinental antecedents, attempted to resolve the problem by defining their temporal or spatial coordinates and by tidying up its pre-national history in the service of Indian nationalistic discourse (Rajadhyaksha 1999; Chakravarty 1996; Vasudevan 2000). These studies offer extremely sophisticated analyses of Indian films, employing the Gellnerian and Andersonian theories of the nation to investigate the extent to which Indian cinematic texts are complicit in the imagining of the national community before and after Independence. At their most effective, they explore tensions within national cinematic texts by engaging with the co-option of Hindi cinema in the ideological discourse of nationalism and the occlusions and erasures of the nationalist project. They retain the category largely to problematize the idea of the nation through focusing on contestations around its meanings, using films as the locus of debates over the history, aspirations, and meanings of the nation to a diverse group of subjects. In the process of critiquing the formation of the nation through the erasure of gender, caste, and regional and sectarian differences in what Chidananda Dasgupta had defined as the 'All-India film' (1968), these studies initiate a rethinking on the nation. However, Manas Ray contends that the globality of such a concept, such as 'Indian' needs be contested and highlights the fact that for Indians (both inside India and outside) such 'Indianness'—as 'a matter of *positioning* and not essence' varies 'with different communities, is used at times for contradictory purposes and quite often gives rise to unintended consequences' (2001).

The rubric of national cinema, under which Indian cinema has been examined, is problematized by the transnationalized production, distribution, and consumption of South Asian cinematic texts in the present and its failure to account for cinematic flows including:

- cross-border movements;
- diasporic flows and contra flows;
- subnational disjunctures that are frequently and increasingly transnational;
- movements to the West and non-West.[5]

CROSS-BORDER MOVEMENTS

The notion of a homogenized, unified, and coherent national cinema can be entertained only through the amnesiac erasure of the hoary legends of Al-Hind and Tamil Eelam that were suppressed under the myth of the Indian nation. The concept of national cinema on the Indian subcontinent requires the overwriting of both undivided memories and post-modern geographies with national histories, which reveal the gaps and erasures necessitated by the appropriation of particular memories and myths in the construction of national identities. However, as the history of the subcontinent imbricates the origins of Indian cinema with those of Pakistan and Bangladesh, the conception of national cinema as a seamless continuity that embraces the concerns and totality of the Indian, Pakistani, or Bangladeshi nations is extremely reductive. The cross-border migration of directorial, lyrical, musical, and acting talent between Lahore and Mumbai, from the 1930s to the present, hints at an umbilical cord connecting the twin cultural capitals more than sixty years after the violent birth of the two nation states. If the failure of the nascent Lahore film industry to emerge as a strong contender to Mumbai is to be attributed as much to the rupture in the Hindi/Urdu cultural memory as to Islamic fundamentalism, Dhaka had to wait for several decades before evolving its version of the Muslim social that could be back-translated in the caste hierarchies of a Hindu West Bengal.

The difference in perception of pre-Independence Mumbai film-makers with post-Independence filmmakers in Kolkata or Chennai is an education in the implication of cultural artefacts in the production of different forms of nationalisms and nation states. In contrast to the films produced after Independence, the films of the 1930s and 1940s, even in Bengali, Marathi, or Tamil, exhibit a multi-ethnic, if not multi-national collaboration and the disengagement of space with language. The internationalism of the pioneers of Indian cinema is epitomized by the original *Devdas* (1936)—a bilingual Bengali/Hindi film produced in Kolkata by a Bengali director starring a Punjabi singer-actor whose untimely death, Vijay Mishra informs us, was mourned in faraway Fiji. Similarly, *Achhoot Kanya* (1936) was designed as a cross-cultural product by a Lahore-based Gujarati financier, who invited a British-educated Bengali producer to collaborate with a German director in a film starring a Eurasian actor. It is now common knowledge that the inspiration for the first silent film *Raja Harishchandra* (1913) came to Dada Saheb Phalke, considered as the father of Indian cinema, after his viewing of *The Life of Christ* (1911). Considering that the history of cinema in India began due to the happy accident of the first screening held at the Watson Hotel in Mumbai in 1896, a year after cinema was born, Indian cinema cannot be placed in a time-space discontinuum with European cinemas like other Third World cinemas. Despite the distribution of production centres in Kolkata, Mumbai, Chennai, and Lahore, films in the colonial era exhibit not only the contamination of *swadeshi* (indigenous) with *pardesi* (alien), but also unusual collaborations between producers, directors, actors, and screenwriters from diverse socioeconomic and linguistic groups that produced the eclectic, autotelic space of Hindi cinema, which Mumbai scriptwriter and lyricist Javed Akhtar described as a different state in an interview (2005). It is more pertinent to inquire how texts of the pre-Independence era, produced through the cross-linguistic, cross-regional, and cross-sectarian collaborations, were appropriated in the construction of the nation and a national cinema. To what extent do these national cinemas constitute postcolonial responses to Empire cinema and how were they produced in conjunction with other national cinemas?

DIASPORIC DESIRES

Vijay Mishra marks a shift in the formal study of Hindi films, extending the imagined community of the nation beyond the borders of the nation state by throwing light on the mediation of the myths of the homeland among the Indian diaspora in Fiji using the visual medium of the film through which the diasporic community was inserted in the nation (2002). Without contesting the formation of a pan-Indian identity through the medium of the Hindi film, Mishra compels a re-thinking on the idea of the nation that is disengaged from territory, echoing Salman Rushdie's deconstruction of the attachment of nation to spatiality in the 1980s. Mishra's assertions about the role of Indian cinema in Indian diasporic identity construction are supported by Ray (2001: 136–84), Velayutham and Devadas (2008), and Ebrahim's (2008) accounts from other places of Indian settlement where Hindi films remained the South Asian migrants' sole link with the homeland in the absence of communication networks. Mishra's incorporation of the diasporic viewer and critic in the cultural economy of Mumbai cinema has set a new direction to South Asian film studies with an increasing number of second- and third-generation British, American, Canadian, and Australian scholars of Indian origin stepping in to fill the lacunae in the India-centric approach to the study of Indian cinema. The academic recognition of the media-invented name for Indian popular film by the title of Mishra's book has made it enter South Asian cinematic vocabulary, particularly in the work of diaspora scholars in which 'Bolly' becomes a convenient prefix for the synchronic and diachronic difference of the 1990s' films from those discussed in earlier studies, including Mishra's own book that concludes with a chapter on the diaspora film. Raminder Kaur's enthusiastic heralding of a 'Bollyworld' in which she locates the new Hindi films makes a strong case for the transnational circulation of popular cultural products among the South Asian diasporas across the world (2005: 309–29). Kaur and Sinha's neologism, Bollyworld, 'to refer to Indian cinema through a transnational lens, at once located in the nation, but also out of the nation in its provenance, orientation, and outreach' (2005) fits the perspective of many of the new works. Rajinder Dudrah (2006) looks at Bollywood film-viewing practices from the perspective of South Asians in UK; Shakuntala Banaji (2006) adopts a comparative perspective to examine Bollywood audience in India and UK; and Jigna Desai (2004) and Tejaswini Ganti (2004) engage with the North American reception of Indian films (Banaji 2006). Another interesting development in South Asian film studies is the examination of the diaspora films and their relationship with mainstream Bollywood cinema (Desai 2004).

SUBNATIONAL TERRAINS

The debates over the nation state grew increasingly intense in the early 1990s following the release of a bilingual film in Hindi and Tamil called *Roja* made by a Mumbai-based filmmaker who inserted the region into the nation and interrogated the boundaries of the nation from the perspective of region, gender, and religion (Niranjana 1994: 1299; Vasudevan 2000). These films and the debates surrounding them not only called attention to the hegemonizing Hindi narrative that elides regional cultural expressions, but also paved the way for sustained explorations of the representations of regional, ethnic, religious, gender, caste, and sexual others in Hindi cinema through which the Hindi/Hindu citizen subject has been normalized. While these studies reflected and contributed to a trend in 1980s film studies that worked with the concept of national cinema, despite the political and economic global transformations that came at the end of the 1980s raising apprehensions about the future of the nation state, their engagement with the conflicts and tensions within the nation inspired the articulation of subnational resistance and transnational revisions in the following decade.

If diasporic scholars have ushered in a new phase in the study of Hindi cinema by framing South Asian cinema within a transnational lens, the inclusion of film studies in south Indian languages in definitive texts on Indian cinema reflects a new thinking within India in which gestures such as these call to attention the Hindi film's textual, discursive, and economic hegemony over the rest of the Indian languages that is mirrored in academic discourse. These differ in their methodical approach and ideological thrust from earlier examinations of non-Hindi cinemas, primarily Bengali, that are inscribed with a different cultural politics in which the Bengali films of Ritwik Ghatak or Satyajit Ray are viewed as providing the template for a meta-discourse on Indian cinema. The essays on Tamil cinema included in Ravi Vasudevan's *Making Meaning in Indian Cinema*, the work of S.V. Srinivas (2000) on Telugu fan cultures, and Sara Dickey's (2000) on MGR films have made way for a book-length work on Tamil cinema edited by Selvaraj Velayutham (2008) that scrutinizes the cultural politics of India's 'other film industry'. Velayutham's book makes a modest beginning in removing the South Asian film from the Hindi, Tamil, or north Indian-south Indian dialectic to an emerging transnational Tamil formation that reverberates with the concerns of the Tamil nation across India, Sri Lanka, Singapore, Malaysia, Middle East, Europe, America, and Canada. Though formal studies of films in other Indian languages have not begun, media reports and articles reveal a parallel transnational economy of films in regional languages that connect the local with the global in a circuit of production and reception quite different from that projected in the Bollywood film industry. If the regional films inscribe a rural, local space that is preserved in the global city on one hand, they mirror the Bollywoodization of the Hindi film on the other through transnationalization of their locales, production, and address. One of the films that emerged as a top grosser globally in 2006 was not one from the more established film industries in Bengali, Tamil, or Telugu, but a launchpad for the newly revived Punjabi film industry called *Mitti Vajaan Mardi* (2006) starring a Canadian-Sikh singer-actor. Despite their weak storylines and histrionic limitations of the lead singer-actors, Punjabi films have not only been playing a major role in mobilizing a global *Panjabiyat*, but have also forged new transnational connections. *Yaariyan* (2008), a recent Punjabi hit, proposes a unique transnational brotherhood through its theme focusing on the relationship between a rural Punjabi with a Punjabi and black Kenyan migrant in Canada symbolically enacted in its *Bhangra* title song. The narrative space of films such as *Jee Aaya Nu* (2003), *Dil Apna Punjabi* (2006), *Mitti Vajaan Mardi* (2006), and *Mera Pind* (2008), though very different, intersects with the diaspora productions of Gurinder Chadha in inscribing the region, or even a city like Amritsar, in the local-global binary. But the most important local global connection is visible in the phenomenal rise of the Bhojpuri film industry in the last decade in which clichéd narratives, 'crude' lyrics, and B-grade Hindi stars do not diminish the films' appeal for their rural Bhojpuri speakers in India and the Bhojpuri diasporas in Trinidad, Guyana, Fiji, Mauritius, and so on.

GLOBAL YEARNINGS

The most significant addition to the body of literature on South Asian cinema is that which brings to light Indian cinema's impact among non-South Asian communities not only in places of South Asian migration, but even in distant regions where South Asian presence is negligible. Brian Larkin's fieldwork in Nigeria on Hausa viewers' preference for Indian melodramas over Hollywood products and their incorporation of Indian cinema in the construction of an Islamic modernity provides a coherent explanation for the popularity of Indian films over their Hollywood counterparts in parts of the world where the sentimental family dramas represented in the film become the signifiers either of tradition through which modernity can be resisted or means of constructing an alternative modernity (Larkin 1997: 46–62). If Larkin's piece in Kaur and Sinha's *Bollyworld* reveals the penetration of the profane world of Hindi film song into the sacred *bandiri* music in Kano with bandiri singers borrowing Indian film songs for singing bandiri praise songs, Dana Rush's essay (2008) on the vodun image makers in Benin unveils a fascinating narrative of the incursion of the Hindi film into the African sacred through the co-option of Hindu imagery by the image makers in vodun art (Larkin in Kaur and Sinha 2005; Rush in Hawley 2008: 155). The popularity of live performances by Indian film stars in Southeast Asia, the Middle East, Africa, and many parts of the Western world was common knowledge. But the extent to which they had invaded the non-South Asian psyche has come to media attention only recently with reports commenting on Egyptian and Ghanaian cabdrivers playing Hindi film songs from the 1970s in New York or Kazakhs, Turk, and even Chinese fans of Raj Kapoor singing the theme song from *Awaara*. As cultures of the Third World become visible to the rest of the world only when they receive visibility, recognition, and acclaim in the first, Indian cinema that has stoked desires in different corners of the globe for nearly a century, attracted media and academic attention only when it caught the fancy of the cynical white viewer sometime in the 1990s. Perhaps the confusion of the diaspora films, particularly *Monsoon Wedding* (2001), *Bend it Like Beckham* (2002), and *Bollywood/Hollywood* (2002), with Indian cinema, familiarized the Western viewer with the space of its ethnic other, thus preparing the grounds for the Bollywood film of the Karan Johar or even Priyadarshan variety. As suspicions about the high ratings enjoyed by Bollywood films at the box office in global cities are confirmed by their predominantly South Asian viewership, the much celebrated Bollyphilia of Andrew Lloyd Webber, Baz Luhrmann, or Danny Boyle must be juxtaposed against the Bollyphobia of the majority of white viewers turned off by the length and non-linearity of the Indian film, notwithstanding the spirited support for 'the cinema of interruptions' by film scholars (Gopalan 2003).

REVISITING THE NATION IN THE ERA OF GLOBALIZATION

Yet theorists of South Asian cinema have made a compelling case for the retention of the category of the nation despite the challenges to the nation state from within and without by showing that the homogenizing drive of globalization is disrupted by the affirmation of national identities. Once again, Rajadhyaksha takes the lead in addressing the issues raised by the 'Bollywoodization' of Indian cinema by deconstructing taxonomies to embed them in the new politics of global capitalism in which the film and other cultural industries are implicated at the end of the twentieth century (1999). The question we need to ask is whether the category of the nation can be sustained in the face of transnational flows of goods, people, and images, or do the global flows of Bollywood require a new vocabulary for imagining the nation that is not rooted in the nation state. With the impending demise of the nation state being thrown in our face by the rise of sub-nationalist separatisms and formation of larger unions and the interdependence of the world that has repercussions in the political, economic, or ecological spheres, the question can no longer be overlooked in the cultural. With all these spheres integrated in global networks of production, markets, and consumption so intricately, can the state-centric division of space of modernity function as a reliable basis for imagined community and forming identities, and can cultures still be construed as discontinuous as the notion of national cultures implies? Rajadhyaksha (2003) and Trivedi (2008) argue for the retention of nation as a political entity that engenders and requires the idea of a national culture through explaining the resurgence of cultural nationalism as traditional cultures' defense mechanism against homogenized identities and globalized economies. Others like Mishra (2002) propose a compromise in which a revision of the idea of the nation by disengaging it from territory can make it serve as a convenient term for imagining collectivity because, as Arjun Appadurai pointed out, the present global process is dominated by the image and the imagination (1996). However, the emergence of new collectivities and identifications in the global era converging on language, religion, ethnicity, gender, caste, and so on point to a redefinition of the idea of the nation rather than cultural homogenization. While Rajadhyaksha and Trivedi's argument about cultural nationalist revivals following the perceived threat of the erosion of local identities are worth serious consideration, localities may be produced in cinematic texts through the consolidation of regional, ethnolinguistic, caste, or village identities. Cultural forms appear to reflect these 'tribal returns' that reflect the counter-movement of globalization towards greater fragmentation in which the desire for locality is translated in particularized narratives of region, ethnicity, or caste, and in which the facelessness of the global village is resisted through the small-place identity of specific neighbourhoods or villages. For this reason, the transnationalization of the Indian film is complemented by the re-emergence of the local through localisms of speech, dress, behaviour, and mores that fragment the homogeneous space of the 'All-India film' in myriad ways. The dream merchants of

Mumbai, Chennai, Kolkata, and Chandigarh cater to a heteroge-
neous transnational or global audience for films as diverse as *Jhankar
Beats* (2005), *Namastey London* (2007), *Vivaah* (2006), and *Welcome to
Sajjanpur* (2008).

TRANSNATIONAL APPROACHES

In this book, we hope to employ a transnational approach to engage the
crossover of Indian cinema by bringing together essays that explore the
meanings produced by Indian commercial cinema in the Indian subcontinent, in Asia, and in the rest of the world. Yet simultaneously, these
essays interrogate the polarized binary of nation and diaspora invoked
in South Asian film studies by following Indian cinema's unruly flows
to local and global sites in the past and the present. For, in existing
scholarship there seems to be somewhat of a lacuna regarding the issue
of nation and identity itself. First, for the most part, films are mostly
seen as implicated in a nationalist ideology and in the production of the
citizen subject within the new political boundaries of the nation state.
While it is true that cultural practices, including cinema, have been effectively deployed by postcolonial states in the management of identity
as cinema scholars have revealed, Indian popular cinema has simultaneously challenged these statist constructions through the mechanics of
its production as well as consumption. It was in the performative space
of Indian popular cinema that the shared cultural memories of its people
were not fissured after Partition as it produced a syncretic space insensi-
tive to caste, creed, class, gender, and ethnicity that made it available for a
variety of uses by diverse ethnic groups. A consequence of the catholicity
of Indian cinema is its decontextualization in the present through which
it is disengaged from the Indian nation state and is transformed into
a 'free-floating signifier' that can be appropriated by filmmakers from
Lahore to Los Angeles (LA) for varied purposes. From vodun image
makers in Benin and feature filmmakers in Ethiopia and Malaysia to
Baz Luhrmann, Andrew Lloyd Webber, and Danny Boyle, the images,
motifs, and conflicts of the oldest and biggest dream machine have invaded
the global cultural imaginary. Our hope is to collect such narratives and
ethnographic data that document and analyse the planetary reach of
a local cinema that alone has been able to challenge Hollywood's dominance in the popular cultural sphere worldwide.

Themes and Issues

The critical importance of this book, thus, lies in bringing together perspectives on Indian cinema from different disciplinary and geographical locations to reconceptualize the understanding of national cinemas. Through examining the meanings of nation, diaspora, home, and identity in cinematic texts and contexts, it examines the ways in which localities are produced in the new global process by broadly addressing the following themes.

The book opens with three essays in the section 'Modernity, Globalization, Globality' that locate Bollywood cinema and its travels within the larger debates on modernity, nation, resistance, and globalizaion. The first essay 'Bollywood, Postcolonial Transformation, and Modernity' by Bill Ashcroft approaches globalization and resistance to globalization from the perspective of postcolonial theory. Arguing that resistance to cultural domination occurs through *transformation* of those influences rather than simple opposition, he cites Bollywood as the most powerful example of 'transformative cultural resistance' as well as of 'alternative modernities', which he defines as the multiple and diverse ways in which modernity multiplies. Through viewing it as a transformation of the institution and technology of cinema to create a total, internally consistent entertainment form with new forms of film narrative and visual styles, Ashcroft disengages Bollywood from its subordination to Hollywood. Contesting the idea of the demise of the idea of the nation in the wake of globalization, Ashcroft also proposes the concept of the 'transnation' or a nation that is deeply rooted in its past and yet crosses borders considering Bollywood as its prime example.

Expanding the term Bollywood to refer to Indian cinema in general, Makarand Paranjape in 'Cultural Flows, Travelling Shows: Bombay Talkies, Global Times', relocates Bollywood's transnationalization in a form of 'internationalism' structuring the Hindi film's borrowings from the Phalke era (Kaur and Sinha 2005). Pointing out that contemporary global flows are not from Hollywood to Bollywood but also from Bollywood to Hollywood, Paranjape demystifies the theory of the unidirectional flow of globalization and cites *Slumdog Millionaire* to make a strong case for the intensification of its reverse or 'contra' flow. He suggests that the difference between Hollywood and Bollywood is not cosmetic but structural, and even civilizational, which is expressed as an aesthetic alterity.

Madhuja Mukherjee's essay 'Mustard Fields, Exotic Tropes, and Travels through Meandering Pathways: Reframing the Yash Raj Trajectory' closely examines the trope of travel, both literal and metaphorical, within the new Bollywood film as well as cinematic travels to South Asian diasporic spaces by focusing on Yash Raj films, particularly *Dilwale Dulhania Le Jayenge* (*DDLJ*, 1995), which triggered Bollywood's travels overseas and has become the template for the new 'travelling' films. Mukherjee demonstrates that the global journey in Yash Raj films appears to anticipate the history of cultural and economic globalization in India and concludes that *DDLJ* has evolved into an allegory of Indian modernities.

The section 'Love Across the Border' posits the problem of using a national framework in constituting a national cinema whose early history reveals a strong imbrication with that of two other national cinemas, namely, those of Pakistan and Bangladesh. The pre-national cinematic map was drawn along the lines of major film production centres in Kolkata, Mumbai, Chennai, and Lahore rather than national borders.

Ishtiaq Ahmed's sweeping historical overview of the flows between Lahore and Bombay before and after 1947 in 'The Lahore Film Industry: A Historical Sketch' shows how two major factors—Partition and the rise of Islamicism in Pakistan—led to the premature demise of a nascent film industry emerging around the Bhati Gate area in Lahore, despite the in-migration of Muslim talent from Bombay, and calls attention to the shared cultural memories that attest to the presence of Lahore in Bombay and Bombay in Lahore. Ahmed argues that in view of its pre-eminent position as the centre of Hindi/Urdu culture, Lahore would have emerged as a strong competitor to Bombay had Partition not occurred and can still become a major production centre for Punjabi films that can cater to a transnational Punjabi population.

Answering Ahmed's hope for a transnational Punjabi cinema, Nicola Mooney's essay 'From Chandigarh to Vancouver: Reimagining Home and Identity in the Films of Harbhajan Mann' throws light on the production of a transnational Punjabi rusticity through the Punjabi film that criss-crosses between villages in Punjab and diasporic Punjabi settlements in Birmingham, California, Vancouver, and Sydney. Mooney's anthropological study of the popularity of the Harbhajan

Mann films connects the revival of an extinct 'vernacular' cinema to the transnational mobilization of a particular ethnic/caste identity through the circulation of images of a Vancouver-born Jat Sikh singer-actor in the Punjabi televisual space.

Anuradha Ghosh, in 'Bollywood, Tollywood, Dollywood: Re-visiting Cross-border Flows and the Beat of the 1970s in the Context of Globalization', re-visits the parallel cinema movement, which portrays the beat of the 1970s, in the three contexts of Bollywood (Bombay), Tollywood (Kolkata), and Dollywood (Dhaka) to explore if their conjunctions and disjunctions can help to build an argument for a kind of cross-border flow. She concludes that the social movements of the 1970s provide a resistance aesthetic connecting alternative cinema practices both in Tollywood and Dollywood with the Hindi language productions from Mumbai.

In 'Cinematic Border Crossings in Two Bengals: Cultural Translation as Communalization?', Zakir Hossain Raju complicates 'cross-border flows' from India to Bangladesh by examining the remakes of Dhaka Muslim socials in Kolkata in the 1990s and opens up the exciting possibilities of dismantling internal hegemonies within South Asia through the reverse flows from Dhaka to Kolkata. However, the deployment of religious difference in the production of nationalist traditions on the subcontinent, highlighted by Raju in his analysis of West Bengal remakes of West Bengal film, fractures the ideological structures underlying Bengali cinema of the 1970s revisited by Ghosh to explore the possibility of a transnational Bengali cinematic sensibility.

The essays in the section 'The Other Film Industry' take a critical look at the relationship between Hindi cinema and 'the other' film industry in the south and between the various south Indian film industries in Tamil, Malayalam, and Kannada to focus on its contestation of the nationalist ideology underpinning the Hindi film while revealing its internal disjunctures.

Devadas and Velayutham have argued that 'the idea of the nation, as reflected through Tamil cinema, intervenes into a specifically ordered version of Indian nationalism and problematizes the notion of a national cinema' (2008). In this volume, Devadas and Velayutham oppose the 'regionalization' of Tamil cinema and trace the transnational flows of Tamil cinema that are seen to be asymptotic with those of Hindi. Defining Tamil cinema as 'a cinema in motion', they provide a fascinating glimpse into different forms of sociality it has produced historically and spatially. The new forms of sociality produced by cinemas in Tamil outlined by them interrupt the ideology of the Hindi film and the conceptualization of the nation state.

Acknowledging that regional cinema addresses regional identities of the people of that region, M.K. Raghavendra, in 'Region, Language, and Indian Cinema: Mysore and Kannada Language Cinema of the 1950s' points out that the discourse formulated in relation to the dominant south Indian cinemas in Tamil or Telugu can prove to be homogenizing when used to analyse other regions, such as Kannada, which emerged before the linguistic organization of the states. He argues that Kannada films of the 1950s, which trace a separate trajectory through displaying a preference for the mythological, folklore, or saint films abandoned in Hindi cinema in the early 1940s, did not address a Kannada identity but one belonging exclusively to 'old Mysore'.

Meena T. Pilliai, in her essay 'Modernity and Male Anxieties in Early Malayalam Cinema', argues that Malayalam films emerging in the 1930s consolidate and enforce the patrifocal ideologies of a society that sought to erase a matrilineal past by imposing a normative, 'native' feminity. Early Malayalam cinema provides useful insights into the construction of the Malayali modern whose logic runs counter to the Indian modern. She shows that in contrast to the deificiation of the mother in Hindi cinema that becomes a metaphor for the nation, Malayalam cinema has been torn between the positive and negative stereotype and preoccupied with the figure of the stepmother.

In sharp opposition to the new Bollywood film with its upper middle class, non-resident Indian (NRI), or global address that presents a designer India, the emergence of films that focus on the local is a novel development which shows that the centrifugal global flows are deflected by centripetal movements. Foucault's notion of heterotopia may be borrowed to show how different worlds are posited next to each other through a history of unequal economic, political, and social developments in the section 'Village in the City'.

D. Parthasarathy notes the growing popularity of Bhojpuri cinema from north Indian villages and north Indian migrants in Ludhiana and Mumbai to indentured diasporas in Fiji, Trinidad, Mauritius, and Guyana in 'Migrant, Diaspora, NRI: Bhojpuri Cinema and the "Local in the Global"'. In his analysis of the rustic Bhojpuri space in the global city of Mumbai and other urban diasporic locations, Parthasarathy suggests that transnational urbanism can provide a more appropriate framework for analysing new forms of sociality and globality in the making.

The wide choice of exhibition practices ranging from the multiplex to B- and C-grade stand-alone theatres has paradoxically facilitated the production and exhibition of a new kind of small budget film with realistic representation targeted at a small, niche middle-class audience. Arguing that these films literally indicate Hindi cinema's return to the local through the representation of theatrical forms that exist on the cultural margins, Nandi Bhatia turns to some of these films in 'Welcome to Sajjanpur: Theatre and Transnational Hindi Cinema' to examine their appropriation of local theatrical traditions such as *nautanki* to represent contemporary social realities.

The final section provides case studies of Bollywood's travels in the present and the past. While transnational economies of production liberate Bollywood from the specific geographies of location shootings in Mumbai or other Indian cities, the global flows facilitated by new technologies produce new Bollywood consumers in the US, the UK, Australia, and Canada whose appropriation of Bollywood as the new Asian 'kool' intersects with that of its loyal fans in Fiji, Africa, and the Middle East.

Manas Ray's essay brings together the past and present travels of Indian cinema through his examination of the function of Hindi films to Fiji Indians in 'Diasporic Bollywood: In the Tracks of a Twice-displaced Community'. Hindi cinema's transformation into Bollywood has not altered its role of identity formation for Fiji Indians who converge on Bollywood films in Australia in their self-definition in ways similar and different from the way they did in Fiji.

Kavita Karan and David Schaefer's ethnographic analysis reveals that the Indian film industry displays a far greater internal segmentation than ever before with films niche-marketed for a particular class, caste, gender, or ethnicity, within and outside the nation. Borrowing categories of Ritzer's concept of the grobal and the global, Karan and Schaefer argue that a key element in the internationalization of films is to draw upon global trends to market global trends for maximum box-office returns and show how the exogamous element increases in the films of the 1990s.

Andrew Hassam argues that though Bollywood might still originate in Mumbai or Chennai, it travels to different locations across the world through its song and dance routines, particularly to diasporic settlements in New York, Sydney, Toronto, London, Vancouver, Durban, and Bangkok. In '"It Was Filmed in My Home Town": Diasporic Audiences and Foreign Locations in Indian Popular Cinema', he juxtaposes the *darshanic* look against Feuer's idea of film audience's identification with the on-screen audience of musical sequences to examine song picturization in Bollywood films. Arguing that diasporic audience is not homogenous, he shows that the cultural background of the spectator and their degree of familiarity with the locations of the song plays a part in how song picturizations set outside of India are received by individual spectators.

In '*Yaari* with *Angrez*: Whiteness for a New Bollywood Hero', Teresa Hubel comments on the relative insignificance of whiteness to Hindi film narratives, with white characters turning up, when they do, often as peripheral figures to create the effect of historical accuracy. She argues that in Hindi cinema, whiteness cannot function as it does in the West, where the legacy of imperialism has made it an unmarked category, whose invisibility allows it to function as a norm against which the aberration of racial others may be measured. In Indian films, on the other hand, whiteness is marked; and it is, increasingly, markedly white—to be resisted, or desired, or dismissed.

Distinguishing between the diasporic viewership of Hindi films in South Africa in the past with the mainstreaming of the new Bollywood 'kool' through its exhibition in cinemas in city centres, Haseenah Ebrahim traces the migration of Bollywood from the 'ghetto' market of the Indian descent population in South Africa to the 'crossover' market of mainstream cinemas, the national television broadcaster, and pay-TV in 'From Ghetto to Mainstream: Bollywood in/and South Africa'. Drawing on Rajadhyaksha's idea of Bollywood as a media assemblage, she throws light on a number of activities attesting to Bollywood's presence in South Africa, such as the use of South Asian locations, influence of the Bollywood style of filmmaking on South-African filmmakers of Indian origin, and India-South Africa collaborations in film production.

Gwenda Vander Steene's essay 'Bollywood Films and African Audiences' on the resurgence of the Indophile phenomenon in Senegal, which involves dressing Indian, dancing to Indian music, in addition to watching Indian films, brings together the historically distinctive narratives of the popularity of Hindi films in Senegal in the 1950s and in the present. Vander Steene engages with Larkin's idea of parallel modernities and cultural proximity to explain why the Senegalese love Indian films.

The literature on transnational cosmopolitanism demands a revisiting of older categories like the nation that were productive in the past but need to be reviewed in light of the new world system. The essays in this collection show that Bollywood's border-crossings in the past and present raise important questions about nation states, borders, and boundaries. In spite of the convincing case made by film scholars such as Chakravarty, Prasad, and Vasudevan for Hindi cinema's complicity in the ideological production of the nation state, a number of questions such as its vast audience among groups and nations not included in its address, or the meanings produced by them, requires a rethinking on the national as a useful category for examining Indian cinema in particular and cinemas in general. Taking into account the above, this book examines the ways in which transnational discourses of cosmopolitanism or locality might offer more productive conceptual tools in reviewing nationality, citizenship, ethnicity, and language through the examination of the travels of Indian popular cinema. Even if nation must be retained as a conceptual category in view of the revival of cultural nationalism in the new wave of Indian films, despite the change in their address, as some have argued, the category needs to be unpacked in order to account for the multiple imaginings of the nation outside the geographical nation.

Notes

1. Derek Bose has traced the etymology of the term to Amit Khanna's use in the 1970s and even earlier to the coinage 'Tollywood' by the *Journal of the Bengal Motion Pictures Association* in the 1930s to refer to Bengali films approximating to Hollywood kind of productions. In Bose's understanding, Bollywood came in the wake of Mollywood to refer to Madras films, Lollywood for Lahore films, and Kollywood for Karachi. Bollywood's global recognition is confirmed by its entry in the Oxford English Dictionary (Bose 2006: 11). For a more contemporary understanding of Bollywood, see Rajadhyaksha (2003) and Madhava Prasad (2003).

2. Masala (spice) is used to refer to a kind of film that uses a formulaic plot, the stipulated number of song and dance sequences, action, melodrama, and all other staples of commercial Hindi cinema that work extremely well at the box office.

3. Despite looking at Bollywood as a brand, Derek Bose places the market share of Bollywood films as barely 2 per cent.

4. Former Pakistani Prime Minister Nawaj Sharief's alleged crooning of the song *'Aise na mujhe tum dekho seene se laga loonga'* (Don't look at me like that/I will embrace you if do) to the Bollywood actor Feroj Khan's attractive sister made headlines in all the major Indiian news channels with both sides refuting the Bollywood style romance probably invented by the Indian media (quoted from memory). A British Australian academic's twelve-year-old sang along to *'Jind mahi'* from *Kal Ho Na Ho* in 2006 to the utter amazement of his Indian visitors.

5. Not only has production of Bollywood films distributed across the world, but the involvement of other nationals such as British, Australians, or Singaporeans in their production disengages Bollywood from Mumbai, Kolkata, or Chennai.

References

Appadurai, Arjun. 1996. *Modernity at Large: Cultural Dimensions of Globalization*, Minneapolis: University of Minnesota Press.

Banaji, Shakuntala. 2006. *Reading 'Bollywood': The Young Audience and Hindi Films*, Basingstoke, Hants: Palgrave Macmillan.

Bose, Derek. 2006. *Brand Bollywood: A New Global Entertainment Order*, New Delhi: Sage.

Brosius, Christiane. 2005. 'The Scattered Homelands of the Migrant: Bollyworld through the Diasporic Lens', in Raminder Kaur and Ajay J. Sinha (eds), *Bollyworld: Popular Indian Cinema through a Transnational Lens*, New Delhi: Sage, pp. 207–38.

Chakravarty, Sumita S. 1996. *National Identity in Indian Popular Cinema, 1947–1987*, New Delhi: Oxford University Press.

Chowdhry, Prem. 2000. *Colonial India and the Making of Empire Cinema: Image, Ideology and Identity*. Manchester: Manchester University Press.

Dasgupta, Chidananda. 1981. 'The Cultural Basis of Indian Cinema', in *Talking about Films*, Delhi: Orient Longman.

Desai, Jigna. 2004. *Beyond Bollywood: The Cultural Politics of South Asian Diasporic Film*, New York: Routledge.

Dickey, Sara. 2002. 'Opposing Faces: Film Star Fan Clubs and the Construction of Class Identities in South India', in Rachel Dwyer and Christopher Pinney (eds), *Pleasure and the Nation: the History, Politics and Consumption of Public Culture in India*, New Delhi: Oxford University Press.

Dudrah, Rajinder. 2006. *Bollywood: Sociology Goes to the Movies*, New Delhi: Sage.

Dwyer, Rachel and Divia Patel. 2002. *Cinema India: the Visual Culture of Hindi Film*, London: Reaktion.

Ebrahim, Haseenah. 2008. 'From Ghetto to Mainstream: Bollywood in South Africa', *Issues in English Studies in Southern Africa*, vol. 13, no. 2.

Ganti, Tejaswani. 2004. *Bollywood: A Guidebook to Popular Hindi Cinema*, London: Routledge.

Gopalan, Lalitha. 2003. *Cinema of Interruptions: Action Genres in Contemporary Indian Cinema*, New Delhi: Oxford University Press.

Jaikumar, Priya. 2006. *At the End of Empire: a Politics of Transition in Britain and India*, Durham: Duke University Press.

Kaali, Sundar. 2000. 'Narrating Seduction: Vicissitudes of the Sexed Subject in Tamil Nativity Film', in Ravi S. Vasudevan (ed.), *Making Meaning in Indian Cinema*, New Delhi: Oxford University Press.

Kabir Nasreen Munni (ed.). 2005. *Talking Films—Conversations on Hindi Cinema with Javed Akhtar*, New Delhi: Oxford University Press.

Kapur, Gita. 1987. 'Mythic Material in Indian Cinema', *Journal of Arts & Ideas*, nos 14–15.

Kaur, Raminder. 2005. 'Cruising on the *Vilayeti* Bandwagon: Diasporic Representations and Reception of Popular Indian Movies', in Raminder Kaur and Ajay J. Sinha (eds), *Bollyworld: Popular Indian Cinema through a Transnational Lens*. New Delhi: Sage.

Kaur, R. and A. Sinha (eds). 2005. *Bollyworld, Popular Indian Cinema through a Transnational Lens*, New Delhi: Sage.

Larkin, Brian. 1997. 'Hausa Dramas and the Rise of Video Culture in Nigeria', *Visual Anthropology Review*, vol. 14, no. 2.

————. 2002. 'Bandiri Music, Globalization and Urban Experience in Nigeria', *Cahiers D'Études africaines* 168 (XLII–4).

Lutgendorf, Philip. 2006. 'Is There an Indian Way of Filmmaking?' *International Journal of Hindu Studies*, vol. 10, no. 3, pp. 227–56.

Majumdar, Ranjani. 2007. *Bombay Cinema: An Archive of the City*, Ranikhet: Permanent Black.

Mishra, Vijay. 2002. *Bollywood Cinema: Temples of Desire*, New York: Routledge.

Prasad, M. Madhava. 1998. *The Ideology of the Hindi Film: A Historical Construction*, New Delhi: Oxford University Press.

————. 2003. 'This Thing Called Bollywood', *Seminar*, May, no. 525. For details: http://www.india-seminar.com/2003/525/525%20Madhavaa%20 prasad.htm.; accessed on 15 March 2009.

Niranjana, Tejaswani. 1994. 'Roja Revisited', *Economic and Political Weekly*, vol. 29, no. 2 (21 May).

Punathambekar, Aswin. 2005. 'Bollywood in the Indian-American Diaspora: Mediating a Transitive Logic of Cultural Citizenship', *International Journal of Cultural Studies*, vol. 8, no. 2, pp. 151–73.

Rajadhyaksha, Ashish. 2003. 'The Bollywoodization of the Indian Cinema: Cultural Nationalism in a Global Arena', *Inter-Asia Cultural Studies*, vol. 4, no. 1 (April).

Rajadhyaksha, Ashish and Paul Willemen. 1999. *Encyclopaedia of Indian Cinema*, New Delhi: Oxford University Press.

Ray, Manas. 2001. 'Bollywood Down Under: Fiji Indian Cultural History and Popular Assertion', in Stuart Cunningham and John Sinclair (eds), *Floating Lives: the Media and Asian Diasporas*, Lanham, MD: Rowman and Littlefield.

Rush, Dana. 2008. 'The Idea of "India" in West African Vodun Art and Thought', in John Hawley (ed.), *India in Africa/Africa in India: Indian Ocean Cosmopolitanisms*, Bloomington & Indianapolis: Indiana University Press.

Srinivas, S.V. 2000. 'Devotion and Defiance in Fan Activity', in Ravi S. Vasudevan (ed.), *Making Meaning in Indian Cinema*, New Delhi: Oxford University Press, pp. 297–317.

Trivedi, Harish. 2008. 'From Bollywood to Hollywood: The Globalization of Hindi Cinema', in Revathi Krishnaswamy and John C. Hawley (eds), *The Postcolonial and the Global*, Minneapolis: University of Minnesota Press.

Vasudevan, Ravi S. (ed.). 2000. *Making Meaning in Indian Cinema*, New Delhi: Oxford University Press.

Velayutham, Selvaraj and Vijay Devadas. 2008. *Tamil Cinema: The Cultural Politics of India's Other Film Industry*, London: Routledge.

FILMS

Barjatya, Sooraj, R. *Vivaah*. 2006.

Barua, P.C. *Devdas*. 1936.

Benegal, Shyam. *Welcome to Sajjanpur*. 2008.

Boyle, Danny. *Slumdog Millionaire*. 2009.

Chadha, Gurinder. *Bend it Like Beckham*. 2002; *Bride and Prejudice*. 2004.

Ghosh, Rituparana. *Chokher Bali*. 2003.

Ghosh, Sujoy. *Jhankaar Beats*. 2003.

Grewal, Deepak. *Yaariyan*. 2008.

Johar, Karan. *Kal Ho Na Ho*. 2005.

Mehta, Deepa. *Bollywood/Hollywood*. 2002.

Murugadoss, A.R. *Ghajini*. 2008.

Nair, Mira. *Monsoon Wedding*. 2001.

Phalke, Dada Saheb. *The Life of Christ*. 1911; *Raja Harishchandra*. 1913.

Roy, Himanshu. *Achhoot Kanya*. 1936.

Shah, Vipul. *Namastey London*. 2007; *Singh is Kinng*. 2008.

Singh, Manmohan. *Mitti Vajaan Mardi*. 2006; *Mera Pind*. 2008; *Jee Aaya Nu*. 2003; *Dil Apna Panjabi*. 2006.

Sivan, Santosh. *Asoka*. 2001.

1 Bollywood, Postcolonial Transformation, and Modernity

BILL ASHCROFT

The battlelines have long been drawn in the argument about whether globalization is the homogenizing spread of US economic and cultural power or a worldwide interaction of local influences; whether it is hierarchical or dynamic; whether it is a cause or an effect; whether it comes from the West or from everywhere. Part of the problem is that there are many globalizations; while the homogenizing pressure of financial markets and neo-liberal ideologies is incontestable, cultural globalization is much more complex and diffuse. Post-colonial theory has an intervention to make in this argument because the debate is very similar to that concerning the relationship of empire and colony. This intervention revolves around the term 'resistance'. Resistance is an overused, even clichéd word in anti-colonial discourse, a word that, in general, oversimplifies the actual power dynamics in colonial relationship. Indisputably, nationalist rhetoric and armed struggle played a significant part in many anti-colonial movements and the rhetoric of resistance itself has been a powerful unifier. But when we observe the cultural production of colonized and formerly colonized societies, we see that 'resistance' to the homogenizing pressures of modernity, imperialism, and colonial culture occurs through *transformation* of those influences rather than simple (and sometimes futile) opposition.

The most fascinating feature of postcolonial societies has been the operation of a 'resistance' that manifests itself as a refusal to be absorbed, a resistance engaging that which is resisted in a different way, taking the array of influences exerted by the dominating power and altering them into tools for expressing a deeply held sense of identity and cultural being. This has been the most widespread, most influential, and most quotidian form of 'resistance' in colonized societies. Sometimes it doesn't look much like resistance and often it doesn't occur to people involved in it that they are 'resisting'. In postcolonial analysis, the supreme model for cultural transformation has been literature: with its appropriation of a dominant language and its transformation by a mother tongue; its adaptation of literary genres; its interpolation of dominant systems of distribution and reading; and the creation of a world audience. These lead to a powerful form of transformation that might be said to demonstrate the way 'local' literary cultures achieve global impact.

However Bollywood, or perhaps more broadly, the South-Asian film industry, provides, if anything, an even more powerful example of transformative cultural resistance. Though very different from literature in terms of its audience, it is more powerful because of the size of that audience. In particular, it provides a very clear case of globalization, or the reciprocal influence of local and global. We can no longer understand the global film industry in terms of 'Hollywood and the rest' because Bollywood has transformed the way we understand the global production of films. Of course, 'Bollywood' is as much a generalization as 'Hollywood', and despite our sense that of some kind of filmic formula operates in both, the specific formula is difficult to pin down. The two words provide us with two very different and very identifiable cultural phenomena, but 'Bollywood' identifies something more specific than 'South Asian Cinema'—the importance of Bombay, a vibrantly energetic postcolonial city, created by colonialism but growing to become the most important city in the empire outside London—'Star of the East/ With her face to the West' (Rushdie 1981: 92–3). The postcolonial city provides the context for a transformative intervention into modernity outside the international function of the nation-state. Bollywood is important in postcolonial terms because it offers a very dynamic example of the transformational and transcultural process by which globalization proceeds. Bollywood demonstrates a form of transformation that has so exceeded its Western origins that it offers a stunning example of the possibilities of transformation. Such transformation explains no less than the nature of contemporary modernity; rather than a linear histori- cal and universal process, extending the taproot of Western modernity, this modernity is multiple, rhizomic, and vibrant, erupting in different places, in different ways.

A note of caution is probably necessary here. There has been a lot of triumphalist breast beating about how India has become the film capital of the world. The figures are impressive. Mihir Bose claims:

> ... every year the Indian film industry produces more than 1,000 feature films, every day fourteen million people see a movie in the country, a billion more people a year buy tickets to Indian movies than they do to Hollywood ones. What is more, while Hollywood is no longer growing, the Indian numbers are likely to grow. (Bose 2006: 26)

He even goes on to say that the Indian film industry has colonized the world. But at the moment, we would have to say that despite this huge domestic market, the influence of this industry on global culture is restricted by its highly formulaic nature and its Hindi medium. If we look at the breadth of distribution and the cultural impact of Indian film, we still have nothing like the impact of Hollywood and neither should we wish it. I am not interested in promoting a new cultural imperialism but in examining the extent to which Bollywood has characterized the emergence of an alternative modernity.

This may be the most significant consequence of the Bollywood phe- nomenon: not only is it an example of cultural transformation but of the way in which modernity multiplies along diverse and culturally distinct lines. Though now, there is a complex array of alternative modernities, modernity, as an epoch, a questioning of the present, an orientation to the future, and at the same time an ethic valuing the present over the past, emerged in the West. But it does remind us that today modernity is plural and it confirms the fact that the historical trajectory of Western modernity was not simply a sign of temporal progress (an assumption embodied in the idea of 'the modern'), but a culturally situated phe- nomenon. Arguments for 'alternative modernities' confirm the need for cultural theories of modernity—theories that foreground place as well as time—but also lead us inevitably to the issue of local agency. This is demonstrated radically by the Indian film industry—a form of modern entertainment that could not have arisen in any other place in the world. Alternative or non-Western modernities emerge out of a *relation* to other modernities, as well as to their own culture and place and the processes of appropriation, adaptation, and transformation have been their characteristic features. Indeed, even where concerted programmes of Westernization have been undertaken by non-Western elites, the cultural transformation of Western models has been almost unavoidable. Thus, like postcolonial literatures, the most characteristic alternative modernities are those we might call 'hybridized', ones that appropriate and transform global cultural forms to local needs, beliefs, and conditions. This does not make them extensions of modernity, but new culturally situated forms of modernization.

Once we understand modernity as plural, we see that it is not so much adopted, as adapted, re-created, and transformed by a range of influences according to the needs of culture and place. These modernities influence each other outside the scope of Western modernity. How they do this is revealed in a story told by Shyam Benegal, one of India's most original filmmakers. He recalls how the Ethiopian filmmaker Haile Gerima told him:

> ... if there was one film that influenced him to the extent that he wanted to become a filmmaker it was the film *Mother India*. In Ethiopia, he said they would view films every month; his grandmother would gather her whole group, children and grandchildren, and they would all go to see *Mother India*. The story ... which somehow expressed the deepest needs and aspirations of the Indian people, had a message not only for the Indian people but for people from outside India like Haile and his fellow Ethiopians. (Bose 2006: 20)

The fascinating thing about this story is that it demonstrates the proliferation of a quintessential modern technology with no reference to the West. Film becomes the way in which the deepest source of national and ethnic identity, an identity very often formed in opposition to the West, can be imagined and depicted, as metonymic of an alternative modernity. And it is transferred from India's filmic *ur-text—Mother India* (1957) to Ethiopia. This is quite different from the kinds of exposure gained in Africa, the Caribbean, Europe, and the US, by films shown to audiences of diasporic Indians, but the exposure is just as lateral. This is the way in which globalization itself proceeds. There is a large body of criticism about *Mother India*'s role in the project of Nehruvian modernization—the reification of the mother figure as the embodiment of an ancient and unified India that was an invention of Nehru's decolonization rhetoric. But apart from its propagandizing role and its use of myth to obscure the actual state of women, the importance of *Mother India* is not what it says, but *the fact that it was made!*

Seeing the impact of *Mother India* in Ethiopia reminds us that modernities emerge from a particular cultural milieu: they are *placed*. Looking at modernity as culturally situated is not only rare but almost counter-intuitive because modernity and the 'march-of-time' seem to go hand in hand: the very idea of the modern is linked to the temporal and to the ideology of development. Yet 'Modernity', as we habitually understand it, has been deeply rooted in Western culture. 'The phenomenon of "political modernity",' says Chakrabarty 'namely, the rule by modern institutions of the state, bureaucracy, and capitalist enterprise—is impossible to *think* of anywhere in the world without invoking certain categories and concepts, the genealogies of which go deep into the intellectual and even theological traditions of Europe' (2000: 4).

The cultural features of Western modernity are deeply embedded as an epoch, a discourse, and concomitant of European political expansion. As cultural formation, Western modernity has been tightly linked to the political concept of the state and to the discourse of imperialism and its practice of territorial expansion. Western modernity, then, may be usefully understood as coterminous with both imperialism and capitalism.[1] The inevitable effect of this was that globalization came to be seen acculturally so that the diffusion of capital, industrialization, urbanization, and the spread of education implied a unified world and a homogeneous programme of 'development' available to all. But neither imperialism nor globalization can be described simply as programmes of homogenization because their operations are characterized by multidirectional and transcultural interactions—operating rhizomically rather than hierarchically or centrifugally. The various transcultural interactions between imperial powers and colonial cultures have a correlation in one of the most interesting features of the present globalized world—the degree to which 'local' modernities have come to characterize the global, in their adaptation of the principles and technologies of modernity to local cultural conditions. Whereas modernity relegated the 'local' to the past 'as an enclave of backwardness left out of progress, as the realm of rural stagnation against the dynamism of the urban, industrial civilization of capitalism' (Dirlik 2005: 464), the local has been the site of the emergence of alternative modernities.

The critical question addressed by the Bollywood phenomenon is: can we talk about modernity without invoking Western modernity? What is the impact of postcolonial transformation on the structure of global relations? The way in which modernity travels and changes can be demonstrated in the emergence of Indian film. The story of India's very early love affair with film is, in an indirect way, a story of its relationship with the Empire and of the contingent moments by which modernities develop. But it is also a stunning example of transformation. Cinema was born in Paris with the Lumière show that opened on 28 December 1885. Maurice Sestiere, the Lumière man, was on his way to Australia, but owing to shipping routes between the colonies had to stop over in Bombay, where he decided to screen the Lumière film. It was first shown to whites only in Watson's Hotel on 30 June 1896, but was soon screened to the general public so that on 7 July 1896, the same day as the Tsar of Russia was seeing the film it was being shown to Indian audiences. Thus virtually by an accident of history and imperial geography, the Indian film industry was born, and from this moment, a culturally situated film industry arose. Obviously, it is a very long way from the Lumière screening to the largest film industry in the world, but this demonstrates how protracted and how internal the process of transformation can be.

The significant feature of transformation is the way it prioritizes the agency of those 'subjected' to dominant influence. These subjects, communities, and cultural histories transform that influence in ways that normal ideas of cultural influence would not expect. Thus, if we view Bollywood as a particular (and particularly vibrant) example of modernity, an adoption and transformation of a modern technology, we can then understand that modernity is not a simple inevitable process of development, a teleological progress of 'modernizing', but a culturally placed event, unfolding 'within a specific cultural or civilizational context and different starting points for the transition to modernity lead to different outcomes' (Taylor 2001: 182). The Indian film may have taken birth by a Lumière screening, but if we are tempted to think it emerged as a simple appropriation from the West it is useful to remember that when *Mother India* was filmed, India, the largest democracy in the world, was in the middle of its second Soviet-style five-year-plan, while the logo of Mehboob Khan's studio was a hammer and sickle with his initials at the centre.

Cultures are not necessarily engulfed by modernity, but creatively transform it to local needs.

Creative adaptation is not simply a matter of adjusting the form or recoding the practice to soften the impact of modernity; rather, ... it is the site where a people 'make' themselves modern, as opposed to being 'made' modern by alien and impersonal forces, and where they give themselves an identity and a destiny. (Gaonkar 2001: 18)

Explaining forms of creative cultural adaptation has been a crucial function of certain forms of postcolonial theory in that they engage with the material realities of colonized and diasporic peoples.

The key site for examining postcolonial transformation has been literature, but comparing film with literature reveals some very clear differences. As technologies of representation, they both reveal dimensions of local agency that contradict the assumption that powerful discourses always exert a homogenizing pressure. Achille Mbembe states that 'Like Islam and Christianity, colonization is a universalizing project. Its ultimate aim is to inscribe the colonized in the space of modernity' (2002: 634). If so, did it succeed? Did it 'inscribe' the colonized in the space of modernity, or did the colonized take hold of the pen and inscribe themselves in that space in a curious act of defiance modelled by postcolonial writers? In terms of Bollywood, did the Indian film not so much inscribe as *refract* the image of India in global visual consciousness? The refraction of this image goes some way to explaining how the colonized are situated in and transform modernity. The Indian appropriation of the technologies of film entailed the continuous selection, reinterpretation, and reformulation of its themes, ideas, and techniques. These amounted to a radical transformation of the institution and practice of cinema, with new forms of filmic narrative and visual styles emerging. This appropriation and transformation was marked by a persistent ambivalence towards both Hollywood and the West, an ambivalence that pivoted on the relationship between resistance and transformation, and led to an entirely new internally referential form.

Despite Indian ambivalence towards both imperial culture and the new technology of film, transformation was a particularly enterprising form of resistance that utilized the technology without being engulfed by it. In this way, Bollywood stands as a metonym for postcolonial transformation. It identifies a range of practices, an enterprise engaged by agents, who locate themselves in a discourse in a resistant, counter-discursive way through the transformation of dominant technologies. They are a specific example of the interactive process by which modernity and globalization proceed. As Marshal Berman describes it:

> Modernism and modernization have nourished an amazing variety of visions and ideas that aim to make men and women the subjects as well as the objects of modernization, to give them the power to change the world that is changing them, to make their way through the maelstrom and make it their own. (1982: 16)

This doesn't mean that they act independently of the forces acting upon them, but they *act*. Whereas 'development'—the 'acultural' theory of modernization—acts to force the local into globally normative patterns, 'transformation' shows that those patterns are adjusted to and by the requirements of local values and needs.

India and China, emerging as two of the largest global participants, reveal with stark clarity something that has been becoming clearer for some time: that modernity can no longer be simply characterized as Western. In addition, just as theories of globalization keep rendering the nation an obsolete category, these countries appear to have re-established the 'nation' as an open *cultural* site taking a significant place in global economics. The nation state, so manifestly abandoned by globalization theory at the turn of the century as an absent structure, has, since the global financial crisis, reasserted its centrality as states have been called to pick up the pieces. But the emergence of India and China lead to a different view of the nation, they may force us to reconsider the importance of the *nation* as a cultural phenomenon, a horizontal reality separate from the vertical authority of the *state*. This different view of nation, one that has its roots deep in ancestral culture and yet exceeds the boundaries of the state, a nation that is in constant flow and migration both within and beyond the borders of the state, perhaps requires a new term, one that accommodates the plural identities of national subjects, the constant movement in which they are engaged, and yet remains culturally identifiable. For this purpose I would suggest the term 'transnation' to emphasize the degree to which the nation always exceeds the boundaries of the state. In this respect, the metonym of the Indian transnation par excellence is Bollywood film, for Bollywood is deeply rooted in Indian culture and mythology, and yet like Bombay itself, seems to dwell somewhere in but beyond the state, while it becomes increasingly globally expansive. Indeed, India has a long history of heterogeneity, argumentative reasoning, and democratic interchange, which reveal a more complicated route to democracy than purely Western inheritance. According to Sen, 'democracy is intimately connected with public discussion and interactive reasoning' (2005: 13)—traditions that have existed in India for millennia. Despite common assumptions, democracy doesn't gain its strength in India from the strength of the modern nation state but from a long history of interacting with, absorbing, and transferring intellectual and cultural practices both internally and externally.

This reality is possibly the source of Nehru's famous statement that 'India is most national when it is international' (cited in Kaur and Sinha 2005: 49). But the spirit of India's fluidity, acceptance, and capacity to change is virtually embodied in the giant figure of Rabindranath Tagore, who made perhaps the defining statement of post-colonial appropriation when he said: 'Whatever we understand and enjoy in human products instantly becomes ours, wherever they might have their origin' (Sen 2005: 86). This may be a common postcolonial, transformatory strategy but it describes 6000 years of India's cultural history as well and it is quite clearly the operating principle of an alternative modernity. In a letter to C.F. Andrews in 1924, Tagore wrote that 'the idea of India itself militates against the intense consciousness of the separateness of one's own people from others' (ibid.: 349). This remarkable statement has two profound implications: first, it asserts itself against an idea of India as a mixture of separated and alienated cultures and communities, sharply distinguished according to religion or caste, or class or gender or language or location; second, it argues against an intense sense of the dissociation of Indians from people elsewhere, particularly the idea that local culture is so fragile that it will break if exposed to outside influences.

Although Tagore's anti-nationalism is often seen to be the polar opposite of the nationalist utopianism that emerged in India in the decades before Independence, it may explain the amazing capacity for transformation displayed by Indian culture. This transformational capacity in Bollywood film demonstrates both practical and ideological features. The most significant practical features concern the script and directorial conventions and the sound. The most significant 'ideological' features concern the audience that the medium 'constructs', and the historical transformation of filmic practice within India itself. The well-established Hollywood practice of scriptwriting is to find a book or play that the director is keen to make into a film, a script is commissioned, funding is found, then actors and actresses are cast, and the film is shot according to a strict timetable. Bollywood, according to Bose (2006), completely reverses the procedure. The script is the last thing written. 'In Bollywood, the starting point is the telling of the story to the male star whose agreement will make or break the film' (ibid.: 31). If the director gets the star, he knows the film will work, and generally, the script is created around the star.

Just as the coming of sound transformed Hollywood, it transformed Bollywood too, but in a quite different way. While the synchronization of picture and sound is critical in Hollywood, 'in Bollywood, as a scene is shot the actors mouth the words they have been given and the sound is recorded later in the studio and superimposed on the film' (ibid.: 32).

But one of the most interesting characteristics of Indian film concerns the audience. Rather than the intense focus required by Western films, Bollywood has a different impact, in a sense it constructs a different audience.

> Hindi films are constructed around set of easily recognizable conventions…
> There is, in other words, a strong ritualistic element in the viewing of Indian films, a light-heartedness, a tongue-in-cheek mimetic relationship to all kinds of styles and genres derived from Western cinema…. Knowledge of these genre conventions and the ability to appreciate films in this relaxed, repetitive, intensely social form is crucial to the larger 'reading competence' that characterises the average, often extremely film-literate spectator in India. (Hansen in Kaur and Sinha 2005: 241)

This difference in audience participation, I would argue, stems from the different but symbiotic roles of reader and writer in literature. This is a situation in which author-function and reader-function mutually constitute the text. However, in the Bollywood film, there is already a high degree of pre-knowledge and expectation occasioned by the conventions of the form. For reasons that have to do with the popularity, the language, and the formulaic nature of the films, Bollywood generates a massive insider group of knowledgeable viewers.

Finally, there is a profound historical sense in which the technology and the discourse of the film are transformed. In other words, there is a diachronic transformation that is itself broadly cultural. To demonstrate this, let us consider two iconic films—*Mother India* and *Lagaan*

(2001)—both nominated for several academy awards, both culturally definitional, and separated by half a century. In a very broad sense, these two films demonstrate something of the historical transformation of India itself. *Mother India* is the product of a nationalist utopianism that had a vision of the future, despite its tragic plot. It was a film for its time, a story of the terrible suffering of the Indian peasants exemplified by a stoic mother who ends up killing her son. But it was a vision of possibility. As Bose (2006: 191) says:

> Mehboob's film was overladen with symbols of modern India—Nehru's India. Indeed, the very first scene in the film shows men wearing the clothing that signi-fied the uniform of Nehru's Congress Party, escorting the mother to inaugurate the arrival of an irrigation canal in the village; just the sort of progress Nehru was seeking as India, finally, took the road towards industrialization.

Independence had come ten years earlier, the future was the nation, and in different ways, the film embodied the India of the time.

Ironically, *Mother India* was the last film to use sync sound until it was revived forty-three years later by another iconic film, *Lagaan*. This unlikely story of a rural village cricket team who learn to play cricket and defeat a team of British district officers to cancel a draconian tax, is the product of a more confident India, a film that can revisit the issues of colonial resistance in a light-hearted way, a film backed by half a century of Indian cricketing success and one secure in the Bollywood formula. But the security of *Lagaan* allows it to revisit the past and it does so ironically within the postcolonial discourse. Cricket is an excellent example of an appropriation and transformation of a cultural form. Today, within a globalized world, the apparently nostalgic view of colonial resistance and the thinly veiled celebration of Indian cricket has a subtle relevance. The urgency of the future drives *Mother India*; the urgency of the present drives *Lagaan* to revisit the strategies of post-colonial resistance. In their different ways, they embody the India of their time. They become specific examples of the historical dimensions of that cultural transformation by which alternative modernities come into being.

From Transformation to Circulation

The principle that complements local transformation and adaptation is global circulation and re-circulation of locally adapted modernities. This circulation is never equal or similar in character. Japan, which has been one of the most energetic adapters of technology, has transformed itself from a copy culture to one in which automotive and electronic products have earned their reputation for reliability. Consequently, Japanese notions and techniques of quality control have greatly influenced European and American industry, as well as consumer behaviour. Srinivas (2002) calls this the principle of 'emission' and although the most prominent emissions from Asia have been those emanating from religious culture, the 'emissions' of Indian fabric, food, and film have reached a truly global span.

The *diffusion* of global influence makes the relationship between the local and the global all the more complex because when we examine local cultures, we find the presence of the global within the local to an extent that compels us to be very clear about our concept of the local. The term 'glocalization' more adequately describes the relationship between the local and the global as one of interaction and interpenetration rather than of binary opposites. 'It makes no good sense,' says Robertson, 'to define the global as if the global excludes the local' (1995: 34). Neither is their interpenetration a one-way process of 'contamination' from an imperial discourse to a colonized subject. The view that the local and the global should not be seen in a simple homogenizing power relationship, but that the local contributes to the character of the global, is now widely held. But how this occurs is less clear and it is precisely this phenomenon that the processes of postcolonial transformation illuminate.

The circulation of the Bollywood film industry, like the global circulation of any 'local' culture occurs in a number of different ways some of which may be regarded as controversial; they can be categorized as distribution, inspiration, influence, and interpolation. Comparing film with postcolonial literatures brings out some quite distinctive features in the former. The global reach of Indian literature is almost entirely limited to Anglophone writing, which is the key model of discursive transformation. The appropriation and transformation of the language; the interpolation of global networks of publishing and distribution; the virtual creation of a world audience of English speakers meant that the production of writers from Raja Rao to Salman Rushdie, from Anita Desai to Kiran Desai have taken prominent place in the genre of world literatures in English. In effect, the appropriation of the language underlay the global distribution and impact of Indian literary writing.

However, for the same reason—the language of the medium—the process has been very different for film. In virtually all these dimensions—distribution, inspiration, and influence—the impact has been one of filtration rather than a more aggressive influence. For instance, the distribution of Bollywood films to diasporic audiences in Africa, Asia, Caribbean Europe, and America led to exposure within those societies simply by the principle of proximity. Proximity may be augmented by exoticism in Europe and America, but in Africa, distribution has led to a form of filtration producing generations of Bollywood fans who do not speak Indian languages but for whom the visual language of the films has been captivating (Larkin 1997: 209–42).[2] Bollywood films have generated considerable identification in audiences in the Third World, and in Asia and Africa in particular, it has confirmed the liberating possibility of a film industry outside Hollywood or Europe.

This exposure may *inspire* a local film industry in the way Haile Gerima told Shyam Benegal of the influence of *Mother India*. But in whatever way the exposure to the film is achieved, this second mode of circulation is in some respects the most potent. Why this inspiration should come from Bollywood rather than the global Hollywood film industry can be explained in a number of ways. The very fact that a dynamic film industry could be evolved outside the West is an inspiration in itself; and it is additionally inspirational when that industry can be built on the basis of a clear cultural, even civilizational, difference. But where *Mother India* is concerned, the inspiration upon people such as Haile Gerima was clearly from its deeply nationalistic aura. This leads us into the controversial territory of Fredric Jameson's notorious designation of Third World literature as 'national allegories' (1986: 69). Aijaz Ahmad was the first to respond, taking Jameson to task for the 'Three Worlds' myth which defined the First and Second Worlds in terms of their economic systems (Capitalism and Communism) but defined the Third World in terms of externally introduced phenomena (Ahmad 1987). Ahmad probably underestimated the importance of the word 'allegory', but 'national allegory' still fails to adequately embrace the complexity of the relationship between literature and the idea of nation. Specifically, the term, as Jean Franco puts it, 'fails to adequately describe the dissolution of the idea of nation and the continuous persistence of national concerns' (1989: 211). Yet despite the controversy surrounding Jameson's claim, it is clear that the inspirational power of classics such as *Mother India*—a film to which Bollywood itself constantly gestures—was the fact that the nation is one of the most readily accessible categories of identification in modernity.

This principle of inspiration is a vigorous form of influence, but the influence I am thinking of is that occurring when the insistent presence of Bollywood impacts on a film produced in another country. In this category I would include *Slumdog Millionaire* in which the subtle allusions to Bollywood are finally confirmed in the only song and dance scene at the closing credits. This film has already aroused considerable controversy, concerning its authenticity, its image of India, and its use of non-Bollywood elements. Curiously, the main criticism of the film that it gives an unflattering picture of Indian life is a de facto assumption that films *about* the 'Third World' as well as *from* the Third World are somehow 'national allegories'. But two things become clear beyond this controversy: the film is aimed at an audience that is in one way or another familiar with the phenomenon of Bollywood; and whatever one thinks about its picture of India, the *feel* of its narrative, its romance, as well as its ugliness is Bollywood-like, while offering at the same time, through the game-show motif, a cultural ethnography of India. The arguments continue to rage on Indian blog sites (where it is just as heavily defended as attacked) but whether lured by exoticism or curiosity, audiences of the film have been introduced to India within the stereotyped conventions of Hollywood. This is an ambivalent form of influence, but it is influence nonetheless.

Finally, the principle of interpolation is one that is much more familiar in literature where writers in English interpolate global systems of genre, production, distribution, and readership. In a sense, Anglo-Indian literature has always engaged in a process of interpolation, with staggering global success. In the case of Bollywood, I would imagine such interpolation is much more open to the accusation of prostitution. The example I am thinking of here is *Bride and Prejudice*. Here the principles of cultural interpolation go hand in hand with a fairly blatant marketing strategy. The script is in English; it falls into a familiar post-colonial genre of writing back to the canon, in this case the very well known *Pride and Prejudice*; Darcy is an American, thus securing the lucrative US audience. I am not sure whether the sound is synced, but by and large, it follows the Bollywood formula of lavish song and dance routines, generously supported by the plot of *Pride and Prejudice*.

The case of *Bride and Prejudice* perhaps confirms that one of the distinguishing features of Bollywood film is its actual disinterest in interpolating global networks. This film falls more easily into the category of replays of *Pride and Prejudice* rather than the category of Bollywood film. Unlike literature, in which interpolation performs the function of representing postcolonial culture to a world audience, Bollywood is too big, too confident in its own formula, too directed at the Indian transnation of Hindi speakers to require interpolation as a strategy. Rather, the transformation of the medium has had a different, an internal and astonishingly focused and confident impact that is disseminated in much the same way as the Indian transnation is disseminated. This then, is the critical distinction between Bollywood and Indian literature. Anglophone literature, in its appropriation and transformation of English, 'constructs'—or chooses—a world audience of English speakers, interpolates the dominant cultural and economic systems of publishing, and represents an Indian reality to that world audience. Indian film, on the other hand, has a different political agenda, ironically, because it has a different economic and consumer base. That political agenda is at once more national and more rooted in a cultural discourse that transcends nation.

A classic demonstration of this supremely confident self-referentiality is *Om Shanti Om* (2007) a tribute to the Bollywood of the 1970s featuring dozens of well-known actors playing themselves. Om Prakash, a budding actor, falls in love with Shanti Priya, the star of a film directed by Mukesh Mehra, who turns out to be her husband and to whom she is pregnant. Shanti is killed in a fire on the set, and Om, who escapes, is taken to hospital by Rajesh Kapoor who is taking his pregnant wife to hospital. Om dies and Kapoor names his son Om. It appears as if Om Prakash has reincarnated and is out now to look for his love and avenge her sufferings, taking revenge from Mukesh Mehra. In true Bollywood fashion, the plot is incidental to the comedy, the songs, and the parade of stars. As one reviewer puts it, Shah Rukh Khan (who plays Om Prakash and Om Kapoor) 'does the most corny things with such conviction that you end up liking them' (Deoshi 2007). But the reincarnation of Om is an allegory of the cyclic continuation of Bollywood film. *Om Shanti Om* points to nothing outside the history of the genre and by including so many stars assumes an audience with highly developed film literacy, in order to make its tongue-in-cheek homage to Bollywood film itself.

If we see this film as an extension of Bollywood's production of an alternative modernity, the implications are significant because it shows a modernity developing in a unique and internally referential way. *Om Shanti Om* is virtually an allegory for this self-referential process. Bollywood, because of its distribution, its wide audience, its cultural integrity, its vibrant, colourful, and completely Indian character shows that the transformation of the technology of film has not led to a transformed version of Hollywood, but to a total, internally consistent entertainment form. The implications of this are that alternative modernities are not merely alternative to the West, not merely versions of Western modernity, but internally coherent, culturally situated, and *placed* modernities. These modernities do not develop as extensions of the historical taproot of the West, but as rhizomic and transformational eruptions.

Taking Bollywood as a model for the development of alternative modernities—modernities that reveal the complex and rhizomic proliferation of modernity in culturally situated forms—shows us that 'alternative' does not mean 'peripheral', nor does it mean small or inconsequential. More importantly, it shows how globalization proceeds through the transformative and circulatory dynamic of local agency. It also reveals something about postcolonial transformation itself: if we are inclined to think that the transformation of dominant discourses, technologies, and creative forms somehow binds the transforming culture to the original, that is, to the West, then Bollywood disproves that. If we are tempted by the erroneous thought that Indian literature in English as somehow a captive of English literature, we cannot make that mistake with Bollywood—a huge, dynamic culturally situated form of a medium that has been regarded as quintessentially modern.

Notes

1. It is important to remember that the concept of 'the West' really rose to prominence in contrast to the Communist 'East' rather than the older 'Orient', and its capitalist modernity should be distinguished from that 'alternative' form of modernity that arose in the USSR.

2. It is a curious sobering fact that the Somalian pirate captured by the American navy in April 2009 and taken to the US for trial had been familiar with Bollywood films with Somalian sub-titles during his childhood. Several inferences could be

made from this but the general cultural connection is of a film industry distributed to an audience that felt itself to be outside the cultural orbit of the West. The fact that Bollywood is Hindu and the Somali audience Islamic is less important than the non-Hollywood character of Indian film.

References

Ahmad, Aijaz. 1987. 'Jameson's Rhetoric of Otherness and the "National Allegory"', *Social Text*, 17: 3–25.

Appadurai, Arjun. 1996. *Modernity at Large: Cultural Dimensions of Globalization*, Minneapolis: University of Minnesota.

Berger, Peter L. and Samuel P. Huntington. 2002. *Many Globalizations: Cultural Diversity in the Contemporary World*, Oxford, New York: Oxford University Press.

Berman, Marshal. 1982. *All that is Solid Melts into Air: the Experience of Modernity*, London: Verso.

Bose, Mihir. 2006. *Bollywood: a History* Stroude. UK: Tempus.

Chakrabarty, Dipesh. 2000. *Provincializing Europe: Post-colonial Thought and Historical Difference*, Princeton, NJ: Princeton University Press.

Cooper, Frederick. 2005. *Colonialism in Question: Theory, Knowledge, History*, Berkeley: University of California.

Deoshi, Naresh Kumar. 2007. '*Om Shanti Om*—A Perfect Diwali Treat', ApunKaChoice.Com, http://www.apunkachoice.com/dyn/movies/hindi/om_shanti_om.

Dirlik, Arif. 2005. 'The Local and the Global', in Bill Ashcroft, Gareth Griffiths, and Helen Tiffin (eds), *The Post-Colonial Studies Reader*, Second Edition, London: Routledge.

Eisenstadt, S.N. 2000. 'Multiple Modernities', *Daedalus*, vol. 129, no. 1 (Winter), pp. 1–29.

————. 2003. *Comparative Civilizations and Multiple Modernities*, Leiden: Boston Brill Academic Publishers.

Featherstone, Mike (ed.). 1990. *Global Culture, Nationalism, Globalization and Modernity*, London: Sage.

Feenberg, Andrew. 1995. *Alternative Modernity: The Technical Turn in Philosophy and Social Theory*, Berkeley: University of California.

France, Jean. 1989. 'The Nation as Imagined Community', in Aram Veeser (ed.), *The New Historicism*, New York: Routledge, pp. 204–12.

Gaonkar, Dilip Parameshwar (ed.). 2001a. *Alternative Modernities*, Durham, NC: Duke University Press.

————. 2001b. 'On Alternative Modernities', in Dilip P. Gaonkar (ed.), *Alternative Modernities*, Durham, N.C.: Duke University Press, pp. 1–16.

Gikandi, Simon. 2001. 'Globalization and the Claims of Postcoloniality', *South Atlantic Quarterly*, vol. 100, no. 3, pp. 627–58.

Habermas, Jurgen. 1981. 'Modernity vs. Postmodernity', *New German Critique*, vol. 22.

————. 1987. *The Philosophical Discourse of Modernity*, Cambridge: Polity.

Jameson, Fredric. 1986. 'Third World Literature in the Era of Multinational Capitalism', *Social Text*, vol. 15 (Fall), pp. 65–88.

Kaur, Raminder and Ajay Sinha. 2005. *Bollyworld: Popular Indian Cinema through a Transnational Lens*, London and New Delhi: Sage.

Kirkland, Frank, M. 1997. 'Modernity and Intellectual Life in Black', in John Pittman (ed.), *African-American Perspectives and Philosophical Traditions*, New York and London: Routledge, pp. 136–65.

Larkin, Brian. 1997. 'Hausa Dramas and the Rise of Video Culture in Nigeria', in Jonathan Haynes (ed.), *Nigerian Video Film*, Ohio: Ohio University Press.

————. 2004. 'Degraded Images, Distorted Sounds: Nigerian Video and the Infrastructure of Piracy', *Public Culture*, vol. 16, no. 2 (Spring), pp. 289–314.

Mbembe, Achille. 2002. 'On the Power of the False', *Public Culture*, vol. 14.

Robertson, Roland. 1995. 'Glocalization: Time-Space and Homogeneity-Heterogeneity', in Mike Featherstone, Scott Lash, and *Roland Robertson* (eds), *Global Modernities*, London: Sage.

Rushdie, Salman. 1981. *Midnight's Children*, London: Jonathan Cape.

Sen, Amartya Kumar. 2005. *The Argumentative Indian: Writings on Indian History, Culture and Identity*, New York: Farrar, Straus, and Giroux.

Smith, Adam. 1776 (1994). *An Inquiry into the Nature and Causes of the Wealth of Nations*, Edwin Cannan (ed.), New York: Modern Library.

Srinivas, Tulasi. 2002. 'A Tryst with Destiny: the Indian Case of Cultural Globalization', in Berger and Huntington (eds), *Many Globalizations: Cultural Diversity in the Contemporary World*, New York: Oxford University Press.

Taylor, Charles. 2001. 'Two Theories of Modernity', in Dilip P. Gaonkar (ed.), *Alternative Modernities*, Durham, NC: Duke University Press.

2 Cultural Flows, Travelling Shows

Bombay Talkies, Global Times

MAKARAND PARANJAPE

The transculturality of Bombay (Mumbai) cinema has been increasingly visible and obvious over the last two decades. What is less understood and explored is its increasing integration with Hollywood, in tune with the broader workings of globalization, which works to integrate markets, economies, and cultures. This chapter attempts to list out the patterns and types of flows of this cinema, with a special emphasis on Mumbai cinema, with the proviso that many of these observations are as yet preliminary and need much more rigorous working out. However, in the process, I would also like to touch upon some vexing issues such as the artistic difference between Bollywood and Hollywood and the (ir)relevance of the notion of national cinemas. The chapter is in three parts. In the first part, two other issues of related interest have been discussed: first, the relationship between the discourse on Bollywood and the movies themselves as discourse; second, the direction and nature of global cultural flows. With particular reference to the relationship between Bollywood and Hollywood, this chapter shows how the travels are not just of Bollywood or South Asian cinema towards Hollywood, but of Hollywood itself towards Bollywood. The second part of the chapter, presents a preliminary taxonomy of the kind of cultural flows between Bollywood and Hollywood. In the concluding third part, not just the differences between Bollywood and Hollywood have been brought out, but an attempt has been made to reformulate our notions of the relationship between the dominant and the subaltern cultures and discourses, between modernity and its discontents, so to speak. By doing so, it may be concluded that Bollywood-Hollywood movements and manoeuvres are not just uni-directional, but they are multi-directional and multinational cultural flows. This chapter, thus, projects the Hollywood to Bollywood movements and manoeuvres, not just of uni-directional cultural flows. Whereas as the discourse on globalization tends to emphasize the West on the rest influence, what we find in the Bollywood-Hollywood relationship is a reverse swing that is becoming increasingly more and more powerful.

At the outset and in the interests of greater clarity, it would be useful to see how Bollywood here refers not only to the Mumbai film industry, but is symbolic of the Indian, to an extent even the South Asian film industry. This may be inferred from the fact that there has always been considerable integration between the different film fraternities in India, especially between Kolkata and Mumbai earlier, and between Chennai and Mumbai to this day, and Hyderabad and Mumbai in the 1970s and 1980s.[1] So, in some sense, despite all the different centres of production and the distinct character of all the different language cinemas of India, there is considerable mixing and amalgamation between them. Similarly, Hollywood refers, in a broader sense, not just to the US film industry, but also symbolizes the interaction and assimilation of several European and international elements including directors, technicians, actors, and so on. Both Bollywood and Hollywood, thus, are generic terms; the former represents an 'inter-Indian', while the latter, an 'inter-Western' cinema. So, in a sense, this chapter deals with the relationship between two larger entities, the first and the second cinemas of the world, without prejudice to which is the first and which the second, since the jury is still out on that one.

Some have argued that Bollywood is actually 'third cinema', that is part of the film industries of the global South. This might have held true for the 'parallel' or 'art' cinema of the 1970s, funded mostly by the National Film Development Corporation (NFDC). This cinema shared a 'progressive', left-wing politics with other cinemas of the global South and did have a social conscience. But with the gradual demise of this parallel, art-house style of filmmaking in India, Bollywood, which is really a commercial enterprise, reigns triumphant. Bollywood, however, is itself experimenting with low-budget, off-beat movies, sometimes financed by big houses. So an alternative within the broadly commercial framework of Bollywood is emerging.

Cinema as Discourse and Discourse as Cinema

As mentioned earlier, in this section, two instances of the relationship between the discourse on cinema and cinema as discourse will be looked into. The first and perhaps most obvious instance of this is the recent, astonishing success of Danny Boyle's *Slumdog Millionaire* (2008) which, it would seem, shows the power of discourse to predict the production and plot lines of real cinematic artifacts. The film was released first in the US, where it has raked in more than US$138 million (A$202.6 million) as of 26 March 2009, then in the UK, where the collections were over £30 million (A$62.6 million) as of 22 March ('Box office/business for *Slumdog Millionaire*'). The film was finally released in India on 22 January, in the original English version and in the dubbed Hindi version. In Australia, it has been showing to packed audiences for several months; as of 14 January, it had already grossed more than A$3 million, but according to noted critic and academic, Vijay Mishra, it has also created among white Australians an unparalleled interest in Bollywood.[2]

Whatever it may or may not do for India's image, *Slumdog Millionaire* has certainly brought Bollywood to the world's centre stage. The film sets itself up as a self-conscious, if slightly parodic, tribute to Bollywood, complete with an improbable plot, song and dance sequences, and the overwhelming force of destiny driving its protagonist from rags to riches. While a postcolonial reading could easily show how the movie misrepresents or distorts Indian realities, the movie marks the coming of age of Bollywood in the Western world, even if it is Hollywood pretending to be Bollywood. It is now clear that the film did not do as well in India, but when one went to see it in January 2009, middle- and upper-class audiences were thronging the theatres in Delhi to catch a glimpse of the Oscar magic, wondering just what had made the film so attractive.

The movie is almost tailor-made to illustrate the movement of Bollywood towards Hollywood. *Slumdog*, no doubt, shows the travel, even 'arrival' of Bollywood to Los Angeles, with the Cinderella-like ascent not only of its protagonist Jamal into a multi-millionaire, but that of the cinematic talent of the Mumbai film industry to the world stage. And yet, I would argue, in the ultimate analysis, *Slumdog* remains an Anglo-American movie about India, not an Indian movie. Apart from the fact that one cannot wish away its politics of representation, it actually represents not so much travels from Mumbai to LA, but from London to Mumbai, then to LA, and to the rest of the world. The cultural flows that it embodies are thus not just multi-directional, but structured on a West to East movement, not the other way round. Bollywood thus circulates in global circuits of dissemination when it is thus repackaged for Western consumption.

Clearly, *Slumdog* does instantiate the travels of Bollywood to Hollywood, not only in terms of its directors, actors, technicians, and musicians, but also in terms of its style and structure, content and technique. The Cinderella-like transformation of a slum child into a multi-millionaire is not only the stuff of the American dream, but also very much of Bollywood fantasy. To put it simply, the game show in the movie is itself a symbol of Bollywood, the world's largest dream factory, which makes the impossible come true. Bollywood, with its links to glamourous film stars and underworld dons, is also depicted in the movie so extensively that it is almost a tribute to the industry. Jamal's initial defining moment is to literally rise out of a pile of shit to get Amitabh Bachchan's autograph. There are several clips from earlier Bachchan movies and one of the early questions in the quiz asks who the star of the superstar's 1970 hit, *Zanjeer*, was. Similarly, the tune of the Surdas bhajan, again a link between Jamal's life and the quiz show, is taken from a Hindi movie. The depiction of the underworld in the movie was also derived, as several critics have pointed out, from earlier Bollywood films like *Satya* (1998) or *D Company* (2005). Although visually, the film is clearly the work of outsiders, the cinematic style mimics Bollywood, as do the dialogues and the improbabilities in the plot. The latter, however, cannot be simply wished away because they are implicated in a politics of representation.

The film has been hailed in India as signifying the arrival of Bollywood in Hollywood. Yet, what is not equally obvious, though it is equally important, is the fact that the movie also illustrates a Hollywood to Bollywood movement. The direction of the cultural flows is not just one-way or two ways, but multidirectional. In *Slumdog Millionaire*, it is the case of a British director, reaching out to Bollywood for its story and setting, using a multinational crew to make a product that is sold all over the world, but chiefly in the US, UK, and India. The travels, hence, are not just from Bollywood to LA, but from London to Mumbai, then Mumbai to LA, Mumbai to London, and then to rest of the world.

Hence, when it comes to contemporary mass culture, more than the power of theory to predict or anticipate reality, we find reality, in this case, the culture industry that is Mumbai cinema, spectacularly able to predict or anticipate theory. The Hindi title of *Bride and Prejudice* (2004), Gurinder Chadha's adaptation of the Jane Austen classic, *Balle Balle: From Amritsar to LA*, highlights a certain kind of mobility, upward and Westward mobility, which not only applied to her characters, but to the culture industry itself. In transposing her setting from early nineteenth-century rural England to early twenty-first-century suburban India, she wanted to augment the span and ambition of the journey from the country to the city, which was the mainstay of a good deal of English literature. Now, such a journey had acquired a truly global dimension. The restricted journeys within provincial England were now transformed into cross-cultural and trans-continental moves in a flatter world, where time and space had shrunk. As if actually to demonstrate the material conditions that enable such flights of imagination, Chadha, herself a Briton of Indian origin, creates and exploits a tri-continental production, with matching histrionic and technical teamwork, to create a commercial product viable in multiple markets and languages across the globe. Observers had to coin a new phrase, cross-over cinema, to come to terms with such a phenomenon.

However, the journey from Mumbai to LA—or, indeed, vice versa, as this chapter would reveal—is of course much more to be expected than from Amritsar to LA. After all, both cities—Mumbai and LA—signify the commercial and cultural capitals of two global cinemas—the second and first respectively—or the other way round, depending on which way you call it, Bollywood and Hollywood. Naturally, one would expect some degree of traffic between the two, if not increasing integration as with other industries and markets. What is more striking is the precocity and ferocity peculiar to its own cultural logic with which Bollywood, or in this case, Hollywood-Bollywood, actually anticipates scholarship. It would seem that the film industry, even in its intellectual formations, whether explicit or implicit, is actually ahead of us. After all, *Slumdog* too, was a couple of years in the making before its late 2008 release. It, therefore, appears that Bollywood leads, while we follow. After all, another trans-continental filmmaker of Indian origin, Deepa Mehta, had already made a movie, *Bollywood/Hollywood* (2002), quite a while before scholars began to speak and write about such integration. Similarly, the title Amritsar to LA is more culturally audacious than Mumbai to LA. From the early Punjabi immigrants to Yuba City, California, to the continued export of brides, as in this movie, and grooms to the Indian diaspora, both the travels and the travails of Indians abroad have a longer and deeper history than the more recent interpenetration of Bollywood and Hollywood. Indeed, the spread of South Asian cinema itself is predicated on prior dispersals of its diaspora across the globe.

But what is as remarkable is that the journey is bi-directional, or rather multi-directional, as all cultural flows usually are. We may see the current moving in one direction, but unlike a stream moving from higher to lower ground until it reaches the sea, culture moves not just from higher to lower, but also from lower to higher ground, so to speak, like that amazing, phantasmagoric boat ride in Shelley's *Alastor*. Hollywood, we also know, has been outsourcing to Bollywood its back office and technical work, such as dubbing, editing, digital enhancement, and other value-addition works are possible because of the relatively inexpensive, technically and artistically skilled labour pool in India. In areas such as animation, for instance, India has been a very active participant in overseas cultural products.

The politically dominant may actually be culturally weaker. It would take another paper to show the many subtle ways in which Bollywood influences Hollywood, but one of these is surely the manner in which the latter wishes to be overtly unlike Bollywood—just as the West has defined itself over the centuries as the not-East and Europe as not-Asia. When Hollywood deigns to be a bit like its other, it does so with parody or irony, as in *Moulin Rouge* (2001), where Bollywood-style sentiment and spectacle are imported into Hollywood in comic vein, or even *Slumdog*'s comic-book-like caricature and distortion of Indian reality. While the ironic distancing in *Moulin Rouge* does add something to our cinematic experience, notably that we never take the plot or the characters seriously, it also takes away from the innocence of Bollywood-style melodrama. The latter is effective precisely because it invites us to suspend disbelief and descend into a sort of childish sentimentality. We know that the real world does not work like that, yet we descend into a maudlin self-indulgence to share our sense of the loss of pre-capitalistic simplicity and our sense of solidarity with the other victims of modernity. *Slumdog*, on the other hand, imports the brutality of modernity into the landscape of the Mumbai slum to show that nothing redeems the lives of the victims except the cultural logic of a foreign film. Jamal has no helpers, no mentors, no friends; his brother and girl-friend both betray him and the game show host, jealous of his success, actually misleads him as he ascends the winnings ladder. His success, then, is both unprecedented and totally irrational. Bollywood, on the other hand, would have provided some helping hand, even a timely *deau-ex-machina* type of intervention. *Slumdog*, lacking this innocence, works for Western audiences, because it makes them feel better about themselves at the expense of the Indians. This is best symbolized by the remarks of the American couple whose Mercedes Benz is stripped by Jamal's friends even as he pretends to be the couple's tour guide. Beaten by the couple's Indian chauffeur, Jamal screams abuses, but is pacified by the American woman, who motions to her husband to help the boy, 'You behaved as you had to; now let us show him how we as Americans behave,' or words to that effect. There were many such improbabilities of the film, including Jamal learning to speak Queen's English by listening to other tour guides at the Taj.

Cultural Flows: Bollywood and Hollywood

In this chapter, Bollywood refers not only to the Hindi film industry, but, in a broader and more nuanced sense, to the multicultural, multilingual, and heterogeneous domain of Indian cinema itself, all of whose filmmak-ing machines are already integrated in complicated ways, even if they are relatively autonomous in production and distribution. Directors, actors, story-writers, technicians, and audiences easily migrate, overlap, and circulate between these cinemas, so that they are not really separate, but must be understood in continuous dialogue with one another. Similarly, Hollywood itself may be seen to be deeply interconnected with British and the continental movie-making process since its very inception, with greater integration more recently with Latin American, Hong Kong, mainland Chinese, Korean, and other Eastern cinemas too. Similarly, there has generally been greater interchange between Hollywood and Bollywood than we fully realize.

There are many types of cross-overs possible between Bollywood and Hollywood. Listed below are a few examples, which will need to be developed and formulated more rigorously.

HOLLYWOOD IN INDIA

The most common of these Hollywood to Bollywood movements has been the many foreign films made on Indian themes and shot on Indian locations. These range from the award-winning (1984) *A Passage to India* (1984) directed by David Lean to the recent *Slumdog Millionaire*. Many other films were shot in India including action thrillers like *Octopussy* (1983) and *Indiana Jones and the Temple of Doom* (1984). But actually, the trend is much older, going back to British films, often based on Anglo-Indian novels on India such as *Bhowani Junction*, *The Far Pavilions*, not to mention TV serials like *Jewel in the Crown* or Richard Attenborough's *Gandhi* (1982). Many of these productions had Indian actors and technicians and were thus truly collaborative.

More recently, there have been many multinational productions mostly by diasporic Indian filmmakers. Of these, the notables include Mira Nair, who has made successful films like *Salaam Bombay!* (1988) and *Monsoon Wedding* (2001), and not so successful ones such as *Kama Sutra* (1996); Deepa Mehta (*Earth* [1998], *Fire* [1996], *Water* [2005]); and Gurinder Chadha (*Bhaji on the Beach* [1993]), *Bride and Prejudice* (2004), *Bend it Like Beckam* (2002). Prior to them there was the unique collaboration between Ismail Merchant and James Ivory. The Merchant-Ivory team made more than forty-five movies over a period of fifty years, many of which were on Indian themes. These include *The Householder* (1963) (Ruth Prawer Jhabvala screenplay, adapted from the novel by Jhabvala); *Shakespeare Wallah* (1965) (Ruth Prawer Jhabvala screenplay); *Bombay Talkie* (1970) (Ruth Prawer Jhabvala screenplay); *Heat and Dust* (1983) (Ruth Prawer Jhabvala based on the novel by Jhabvala); *The Perfect Murder* (1988) (H.R.F. Keating and Zafar Hai screenplay, based on the novel by Keating); *In Custody* (1994) (Shahrukh Husain and Anita Desai screenplay, based on the novel by Anita Desai, directed by Ismail Merchant); and *The Mystic Masseur* (2002) (Caryl Phillips screenplay, based on a novel by V.S. Naipaul). The Merchant-Ivory team was the most impressive of all collaborative ventures between Bollywood and Hollywood; their very impressive oeuvre deserves to be studied at length.

FOREIGN TECHNICIANS IN BOLLYWOOD

There was recently a news item that Western India Cinematographers' Association (WICA) had decided to protest against foreign technicians working in India without work permits or without being members of the WICA. The Indian technicians pointed out that no Indian can work in any film industry aborad without work permits or union memberships; in fact, Indian technicians were often denied such guild memberships to prevent them from finding work abroad. The report also added that that there are more than fifty women from abroad working as extras or dance girls in Bollywood movies, once again, without work permits.[3] What this shows is that Bollywood employs, mostly informally, a large number of foreign actors and technicians, all of whom have contributed to the new style of filmmaking in India, which makes the final product more global in idiom.

Actually, from its inception, the Indian film industry has employed such foreigners. One of the most famous of these is Franz Osten, whose real name was Franz Ostermayr. Born in Munich on 23 December 1876, he established what was the precursor to the Bavaria Film Studies, still one of the largest in Germany. Osten's career in Germany was disrupted by World War I, after which he made *Prem Sanyas* (1925), better known in its English version as *The Light of Asia* (1926). This film was made because a young solicitor from Calcutta, Himanshu Roy, went to Munich in 1924 looking for collaborators to make movies on world religions. Osten returned with Roy to India, with his two cameramen, Willi Kiermeier and Josef Wirsching. Based on the life of the Buddha, *The Light of Asia*, is considered to be one of the more important films of the silent era, though it flopped in India and in the US. But the Himanshu Roy-Franz Osten team went on to make *Shiraz* (1928)/*Das Grabmal einer Großen Liebe* (German title), *Prapancha Pash* (1929)/*Schicksalswürfel* (German title)/*A Throw of Dice* (English title), and *Achhoot Kanya* (1936)/*Untouchable Girl* (English title)/*Die Unberührbare* (German title). Of these three films, all of them were made in English in addition to Hindi and two were made in German and English. What is more, these films were quite liberal for their times, showing scenes of kissing, which until recently was always censored out of Indian movies. The 1920s and 1930s, just before the talkies, were thus a uniquely cosmopolitan period in Indian movies, which anticipate, by many decades, the more recent cross-over movies. Osten, who began with Orientalist gestures, ended up fully absorbed into Bombay cinema. In addition to *Achhoot Kanya*, he went on to make movies like *Kangan* (1939) and *Durga*. Scripted and produced by Indians, these films are hardly distinguishable from the normal run of Hindi movies. But Osten's peculiar cinematic imprint is recognizable to those who know his style.

The flip side of this has been the overtures by the French film industry to Bollywood to use both French locations and technicians, now that the latter have lost a lot of business to the recession in Hollywood. There are over 1,00,000 skilled technicians who live in and around Paris, who are eager to work for Bollywood (Iyer 2008).

BOLLYWOOD ABROAD

Since the 1960s, many Bollywood films have been shot abroad, usually in exotic locations. This trend follows two distinct phases. In the first phase, lasting till the 1980s, foreign locations were merely backdrops, while in the last twenty years, with the growing affluence and clout of the Indian diaspora, Bollywood has not only set films exclusively in foreign locations, but also changed its representation of overseas Indians.

BORROWING OF STORIES, THEMES, REMAKES, AND ADAPTATIONS

From the early days, Bollywood has looked to the West for inspiration when it came to story ideas. Such borrowing actually includes Indian adaptations of famous Western works. If we take the case of Shakespeare alone, from Sohrab Modi to Vishal Bharadwaj, Bollywood has produced notable adaptations of the great bard's plays. Numerous Indian movies have also copied, adapted, pillaged, and cannibalized Hollywood movies in a variety of ways. The latest example of such borrowing is *Ghajini* (2008), whose main plot idea is based on *Memento* (2000). Directed by Christopher Nolan, the film is about a man who suffers from a peculiar form of short-term memory loss, to offset which he tattoos important information on his body in order to track the man he believes had killed his wife.[4]

COLLABORATIVE DISTRIBUTION ARRANGEMENTS

A new trend is for Bollywood films to be sold to major Hollywood companies for distribution or DVD rights. *Taare Zameen Par* (2007), Aamir Khan's production, for instance, was bought by Disney. Similarly, *Lagaan* was distributed by Paramount, and *From Chandni Chowk to China* (2009) was actually produced by Warner Brothers.

BOLLYWOOD BUYS HOLLYWOOD

More audacious are Bollywood's attempts to buy a piece of Hollywood. Karan Johar bought the song rights of 'Pretty Woman', which he remade in his hugely successful *Kal Ho Naa Ho*. More recently, Anil Dhirubhai Ambani Group (ADAG) signed a deal with Hollywood's leading director, Stephen Spielberg, to set up a new studio. The deal worth $1.5 billion was inked after three months of negotiations and will result in the production company, owned in large part by the ADA Reliance group, which has agreed to invest $500 million in the venture. The deal frees Spielberg, the most successful director in the history of Hollywood, from Dreamworks, which was sold to Viacom. Whether this company will also make Hindi movies is not clear, but it does herald a new era of collaboration between Bollywood and Hollywood, besides providing an Indian business group with unprecedented access to the entertainment business in the US and the rest of the world.

HOLLYWOOD–BOLLYWOOD: MULTI-DIRECTIONAL MANOEUVRES

This chapter has emphasized the fact that cultural flows are not uni-directional, but multi-directional. 'Bollywood' and 'Hollywood' have been used as generic points of reference and difference; neither are they essentialized nor considered, in the ultimate analysis, entirely and clearly distinguishable from one another. Rather, they form a grid or network of mutually influencing and influenced global cultural patterns. It is not that all cultures are alike or homogenous, but that their entity or distinctiveness is neither absolute nor unchanging. Cultures are constantly in the process of self-transformation and interaction with other cultures. Both Bollywood and Hollywood are no exception to this rule. While they each have distinctive and identifiable features, their borders are porous and inviting. The real challenge for cultural analysts is to describe the distinctiveness of cultures without succumbing to the temptation of reducing them to some simple model of norm and deviation, source and dissemination, or origin and transformation. What is needed, instead, is to see influences, convergences, flows, and interactions without either essentializing differences, or collapsing all differences so as to produce one global cultural mush. That is why, the concluding section of this chapter tries to point precisely to the difference between Bollywood and Hollywood, as two distinct and competing styles of world cinema.

One may disagree with the idea that given the varieties and degrees of integration between Bollywood and Hollywood, some believe that a national cinema is no longer viable, let alone relevant. However, it must be understood that the difference between the two cinemas is not just cosmetic, but structural. It is actually grounded in a civilizational difference, expressed as an aesthetic alterity. It may be argued that postcolonial difference too is predicated on civilizational dissimilarity (Paranjape 1998). Bollywood remains a cinema of emotion, of *rasa*, rather than of action or plot. It is an old difference between Aristotle's *Poetics* in which action is most important as opposed to Bharata's *Natyasastra* in which the relish of art lies in its ability to produce states of mind which can be 'tasted'.[5] In Bollywood, script, dialogue, songs, and other emotive affects are paramount. In contrast, Hollywood relies much more on technology, special effects, and what we might term the manipulation of material affects. Hollywood is a cinema of action, while Bollywood is still a cinema of feelings, moods, emotions, and sympathy.

Hence, Hollywood may be considered a predominantly masculinist or macho cinema, while Bollywood is more properly feminine or androgynous.[6] Structurally, too, the narrative of Bollywood remains synthetic or synesthetic, with song, dance, poetry, spectacle, dialogue, action, all fused together to form one unified aesthetic experience. Indeed, the musical element is a key difference between the two cinemas. Without song and dance, there is no Bollywood, while in Hollywood, only musicals can afford to accord primacy to them. Furthermore, in Bollywood there remains some contestatory possibilities as it represents the cinema of the dominated, not the dominant; and yet, this is a culture that does not strive to become like its dominant Other.

Many of these issues can be brought into sharper focus when the audience reception of the two cinemas are compared. This topic has come in for close study in recent years. For instance, Lalitha Gopalan (2002) argues that in *Rangeela* (2000), Mili and Munna are the natural pair because both love cinema. Kamal, the third point of this love tri-angle loses because he loves Mili and not cinema! (p. 2). Similarly, in the earlier superhit, *Hum Aapke Hain Kaun...!* (1994), the spectator is assumed to be both a lover and a knower of Bollywood cinema

> The opening credit sequence has both leads, Madhuri Dixit and Salman Khan, looking straight at us singing '*Hum aapke hain koun?*' 'Who am I to you?'; asking us to reflect on our relationship to cinema, the film draws us into a triangular economy of desire, making us an integral part of its love story. (p. 3)

This question—'*Hum aapke hain kaun?*'—is crucial not only to Gopalan's argument, but to our whole viewing experience of Bollywood. Accord-ing to Gopalan, not only does this question acknowledge the specta-tors' amorous relationship to Bollywood cinema, but it also shows an intelligence, self-reflexivity, and ironic distancing that the so-called 'low brow' commercial cinema is capable of exhibiting in thus foregrounding its own artificiality. Bollywood relies on a long and shared relationship between viewer and film, with a knowledge and familiarity on the part of the former of its codes and conventions. An example from the same movie is the *antakshari* scene in which both the characters on screen and the audience share the rich history of Bollywood cinema. While we might argue that Hollywood requires a distancing, Bollywood invites identification, particularly a film like *Hum Aapke Hain Kaun...!* as in-deed do other Bollywood movies such as *Om Shanti Om* (2008). Such movies invite us to reflect on our viewing practices. As Gopalan (2002) observes, 'More often than not, by calling attention to our viewing habits within the diegesis and naming it love, contemporary Indian films have closed the gap between the screen and the spectator.' Gopalan enjoins upon us to read Bollywood from the point of view of a cinephiliac. As Megan Carrigy (2009) recounts, repeat viewing of familiar films and favours reading them by way of particular, perhaps peripheral (what she terms ornamental) details—a kind of cinephiliac's fetishization. It is

Gopalan's conspicuous interweaving of matters conceptual and personal that keeps both love and theory in sight of each other.

Audiences go to a Bollywood movie to laugh and weep, to rejoice and mourn, to celebrate and grieve. It is, to them, primarily an emotional experience that is cathartic, restorative, and recreational. It is both an escape from the world and an affirmation of the world, with all its drawbacks and challenges. And, in the end, as in the traditional rasa aesthetics, a moral order is upheld and restored. There is no ultimate loss because the universe is governed by dharma.

The narrative grammar of Bollywood is thus much different from that of Hollywood. What is more, all the different South Asian cinemas share this grammar more or less. This is possible owing to the civilizational similarities, which are revealed upon careful scrutiny despite obvious political, linguistic, regional, and religious differences. Yet, what was once thought of only as an ethnic cinema abroad is increasingly seen today as a global alternative to Hollywood. It is Mumbai's Hindi cinema, along with Telugu and Tamil film industries in the south, and, to a lesser extent, contemporary Bengali movies that together have the best claims to constitute this global alternative. All these cinemas cater not just to local audiences but to diasporas within India and abroad. They have thus a trans-regional and trans-national reach. And of all these cinemas, it is the Mumbai film industry which is the most widespread, creative, powerful, and technologically advanced that poses the real challenge to Hollywood. It is in this sense that Bollywood virtually embodies the cultural aspirations of not just a nation, India, but that of a whole subcontinent and a civilization.

Notes

1. These connections are well-documented; see, for instance, Ashish Rajadhyaksha et al. (1999).

2. As mentioned during a personal conversation, 25 March 2009.

3. See 'Cameramen unite against foreign technicians in Bollywood'.

4. For a more detailed study of how Bollywood transforms Western cinema, see Ashish Rajadhyaksha (1994) (http://www.anukriti.net/tt/bollywood.asp) and Lalitha Gopalan (2002).

5. On the exposition of the rasa aesthetics elsewhere, see Makarand Paranjape (2007a). Other critics such as Ravi Vasudevan have noted the predominance of excessive emotion and melodrama in Bollywood. See Vasudevan (1989).

6. See Makarand Paranjape, 'Balle Bollywood: Bollywood Dreams and Post-colonial Realities', *The Narrator* (1995); there is a reading of major Bollywood movies, including *Sholay* (1975), as homoerotic, but heterosexual texts.

References

Anil Ambani Group, 'Spielberg To Set Up $1.5 billion Studio', http://in.movies. yahoo.com/news-detail/34260/Anil-Ambani-group-Spielberg-set-up-1-5-billion-studio.html; accessed on 12 February 2009.

Ashcroft, Bill. 2001. *On Post-Colonial Futures: Transformation of Colonial Culture*, London: Continuum.

————. 2001. *Post-colonial Transformation*, London: Routledge.

Ashcroft, Bill, Gareth Griffiths, and Helen Tiffin. 2002 (1989). *The Empire Writes Back: Theory and Practice in Post-Colonial Literatures*, London: Routledge.

Carrigy, Megan. 'Senses of Cinema', http://archive.sensesofcinema.com/ contents/books/03/28/cinema_of_interruptions.html; accessed on 22 May 2009.

'Box office/business for *Slumdog Millionaire*', Internet Movie Database, http:// www.imdb.com/title/tt1010048/business; accessed on 23 March 2009.

'Cameramen unite against foreign technicians in Bollywood', 27 January 2008. http://www.realbollywood.com/news/2008/01/cameramen-unite-against-foreign-technicians-in-bollywood.html; accessed on 16 March 2009.

'Franz Osten'. http://en.wikipedia.org/wiki/Franz_Osten; accessed on 15 March 2009.

Gopalan, Lalitha. 2002. *A Cinema of Interruptions: Action Genres in Contem-porary Indian Cinema*. London: British Film Institute. 'Merchant Ivory Productions'. http://en.wikipedia.org/wiki/Merchant_Ivory_Productions; accessed on 10 March 2009.

Iyer, Meena. 2008. 'Paris woos Bollywood with Hi-Tech Special Effects', *Times of India*, 26 November, http://timesofindia.indiatimes.com/Mumbai/Paris_woos_Bollywood_with_hi-tech_special_effects/articleshow/3757265.cms; accessed on 3 February 2009.

Paranjape, Makarand. 1995. *The Narrator: A Novel*, New Delhi: Rupa and Company.

————. 1998. 'Theorising Postcolonial Difference: Culture, Nation, Civilization', *SPAN*, vol. 47 (October), pp. 1–17.

————. 2004. '*Balle* Bollywood: Mumbai Dreams and Postcolonial Realities', in Udaya Narayana Singh, et al. (eds), *Language, Society and Culture*, Mysore: Central Institute of Indian Languages and Mahatma Gandhi International Hindi University, pp. 96–105.

Paranjape, Makarand. 2005. *Europe in the Second Millenium: a Hegemony Achieved?*, Rila Mukherjee and Kunal Chattopadhyay (eds), in Kolkata: Progressive Publishers and Centre for European Studies, pp. 224–41.

————— (ed.) 2005. *English Studies, Indian Perspectives*, New Delhi: Mantra Books, pp. 487–503.

—————. 2007a. 'The Philosophy and Aesthetics of Rasa', *Prabuddha Bharata*, September, pp. 524–9.

—————. 2007b. 'The Philosophy and Aesthetics of Rasa: A Note', *Sanskrit Studies*, vol. 2, New Delhi: Special Centre for Sanskrit Studies, JNU and D.K. Printworld, pp. 205–19.

Raghavendra, M.K. 2009. 'Plagiarizing for Bollywood', http://www.anukriti. net/tt/bollywood.asp; accessed on 31 March.

Rajadhyaksha, Ashish. 1994. 'India's Silent Cinema: a "Viewers View"', *Light of Asia: Indian Silent Cinema, 1912–1934*, Pune: National Film Archive of India, pp. 25–40.

Rajadhyaksha, Ashish and Paul Willemen. 1999. *The Encyclopedia of Indian Cinema*, second revised edn, London: The British Film Institute.

Vasudevan, Ravi. 1989. 'The Melodramatic Mode and the Commercial Hindi Cinema: Notes on Film History, Narrative and Performance in the 1950s', *Screen*, vol. 30, no. 3, pp. 29–50.

—————. 1995. 'Film Studies, New Cultural History and Experience of Modernity', *Economic and Political Weekly*, 4 November, pp. 2809–14.

3   Mustard Fields, Exotic Tropes,
      and Travels through Meandering
      Pathways

      Reframing the Yash Raj Trajectory

MADHUJA MUKHERJEE

The one who haunts my dreams
And torments me
Tell him to appear before me
                        (Simran singing in *Dilwale Dulhania Le Jayenge*, 1995)

While Bollywood has been read as a particular kind of branding of
Mumbai cinema, it might be worthwhile to closely examine a select
Yash Raj films in order to understand their popularity in the context
of global-local dichotomies. It is imperative that these films be studied as they have been crucial in producing certain ideas of romance
and narrative that have been influential in reproducing specific signs
about the performance and enunciation of romantic love, which are, in
turn, connected to a series of cultural practices.[1] Beginning with *Silsila*
(1981), *Chandni* (1989), *Dilwale Dulhania Le Jayenge* (*DDLJ*, 1995),
and later with *Neal n Nikki* (2005), *Bachna Ae Haseeno* (2008), and
so on, Yash Raj productions have successfully fashioned certain visual,
narrative, and musical tropes about love and romance. Equally signifi-

cant in these films is the journey that the protagonist undertakes as in *DDLJ*, which is reworked with a difference in *Neal n Nikki*, or even further in non-Yash Raj films like *Jab We Met* (2007) or *Love Aaj Kal* (2009). The 'travel and living' excursion and the quest for forbidden pleasures (of sex, adventure, money, freedom, and so on) is gendered and tagged with a 'telos' or a promise that the explorers would return home wiser and 'settled'.[2] This chapter analyses such tropes in order to make meaning of the idea of travel (and love) as portrayed in recent Hindi films.

Rachel Dwyer (2002) reasserts that romance is part of a contemporary consumerist culture and is associated with activities such as travel, going out, and so on that are 'essential components of courtship'. To quote her,

> [T]ravel is one of many ways in which Hindi films depict space and place, in particular places suitable for love and romance, and the idea of transnational Indian.
>
> In addition to movement of media [or 'mediascapes' as described by Appadurai] and other flows, we also see the actual movement of people. To be part of a transnational family is almost hallmark of being middle class in India, ...

Dwyer also shows how,

> Travel and romance have been linked in Western culture as consumerist activities. This is also seen in Hindi films, where travel is associated with consumerism, ranging from shopping in duty-free shops, eating and drinking out....[3]

Hence, if one were to analyse the Yash Raj Chopra trajectory, such travels (first to Europe, then to Canada, and elsewhere subsequently), were launched through one of Yash Raj's most talked about films *Silsila* that depicted its characters dancing and romancing in Amsterdam's tulip fields. This was followed by a honeymoon-like romance and song and dance in Switzerland in *Chandni* which culminated in the violence and fear of *Darr* (1993). Not only did Yash Raj single-handedly popularize the idea of Switzerland as a marker of romance in the psyche of the Indian masses (especially in the absence of Kashmir during that period), but Yash Raj productions and these three landmark films also chalked out a global market for Bollywood.[4] Briefly, Bollywood seems to flag mark its market through its own narratives. Moreover, and more significantly, this global journey appears to predate and coincide with the history of cultural and economic globalization in the country. *Darr* (released before

DDLJ) in 1993, at the point when India's cultural-political histories were being completely transformed, appears like an alarming premonition.[5] *Dilwale Dulhania Le Jayenge*, however, is *the* landmark film, after which Mumbai cinema took its global turn.[6] While a complete study of the unprecedented and unparallel success of *DDLJ* is outside the purview of this chapter, *DDLJ*'s own travels in time has been referred to. Before proceeding to examine *DDLJ*, the history of the travels of Hindi cinema from the 1960s to the present has been outlined below.

Detouring the Diaspora: The Joy of Travel, the Fear of Migration

Depictions of foreign locales were quite popular in 'old' Hindi films targeted at the domestic market such as *Sangam* (Raj Kapoor, 1964) in which, post interval, the young couple goes on an exotic picturesque honeymoon trip to the West. The song '*Main kya karoon Ram…*' articulates the pleasures and transgressions offered by the undefined West. Such locales in the Hindi film not only offered visual pleasures but also became signs that chronicled the differences between the self and the other. Manoj Kumar's *Purab Aur Pacchim* (1970) is a quintessential example of this category. In *Love in Tokyo* (Pramod Chakravorty, 1966), the spectators get glimpses of ropeways, entertainment parks, bridges, monorail, Japanese theatre, *geisha* dances and *sake*, along with snatches of Japanese speech like 'Sayonara'. The protagonist in these films is like a 'tourist', gathering mementos and photographs without interacting with the local people. Alternatively, in *An Evening in Paris* (Shakti Samanta, 1967), the heroine Deepa comes to Paris in search of love where she meets Sam/Shyam, an Indian from Lucknow, who masquerades as a Frenchman. It is through their experiences and the song ('*Dekho, dekho…*) that the spectators get to see disparate objects and spaces like the traditional dances of Switzerland, the Virgin Girl Mountains of Jungfraw, Beirut, fights around Niagara falls, romantic scenes at the Eiffel Tower, women water skiing, and buses and boats of Paris. Moreover, films like *Prem Pujari* (Dev Anand, 1970) or the Amitabh Bachchan starrer *The Great Gambler* (Shakti Samanta, 1979) essentially have nationalist texts that translate European images, metaphors, and expressions into Hindi. For instance, the hit song '*Do lafzon ki…*' shot in Venice, attempts to transport the 'feel' of Italian romance into Hindi cinema. These films chart the passage from India to Europe via the Middle East and present the West as alluring, elusive, dangerous, and exciting. Hence, Inspector Vijay's experiences are intertwined with the exploits of the great gambler Jay (both played by Bachchan) in the film in curious ways. This motif is also visible in a film like *Charas* (Ramanand Sagar, 1976), which narrates the story of a non-resident Indian (NRI) Vijay (Dharmendra) and his tussle over his ancestral property. The narratives of such films move in diverse directions and to different places to tell the tale of diaspora unease about migrating to different parts of the world in search of livelihood: though such travels, as it is evident from such narratives, are never without the mystifying excitement of the unknown.[7]

Although the South Asian migration to the Middle East is a comparatively recent phenomenon, South Asians sailed to the Caribbean as indentured workers during the colonial period.[8] They also migrated to Fiji, Southeast Asia, North and South America, the Caribbean, East and South Africa as well as to the UK during the nineteenth century and early twentieth century, and some, expelled from Uganda, migrated again and settled in Britain. Indians or South Asians also travelled to the North and West of the world and to countries like the US, Canada, and the UK for work in addition to Fiji, Mauritius, Guyana, Malaysia, Singapore, and other East Asian countries as well as to the Middle East for livelihood. The post World War II mass exodus from South Asian countries to the West and to the North produced a new kind of public, spaces, and cultures in those countries over the years.

However, it was the global-local dialogues in the 1990s that prompted the new Hindi films that some have described as Bollywood to include a diasporic *imaginaire* to address their burgeoning worldwide market.[9] Post *DDLJ*, Bollywood often sets its narratives in the West (as in *Kabhi Alvidha Na Kehena* [*KANK*, Karan Johar, 2006]; *Kal Ho Naa Ho* [*KHNH*, Nikhil Advani, 2003]; *Salaam Namaste* [Siddharth Anand, 2005], and so on) and the protagonist is frequently a diasporic youth, who comes to represent the NRI but could also be a 'resident urban Indian'. For example, Shah Rukh Khan (SRK) plays a NRI caught in an extra-marital relationship in *KANK* and travels to the US to seek a cure for a terminal disease in *KHNH*. In both films, he manages to hold up a mirror to both the NRI and the resident urban Indian. This occurs due to a hegemonizing global culture identifiable beyond the plot and character.

Interestingly, one of the biggest hits in the last decade, *Kuch Kuch Hota Hai* (*KKHH*, Karan Johar, 1998) traverses the East/West cycle not by travelling to the West physically but by manufacturing a 'virtual West' within India. In fact, the film has incorporated the West into India through its settings, locations, and movements so completely that it does not even have to produce a West existing 'outside' the East. The film features an urbanized and globalized (playing basketball, wearing baseball cap) female protagonist and an Oxford returned, guitar-strumming second female protagonist who can switch over to singing bhajans with consummate ease. The Oxford-returned protagonist is not represented as a NRI corrupted by 'Western' influences but a loving and lovely young woman who merely sports short, skimpy outfits normalized in the West.[10] She has been internalized in the *Indian imaginary* not as a signifier of the West but as an Indian who has temporarily resided there. Such Bollywood representations establish the diaspora community as national and the local communities as global (Ray 2002).

Transnational Travels and Longings of (Non)Migratory People

Dilwale Dulhania Le Jayenge is a cult film in more ways than one (Chopra 2002). The film, which has been running in a Mumbai theatre for the last fifteen years and more (in Maratha Mandir, for one show), involves multiple issues of cultural practices and economy. Ideologically, the film produces an audience located on the margins of shifting cinematic modes and evolving global conditions. It includes several concerns pertaining to contemporary transformations within nationalist discourses and spaces as well as the growing problems of global-local geopolitics. In fact, it is symptomatic of the concerns that have been tackled by local global, postcolonial Indians. Moreover, its style of narration (that is, the structuring of situations, characterization, the entire mise-en-scène, use of songs, and so on) introduces certain new codes about lifestyle, friendship, love, travel, freedom, and marriage.[11]

The film opens with shots of London's city square and closes in on Baldev Singh feeding pigeons. These images dissolve into a reverie or images of Punjab and its sense of plenitude (and the song '*Ghar aa ja pardesi...*'). Several scholars have examined the monologue delivered here by Baldev (Uberoi 2006; Desai 2004). While feeding the pigeons Baldev says,

> This is London ...
> I have been here for the last twenty-two years ...
> This street asks me my name ...
> From where do I come? ...
> Why am I here? ...
> After all these years, I am still a stranger here ...
> Nobody knows me here, excepting these pigeons.
> They do not have a country like me; they go to the place where they get food ...
> When can I fly (back)? My needs have cut my wings ...
> But one day, I shall definitely return to my country, to my Punjab!

Yash Raj's own nostalgia for his pre-Partition homeland produces an imaginary and a layered topography for Punjab through recurring images in many of his films, including *Veer Zaara* (2004).[12] The film addresses the diaspora crisis of migration, displacement, and labour at the very outset through Baldev's character. But eventually, Baldev severes his ties with UK and returns to Punjab to get his daughter married off to the son of an old friend in an evident attempt to legitimize his claim to come back to the lost homeland. His daughter Simran, the second-generation diaspora, is a cheerful young girl (also a poet), who embodies the alleged diaspora dichotomy about being 'Western outside-*phir bhi dil hai histdutani*'.[13] Hence, although she is shown floating about singing the popular song quoted earlier in the beginning, she appears to be petrified of her father. She seeks his permission to travel and experience the world before she is married off to a person she has never seen in an attempt to live her own life on her own terms even though temporarily.[14] What follows this is one of the most exciting journeys across Europe with expressions like 'Euro-rail invites you to Paris' and 'Euro-rail, Paris-Rome' evoking the idea of adventure and anticipation. Moreover, crucial sequences are built around the suggestion that Simran and Raj would be travelling to Zurich, Switzerland, Bonn, Germany, and so on. The motif of pilgrimage is inverted as a passage through high consumerism. While the first half of the film takes the audience through a memorable trip by Euro-rail (actually by car and also by foot), the narrative moves to the mustard fields of Punjab in the second. The patriarchal moral scheme of the film, the function of the domineering father-figure, and Raj's insistence that he would marry Simran only after obtaining parental consent have been debated at length.[15] But the pleasures that such two-fold travel appears to offer remain unaddressed and the larger political history that they can portray have been inadequately explored.

One of the most significant aspects of *DDLJ* is the subject of travel and how the Indian diaspora travels back to India (largely figuratively) to relocate its ambivalent self. At one level, it is the story of Raj and Simran, who meet as they tour across Europe, quarrel, and then, fall in love. However, they express their love for each other only at the point when Simran is forcibly brought to India and is about to be married off to the groom of her father's choice. In India, Simran and Raj meet surreptiously in spaces milling with relatives as she goes through pre-marital rituals. Raj actively participates in the wedding and other rituals in his attempt to demonstrate his Indianness, in order to impress his future father-in-law and win the bride or the *dulhania* over. The narrative does not repeat the older Hindi cinema formula of resolving the romantic plot with the couple's elopement despite the girl's mother encouraging the young couple to do so by invoking similar instances from popular Hindi films.[16] The last sequence of the film is an elaborate display of Raj's allegiance to the family structure as he waits for the consent of the bride's father to their marriage even at the moment of his boarding the train from Punjab. Simran's run to catch-up with Raj after her father permits her to join him has now become an iconic image that recurs in many films as a sub-text. This ending might appear like a weak dénouement but its meaning must not be read in the 'bloody proof' of one's loyalty towards the father because a certain value is attached to the face of the star and on the audience that has its gaze fixed on SRK (like Amrish Puri). The effect produced by the face of the star appears to play a considerable role in the way in which Baldev urges his daughter (while he continues to gaze at Raj intensely) to 'go my dear, go ....' While the function of the star is a complex issue, the conflict between traditional values and (post) modern conditions is clearly visible in this encounter. Undoubtedly, post-*Hum Aapke Hain Kaun...!* (Sooraj Barjatya, 1994), it was *DDLJ* that became a remarkable instance of the re-working of the wedding theme and the patriarchal moral scheme (Majumdar 2007). To quote Aditya Chopra,

> I was also trying to get something out of my system. I'd be quite troubled by watching those love stories in which the boy and the girl elope. I'd wonder how can they just cut themselves off from their parents who've done so much for

them? How can they be so callous? They have no right to break the hearts of their parents. I wanted to say that if your love is strong enough, your parents will be convinced about your love ultimately.[17]

In one of the crucial sequences in the film, Simran and Raj are forced to share a room for the night after missing their train to Zurich. While Simran, as befitting an Indian girl, is initially unwilling to share a room with Raj, she eventually agrees to consume brandy to save herself from the severe cold. What follows is the memorable song *'Zara sa jhum lu main ... aa tujhe chum lu main'* in which she keeps falling all over Raj and tries to kiss him.[18] After this fantasy song and dance sequence articulating her sexual adventurism, the following morning (post-intoxication), Simran is revealed to be terrified as she finds herself alone in a room with Raj wearing his shirt. After making some flirtatious comments in typical SRK style, Raj assures her that he understands the value of *izzat* (honour) for an Indian woman and that he would never transgress Indian codes. While the idea of Raj's Indian identity emerges gradually through his interactions with Baldev and his visit to Punjab, the 'West', underpinning her diasporic subjectivity, erupts occasionally in Simran and is eventually subsumed under her acceptance of patriarchal moral values. For instance, Simran continuously denies the presence of Raj's image as well as the sound of the instrument he plays in both the romantic songs set in Europe (*Ho gaaya hai tujhko to pyaar sajna ...*) and in India (*Tujhe dekha to yeh jana sanam ...*). One may hence suggest that there are two sets of diaspora identities in this film: (a) of Raj, a mis-directed youth, who loves his beer and is yet to find his 'true identity', regard for elders and traditional-cultural values, and so on; and (b) of Simran, who is perfectly aware of her role within the patriarchal order and, therefore, suppresses her desires, which, nonetheless, erupt in certain inexplicable situations. While Raj finally learns to subjugate his will, Simran learns to articulate her desires despite her initial reservations through their entire journey. Moreover, the role of Malhotra, Raj's father, as the liberal-modern, English (un)educated diasporic figure is crucial as an alterity to Baldev. First, his diaspora identity appears both economically as well as emotionally more 'settled' than Baldev. Second, his support for the match and his comic actions problematize the patriarchal order, which has been largely ignored by most scholars.[19] Thus, Raj's growth as the 'émigré, or foreign-returned [born] Indian', appears somewhat linear (failing in the examination, travelling across Europe, meeting the girl, falling in love, attempting to woo the girl, learning to accept his nascent Indianness, and eventually taking the bride home, and so on). For Simran, the diasporic condition is more complex, since she both conforms to and denies her Indianness. Her sister appears like her mirror image and is indeed the idealized Indian diaspora, though the mother voices sentiments of unease in certain scenes. To use Uberoi's (2006: 182, Chapter 6) words,

> [t]his projection of the anxieties of modernization and identity loss, typically focused on women's sexuality, has been a fairly consistent theme in the Indian commercial cinema and other media of the popular culture over the last half-century or so ...

However, as Desai (2004) has pointed out, diaspora studies have largely dealt with issues of community disregarding the question of gender, which can help us re-read problems of dislocation and a profound sense of emotional loss. For instance, Baldev's job as a storekeeper and his love for Hindi film songs dramatize the economic pressures and emotional conflicts of the migrant and Indian diaspora.

On the other hand, the fact that *DDLJ* is running in a local theatre for the last fifteen years or more underlines the fact that it is equally important at 'home' because it projects the uncertainties of local Indians and their emergent global identities.[20] SRK himself has said,

> I'm like Raj in the film. I live recklessly like him. Like Raj who was so confident about winning over Simran's parents, I knew I could win over her parents and Gauri would be mine.[21]

He also confesses how Gauri was locked up in her house by her parents just like Simran and how he, nevertheless, felt that he could never love her as much as her parents did. While most discussions on Bollywood focus on the emergence of diaspora films, the corporatization of Bombay cinema and its reception as the major feature of brand Bollywood, *DDLJ* seems to hold up a mirror to the developing transnational culture, its political-economy, the dilemma of subjectivity, identity, and questions of gender. Here, it is imperative to refer to the conditions of migration in historical terms and understand that South Asian diasporas are heterogeneous and mixed in terms of languages, religions, castes, classes, cultures, and so on. In fact, the economic and psychological losses produced through postcolonial displacements remain ineffectually examined within diaspora studies. To use Lowe's (1998) words, as quoted by Desai (2004: 12),

> Despite the common conjecture that Asians immigrate from secure, seamlessly 'traditional' cultures, most of the post-1965 Asian displacements come from countries already ravaged by colonialism and now repeated devastated by disruptions caused by neocolonial capitalism, and [media] wars.

Displacement and diasporic circumstances need to be studied in the context of the manifold forms of violence produced through colonialism and how such matters have re-emerged economically and culturally in the era of globalization. This transnational phenomenon is indeed a 'contradictory, fragmented, and heterogeneous' global condition. As Desai has argued in her book (2004), the 'flow of capital, cultural productions, and [the ways in which] people cross state borders in mass migration' are important points for deliberation.

In this context, the subject of home and homecoming become significant. *Dilwale Dulhania Le Jayenge* portrays such 'fluidity of the home' and journeys, which are marked with homesickness. However, diasporic situations do not necessarily involve a physical return but rather a re-turn,[22] or 'a repeated turning to the concept and/or relation of the homeland and the diasporic kin'.[23] What become significant are questions of memory, nostalgia, narratives of history, and imaginings of a 'lost' homeland, which are connected to the desire for, as well as, the fear of travel. This sense of loss often culturally reproduces images of a past and home occasionally inventing the idea of 'origin and authenticity' and, therefore, making the 're-turn' a mythical turn. Kaplan (2000) writes about the meaning of such displacements and travels. She argues that such travels produce a complex structure of representations within an ambivalent historical and personal context in which home is not simply produced as a location, community, culture, landscape, and nation state, but as a structure of feeling. Baldev's displacement and loss of home apparently destabilizes the patriarchal and heteronormative order. Return and travel (as a quest for identity) are, thus, attempts to re-establish these values. However, the journey is not without excitement, surprise, sexual exuberance, permissiveness, transgression, fun, exploration of new places and cultures, objects, consumer goods, and other pleasures. Therefore, Raj and Simran's journey is like a quest for the Utopia of romantic love in the era of globalization. The transformations of Dystopia into Utopia and the transmutation of the memory of violence into a pursuit for happiness and love are significant aspects of *DDLJ*.[24]

Beyond Disruptions: Travels and Tours Unlimited

A 'lesser' film like *Neal 'N' Nikki* (Arjun Sablok) from the Yash Raj banner opens up interesting issues including the ways in which travel becomes a metaphor for identity formation and becomes interlinked with the question of local-global struggles, consumerism, sexuality, and so on. The film *Neal 'N' Nikki* begins by quoting *DDLJ* and displaying a visually unexplored landscape. In fact, the male protagonist Neal re-enacts a scene from *DDLJ* by seeking his father's permission to travel to Vancouver and to experience unrestrained pleasures before he gets married. While Vancouver is no 'Las Vegas', he unwittingly encounters Nikki, a 'virgin in bikini tops', a point that gains significance within the film's discourse. What is intriguing about this film is that Neal and Nikki fall in love via Yash Raj films like *Silsila* and *Chandni* projected on a laptop and through their own re-enactments of the films against the lush Canadian topography. This sequence is engaging in the sense that Nikki requests Neal to do *what they do* in Yash Raj films in order to make her ex-boyfriend jealous. In this process of re-enactment, Neal and Nikki actually fall in love with each other as does her ex with her. This forceful acknowledgment of Hindi/Yash Raj films and its projection as a 'love potion' reconfirms the connections between cinema, consumerism, culture, sexuality, and problems of identity. Interestingly, while Nikki, like Simran of *DDLJ*, retains her virginity despite many temptations, Neal and Nikki, unlike Raj and Simran, do not actually travel to Punjab to experience a sense of nostalgia and belonging. This journey, which never takes place, refigures in the global market where one can discover Punjab without travelling there physically. If (as discussed earlier and elsewhere), *KKHH* addresses the East/West cycle by not going to the West, *Neal 'N' Nikki* negotiates the problem of diasporic re-turn by not coming to the East at all. This seamless suturing of East-West and vice versa truly projects the altered global scenario. While Canada is not exceptional in any way, it is projected as a section of the continuum or as a part of the whole trajectory that connects the diaspora, particularly the Punjabi diasporas, with one another. Sometimes, the place, with its blossoming green pastures, is presented as a spa or health resort, which is juxtaposed with the fields of the idealized Punjab and the Punjabi *kudi* (girl). The gory, bloody, and meaty climaxes of *Darr* or *DDLJ* dissolve into a somewhat insipid happy ending where the 'Sardar with a Guitar' resolves the crisis by claiming his bride. A kiss seals the romance and all ends more or less happily. Certainly, a straightforward reaction to this would be that debates on identity and choices appear to have been resolved by 2005. Hence, *Neal n Nikki*, despite its self-reflexivity and references to *DDLJ* and earlier Yash Raj films, need not traverse through an intense climax. Nevertheless, since the film did not fare particularly well at the box office, one may argue that either this is not a representative Yash Raj film or that the reception of Bollywood films is extremely complicated. Moreover, the successes of films like *Bunty Aur Babli* (Shaad Ali, 2005) in the same year and *Chak De! India* (Shimit Amin, 2007) a couple of years later, highlights the fact that global cinematic passages in terms of spaces and places are complicated and multifarious. Furthermore, both the films underline the journeys that women make. Often, ethnoscapes (spaces produced through flows of people like immigrants and so on) and finanscapes (flow of global capital and so on) merge with technoscapes (flows of technology and so on), mediascapes (the 'repertoires of images and information'), and ideoscapes (ideological shifts connected to Western world-views), to borrow Appardurai's (1990) now familiar notion of 'scapes', to produce a 'landscape' of flustered desires. Thus, the journeys that the young aspirants make from small towns (Benaras, Kanpur, and so on, as in *Bunty Aur Babli*) to metro cities (like Mumbai) and to the north and elsewhere thereafter, or from London to the US after exotic travels and tours in Delhi (as in *Bride and Prejudice*, Gurinder Chadha, 2004), need further elaboration. Besides, such plays of the domains like 'ethnoscapes' 'mediascapes', 'ideoscapes', and so on produce an environment in which aspiring global citizens such as those in *Rab Ne Bana Di Jodi* (Aditya Chopra, 2008) can embark on an imaginary journey through the media. In this film, the young dissatisfied bride (married to a glamourized SRK) participates in a reality dance show to move up the social ladder. In some ways, this woman is very much an Emma Bovary (Gustave Flaubert, 1857) who has now been re-located to the margins after liberalization in India. However, the question of crossing borders is displaced on to a 'media-trope'. Thus, the protagonist hopes to travel the world without actually moving anywhere. Certainly, such travel motifs highlight the history of migration in the colonial and postcolonial period, as well as the complicated meanings of travel in the contemporary ever-changing global conditions.

Travelling without Travel: The Case of *DDLJ* as a Movie Event

On 20 October 2009, *DDLJ* completed fifteen years of continuous screening in Mumbai. Since then, several months have passed and *DDLJ* is still running in Maratha Mandir. The managing director of Maratha Mandir had commented:

> The film completes fourteen years in our cinema hall and we still get at least 60–70 per cent occupancy on weekdays and a houseful board on weekends and holidays. Whoever claims that it is not doing well can come and check our cinema hall.[25]

However, some producers-distributors disagree with this and claim that only about 40 per cent of the seats are occupied on any given day (personal communication). Moreover, a local resident insists that Maratha Mandir is like a covered air-conditioned park. Since it is located near the Mumbai central station, transit passengers pour in and out or lovers walk in to snatch some intimate moments with the *DDLJ* music producing a romantic environment. Apparently, its location, air-conditioning, and the ticket pricing play an important role in *DDLJ*'s uninterrupted run in the theatre.[26] Only *Sholay* (Ramesh Sippy, 1975) and *Mughal-e-Azam* (K. Asif, 1960) appear to have enjoyed equally long runs.[27] In one of his interviews, the projectionist, Jagjivan Vitthaldas Maru, states,

> 'I still can't believe how this movie attracts such a huge audience; the halls still go jam-packed on festival days occasions and weekends. Will you believe it, the film actually did not do well in the first week of its release in our theatre,' he wonders aloud.[28]

The cultural meaning of this phenomenon may be partially understood through what Prachul Goel writes on his blog. His shares his experiences of watching *DDLJ* in Maratha Mandir on Thursday, 19 November 2009:

> This Sunday, Neha and I saw *Dilwale Dulhania Le Jayenge* at Maratha Mandir. Yes, the same cinema that has been showing the movie for the past fourteen to fifteen years. I so wanted to see *DDLJ* on the big screen as I had missed out on

it when I was young, and I really love the movie. So this Sunday, we landed at central station with that sole purpose.... Imagine our surprise when we entered the gates of the cinema to find that it was HOUSEFULL!!! Years after the release of the movie, with the balcony rates reduced to Rs 25, DDLJ with its tagline of 'Come, fall in love...' still goes housefull [sic] on a Sunday morning.[29]

My own subsequent visits to the Maratha Mandir revealed that the house is at least 52 per cent full on any given Saturday afternoon (for instance on 2 October 2010). With 810 tickets out of 1100 sold for *DDLJ* on Sunday 26 September 2010 out of its 1100 capacity, it was successfully competing with *Dabaang* (Abhinav Kashyup, 2010), one of the biggest Bollywood films ever, which had about 843 takers (for the matinee show).[30] Moreover, the balcony is usually full and *DDLJ* continues to engage the crowds inviting hoots, whistles, and laughter. Certainly, *DDLJ*, with its familiar plot and each character, situation, dialogue, and song acquiring the status of a culturally symbolic narrative, functions like a fairy tale. *Dilwale Dulhania Le Jayenge* is a time machine through which one may travel back and forth. The film seems to have transcended its immediate meanings and has evolved into an allegory of Indian modernities. In addition to the low ticket pricing, Maratha Mandir's location and its proximity to working class living quarters appear to have played a crucial role in the meanings it has for people who come to view the film. My personal conversations confirmed that the site of Maratha Mandir—the theatre itself—has attained a kind of social centrality for its viewers. The popularity of this location appears to be significant as people return here to celebrate anniversaries, to rekindle personal memories, or even to produce their own personal records.[31] In a personal conversation, the manager of the theatre stated:

> For the first six or seven years all the shows for the film were houseful. Even for the next five years the house was always eighty per cent full. And, till date, for this one noon show, there have been no losses. While Fridays, which is the Jumma day, are dull days for us, on the Sundays we still have houseful! You can check it yourself....[32]

With reference to this, in a dialogue triggered on a popular networking site (*Facebook*),[33] most respondents mentioned that they have seen *DDLJ* more than fifteen times (mostly on TV though). The film remains a signpost of idealized love largely because most youngsters have literally grown up in the (omni)*present* gaze of *DDLJ*. This strong sense of identification with the film, characters, and the topos belongs to the realm of the *imaginary* to some extent. In view of the above, it might be safely inferred that *DDLJ* has been watching us like a deity and overseeing our cultural transmutations ever since it heralded the formation as well as the consolidation of a global identity when it was first released.

Notes

1. For instance, they do this by reworking certain 'Mills and Boons' strategies—romantic locations (Europe, Canada, and Punjab) and images of romantic love (chiffon saris, singing in the Alps, and so on).

2. For instance, *Neal 'N' Nikki* set in Canada, refers back to *DDLJ* and to the journeys that the diaspora and the next generation make in a self-conscious way, only to escape *DDLJ*'s much talked about climax set in Punjab.

3. Moreover, about Farhan Akhtar's *Dil Chahata Hai* (2001), Majumdar (2007: 142) observes: 'Air travel, car travel, leisure, art, discos, music fashion, style attitude, grace, love, and desire-DCH is a combination of all these....'

4. See Kavoori and Punathambekar (2008) and my essay (2009) on discussions on the contemporary industrial shifts in Mumbai cinema.

5. *Newsweek* report of 2000 (as stated by Rajadhyaksha 2009: 70), mentioned four films which made history in the West as far as distribution of Hindi movies were concerned—three of them being directly or indirectly Yash Chopra productions—*Dilwale Dulhania Le Jayenge* (*DDLJ*, 1995), the film which in some ways started it all; *Dil to Pagal Hai* (*DTPH*, 1997); Karan Johar's *Kuch Kuch Hota Hai* (*KKHH*, 1998); and Subhash Ghai's *Taal* (1998).

6. Chopra (2002: 56) writes, 'DDLJ worked as a fantasy for Indian audiences both inside and outside India.'

7. This has also been discussed in my article (2009: 50–72).

8. Travels for trade, religion, and so on was actually common in the pre-modern era. However, there is a specificity in the ways in which the mass migration of the working class people took place during the colonial period, which in turn produced a new map for transactions.

9. See Preben Kaarsholm (ed.). 2002. *City Flicks: Cinema, Urban Worlds and Modernities in India and Beyond*, Occasional Paper no. 22, Denmark, Roskilde University, and R. Kaur and A. Sinha (eds). 2005. *Bollyworld, Popular Indian Cinema through a Transnational Lens*, New Delhi, Thousand Oaks, and London: Sage, for discussions on the phenomena of the reception of Bollywood by the Indian diaspora in the countries mentioned in the text.

10. One of the biggest hit of the 1970s, *Hare Rama Hare Krishna* (*HRHK* Dev Anand, 1970), however, sees such influences as degradation. The female protagonist of *HRHK*, Jesse/Janice/Jasbir, is an iconic guitar-strumming, beer-guzzling, cigarette-puffing figure of the 1970s. The establishing sequence analyses the causes for Jesse's rebellion and presents Western influences as the reason of her

moral disintegration. Eventually, Jesse has to kill herself and is therefore offered a moralist ending by the narrative, which appears to grow from the fatalistic endings the vamps or transgressive women usually suffer in Hindi mainstream films.

11. See Majumdar (2007) for discussions on 'aestheticization of commodity', the designs and the 'rise of scenic interiors', and the 'new political economy of design' in contemporary Mumbai cinema.

12. See Brown (2007).

13. Besides the fact that this is an oblique reference to the film song '*Mera joota hai Japani...phir bhi dil hai Hindustani*', I also wish to highlight the shifts from an international self-projection (*Japani, English, Russi*) to a more contemporary, diffused, and transnational identity.

14. In my understanding, the film does not necessarily attempt to dwell elaborately on Baldev's character and establish it. Instead, it uses the star value of Amrish Puri and his iconic visage to produce a sense of respect for the great father-figure.

15. See Vasudevan (2010) and Uberoi (2006). Also see my article (Mukherjee 2009) with Manas Ray (2002).

16. In several films like *Bobby* (Raj Kapoor, 1973), *Love Story* (Rajendra Kumar, 1981), *Qayamat Se Qayamat Tak* (*QSQT*, Mansoor Khan, 1988), and so on, the entire climax is built around a thriller like chase between the absconding lovers and the disapproving parents. The closure would alternately be either the acceptance of the love or a brutal murder. Even films like *Dil Hai Ki Manta Nahin* (Mahesh Bhatt, 1991) and *Jab We Met* (Imtiaz Ali, 2007) rework the theme of elopement.

17. As quoted by Uberoi (2006: 185–6, Chapter 6).

18. Prasad's (1998) rather well-known theorization brings up issues of morality and the problem of 'kiss' in Indian cinema in his chapter on feudal family romances.

19. Vasudevan (2010) does discuss Malhotra in p. 369.

20. Vasudevan (2010: 372–3) writes:

The concluding gesture of the film, the exchange of thumps up sign between father and son, then suggests that the acknowledging of the next, globalized generation as legitimate successors comes under the sign not only of patriarchal sanction, but of integration and, indeed, assertion, of local product in the global commodity constellation.

However, he adds, '[w]e should not allow this concluding semiotics to obscure the complexity of the new assemblage of the cinema in the contemporary epoch'.

21. As quoted by Uberoi (2006: 195, Chapter 6).

22. *Namesake* (Mira Nair, 2006), deals with this question of diaspora problems—return and homesickness. It shows the journeys both Ashima and her son Gogol make. Ashima has migrated to the US through marriage and her sense of longing for Kolkata, India is strongly rooted as opposed to Gogol who re-turns to his Indian identity after a series of personal losses.

23. As quoted from Tololyan (1996) in Desai (2004: 19).

24. Such fluidity of travels and identities, however, cannot compensate for the fear and everyday problems of the diaspora. While films produced by Dharma Productions and made by Karan Johar are often read as the examples of lifestyle

advertisements, some of their films do show irrepressible anxieties. For instance, *KHNH* shows the disruptions within the Punjabi and Gujarati diasporas. Moreover, in *My Name is Khan* (Karan Johar, 2010) he embarks on a reverse journey. Initially, Khan travels from India to the US for work (besides the fact that both his wife and brother are into business there) with a certain condition. Later, when his son is killed in a racist violence post 9/11, he moves into the interiors of the US, through floods, cyclones, and hostility to meet the President (George W. Bush) and establish the simple fact that though his surname is Khan, he is 'not a terrorist'. This mythical passage that culminates into the meeting with the black President (Barack H. Obama) underlines the suffering, pain, and bloodshed involved in such travels. In short, such films seem to narrate more than they attempt to narrate, just as such composite and convoluted narratives produce dream-like distortions.

25. 'DDLJ Turns 15 at Maratha Mandir Today', *TNN*, 20 October 2009. For details: http://timesofindia.indiatimes.com/city/mumbai/DDLJ-turns-15-at-Maratha-Mandir-today/articleshow/5140042.cms; accessed on 1 March 2010.

26. Manager Ramesh Vajpayee says, 'Balcony tickets are for Rs 22, Dress circle for Rs 20 and stall tickets for Rs 18', during 2009. (http://timesofindia.indiatimes.com/city/mumbai/DDLJ-turns-15-at-Maratha-Mandir-today/articleshow/5140042.cms).

27. However note that presently the ticket have gone down to Rs 20 for Balcony, Rs 17 for Dress Circle, and Rs 15 for the stalls. Also, Ravi Vasudevan in 'The Contemporary Film Industry-II: ...', published in *The Melodramatic Public, Film Form and Spectatorship in Indian Cinema*, 2010, New Delhi: Permanent Black, p. 374, quotes extensively from *Hindu Business Line Internet Edition*, 28 April 2004. He writes about the public in Maratha Mandir.

> [N]ot an all-male audience. There are courting couples, co-eds, traveling salesman and a whole lot of other movie-watchers. Almost 40 per cent of the audience comprises casual vistors from outside Mumbai. Since Maratha Mandir lies close to Mumbai Central and the State Transport Bus Stand ... From, http://timesofindia.indiatimes.com/city/mumbai/DDLJ-turns-15-at-Maratha-Mandir-today/articleshow/5140042.cms (accessed on 1 March 2010).

28. He remembers rolling out the *Sholay* reels in 1982 for two weeks, but says that, 'Sholay's popularity is nothing in comparison to DDLJ's. Now, there are dozens of familiar faces that I can spot here every weekend, some have been coming for years.' http://entertainment.oneindia.in/bollywood/features/2008/dilwale-dulhania-le-jayenge-654-weeks-050608.html; accessed on 2 March 2010.

29. http://prachurgoel.blogspot.com/2009/11/ddlj-at-maratha-mandir.html; accessed on 2 March 2010. Goel further writes, 'The balcony was full, as expected, with a less-than-IIT ratio of girls to boys. The movie was, to say the least, entertaining. We were mouthing almost all the dialogues along with rest of the crowd. The cheering and whistling at some points was incredible, especially the legendary train scene. It was so much better than the crappy wannabe-Hollywood-cool movies that have no heart and originality that one gets to see these days.'

30. Maratha Mandir official records, courtesy manager Pravin V. Rane.

31. As told by the manager of the house.

52   Madhuja Mukherjee

32. Note Yash Raj provides them with a fresh print of *DDLJ* every year.
33· From, http://www.facebook.com/home.php?#!/profile.php?id=605217723
&ref=profile

Amrita Ghosh writes (19 April 2010 at 12:46 p.m.):
> '15–20, can't remember! i love the airport/station scene when Simran asks for Raj's address to send him her wedding invite. The way Raj says—*"main nahin aaunga"*—and then that song...(sigh)...my heart is fluttering as i post this!'

Anurima Das writes (19 April 2010 at 9:59 p.m.):
> 'almost everyday 1nc i watch a few scenes of the film. i carry the cd with me each time i have some important thing happening to me- exams, any important interview etc. each time i watch the film its a new experience all together. my favourite scene is the first scene after "tujhe dekha toh ..." tht smile those silent moments sum everything up. and....'

Rimjhim Chatterjee writes (20 April 2010 at 10:27a.m.):
> 'easily twenty times n counting...i cn watch whnevr it come on tv. d scene whr shahrukh helps d *kunwari* bua 2 help select saris frm d window...d scene in d barn... of course d mustard field scenes...n church scene...d scene whr he tricks amrish puri 2 get d beer ... man!i cn go on...shahrukh's best!'

References

Appadurai, Arjun. 1990. 'Disjuncture and Difference in the Global Cultural Economy', in Mike Featherstone (ed.), *Global Culture, Nationalism, Globalisation and Modernity*, London: Sage.

Brown, Rebecca M. 2007. 'Partition and the Uses of History in *Waqt/time*', *Screen*, Summer, vol. 48, no. 2.

Chopra, Anupama. 2002. *Dilwale Dulhania Le Jayenge*, London: BFI Publishing.

Desai, Jigna. 2004. *Beyond Bollywood: The Cultural Politics of the South Asian Diasporic Film*, New York and London: Routledge.

Dwyer, Rachel. 2002. *Yash Chopra*, London: BFI Publishing.

Kaarsholm, Preben (ed.). 2002. *City Flicks: Cinema, Urban Worlds and Modernities in India and Beyond*, Occasional Paper, no. 22, Denmark: Roskilde University.

Kaplan, Caren. 2000. *Questions of Travel: Postmodern Discourses of Displacement*, USA: Duke University Press.

Kaur, R. and A. Sinha (eds). 2005. *Bollyworld, Popular Indian Cinema through a Transnational Lens*, New Delhi: Sage.

Kavoori, A.P. and A. Punathambekar (eds). 2008. *Global Bollywood*, New Delhi: Oxford University Press.

Majumdar, Ranjani. 2007. *Bombay Cinema: an Archive of the City*, Ranikhet: Permanent Black.

Mukherjee, Madhuja. 2009. 'Photoshop Landscapes: Digital Mediations and Bollywood Cities', *Journal of the Moving Image*, no. 8.

Prasad, M. Madhava. 1998. *The Ideology of the Hindi Film: A Historical Construction*, New Delhi: Oxford University Press.

Rajadhyaksha, A. 2009. *Indian Cinema in the Time of Celluloid, From Bollywood to the Emergency*, New Delhi: Tulika Books.

Ray, Manas. 2002. 'Bollywood in Diaspora: in the Tracks of a Twice Displaced Community', in Preben Kaarsholm (ed.), *City Flicks: Cinema, Urban Worlds and Modernities in India and Beyond*, Occasional Paper, no. 22, Denmark: Roskilde University.

Uberoi, Patricia. 2006. *Freedom and Destiny: Gender, Family and Popular Culture in India*, New Delhi: Oxford University Press.

Vasudevan, Ravi. 2011. 'The Contemporary Film Industry-II: Textual Form, Genre Diversity and Industrial Strategies', *The Melodramatic Public: Film Form and Spectatorship in Indian Cinema*, New York: Palgrove Macmillan.

4   The Lahore Film Industry

A Historical Sketch

ISHTIAQ AHMED

Films, State, and Religion

Given the multifarious roles that the film industry plays in millions of lives, its importance as a rival to political and religious establishments in influencing and shaping opinion needs to be noted. In fact, film theatres probably have a larger, more loyal, captive audience on a regular basis than political parties and religious institutions. The choice of themes and subjects taken up by films are as much a reflection of the material and intellectual resources available within the film industry as of the wider social, religious, and political contexts in which films are made. It is, therefore, not surprising that film production and the film industry draw the interest both of the state and the religious establishment.

In ideological states, not only documentary films, but even feature films have to conform to an officially-sanctioned political and moral code. Thus, for example, the Soviet Union tightly curtailed artistic freedom, even though Russian filmmakers were pioneers in technical innovations. The Nazis exploited that medium grotesquely to propagate their racial ideology and glorify violence and war. Even in liberal societies, the film industry is not entirely free to choose themes and subjects. On the contrary, it is expected to cultivate patriotism, uphold mainstream social and moral values, and avoid too harsh a criticism of the dominant economic philosophy and social mores. In one sense, the film industry is part of the nationalist project and cannot deviate from it too drastically. During periods of political tension and insecurity, apprehensive liberal-democratic societies can exhibit great intolerance of dissent and even persecute alleged unpatriotic film professionals. The classic case is that of the McCarthyism Era (late 1940s to late 1950s) in the US. It un-leashed a witch hunt for real and imagined communists and leftists in all walks of life and particularly targeted entertainment professionals in Hollywood. Hundreds of screenwriters, actors, directors, musicians, and others were blacklisted and denied employment in the field because of their political beliefs or associations, real or suspected (Buhle and Wagner 2003).

In South Asia, such a concerted onslaught on film professionals has not taken place, though polarization between leftists and rightists has existed in the various filmmaking centres. In the early years after Inde-pendence, the left-leaning Indian People's Theatre Association (IPTA), affiliated to the Communist Party of India, had a significant following among Bombay film professionals, which also included sympathizers charmed by Nehruvian rationalism and socialism. Bollywood actors and other professionals have been involved in active politics since the very beginning. Some were nominated by the Congress Party to the Rajya Sabha, the upper house of parliament, while some directly contested seats in the Lok Sabha, the lower house.[1]

However, the state in South Asia also monitors the film industry in a more direct manner through national film censor boards. These censor boards act as gatekeepers that assess the moral, political, and religious correctness of motion films before they can be shown to the public. From time to time, films are banned or drastically censored if they are deemed to offend public sensibilities and sensitivities.

In the case of the Lahore film industry, the role of politics and religion in determining its fortunes and destiny has been far greater than in any other South Asian film production centre. The reasons for that are many, but the most basic has been the overall ideological growth of Islamism in Pakistani politics. This chapter provides a historical sketch of the vicis-situdes attended upon the Lahore film industry from its inception to the present times.

The Cultural Heritage of Pre-partition Punjab and Lahore

Pre-colonial Punjab was a stronghold of popular syncretic movements, which held rigid orthodoxy and dogmatism of both Hinduism and Islam at bay. The large following of complementary movements like Sufism, Bhaktism, and Sikhism in Punjab, encouraged a lifestyle tolerant and accommodative of the diversity of customs, traditions, and beliefs. No doubt, orthodox faith held sway for short spurts of time in Punjab but such aberrations were soon thereafter superseded by the revival of popular cults and people returned to the traditional pluralist fold.[2] A vibrant tradition of story-telling and melodic rendering of heroic and romantic epics was prevalent in the Punjab. Thus, epics such as Heer Ranjha, Sohni Mahiwal, Sassi Punnu, Puran Bhagat, and other such tales were recited in the evening in *baithak*s (private sittings) or in the village square under a tall and big tree. Also, professional story-tellers would wander around the Punjab narrating tales from the Mahabharata, the Ramayana, the tragedy of Karbala, as well as the *Dastan-e-Amir Hamza*, and many other such stories. On the occasion of Ram Lila and the annual gatherings at Sufi shrines, wandering actors would perform before eager audiences. The *mirasi* or bard was an essential component of the social order who, alone from among the lower order, could take liberties with the landowning castes and *biradari*s (kinship lineages).

What was true of the Punjab as a whole was especially true of Lahore, its traditional capital, since the time of Emperor Akbar, if not earlier (1556–1603). A contemporary of Akbar, Shah Hussain, a rebel Sufi, who had fallen in love with a beautiful Brahmin boy, Madho, drank wine and danced ecstatically in the streets of Lahore. His idiosyncratic behaviour and defiant lifestyle earned him the ire of the conservative sections of society, who approached Akbar to chastise him but the Emperor ignored their protests. Both Shah Hussain and Madho are buried in the same tomb and an annual festival attracts a large number of people to their resting place (Yunus 1991: 136–44). Later, Bulleh Shah, another rebel Sufi and poet par excellence, migrated from nearby Kasur and lived in Lahore where he, too, gathered a large following of non-conformists (Ahmed 2006). As the capital of Maharaja Ranjit Singh's kingdom, Lahore continued to be a city known for its large number of courtesans and musicians and there was much conviviality and entertainment prevalent at his court (Sheikh 2006).

Colonial Lahore

There can be no denying that the Punjab in general and Lahore in particular benefited the most from colonial modernization and development policies. The British decided to recruit a major portion of its army from the Punjab and continue with Urdu as the medium of instruction in schools. The Urdu Board was not established in Delhi or Lucknow, the centres of the Urdu-speaking homeland in northern India, but in Lahore. As a result, educated Punjabi Hindus, Muslims, and Sikhs, were invariably literate in Urdu. By the beginning of the twentieth century, Lahore had turned into the cultural and educational capital of north-western India; Calcutta being the centre in the north-east; whereas Delhi was reduced to being the administrative capital. Although the majority of the population of Lahore was Muslim, the nearly 40 per cent Hindus and Sikhs owned around 80 per cent of modern buildings, commercial enterprises, and businesses (Ahmed 1999: 116–67). They also owned the cinema houses and studios.

Establishment of the Lahore Film Industry

By the early 1920s, there were nine film theatres in Lahore. It was the era of silent films, made in Hollywood, London, Bombay, or Calcutta. The first silent film in Lahore, *The Daughters of Today*, was produced by a former officer of the North-Western Railway, G.K. Mehta, who had imported a camera from London, and the film was released in 1924. The lead role was played by the future legendary Bombay filmmaker, Mian Abdur Rashid Kardar, famously known as A.R. Kardar, who also assisted Mehta as assistant director. The film was produced largely in the open air as there was no studio in Lahore at that time. Kardar and his fellow artist and calligraphist, M. Ismail, later a noted character actor in post-Partition Pakistani films, sold their properties, and in 1928, established a studio on Ravi Road, near Bhati Gate where they lived and founded a film production company called United Players Corporation (Hameed 2006). The lighting facilities in the studios were not very good and shootings were possible only in the daylight. The choice of Ravi Road was partly dictated by the fact that the thick forest along the banks of the River Ravi and the mausoleums of Mughal Emperor Jehangir and his wife Nur Jahan across the bridge provided excellent locations for shooting action-packed melodramas.

The first film produced at the Ravi Road Studios was *Husn Ka Daku* (1929) or Mysterious Eagle. This time, Kardar was the director himself as well as the leading male actor opposite Gulzar Begum. Ismail played a supporting role. An American actor, Iris Crawford, also acted in the film. The film did quite well, but Kardar decided not to act in films and instead concentrate on direction. Kardar also produced *Sarfarosh* (1930) or Brave Heart with Gul Hameed playing the lead role. It was noticed in Bombay and Calcutta and Lahore began to receive greater attention. In 1932, Kardar produced the first talkie from Lahore, *Heer Ranjha*.[3]

But Lahore's reputation as a filmmaking centre was established firmly when Roop Lal Shori, a resident of Brandreth Road, Lahore, began to produce films such as *Qismat Ke Her Pher* (1931), also known as *Life After Death*. Later, D.M. Pancholi, a Gujarati, set up a studio in Lahore, and suddenly, the Lahore industry began to be viewed as an up-and -coming competitor to Bombay. Himanshu Roy, a Bengali, who later founded the famous Bombay Talkies in Bombay, also started his career in Lahore.[4]

Nevile (1993: 98–110) has vividly described the vibrant cinema culture that had evolved in Lahore. People thronged to its various theatres in large numbers and visits by leading Bombay film stars became memorable social events. Among them the visit on 2 December 1937 by the legendary singer-actor K.L. Saigal, a Punjabi from Jullundur, attracted huge crowds as Lahoris came to see him and listen to him. As the reputation of the Lahore film industry spread, it began to attract poets, writers, and intellectuals. In the beginning, films produced in Lahore were mainly in the Punjabi language. Till 1947, Punjabi films were shown in the whole of undivided Punjab as well as in Delhi, Calcutta, Bombay, and Kanpur, where Punjabis had been settling in significant numbers since early twentieth century. However, in the 1940s some very successful Urdu/Hindi films were also produced from Lahore. Among those were *Khandaan* (1942), *Khazanchi* (1941), and *Dasi* (1944).

Lahore–Bombay Connection

Bombay, Calcutta, and Madras emerged as film production centres earlier than Lahore. Although Bombay became the film capital, Lahore enjoyed an advantage over Calcutta and Madras and seemed poised to become the second most important filmmaking city. The advantage was that while Bombay was the undisputed capital of Hindi-Urdu films it was located far away from the Hindi-Urdu language heartland of Uttar Pradesh. Calcutta was essentially the cultural capital of the Bengali renaissance while Madras catered to the Tamil-speaking audiences of southern India. On the other hand, Punjabis were conversant in Urdu, the actual lingua franca of northern India, which was largely identical with spoken Hindi or Hindustani. Therefore, Lahore, other than Delhi, Uttar Pradesh, and Hyderabad Deccan, provided the Hindi-Urdu talent which could be absorbed easily by the Bombay film industry. Therefore, several generations of Punjabi Hindus, Muslims, and some Sikhs with a Lahore connection have been employed in Bombay.

Among them were actors like K.L. Saigal, Prithviraj Kapoor, Dilip Kumar,[5] Shyam Khurshid,[6] Suraiya, Shyama (Khurshid Akhtar), Manorama (a Christian from Lahore), and many others; lyricist Qamar Jalalabadi and music director Vinod (real name Eric Roberts). A Christian from Lahore, Vinod composed the famous 'Lara Lappa Lara Lappa layee rakhda, Additappa, additappa payee rakhda', after he shifted to Bombay where he composed music for some memorable Punjabi films as well.[7] Another Punjabi stalwart among music directors who began his career in Lahore was Shyam Sunder whose immortal songs in films such as Gaon ki Gori (1945), Lahore (1948), produced in Bombay, but shot on locations in Lahore (at that time things were not so bad between India and Pakistan despite the bloody riots of 1947), and Bazaar (1949) have earned him a lasting place in the annals of Hindi film music.[8]

Even the pioneer of the Lahore film industry, A.R. Kardar had settled in Bombay in the early 1940s where he established his Kardar Studios. He went on to make music classics such as Shah Jahan in which K.L. Saigal played his last role before his death in January 1947. Dulari (1949), Dillagi (1949), Dard (1947), Dastan (1950), Dil Diya Dard Liya (1966) followed later. Kardar never returned to Lahore despite belonging to a leading Muslim family of that city. His presence in Bombay helped to establish a large Muslim Lahori group of big and small actors, directors, and music personalities. Among them was Kardar's assistant and fellow Bhati Gate resident, M. Sadiq of 'Chaudhvin ka Chand' (1960) fame (Hameed 2006). Legendary singers like Mohammad Rafi and Noorjahan moved to Bombay in the 1940s as did Shamshad Begum. Music director Jhandey Khan and Master Ghulam Haider also shifted to Bombay. Ghulam Haider's innovative Punjabi tunes and fast beats became a craze. Other noted music directors from Lahore were Feroze Nizami and Khurshid Anwar. Lyricist Tanveer Naqvi had also settled in Bombay (Ahmed 2006). At that time, nobody had any inkling of the fact that India would be partitioned with Lahore and Bombay ending up in two different states.

Partition Riots and Exodus of Hindus and Sikhs

The 1947 Partition of India also resulted in the partition of the Punjab. Hindus and Sikhs who began their careers in Lahore, but later went on to become famous in Bombay were Pran, Om Prakash, Jivan, Hiralal, Meena Shori, Qamar Jalalabadi, Chetan Anand, Ramanand Sagar*, B.R. Chopra* and I.S. Johar. The central role that Lahore played in inducting Bollywood's most famous bad man, Pran, into films is vividly described in his biography (Rueben 2005: 33–43). Music directors Pandit Amarnath and his brothers Husnlal and Bhagat Ram also fled Lahore in 1947 as did Hanslal Behl. O.P. Nayyar recorded his first song, 'Preetam aan milo, dukhia jiya bullai, aan milo' at the His Master's Voice studio in Lahore. He left Lahore only in 1948, when it became clear that people were not going to return to their homes on either side of the Punjab and that the borders, demarcated along national boundaries, would become permanent (interview relayed on Indian Zee TV in 2002).

On the other hand, Hindus and Sikhs of Lahore-Punjabi connection who started their film careers first in Bombay included actors Dev Anand, Balraj Sahni, Geeta Bali, Kamini Kaushal, Rajendra Kumar, Manmohan Krishan, Gulshan Rai, and many others. Novelists and script writers Krishan Chander and Rajinder Singh Bedi and lyricist Naqsh Lyallpuri* began their literary careers in Lahore. Music director Roshan was born not far from Lahore in a village near Gujranwala. (Some sources mention Jalalpur Jattan, in the adjacent Gujarat district, as his place of birth.) The lyricist Rajendra Krishan who wrote some immortal romantic songs for Bollywood was born in Jalalpur Jattan. The Lahore connection continued much later also when Kabir Bedi, Prem Chopra, Simi Garewal, Shekhar Kapur—all Lahore-born—gained fame in Bombay.

Interviews on Leaving Lahore in 1947

The present author visited Bombay in 1997 and again in 1999 and 2001. On these occasions, three interviews were conducted. I had always wondered why neither B.R. Chopra nor Ramanand Sagar had made any films on Partition and especially on Lahore. I met Mr Chopra* in his office in Mumbai on 4 January 1997 to talk about his memories of Lahore. After the customary greetings, he gave me a very moving narrative of Lahore and its nascent film industry. He had started working as a journalist for a film magazine in Lahore and had also launched a film in cooperation with I.S. Johar, but the rioting dashed his dreams and he had to flee from Lahore. He told me that he could contemplate visiting Lahore, but his wife, who belonged to Shahalmi Gate where Hindus and Sikhs were once concentrated, would never be willing to do so. This is because she was haunted by the cries and wailing that broke out when Shahalmi was set ablaze in the summer of 1947. It had traumatized her completely. I then cautiously probed him about why he continued to take up progressive subjects in his films in his long film career as a director and producer and had never succumbed to the communal virus. He wore a wry smile that betrayed sadness as well and said that since all communities were victims as well as culprits of violence, he preferred not to stoke old wounds.

Another outstanding Lahore-born Bombay filmmaker that I talked to was Ramanand Sagar.* I met him on 25 October 1999 in Delhi and again in his home in Mumbai on 20 October 2001. He spoke to me in an accent which was not only *teth* (native) Lahori Punjabi but also of Mozang, one of the old localities of Lahore. Sagar was born in a village, Asal Guru Key, on the outskirts of Lahore but grew up in his grand-parents' house in Chha Pichwara, off Lyyton Road, which, along with Temple Road, and Queen's Road forks off from Mozang Chungi. To my very great surprise, his grandparents' house and our house on Temple Road in which I was born in 1947 were not more than a kilometre apart from each other.

Sagar had been a member of the Progressive Writers Movement and was, for a while, a sympathizer of the Communist Party. His novel, *Aur Insaan Marr Gya* (And Humanity Died) is considered a classic on the partition of Punjab. The first part of the novel is a very moving account of the Partition riots in Lahore. It is generally acclaimed that *Aur Insaan Marr Gya* is one of the most neutral though deeply moving and shocking portrayal of the events in Lahore and other parts of the Punjab. I asked him, too, why he never went on to make a film based on that great novel. He told me that he feared it would stir the vile passions and hatreds of 1947. He made a very interesting observation that what can be read as a piece of literature could prove to be an igniter of communal and atavistic feelings when transmitted through motion pictures. Therefore, he asserted, it was best that *Aur Insaan Marr Gya* remained a novel and was not made into a film.

Lyricist Naqsh Lyallpuri* was working as a journalist in Lahore when Partition took place. I met him in Bombay on 2 January 1997. He gave me a detailed account of how he and his family had escaped from Lyallpur (now known as Faisalabad) as part of a long caravan comprising Hindus and Sikhs. As in many other cases, his account brought out the evil nature of mob violence that was let loose on them as well as some magnificent examples of human mercy and solidarity by Muslims who gave them food and other help and thus enabled them to cross safely into India. He told me he wrote only romantic songs and kept away from politics. In any case, his experience as a 23-year-old young man who had crossed the border from Pakistan to India was that there were good and bad people on both sides. He also saw thousands of Muslim corpses on the Indian side of the Punjab and realized that no one community could be blamed for what happened in 1947.

The same feeling was expressed by Sunil Dutt who was born in village Khurd of Jhelum district north of Lahore. Sunil Dutt visited Pakistan along with Dilip Kumar in 1998 and was very well received by his Pakistani counterparts in the Lahore film industry as well as the people of his village, which he visited after more than fifty years. They called him the lost son who had come back home.* Other Bollywood actors who have visited Lahore include the heartthrob of the 1960s Rajendra Kumar and veteran actresses Kamini Kaushal and Shyama. Rajendra Kumar was born in Sialkot but grew up in the Hindu-majority Lahore locality of Krishan Nagar. He paid a visit to Krishan Nagar to see his old home. People saw tears roll down his cheeks. The locals treated him with a lot of affection. Kamini Kaushal was invited by her alma mater, Kinnard College for Women (founded 1913), to attend the seventy-five-year Jubilee. Not surprisingly, she attracted a lot of attention and met many of her old class-fellows. Shyama (Khurshid Akhtar) visited her relatives. That visit was kept rather private.

Sahir Ludhianvi Emigrated from Lahore to Bombay

The crude logic of the Partition killings, loot, and plunder in Punjab was that if you were a Hindu or Sikh you had to flee to India and if a Muslim to Pakistan. However, the famous poet Sahir Ludhianvi (real name Abdul Haye), first brought his mother to Lahore from Ludhiana because as Muslims there was no place for them in East Punjab. However, Sahir's humanist-socialist poetry was too radical for an ideological state like Pakistan. Even in 1947–8, he had felt that Islamism will come to figure prominently in Pakistani cultural and political life. Therefore, Sahir crossed the border into India in 1948 (some accounts mention 1949). I talked at length about Sahir's exit from Lahore with his bosom friend from Ludhiana, the veteran Pakistani journalist and literature critic Hamid Akhtar, on 18 May 2003 in London during the Punjabi International Congress.* Sahir stayed in Delhi briefly before leaving for Bombay. He was soon to become one of the most sought-after lyricists in Bombay. The Nehruvian type of intellectualism that pervaded the Bombay film industry proved to be fertile ground for his progressive and revolutionary poetry. Some of the songs that he penned for Hindi films remain gems of visionary composition.

Lahore Film Industry after Partition

Apart from Punjab and Bengal, communal rioting also wrecked lives in Hindu-majority Bombay, where Hindu extremists attacked Muslim localities. The famous short story-writer Saadat Hasan Manto escaped with his life and ended up in Lahore. Manto belonged to Amritsar, now on the Indian side of the Punjab. His relatives were already settled in Lahore. In Pakistan, Manto, whose potent pen had sketched some of the most graphic scenes of Partition brutality, was accused of promoting obscenity in his short stories and began to be harassed by the authorities and right-wing elements. He did get some assignments in Lahore films, but died a few years later in 1955 apparently because of alcoholism. In any case, the productive capacity of the Lahore film industry was severely debilitated in the aftermath of the 1947 riots. The flight of artistes, technicians, producers, and indeed capital from the Lahore film industry to Bombay nearly crippled it. However, it kept going on. In 1948, *Teri Yaad*, produced by Diwan Sardari Lal, was released. Some

Hindus had stayed on in Lahore and Diwan Sardari Lal was one of them. Dilip Kumar's younger brother, Nasir Khan, who was then a student at the Hailey College of Commerce in Lahore, played the lead role.[9] *Teri Yaad* did not do well at the box office.

At any rate, migration from Bombay to Lahore picked up momentum gradually. Among the returnees were music director Ghulam Haider, Noorjahan and her husband Shaukat Husain Rizvi, Nazir and his wife Swarnalata, character actor Alauddin, and some others. Later, Khurshid Anwar (1952) and M. Sadiq also came back (probably in 1969 or 1970). Before Partition, some Muslim actors used to assume Hindu names. This tradition continued even in the early years after Pakistan came into being. Thus, the two most famous male stars, Santosh Kumar (Musa Raza) and Sudhir (Shah Zaman) continued with that trend.

Lahore became the centre of both Urdu and Punjabi films. By 1956, thirty-one films were released; eleven ran long enough to celebrate silver jubilees. By 1957, fifteen film companies, five studios, and fifty distribution companies existed in Lahore; but the content was poor and there was hardly anything new. So in 1961, out of thirty-eight films, only five made some money. Until then, Bombay films were shown in Lahore theatres and Indian film songs were played from Lahore and other Pakistani Radio stations. On the other hand, after the Partition of Punjab in 1947, no comparable Punjabi-language film industry came up in the Indian Punjab. Some Punjabi films continued to be made in Bombay, but as a whole, the Partition of the Punjab was a major blow to regional language cinema in India.

Pakistan—An Ideological State and Films

A problem that cropped up in Pakistani politics was that if Pakistan was made for the Muslim nation of India as a state where they could practise their Islam-based distinct way of life, then what all was needed to consolidate such an identity? No consensus existed on this subject. While the modernist ruling elite interpreted such a connection between religion and state in largely symbolic and cosmetic terms, the ulema were convinced that all un-Islamic ways and forms of life had to be eradicated and instead a chaste social and political order permeated by Islamic moral and legal principles needed to be established. In their opinion, music, dance, romantic theatre, representations of the human form, photography were forbidden in Islam and had no place in an Islamic milieu. Therefore, they ruled that filmmaking was un-Islamic. However, a novel interpretation of cinematography by the fundamentalist ideologue, Maulana Abul Ala Maududi, in 1960, helped to generate enough confusion that the issue receded into the background. Maududi opined that Islam forbade the painting of the human figure and face. However, motion pictures threw an image of the human person on the screen and did not reproduce it as a hard picture. Therefore, just as Islam did not ban the use of a mirror which produced an image and not a picture, cinematography was permissible provided that it was exploited to propagate Islamic ideals and themes, and the plays were consistent with Islamic chastity and morality. Moreover, since Islam was against the mixing of the sexes normally films should have no role for females. However, if a female character was absolutely essential, then male actors should dress up as women and play those roles (Maududi 1982: 262–7).

In those early years, the government resisted pressure from religious forces and filmmaking could continue undisturbed. Pakistani film professionals generally kept away from politics. Some, such as character actors Allauddin and Agha Talish, harboured leftist sympathies. Filmmakers and directors Riaz Shahid and Khaleel Qaiser were also of a progressive bent of mind, but, on the whole, Pakistani film industry was apolitical. This remained true even in later years although exceptions were there, such as the leading star Muhammad Ali, becoming an active member of the left-leaning Pakistan People's Party led by late Zulfikar Ali Bhutto and later becoming the cultural minister in the government of Prime Minister Nawaz Sharif.

On the whole, the Lahore film industry primarily produced films based on the boy-meets-girl formula, with a nasty villain plotting to harm the love birds and the hero's sidekick, providing comedy and humour with his antics. Social themes were rarely touched. In this regard, two films from the early phase stand out as exceptions to the rule.

JAGO HUA SAVERA (THE DAY SHALL DAWN, 1959)

Jago Hua Savera was produced by two Lahore intellectuals, A.J. Kardar who directed the film and the celebrated poet Faiz Ahmed Faiz who wrote its story. Shot mostly in a village of East Pakistan, it was a neo-realist critique of the hard lives of poor fishermen. Though understandably not a box office success, it received an award at the Moscow Film Festival and favourable reviews elsewhere internationally.[10]

KARTAR SINGH (1959)

One film dared to probe the Punjab Partition in an unorthodox way and that did not conform to the Pakistani establishment's one-sided standpoint of blaming only Hindus and Sikhs for the violence in 1947. Written and produced by the poet Saifuddin Saif, himself a refugee in Lahore from nearby Amritsar, *Kartar Singh* was a very delicately balanced portrayal of the Partition on the one hand and an expression of a positive aspiration to a separate homeland for Muslims in the subcontinent on the other. The Hindu medicine man, the *vaid*, and the Hindu shopkeeper are portrayed as sincere and caring human beings. The Sikh, Kartar Singh, is the bad character of the village. He has a change of heart towards the end of the film. The Partition takes place and the Muslims of the village leave for Pakistan. Kartar Singh brings a Muslim boy who had been separated from his family to the international border to return him. Tragically, he is shot dead by the elder brother of that boy, the hero Umar Din, who works as a border guard. He mistakenly believes that Kartar Singh is looking for some new opportunity to do mischief. It must be said to the credit of the Pakistan film censor board that it let *Kartar Singh* tell a story that was closer to the truth than what the Pakistani official position has been. Kartar Singh was one Pakistani film that was also imported into India and became very popular in East Punjab.[11]

Ban on Import of Indian Films (1962)

The film community in Lahore had been complaining for a long time that it needed protection and government support to establish itself and that competition from India prevented its growth. This objection was partly correct in that the relationship between Bollywood and Lollywood was not reciprocal and balanced. Very few Pakistani films were bought by Indian distributors while Bollywood films were shown all over Pakistan. Constant lobbying and public demonstrations by the

Pakistani film community finally prompted the Pakistani government, in 1962, to impose a ban on the import of Indian films. In 1963, the government made the rule that every theatre had to devote 85 per cent of the playing time to Pakistani films.[12] It meant that those Indian films that were already in Pakistan could be shown for the rest of the playing time. However, no such quota system was introduced with regard to the playing of Bollywood film songs in Lahore and other Pakistani radio stations.

The 1960s: The Golden Period of Lahore Film Industry

Pakistan's overall socioeconomic indicators in general and economic development in particular during the 1960s were very impressive. The general optimism also pervaded the Lahore film industry. Karachi had started producing films but Lahore remained the capital of the film industry. Both Urdu and Punjabi films made significant improvements in technical areas and many new talented individuals had made their mark in the departments of acting and music. Riaz Shahid experimented with progressive themes based on Palestine (*Zarqa*, 1969) and composite secular Kashmiri nationalism (*Ye Aman*, 1969), and took up class oppression and other forms of oppression in most of his films.[13] Riaz Shahid fell in love with the actress Neelo who was a Christian but converted to Islam when she married Riaz Shahid. Neelo gained great sympathy of the public and won Riaz Shahid's heart when she refused the invitation by the then Governor of West Pakistan, Nawab Amir Muhammad Khan Kalabagh to dance before the Shah of Iran who was visiting Pakistan. She refused and the governor sent the police to bring her, which led to a suicide attempt on her part. This incident inspired a poem by the people's poet Habib Jalib. The opening lyrics were:

Tu kay nawaqif-e-aadab-e-ghulami hae abhi
Raqs zanjeer pehan kar bhi kiya jata hai.

(You are not aware of the protocol of a king's court. Sometimes one has to dance with the fetters on.)

Their extremely talented son, Shan, is currently one of the leading stars of Lollywood. He recently acted in a progressive film, *Khuda ke Liye* (In the Name of God, 2007), which is a scathing criticism of Islamism and extremism.

Complete Ban on Indian Films and Songs, 1965

Things came to a head in terms of the Bollywood-Lollywood relationship when India and Pakistan fought a full-scale war in September 1965 after several months of heightened tensions and military skirmishes in the disputed Kashmir state and in the marshes of the Rann of Kutch on the Rajasthan-Sindh border. Pakistani film artistes took an active part in the radio and television programmes devoted to patriotic themes. The singers in particular rendered many songs extolling Pakistanis to fight for their nation's honour and integrity. Noorjahan lent her rich melodious voice to many such songs. In one, she heaped praise on military officers:

Mera mahi rang rangeela, mera mahi cchaen cchabilla
Haye in karnal ni, gernail ni

(My love is full of joy, fun and passion
He is a general or a colonel.)

In a chorus sung by radio artistes, Hindus were reminded that war and fighting were not activities they were suited for:

Lalaji, jaan deo, larna kee jano
Tussi murli wajjawan wale
Aye gall tuhadey vass di nahin

(My dear Hindu friend, you are no good as a fighter
You are good at playing the flute
War and fighting is not your trade.)

A blockbuster Punjabi film, *Malangi*, released soon after the 1965 war on 14 December 1965 reflected a marked change with regard to pre-partition Punjab. In sharp contrast to *Kartar Singh* (1959) in which the main Hindu characters were presented as good human beings and the Sikh, Kartar Singh, played the roughneck. In *Malangi*, Hindus are stereotyped through the village moneylender as greedy and cunning while the Sikhs continue to play the role of roughnecks and criminals. In any case, the 1965 war greatly exacerbated relations between India and Pakistan. It brought down the curtain completely on Indian films and songs.[14]

After the 1971 war in which the Pakistan military suffered defeat in East Pakistan and lost that wing of the country, relations between India and Pakistan became even more unfriendly and hostile. In 1976, the National Film Development Corporation, headed ironically at that time by the leftist poet Faiz Ahmed Faiz, produced the film

Khak-o-Khoon based on a novel by the right-wing romantic writer Nasim Hijazi in which Hindus during the pre-Partition era were, as a community, portrayed as scheming and cunning and always on the lookout for an opportunity to harm Muslims. Such stereotyping reflected the anti-India and anti-Hindu national mood that state-sponsored films projected.

However, Lahore and other parts of Pakistan could access Bollywood films from two sources between 1971 and now. The first was when the Indian state television, Doordarshan, began to beam famous Bollywood films across the border in the early 1970s. Initially, they created such a stir that government offices and departments would mysteriously become understaffed when Indian films were being shown. The absentees would submit applications pleading the need to attend the funeral of some close relative. Later, it was found that in many cases, the applications were fake as the same relatives—grandparents, in-laws, and even parents—had been declared dead earlier. The second route was the inflow of pirated Bollywood films on video-cassettes via Dubai, Abu Dhabi, and other such places where thousands of Indian and Pakistani workers had settled. In fact, with the introduction of films on CDs and DVDs, the sale of Bollywood films in Lahore and other parts of Pakistan became a most lucrative business.

The Assault on Lahore Cinemas

In 1977, right-wing political forces including Islamist parties embarked upon mass protests aiming to bring down the government of Z.A. Bhutto. He was accused of authoritarianism, bad government, and promoting un-Islamic ideas such as Islamic Socialism. The demonstrations in Lahore were particularly unruly and the wrath of the protestors, during the several weeks of street demonstrations, was particularly unleashed on the cinemas. Forty film theatres were badly burnt in Lahore alone.[15] Mohammad Ali was especially targeted. The film industry virtually came to a standstill.

General Zia's Islamization and the Lahore Film Industry

In July 1977, General Muhammad Zia-ul-Haq overthrew Z.A. Bhutto and established a military government that declared its mission to

'Islamize' all sectors of society. For the film industry it did not mean any direct prohibitions. But the subjects that began to be taken up were increasingly infused with crime and violence, and recourse to Islamist jargon. Ironically, the veteran actress Bahar, who had played the role of a Hindu girl in *Kartar Singh*, was seen accusing someone of apostasy in a film in the 1980s! Government policy discouraged 'too much romance' while Punjabi cinema degenerated into the wild-West type of stories about outlaws and criminal gangs. In the mid-1980s, Babra Sharif, a top star of that era, acknowledged that films' quality had deteriorated. There was a serious dearth of good scripts and that films were being based on gimmicks and action.

The irony, of course, was that General Zia privately had no qualms about inviting Bollywood superstar Shatrughan Sinha to his home to meet his mentally challenged daughter who adored Indian film stars and especially Shatrughan. He became a family friend and used to visit Pakistan regularly.[16] That connection has continued even after General Zia's death and he has regular contact with the late general's children. Some rumours suggest that Zia himself was addicted to Bollywood films.

Murder of Sultan Rahi

One of the most popular heroes of Punjabi films was Sultan Rahi. He is said to have appeared in more than 700 movies and was named in the *Guinness Book of Records* for being the most prolific actor. Some of his major films include *Maula Jatt* (1979), *Sher Khan* (1981), *Chan Veryam* (1981), *Kaley Chore* (1990), and *The Godfather* (1992). His extremely successful film career came to a tragic end on 9 January 1996, when he was shot dead by unidentified persons in a highway robbery on the G.T. Road near Gujranwala. He was on his way to Lahore from Islamabad. At the time of death, he was 58. His fans were devastated. Bollywood superstars such as Amitabh Bacchan and Dharmendra paid tribute to him in an Indian Zee TV programme aired immediately after his death was announced. To this day, his murder remains unsolved.

Pakistan Television Takes Over

At any rate, decay had set in from the early 1980s and few quality films were made. By the late 1990s, the industry was in a state of paralysis.

Third-rate Punjabi and Urdu films continued to be produced, but most talent sought opportunities in television serials and plays. In fact, Pakistani serials attained such good quality that they found eager audiences in Indian homes. Controlling television production was easier because all production was for the state-owned Pakistan Television (PTV) at that time. In TV serials, the writers had a more or less free hand to criticize feudal oppression but had to foster a conservative middle-class urban ethic. The veteran A. Hamid* who produced many serials for PTV told me that government instructions were not to show any love affair unless it was made clear that the boy and girl were in the process of getting engaged and were going to marry each other!

Bombay and Lahore Re-connect

Meanwhile, the Lahori-Punjabi presence in Bollywood had not faded out altogether. In particular, Punjabi producers and directors such as B.R. Chopra and his brother Yash Chopra, the Kapoor clan, the Anand brothers and many others, in one way or another, took up Punjabi themes, especially in film music and lyrics, where Punjabi continued to figure prominently. The first important re-link between Bombay and Lahore was re-established when Salma Agha, a Pakistani and a niece of Raj Kapoor through an uncle who had married a Muslim and converted to Islam, 'who also carried a British passport', arrived in Bombay and was cast in *Nikah* (1982) produced by B.R. Chopra.[17] Meanwhile, Bollywood actress Reena Roy moved to Pakistan after marrying Pakistani cricketer Mohsin Khan. They later divorced and Reena Roy returned to Bombay.

Another Pakistani actress, Zeba Bakhtiar was invited by Raj Kapoor to act in his film *Henna* (1991), which promoted India-Pakistan concord. Raj Kapoor died suddenly in 1988 and Zeba Bakhtiar then acted under the direction of his eldest son, Randhir Kapoor, and played the lead role against Randhir's younger brother, Rishi Kapoor. Angry voices were raised in Pakistan, but the government did not hinder her from working in India. It was a time when a thaw in the India-Pakistan estrangement seemed to be on the cards. First, the Indian Prime Minister Inder Kumar Gujral and the Pakistani Prime Minister Nawaz Sharif met and declared their intention to work for peace and normalization. Dilip Kumar, Rajendra Kumar, Sunil Dutt, Raj Babbar, Randhir Kapoor, and Rishi Kapoor visited their ancestral homes in the Pakistani Punjab and

North-West Frontier Province. The late Nusrat Ali Khan and singers Mehdi Hassan and Ghulam Ali enthralled Indian audiences in Bombay and other parts of India.

Prime Minister Atal Bihari Vajpayee's visit to Lahore in February 1999 culminated in the Lahore Accord, which reiterated the intention to live in peace and to seek a peaceful resolution of the disputes between the two countries. Among those who accompanied him to Lahore was veteran actor Dev Anand who had studied in the famous Government College, Lahore. Dev Anand has described his emotions and sentiments as he set his foot again in his alma mater after more than half a century in very moving words in his autobiography (2007). However, that process was scuttled once again by the outbreak of hostilities at Kargil in May 1999. A Bollywood film, *Earth* (1998), written by the Lahore-born Pakistani Parsi writer, Bapsi Sidhwa, and the Indian-Canadian Deepa Mehta, also of Lahore origin, starring Aamir Khan, Nandita Das, and Rahul Khanna portrayed the grim reality of the riots of 1947 as seen by a physically-challenged young Parsi girl.

Anti-Pakistan Themes in Bollywood Films and Anti-Hindu Themes in Lollywood

However, the rapid tempo of good relations received a rude shock when the Kargil mini-war of May 1999 broke out. It greatly accentuated anti-Pakistan feelings in India. Not surprisingly, such feelings were expressed blatantly in some Bollywood films such as *Gadar* (2001). Others such as *Border* (1997) and *Refugee* (2000) touched India-Pakistan relations and generated controversy but their maker, J.P. Dutta denied any intention of maligning Pakistan and insisted that his real intention was to promote peace between the two countries and their people. In any case, concerts in Bombay given by Pakistani artistes such as the singer Ghulam Ali were disrupted on a number of occasions by goons sent by the Mumbai-based neo-fascist, anti-Muslim Shiv Sena.

Fanatical themes found their way into Lollywood as well. In 2002, *Ghazi Ilam-ud-Din Shaheed*, produced in Lollywood and based on a historical incident in Lahore from the late 1920s, was released. A Hindu, Rajpal, had published a book, *Rangeela Rasul* (The Pleasure Loving Messenger of God), which was highly scurrilous to the founder of Islam, the Prophet Muhammad. It enraged the Muslims who began to agitate against Rajpal. On 6 April 1929, a Muslim youth, Ilam-ud-Din, stabbed Rajpal to death. He was sentenced to death by the courts and was hanged. The film was a eulogy to Ilam-ud-Din's love for the Prophet of Islam.

The Peace Process Rekindled the Bollywood-Lollywood Connection

Things, however, improved once again after the Agra Summit of July 2001, but then deteriorated after a few months when both countries ordered their troops to their shared border following the terrorist attacks on the Indian Parliament on 13 December 2001. Conflict and war were in the air for some months but then the peace process was again revived. Thus, a number of Lahore film artistes began to establish themselves from 2003 onwards. Some Indian artistes such as Divya Dutta went to Lahore to act in some films and TV plays. Bollywood director Mahesh Bhatt and actress Urmila Matondkar visited Lahore and were received very warmly. Lollywood actress Meera created a sensation by agreeing to a kissing scene in a Bollywood film. There were loud protests in Pakistan and attempts to declare her an infidel, but Meera refused to be cowed down.[18]

The Mumbai Terrorist Attack and the Explusion of Pakistani Artistes

As is obvious from the earlier discussion, the Bollywood-Lollywood connection has been hostage to the politics between India and Pakistan. Nothing expresses this sad reality more tragically than the fact the terrorist attacks launched on November 2008 by the suspected Pakistan-based group, Lashkar-e-Toiba, which resulted in more than 150 deaths and injury to more than 500, unleashed a very strong anti-Pakistan wave. Pakistani artistes working in Bombay were ordered to leave India almost immediately. It will be quite some time before the current situation is superseded by a normalization of the Bollywood-Lollywood interaction.

Conclusion

It has been demonstrated above that Lahore held out great promise of becoming the second most important film centre after Bombay, if

India had remained united. The reasons for that was partly the fact that historically Punjab already had a very vibrant tradition of performing artistes. Cinema providing a new forum for them would have been a natural evolution. Second, Lahore, due to Urdu being the main medium of education and literacy in the Punjab, had an advantage over many other parts of India in catering to the Bombay-based Hindu-Urdu (or rather Hindustani) language film industry with actors, song, story and script writers, singers, lyricists, and so on. Third, an exodus of many gifted non-Muslim film professionals also took place at the time of Partition in 1947.

However, on the positive side, Lahore became the number one film centre in Pakistan; only much later films at Karachi, Hyderabad Sindh, and Peshawar began to be made, but Lahore's leading position remained challenged. The Lahore film industry grew and prospered during the 1960s. However, from the second half of the 1970s, Islamism began to gain momentum in Pakistani politics largely as a reaction to a perceived threat posed by the populist ideology of Islamic Socialism propagated by the Pakistan Peoples Party led by the late Zulfikar Ali Bhutto. It radicalized a noticeable number of intellectuals and intelligentsia, as well as workers and peasants. General Zia-ul-Haq came to power in July 1977 after overthrowing Z.A. Bhutto. He initiated the so-called Islamization process purporting to mould all aspects of life into a coherent framework, commensurate with a puritanical and austere version of Islam. Not surprisingly, the Lahore film industry and other forms of popular art were adversely affected by the right-wing politics and policies upheld by the Pakistani state. The Lahore film industry has never recovered from that and has become a producer of mediocre Urdu and Punjabi films. Needless to say, that expecting the film industry to flourish on its own without the consolidation of an enlightened and liberal society is rather unrealistic. Therefore, the revival of a strong film industry in Lahore in terms of internal stimuli is dependent on Pakistani society becoming receptive to artistic creativity and freedom of expression.

On the other hand, the linkage between Lahore and Bombay has been revived several times, but the politics of hostility and war has subverted it each time. That linkage will revive and thrive only if the two countries can sort out their differences and learn to live in peace as good and caring neighbours.

The fact remains that the Lahore film industry can potentially become once again the hub of Punjabi films, and if the quality is good, the 120 million Punjabis living in India, Pakistan, and in the diaspora can become a very large market for its products. The Punjabis are the most affluent cultural group among South Asian linguistic nationalities and entertainment in Punjabi can be a veritable source of wealth generation and prosperity. For that to happen both the internal and external factors have to converge harmoniously. That will probably take some time.

Notes

1. The late Sunil Dutt, a Congress Party office-holder in Mumbai, held the portfolio of sports minister in the federal government when he died some years ago. Similarly, Shatrughan Sinha served as a minister in the rightwing Hindu nationalist Bharatiya Janata Party.

2. The present author met an elderly Muslim gentleman, Mashkoor Sabri, in Multan in December 2004, who told him that he had played the character of Lord Ram in his native Toba Tek Singh as a young lad, much to the consternation of orthodox Hindus. However, by and large, other Hindus and Sikhs enjoyed his performance and there was never a real problem with Muslims playing the role of sacred Hindu personalities.

3. For more details: http://www.mazhar.dk/film/history/40s/1947.htm; accessed on 16 May 2009.

4. For details: http://pakfilms.tripod.com/the_silent_era.htm; accessed on 16 May 2009.

5. Dilip Kumar's mother-tongue is Hindko, a Punjabi dialect spoken in northern Punjab and many parts of the North-West Frontier Province.

6. He started his career in Lahore, married a Muslim, but after his early death, his wife returned to Pakistan. Their daughter later became a famous TV star known by the name of Saira Kazmi.

7. Harjap Singh Aujla. 2009. 'Vinod—A Brilliant Music Director Who Never Got His Due,' For details see: http://www.apnaorg.com/articles/aujla-5/; accessed on 17 May.

8. Satish Chopra. 2011. 'In search of a genius—Shyam Sunder', For details see: http://www.apnaorg.com/research-papers/satish-2/; accessed on 12 March.

9. For details see: http://www.panjabilok.net/misc/movies/landmarks_pak_cinema.htm; accessed on 17 May 2009.

10. *Daily Times*, 22 August 2008, Lahore.

11. For details see: http://www.upperstall.com/films/1959/kartar-singh; accessed on 17 May 2009.

12. For details see: http://www.punjabi.net/talk/messages/45135/20.html/; accessed on 17 May 2009.

13. For details see: http://anisshakur.tripod.com/id20.html; accessed on 17 May 2009.

14. For details see: http://www.robertjsteiner.com/lifestyle/interests/movies/ 50317/india_gives_full_release_of_first_pakistani_film_in____years/; accessed on 17 May 2009.

15. For details see: http://www.panjabilok.net/art/pun_cine2.htm; accessed on 17 May 2009.

16. *Tribune,* 4 August 2005, Chandigarh.

17. For details see: http://en.wikipedia.org/wiki/Salma_Agha; accessed on 18 May 2009.

18. For details see: http://www.santabanta.com/cinema.asp?pid=5493; accessed on 18 May 2009.

References

Adeeb, Yunus. 1991. *Mere Shehr Lahore* (My City of Lahore), Lahore: Atish Fishan Publications.

Ahmed, Ishtiaq. 1999. 'The 1947 Partition of Punjab: Arguments Put Forth before the Punjab Boundary Commission by the Parties Involved', in Ian Talbot and Gurharpal Singh (eds), *Region and Partition: Bengal, Punjab and the Partition of the Subcontinent,* Karachi: Oxford University Press.

—————. 2006. 'The Rebel Sufis of Punjab', *The News International,* 2 December, Karachi.

Ahmed, Shoaib. 2006. 'Lahore Launchpad for Many Filmstars and Singers', *Daily Time,* 2 May, Lahore.

Anand, Dev. 2007. *Romancing with Life: An Autobiography,* New Delhi: Viking/ Penguin.

Ashraf, Agha. 1989. *Aik Dil Hazaar Dastan* (One Heart and a Thousand Stories), Lahore: Atish Fishan Publications.

Buhle, Paul and David Wagner David. 2003. *Hide in Plain Sight: The Hollywood Blacklistees in Film and Television, 1950–2002.* New York: Palgrave Macmillan.

Hameed, A. 2006. 'Lahore Lahore Aye: Bhati Gate—Lahore's Chelsea', *Daily Times,* 24 December, Lahore.

Maududi, Syed Abul Ala. 1982. *Rasail-o-Masail,* vol. 2, Lahore: Islamic Publications.

Nevile, Pran. 1993. *Lahore: A Sentimental Journey,* New Delhi: Allied Publishers Limited and Karachi: Indus Publications.

Pande, Alka. 1998. 'Languishing Tradition', *The Hindu* (Sunday Magazine), 29 November, Delhi.

Rueben, Bunny. 2005. *... and Pran: A Biography,* New Delhi: Harper Collins Publishers India.

Sheikh, Majid. 2006. 'The Rise and Fall of Courtesans', *Dawn,* 17 June, Karachi.

Tandon, Prakash. 1969. *Punjabi Century 1857–1947,* Berkeley: University of California Press.

5   From Chandigarh to Vancouver

Reimagining Home and Identity in the Films of Harbhajan Mann

NICOLA MOONEY

Give a cheer for Punjab, children of the lion,
Dance the bhangra one more time,
Dance the bhangra once again.
Wherever we go, we create a new Punjab.
We earn our livings honestly and invoke our Gurus' names.
We are always in good spirits, we laugh and sing with every moment.
Like pink roses in bloom, we have a regal bearing.
Friends, our hearts are Punjabi,
We live with pride.

After discoursing on the importance of the turban, skill in *bhangra*, and the charms of young Punjabi women to young Punjabi men, so concludes the song '*Gabroo Jawan*' (Young Men) which is featured in the film *Dil Apna Punjabi* (Our Hearts Are Punjabi), starring the popular Indo-Canadian Jat Sikh singer and actor Harbhajan Mann. Arguably part of a recent renaissance of this regional Indian film genre, contemporary Punjabi films such as this one reflect on many of the diasporic issues and themes important to this increasingly transnational community, as articulated here. In particular, '*Gabroo Jawan*' expresses the cultural practices, symbols, and socio-religious values of Punjabis, Sikhs, and particularly

Jat Sikhs, such as bhangra and its feminine corollary *giddha*; the appellation 'Singh' (lion) bestowed on Sikhs by Guru Gobind Singh, and the practice of *naam simran* (invoking the Guru's name); ethical and spiritual notions of *kiraat kamai* (honest labour), and *chardi kalaa* (aspirations of contentment); land, place, home, and identity and the importance of maintaining autocthony and authenticity in contexts of migration; and, the unwavering pride of a people in some ways marginalized by both the Indian nation-state and diasporic modernity. This chapter begins with an exploration of the significance of a notion of home, produced and consumed in contemporary Punjabi cinema, and particularly in those films starring Harbhajan Mann, which target both recently and soon-to-be migrant Punjabi, and particularly Jat Sikh, audiences. Further, how the diasporic imaginings of home, identity, belonging, emplacement, and authenticity are created and deployed across and beyond—to the borders of the Indian, diasporic—and the frequent Canadian contexts of these films are closely analysed. The chapter also demonstrates how both characters and audiences occupy a complex, interstitial symbolic space of departure, nostalgia, and utopian return that is simultaneously a site (however incipient) of experimentation with settlement, citizenship, and transnationality, and the reconfiguration of regional, national, diasporic, and modern identities therein. Across the diverse spaces and temporalities of modernity and diaspora, Jat Sikhs construct their hearts and thus their very beings as completely and ineffably Punjabi.

Positioning the Filmic Diaspora

Modern and diasporic Punjabi life is characterized, in India as elsewhere, by 'global flows' (Hannerz 1992) of capital, goods, technologies, media, and ideas. Relatedly, identities are produced, reproduced, and contextualized through the globalized networks and constant motion of people in the diasporic Punjabi 'ethnoscape' (Appadurai 1996). Diasporic identities are embedded in broad discourses of fixity and movement, origin and destination, territoriality and deterritorialization, roots and routes, global and local; terminologies of place, locality, sitedness and ultimately, identity, are engaged in the conceptualization and reimagining of home (cf. Appadurai 1996; Clifford 1994; Lavie and Swedenburg 1996; Lovell 1998; Meyer and Geschiere 1999; Rapport and Dawson 1998). Relationships between places and identities are transformed as homes old and new become sites for the attachment of identities to places through everyday practices, enactments, embodiments, and discourses (cf. Bahloul 1996; Lovell 1998; Rapport and Dawson 1998). The 'imaginary homelands' (Rushdie 1991) of diaspora are places in which notions of identity, belonging, and emplacement are continually inscribed and reinscribed against contemporary contexts of transnational movement and histories of—what is often violent—modern displacement. But whatever the displacements of home, diaspora does not entail the dissolving of 'homogeneous, discrete and tightly bounded' cultures (Levin 2002: 7), for the ethnographic subjects of diaspora often regard themselves as culturally essential, primordial, and frequently autochthonous entities (Clifford 1994; Fog Olwig and Hastrup 1997; Lovell 1998). Globalized movement reinforces cultural difference (Appadurai 1999; Meyer and Geschiere 1999), as 'there is much empirical evidence that people's awareness of being involved in open-ended global flows seems to trigger a search for fixed orientation points and action frames, as well as determined efforts to affirm old and construct new boundaries' (Meyer and Geschiere 1999: 2). As the remainder of this chapter will suggest, the recent popular cinema of India and in particular of the Punjab region have much to say to these theoretical concerns.

Indian cinema, if situated in its significant contexts of coloniality and postcoloniality, tradition and modernity, and the nation and its discontents (or the centre and its peripheries), can be read as a form of social commentary. Indian films have an 'implicit politics' (Dhondy 1985: 127), wherein film is 'a microcosm of the social, political, economic, and cultural life of [the] nation .... the contested site where meanings are negotiated, traditions made and remade, identities affirmed or rejected' (Chakravarty 1993: 32). Film is also a means of processing transitions to modernity as well as of creating a modernity uniquely Indian. Popular Indian cinema thus provides audiences with the cultural categories with which to order and interpret their lives (cf. Nandy 1998). Film is 'part of a new staging of narratives surrounding Indianness as a problematic field of identity construction in a globalizing world' (Brosius and Butcher 1999: 32). Following Anderson (1983 [1991]), imagination is a central part of this construction of identity and community.

Contemporary Bollywood films, most in the vein of romantic comedies or family-themed comedy-dramas, frequently have transnational plots and characters. They feature stories about globalized Indians in full possession of the forms of elite cultural capital—in which filmic images are themselves important—demanded of transnational others by the West: they are materially and technologically savvy, fluent in English, educated in the right schools (or locations), pursuing the right careers, and living in the right countries. Diasporic Bollywood films construct what Shakuntala Rao has called 'a ubiquitously wealthy and consumption-oriented dreamworld' in which non-resident Indians (NRIs) gain 'meaning from ... [the] state of being abroad' and yet are 'unproblematically represented' as Indian nationals (2007: 66–7). The nation is idealized, celebrated, unified, and, paradoxically, left behind by contemporary Bollywood film's diasporic themes, characters, modes of production, and audiences. Explicitly concerned with a totalizing, consumptive, and cosmopolitan modernity, the film produces a sort of utopian fantasy, the 'emergent paradises' of which are constructed through the social figurations available in family, village, temple, occupation, and public and civic culture (Inden 1999: 43–4). Yet the narratives of Hindi film nevertheless thus exercise struggles over the processes, natures, meanings, and experiences of postcolonial modernity, the nation, and diaspora, representing and negotiating important conflicts between the 'rationalist modern state' and particular attachments to community, locality, language, culture, and morality (Nandy 1998), as well as within the diasporic condition. As the subjectivity of Indian film heroes and heroines is dependent on the collective (Vasudevan 2000), Hindi films are significant venues for the development, representation, and at times, contestation of both national and communal subjectivities.

While the transnational emphasis of Indian film is new, urbanization has been an ongoing theme of the cinema, reflecting that the process is an important part of many Indian modernization and development trajectories and often precedes transnational migration. Dwyer and Patel (2002: 63) note that 'the opposition between the city and the village is frequently made in Hindi film.... [contrasting] the pre-modern or timeless village and the city as an icon of modernity.' As a result, the hero—who is always engaged in working out the various conflicts of modernity—must leave the village, which is now, filmically at least, only what Nandy has called a 'fantasy of a peasant or rural past... a lost paradise' (cited in ibid.: 64). Nevertheless, the rural hero typically triumphs in this new setting, thematically overcoming the dystopia that is urban life and becoming skilled in the practice of modernity, developing new forms of individual subjectivity in honing this expertise (Vasudevan 2000: 12). These transitions are further exaggerated in diasporically themed films. Village forms of sociality are reconstructed and idealized in urban—and diasporic—places as a means of negotiating unsettling encounters with social diversity and cultural alienation (cf. Nandy 1998: 6). This is certainly the case with contemporary Punjabi films focusing on Jat Sikhs, in which working out relationships with the village from the vantage of diasporic locations and experiences are often central to the narrative.

The Indian film is a 'temple of desire' that must 'accommodate deep fantasies belonging to an extraordinarily varied group of people, from illiterate workers to sophisticated urbanites' (Mishra 2002: 29). But because 'the [new] cosmopolitanism of the NRI consists of the ability to move back and forth almost effortlessly between India and the Westernized world', the contemporary diasporic film 'evade[s] the problems of social antagonism and justice' (Inden 1999: 56, 61). As a result, communal and mass audiences and their triumphs and problems are essentially eliminated and alienated from cinematic consideration (cf. Rao 2007). Indian cinema audiences are positioned in part according to their comparative mobility and place vis-à-vis the nation: Indian villagers imagine life in Indian and transnational metropolises via film, urban Indians look home to their villages and out to the world of the transnational diaspora, and NRIs imagine both village and urban Indian homes, as well as cities in other parts of the diasporic world. These positionings and their potential intersections and negotiations are especially complex for Jat Sikhs, who are often privileged in terms of transnational citizenship, but are marginalized within the nation. Across the diverse representations of the Indian film, for several reasons that I will not examine here, Punjab is featured very prominently. Suffice to say that Hindi films of the 1990s and 2000s, in effect 'inscrib[e] Punjabi culture as the national public culture of India' (Dwyer and Patel 2002: 19). This reflects, in part, an ongoing process of struggle and accommodation between the national centre and the regional, ethnic, and religious margin. To better understand this dynamic, I now turn to a brief consideration of *Punjabiyat* (or Punjabi identity) and *Jatpana* (or Jat-ness).

Positioning the Filmic Jat Sikh

A region of northwestern South Asia, Punjab straddles the post-Partition Indo-Pakistani border and both India and Pakistan have present-day states called Punjab. On both sides of this border, Punjabis share a history and language, as well as numerous features of everyday life such as kinship structures, family values, and notions of social virtue; adherence to caste endogamy; notions of gender; folk practices and traditions; material and popular cultures; and, a predominantly rural economy. Indeed, one of the central qualities of being Punjabi is being an autochthonous people, rooted in rural lands and agricultural lifeways, despite a century-old history and tradition of diaspora, which many contemporary Punjabis feel an impulse to join. The notion of Punjabiyat or a unified Punjabi culture recognizes and expresses the region's cultural commonalities (among which we might include the diaspora), such that with the exception of the formal religious affiliations of Sikh, Hindu, or Muslim, the designation Punjabi articulates an ethnic category.

But despite these broad similarities among Punjabis, the possibilities of Punjabi community are intersected and challenged by historical and postcolonial distinctions of religion, caste, nation, politics, and territory. In relation, particular local identities are constructed in which Muslim Pakistanis are differentiated from Hindu and Sikh Indians, Indian Hindus and Sikhs differentiate themselves from each other, and various Indian Punjabi caste communities (whether Hindu or Sikh) assert their further differences. Thus, although the claim to being Punjabi remains a link between Sikhs, Hindus, and Muslims from greater Punjab, and despite the fact that many Punjabis claim an attachment to the common cultural identity expressed in Punjabiyat, each community also attempts to demarcate its boundaries clearly from each other.

Among these various Punjabi communities, it is perhaps Jat Sikhs that make the broadest and loudest claims to being at the heart of Pun-jabi traditions and thus the most Punjabi of Punjabis. A caste of farmers and landlords with significant regional socioeconomic status, Jat Sikhs embody the autochthonous Punjabi identity, but now frequently live urban and transnational lives, although they construct and maintain rural affiliations. In their landed attachments to the region, whether expressed actively in agricultural practices, the social value attached to rural land ownership regardless of occupation and residence, emotive rural nostalgias—or even religiously-nationalist Khalistani aspirations (Mooney, forthcoming)—Jats[1] are emblematic of and perhaps even synonymous with Indian Punjab. While they share in the commonalities of Punjabiyat, their solidarities also manifest an awareness of regional sociopolitical distinctions arising in colonial and national oppressions, notions of religious orthodoxy, modes of linguistic expression, economic discriminations, and perceptions of social marginalization. These challenges forge a notion of Jatpana based in a sense of common interest, shared identity, and ethnic solidarity among Jats that firmly differentiate them from other Punjabis and at the same time encourage their assertions to being representative of Punjabi identity.

Performance traditions and popular culture are central modes of both Punjabiyat and Jatpana. Utilizing regional linguistic, oral, poetic, musical, and dance forms, these are important means of expressing and reinforcing particular forms of Punjabi culture. Today, Punjabi films employ these cultural devices to construct regional identifications among diverse Punjabi audiences. For those still living in villages, the reification of the *pind* (village) and its way of life reaffirms that although farming is an increasingly difficult pursuit, this is the most authentic and pleasurable manner of being Punjabi, and moreover, essential to the retention of Punjabi culture against urban and diasporic incursions. Meanwhile, those living abroad are portrayed to work hard in the pursuit of progress—often of a material nature—and succeed in each instance, with few difficulties in rendering their second-generation children authentically Punjabi. The emotional difficulties of diasporic life—separation from beloved relatives and the land and thus the psychologically grounding senses of belonging, emplacement, and being at home—make profound contributions to the 'rural nostalgias' (Mooney 2011) cultivated through a telescoping emphasis on India, Punjab, and the pind. The urban middle class is given comparatively little attention in Punjabi film (perhaps because Punjabi towns are far less picturesque than its villages) but is in essence diasporic in its separation from the village and its authenticity-producing practices and lifeways.

As in their Bollywood counterparts, song and dance sequences are essential to the character of Punjabi films. Songs are Indian cinema's best devices for the deployment of arcadias and utopias (Inden 1999: 51). It is in film songs that the unique regional traits of Punjab are constructed and expressed, often very explicitly. Although like their

Hindi counterparts, Punjabi films frequently manufacture tenuous plot devices to include songs, these are rarely flashy item numbers of the typical Bollywood variety. Significantly, Punjabi films songs often utilize regional performance traditions: bhangra, giddha, *jaggo*, and *ghazal* in which rural traditions are imagined and reconstructed through an emphasis on an inherently rural character and an encapsulation of autochthonous Punjabi traits, each primordially felt, if demonstrably constructed. Bhangra has been described as 'earthy and robust', reflecting the 'daredevilry... confidence... gusto and overflowing energy' of Punjabis (Khokar 2003: 19–20). These descriptions might be applied to the bhangra performances in Punjabi cinema, which usually outdoes its depiction in Bollywood cinema in a quest for and proof of regional authenticity. Like '*Gabroo Jawan*', many bhangra and film songs feature similar sorts of generalizations about the boisterous and lively nature of Punjabiyat—or perhaps more appropriately, for these films are often Jat-centric, Jatpana—that express not only its autocthonous associations with the Punjab region, but also certain qualities and characteristics that are taken among Punjabis to be authentic and primordial even as they might be essentialist and stereotypical. Watching bhangra performed in film and singing along with the songs contributes to the maintenance and reconstruction of Punjabiyat (cf. Roy 2005: 5), as the songs not only mark the viewer's origins, ancestry, linguistic and performative competences, and identity, they also delineate important social and cultural aspects of being Punjabi. But among Jats, bhangra performed by Jats occupies a particularly privileged position for it is considered most accurate in its linguistic competence, most authentic in its themes and representations, and thus most appropriate to Jat claims of regional dominance.

These claims are developed in marginalizing and dystopic post-colonial historical experiences and collective memories of what were in many cases multiple losses of life, land, and power for Jats against the political and social divisions of post-Independence India, as well as in the regional history of Sikhism. Both Sikh theology and its regional history are meaningful in framing Jat Sikh perceptions of marginality, for Sikhism includes religiously sanctioned formations of militancy and martyrdom, along with a theology of the indivisibility of faith and politics, and the religion developed amid a history of alternating Mughul oppression, self-determination under Maharaja Ranjit Singh, and British colonization. More recently, Sikhs have been marginalized by both hegemony and negligence within the Indian state. It is a matter of conventional wisdom, as well as the position of most scholarship on recent Punjabi history (for example, Axel 2001; Gupta 1996; Mahmood 1996; Pettigrew 1995; Tatla 1999) that the Khalistani Sikh separatist movement has been important in defending against the encroaching peripheralization of the Sikh community within the Indian state, as well as in response to the environmental and social 'violence of the Green Revolution', a Western development intervention spectacularly deployed in but ecologically unsuited to the region (Shiva 1989). The Utopian premise of Khalistan originated in a situation of increasing socioeconomic, political, and religious marginalization in Punjab. The state is one of the more prosperous and socially developed in India and Jats have historically been comparatively wealthy farmers and landlords. But they have been forced into increased urban and transnational migration over the past century, most often as a result of increasing economic hardship related to population growth, land division, and increased debt during the colonial period; land and other property losses at Partition; post-Green Revolution land degradation and capital costs of modern farming; the failure of the nation state to invest in Punjab as both border region and apparent exemplar of modernity; and, status-based aspirations of participation in middle-class and more recently diasporic lifestyles. Contributing further to these marginalizations, Sikhs failed to realize an independent state at Partition, when the region was bitterly divided on the basis of religious demography to much loss of limb, life, and land, not to mention sacred sites; two decades later, in 1966, the postcolonial state was further reduced in area on (what Jat Sikhs claim were false) linguistic premises. Then, in June 1984, the most sacred site of Sikhism, Amritsar's Golden Temple, was invaded by the Indian army in a bloody attempt to flush out the famed Khalistani militant Jarnail Singh Bhindranwala who had taken refuge there after falling out with Indira Gandhi's Congress government which had installed him as a puppet leader in the first place. Five months later, Gandhi was killed in revenge by her Sikh bodyguards, resulting in the mass killing of several thousand Sikhs in targeted pogroms facilitated by local government officials and the armed forces in the capital and throughout north India and triggering what many Sikhs refer to as a period of genocide in the region.

Importantly, the Jat diaspora permits the imaginative possibility of a sovereign community beyond the oppressions of the Indian state (Mooney 2011). New boundaries from other Punjabis and Indians have been constructed and enforced in response and these in themselves encourage migratory displacements. The diaspora condition is one of both Utopia and dystopia (Safran 1991): recently-migrant Jats are embedded as much in the painful moment of departure as in any arcadian reverie or utopian hope of return, and relatedly, attempt to construct cohesive, singular, authentic, primordial, and thus reassuring and comfortable identities for themselves through nostalgic discourses, acts, performances, and images of self-preservation. In this sense, the contemporary Punjabi cinema intends to both represent globalized Punjabi modernity and to reclaim Jat centrality in the project of Punjabi tradition. In doing this, it employs what I call a 'rural imaginary' (Mooney 2011), an active practice, nostalgic discourse, and timeless imagining of Jatpana. The rural imaginary is expressed and reconstructed through the maintenance of socioeconomic links to land and villages and visits home, as well as speech, diet, dress, music, ritual, and of course film. As the originary reference point for the articulation of the rural imaginary is leaving the land—and thus one's traditional caste identity as a Jat—urban Jats in India as well as globally diasporic Jats manifest and participate in the rural imaginary. Inventing traditions (Hobsbawm 1983 [1997]), which simultaneously mark modern separations from land and rural tradition and the reconstruction of a unique, landed, and rural Jat identity in diaspora, the rural landscapes of Jat transnationalism are imagined as akin to the rural homescapes of Punjab (Leonard 1997), thus making home and place continuous against diasporic displacements. Such rural connections and imaginings construct authentic Jat homes and rooted identities on an everyday basis in Indian cities close to Punjabi rurality, as well as in leisure-time, ceremonials, and reminiscent recognition in London, Toronto, Vancouver, or San Francisco. While a hierarchy of displacements may distinguish between the transnational experiences of urban Indian and transnational Jats, they nevertheless narrate very similar rural imaginings and participate in common practices of rural attachment. Urban Sikhs in India as well as abroad share the convention of 'imaginative unity' collectively developed 'from sacred time-space chronotopes of shared genesis, homelands, sacred centres and cataclysmic events of suffering' (Werbner 2002: 11). Indeed, the rural imaginary may be a place of solace from—and perhaps even erasure of—the slights and traumas of Jat history. The rural imaginary thus attempts an imaginative, nostalgic, and utopian Jat reterritorialization of Punjab, and Punjabi cinema, like bhangra (Mooney 2008b), is a key site for this redeployment of Jat identity, uniting the Jat Sikh diaspora in shared imaginings of the homeland and empowering its members through the creation of everyday spaces for the development and assertion of solidarity, difference, and even alternate forms of sovereignty.

The Punjabi Films of Harbhajan Mann

While the Hindi film industry is populated with Punjabis, the regional cinema has not seen as much success as that produced in Mumbai. Although Punjab has long had a regional cinema, it was often subject to critical disdain and significant popular derision among its middle-class audience. While several critically-acclaimed films—such as *Nanak Naam Jahaaz Hai* (1969), *Shaheed-e-Mohabbat* (1999), and *Waris Shah* (2007)—punctuate the Punjabi genre's filmography, the majority of Punjabi language films are considered run of the mill and receive even little popular acclaim. However, something of a renaissance of Punjabi film has occurred over the last decade, perhaps in conjunction with the ongoing development of a pre-eminence of Punjabi characterizations and bhangra-based item numbers in Bollywood cinema. This renewal of regional popular culture most clearly begins with *Shaheed-e-Mohabbat*, a critically acclaimed and popularly beloved tale of an ill-fated Partition romance that metaphorically invokes the displacement and disenfranchisement of (Jat) Sikhs in postcolonial India (Mooney 2008a). As in Hindi cinema, hits often depend on particular constellations and combinations of stars. Those films based on characterizations and plots featuring Jat Sikhs—and often starring them—are among the most successful Punjabi films as there is a large Jat Sikh audience that claims socioeconomic and political centrality in the region, as well as in the South Asian diaspora. Along with this, Hindi films focusing on Punjabi characters, landscapes, and histories are also popular. Conversations with Jat Sikhs during a short visit to Punjab in the winter of 2006/7 suggested to me that regional appreciation of Punjabi cinema is growing.[2] There is even some evidence that Punjabi cinema, like that of Bollywood, is making inroads with global, non-Indian audiences. Punjabi films routinely play in urban multiplexes in the greater Toronto and Vancouver areas, and in April 2009, *Tere Mere Ki Rishta* was reviewed, and recommended, in the *Georgia Straight*, an alternative Vancouver weekly.

Punjabi cinema, and particularly that featuring and produced primarily for Jat Sikhs, must be viewed from the troubled perspective of religious and regional postcolonial marginality as outlined above. Brosius and Butcher advise us that—

> audiences derive meaning from audio-visual media by using a perspective oriented by belief, common sense, and local everyday practices in which visual codes play an important role .... The mediascape ... is situated within a larger field in which culture is translated, negotiated, and continuously renewed and re-invented (1999: 12–13).

While they recently share similar themes, plots, characters, and images, Bollywood and Punjabi mediascapes are at times at significant odds. Despite its importance to national development and modernity, Punjab is often imagined by the nation at large as being populated by rubes and bumpkins living in various states of rural retrogression and backwardness. This stereotype is particularly attached to Jats and is commonly exploited in the *sardarji* joke (a large category of jokes in which Jat Sikh traits are both propagated and ridiculed), as well as in the filmic sidekick. Sikhs frequently complain about their (mis-)representation in Bollywood films in general and in song and dance scenes in particular. One particular criticism focuses on the *nakli sardarji* (fake Sikh) who does not have a real beard. Despite this, Bollywood continues to produce films with central Sikh characters, including the recent comedies *Out of Control, Jo Bole So Nihal*,[3] and *Singh is Kinng*; in these latter two, Sunny Deol (a Jat Sikh) and Akshay Kumar (an Arora Sikh whose real name is Rajiv Bhatia) grew 'respectable' beards for their starring roles, although the characters they played were accused in the community of maligning Sikhs. Occasionally, more serious films dealing with the region's contested history are produced in Bollywood, such as *The Legend of Bhagat Singh, 23ʳᵈ March 1931: Shaheed, Maachis, Gadar, Veer-Zaara*, and *Rang de Basanti*.

Punjabi cinema also produces serious reflections on regional histories, such as *Shaheed Udham Singh, Des Hoya Pardes, Hawayein*, and *Mannat*. And of course, the Punjabi cinema also produces its share of lighthearted films, including *Pind Di Kudi, Munde U.K. De*, and *Tera Mera Ki Rishta*. Indo-Canadian singer-turned-actor and recently producer, Harbhajan

Mann has played the lead role in half a dozen Punjabi feature films since 2002: *Jee Aayan Nu* (Welcome, 2002), *Asaan Nu Maan Watna Da* (We're Proud of Our Homeland, 2004), *Dil Apna Punjabi* (My Heart Is Punjabi, 2006), *Mitti Wajan Mardi* (The Earth/Land Beckons), *Mera Pind* (My Village, colloquially, My Home, 2008), and *Jag Jeondiyan Di Mele* (The World Is A Festival/Place For The Living, 2009). To Jat audiences, it is important that Mann himself is a Jat, and a transnational one at that, as this lends his characters empathy and authenticity; an oft-utilized support cast—again largely Jat—seems to extend this effect. Mann has been among the most successful, consistent, and popularly acclaimed Punjabi actors outside of Bollywood, even if to a Western viewer his characters are perhaps somewhat typecast and his acting at times rather stilted. Importantly, each of his films touches upon significant regional and diasporic social issues, including internecine land disputes, unemployment among educated Punjabi youth, arranged marriage and other gender issues, rural development strategies, alcoholism, the often questionable means of Punjabi emigration, the problem of maintaining Punjabi culture abroad, and particularly in the second generation, and in his latest film, the ongoing scourge of caste in the ostensibly casteless Sikh society.

In a 2006 interview with BBC Leicester, Harbhajan Mann remarked 'we used to talk about the poor quality of Punjabi films and how people used to just laugh at them', and claimed that his 'films are very real, the people, locations, and acting provide something we can all relate to in our lives', thus positioning himself as central to the re-emergence of the regional cinema. In another interview with Canada's *Mehfil* magazine, Mann commented in a similar vein that 'we are trying to get cinema to be not only entertainment but also convey a message through movies'. Asserting the cultural and commercial wisdom of this approach, Mann also stated: 'when I took on Punjabi cinema, no one took me seriously; they told me I was wasting my time and that no one was going to go see a Punjabi movie. And now I have Yash Chopra and big production companies to work with, and this movie was produced by TIPS, one of the biggest producers in Bollywood'. Meanwhile, situating Mann as an everyman rightfully beloved by his community, interviewer Kuljeet Kaila noted that 'Mann may be a Punjabi superstar, but he still answers his own door and lives in a neighbourhood much like that of many of his Canadian fans'. Of course, that is, when he is neither filming nor performing in India; despite having grown up in Canada, in a trajectory entirely counter to that of other diasporic Punjabis for whom there is often no return, Mann's success as a Punjabi artist demands that he spend most of his time in India.

Let us turn now briefly to the films themselves. While each no doubt deserves a more thorough analysis, the films here are dealt in terms of their obvious thematic relevance to questions of home and identity in the Jat Sikh diaspora. Just as nation and modernity are imagined and narrated in Indian popular cinema 'through a visual shorthand of landscape, maps, particularities of dress, and utterance used to evoke feelings of identification' (Chakravarty 1993: 14), the regional cinema is similarly imagined and narrated. Moreover, 'question[s] of fact' are 'not so much related to the question of veridicality or truth but to the issue[s] of memory' (Menon 2003) and experience. Importantly, despite the globalized movement and incipient transnational citizenships of Jat Sikhs and other Punjabis, Punjab remains a village-based society with village-based identities. Indeed, each of the films navigates and struggles with transitions from rural to urban diasporic settings, exploring the potentialities of home and belonging in each.

Mann's earliest two films, *Jee Aayan Nu* and *Asaan Nu Maan Watna Da* are clearly, even self-consciously, concerned with demonstrations of pronounced transnational success, rural nostalgias, and longings, and the discomforts provoked across diasporic locations by personal relationships. In both films, members of the Punjabi Canadian second generation accompany their parents on visits to Punjab and there meet marriage partners in the pind. In *Jee Aayan Nu*, the uncomfortable de-territorializations that accompany transnational marriage are explored, while in *Asaan Nu Maan Watna Da*, idealistically and perhaps somewhat fantastically, an adult brother and sister accompany their parents to Punjab after their respective graduations, cast aside their Canadian love interests, and meet love-come-arranged marriage partners in the village. Meanwhile an internecine land dispute erupts between their father and his younger brother (*chacha*) who, resentful of his elder brother's diasporic success, and prompted by his wife, bribes the village *patwari* to declare the land part of a government expropriation scheme. The ineffective, resource-hungry, and Punjabi-marginalizing state thus provided the means of this deeply unfilial and profoundly un-Jat behaviour in which brothers become others.

Mitti Wajan Mardi is a more complex film, dealing with concealments of plot and twists of narrative. In part a critique of diasporic life for those remaining in Punjabi villages and towns, this film also presents the village to diasporic audiences in terms of some problematic realities. In the film's opening scenes, shortly after Varyam graduates from medical school, we learn that his father, an apparently wealthy farmer, came to the US illegally, contracted a fake marriage to gain immigration, as a result was estranged from his first wife and Varyam's elder sister in Punjab, and thus remained in his second, American marriage of which 'Dr Varyam' was the fine progeny. An alcoholic and widower, Varyam's father urges his son to return to Punjab and right this family wrong by having his first wife immerse his ashes at Kiratpur Sahib and promptly dies; the film thus presents an important message of responsibility—if not quite sobriety—to the macho Jat practice of drinking. It also touches upon humorous, but very real issues of culture shock when Varyam travels to Punjab: he cannot read Punjabi, tolerate the food, or drink the water, and his driver pesters him for foreign liquor. Meanwhile, Varyam finds a love interest in Preet, a teacher in the village school who at one point chides Varyam 'he who fails in Punjabi fails in everything'. Positioning himself as a Canadian doctor who wants to work in the village, Varyam establishes himself under false pretenses and proceeds to ingratiate himself with his step-family, eventually enlisting his sister Rani's aid. Thus in a significant plot twist, a generalized Canada appears to stand in for San Francisco, commenting on the indistinct and interchangeable nature of all places other than those in Punjab; yet, it is their crucial difference that permits the narrative to proceed. Returning to one of the themes of *Asaan Nu Maan Watna Da*, we also learn that the film's title intends a double entendre: responding to their rural imaginaries—the earth of Punjab beckons the members of its diaspora home—but also calls out to land-greed and thus disputes among the locals. In a flagrant and violent land grab, Varyam's *mama* (maternal uncle) cast Varyam's father out after learning of his second marriage and then killed Varyam's sister's fiancé so that she would not have children to claim an inheritance. Both the village and diasporic life are unhomely in this film and Varyam—returning to the US with a heavy heart at leaving his newfound family—is ultimately at home in neither.

In something of a departure from these characterizations of the village, *Mera Pind* emulates the acclaimed Hindi film *Swades* in that the diasporic hero forgoes his transnational success and returns to the village to champion the cause of development. It seems that the village is a place to which return is possible after all. And yet, in *Jag Jeondiyan Di Mele*, Mann's most recent, and arguably most complex film, we see preliminary signs of an accommodation to and acceptance of diasporic life, if not merely a resignation to it. Arguably the most melodramatic and thus 'Bollywood' of themes yet in Mann's body of work, this film nevertheless develops a notion of Sikhcentrism throughout. Visiting a *samadh* (rural gravesite or shrine) in India, an elderly Abhaijyot begins to recount the tale of the ill-fated romance of his youth to his daughter; later the narrative is recounted in several sites on the Canadian west coast and much of the subsequent action is located here. We learn through flashbacks that a young Abhaijyot fell in love with a Banjara (gypsy) girl, Mittro, but their marriage was prohibited by both families, and in tragic response, Mittro took poison, promising Abhaijyot in her last breath that she would meet him again within that very lifetime. Distraught, Abhaijyot flies to Vancouver (apparently sans visa) to work for his mama. Here, he meets Ekam, a blind Sikh girl who is the physical verisimilitude of Mittro. He pursues a romance with her and through a series of narrative developments she regains her sight and ultimately with the approval of both his parents and Mittro's family, marries Abhaijyot, returns to Canada, and has their daughter. The village is a place of outmoded traditions, although parental approvals are still important, while Canada is on the one hand an accepting place where Abhaijyot can mourn and later pursue both success and happiness and Mittro can live again as Ekam, but only transformed into a Sikh and thus an appropriate wife for Abhaijyot, such that particular traditions are restored to inviolability. The now common motifs of transnational Jat success, disputes within Jat families, and the education of children in Punjabi values make their usual reappearances, while in new twists there is significant Canadian product placement and the cameo appearances of two Indo-Canadian Jat Sikh media personalities Baljinder Atwal and Harjinder Thind. These attest to the imbrication of consumerist modernity and diaspora, an expanded commercial significance of diasporic Punjabi film, and a growing Jat adaptation to and comfort with diasporic life.

We may conclude with a few reflections on *Dil Apna Punjabi*, with which this chapter opened. As I have described, the song and dance sequence of '*Gabroo Jawan*' provides a unique area for the reappropriation, reinterpretation, and reassertion of both Jatpana and Punjabiyat amid a troubled regional history and the displacements of diasporic modernity. It is important that the song is deployed following a turban-tying competition for village youth. Mann typically wears turbans only in scenes where he performs bhangra in public settings in his films and the only routinely turban-wearing characters are village elders, strict fathers, and the role of the comic sidekick. Significantly, while his village offers him little more than a life of unemployment, idleness, and paternal castigation—little to support a turban with pride—after a brief sojourn to work abroad, experiencing success as a singer, and in thus 'finding himself' developing a more personal sense of subjectivity, the lead character Kanwal returns to Punjab where he is warmly reincorporated into the patriline, restored to health and self by his mother's love and cooking, and just manages to avert the arranged marriage of his love interest Laddi to another man; thus he is quite markedly re-embedded in land, home, and village. This is the utopian fantasy of diaspora in perhaps its most flagrant state. Because of his skill, and luck, in an especially lucrative occupation, Kanwal can return to the village after only a brief time away, having made good. Despite being an overtly Punjabi film, in the best Bollywood fashion, art has little reference to life in *Dil Apna Punjabi*. While Kanwal's identity is quickly re-authenticated and he is promptly re-ensconced in his home, the diasporic poesis of other '*Gabroo Jawans*', owing to the comparative permanence of their urban, transnational migrations, is given not only to a bittersweet nostalgic longing for the Punjabi pind, but also to the possibilities of subjective authority, cultural authenticity, and sovereign citizenship in diaspora.

Notes

1. Hereon, wherever religious identity is not primary, I refer simply to Jats.

2. Indeed, in April 2007, the *World Sikh News* reported that a Punjabi Film Festival had been initiated in Amritsar.

3. A particularly contentious film linked to the 22 May 2005 bombing by the Babbar Khalsa of the Liberty Cinema Hall in Delhi, killing one person and injuring fifty more, as the audience watched the film's opening scenes.

References

Anderson, Benedict. 1991 (1983). *Imagined Communities: Reflections on the Origin and Spread of Nationalism*, London: Verso.

Appadurai, Arjun. 1996. *Modernity at Large: Cultural Dimensions of Globalization*. Minneapolis: University of Minnesota Press.

————. 1999. 'Dead Certainty: Ethnic Violence in the Era of Globalization', in Birgit Meyer and Peter Geschiere (eds), *Globalization and Identity: Dialectics of Flow and Closure*, Oxford: Blackwell Publishers.

Axel, Brian Keith. 2001. *The Nation's Tortured Body: Violence, Representation and the Formation of a Sikh 'Diaspora'*, Durham: Duke University Press.

Bahloul, Joelle. 1996. *The Architecture of Memory: A Jewish-Muslim Household in Colonial Algeria, 1937–62*, Cambridge University Press.

Brosius, Christiane and Melissa Butcher. 1999. 'Introduction: Image Journeys', in Christiane Brosius and Melissa Butcher (eds), *Image Journeys*, New Delhi: Sage Publications.

Chakravarty, Sumita. 1993. *National Identity in Indian Popular Cinema (1947–1987)*, Austin, TX: University of Texas Press.

Clifford, James. 1994. 'Diasporas', *Cultural Anthropology*, vol. 9, no. 3, pp. 302–38.

Dhondy, Farrukh. 1985. 'Keeping Faith: Indian Film and its World', *Daedalus*, vol. 114, no. 4, pp. 125–40.

Dwyer, Rachel and Divia Patel. 2002. *Cinema India: The Visual Culture of Hindi Film*, New Brunswick, NJ: Rutgers Press.

Fog Olwig, Karen and Kirsten Hastrup (eds). 1997. *Sitting Culture: The Shifting Anthropological Object*, London: Routledge.

Gupta, Dipankar. 1996. *The Context of Ethnicity: Sikh Identity in a Comparative Perspective*, New Delhi: Oxford University Press.

Hannerz, Ulf. 1992. *Cultural Complexity: Studies in the Social Organization of Meaning*, New York: Columbia University Press.

Hobsbawm, Eric. 1983 [1997 reprint]. 'Introduction: Inventing Traditions', in Eric Hobsbawm and Terence Ranger (eds), *The Invention of Tradition*, Cambridge: Canto/Cambridge University Press.

Inden, Ronald. 1999. 'Transnational Cinema, Erotic Arcadia and Commercial Utopia in Hindi Films', in Christiane Brosius and Melissa Butcher (eds), *Image Journeys*, New Delhi: Sage Publications.

Kaila, Kuljeet. 2003. 'Harbhajan Mann, Music Mann', *Mehfil Magazine*; http://www.mehfilmagazine.com/featurestory05.cfm.

Khokar, Ashish Mohan. 2003. *Folk Dance: Tribal, Ritual and Martial Forms*, New Delhi: Rupa & Co.

Lavie, Smadar and Ted Swedenburg (eds). 1996. *Displacement, Diaspora and Geographies of Identity*, Durham, NC: Duke University Press.

Leonard, Karen. 1997. 'Finding One's Own Place: Asian Landscapes Re-Visioned in Rural California', in Akhil Gupta and James Ferguson (eds), *Culture, Power, Place: Explorations in Critical Anthropology*, Durham, NC: Duke University Press.

Levin, Michael. 2002. 'Flow and Place: Transnationalism in Four Places', *Anthropologica*, vol. 44, no. 1, pp. 3–12.

Lovell, Nadia (ed.). 1998. *Locality and Belonging*, London: Routledge.

Mahmood, Cynthia Keppeley. 1996. *Fighting for Faith and Nation: Dialogues with Sikh Militants*, Philadelphia: University of Pennsylvania Press.

Mann, Harbhajan. 2006. Interview with BBC Leicester. http://www.bbc.co.uk/leicester/content/articles/2006/04/15/harbhajan_mann_qa.shtml.

Menon, Dilip. 2003. 'The Kiss and Bhagat Singh', *Seminar*, no. 525.

Meyer, Birgit and Peter Geschiere (eds). 1999. *Globalization and Identity: Dialectics of Flow and Closure*, Oxford: Blackwell Publishers.

Mishra, Vijay. 2002. *Bollywood Cinema: Temples of Desire*, New York: Routledge.

Mooney, Nicola. 2008a. 'Of Love, Martyrdom, and (In)Subordination: Sikh Experiences of Partition in the Films Shaheed-e-Mohabbat and Gadar: Ek Prem Katha', in Nandi Bhatia and Anjali Gera Roy (eds), *Partitioned Lives: Narratives of Home, Displacement, and Resettlement*, Delhi: Dorling Kindersley/Pearson.

————. 2008b. 'Aaja Nach Lai (Come Dance): Performing Dance and Practicing Identity among Punjabis in Canada', *Ethnologies*, vol. 30, no. 1, pp. 103–24.

————. 2011. *Rural Nostalgias and Transnational Dreams: Identity and Modernity among Jat Sikhs*, Toronto: University of Toronto Press.

————. (Forthcoming) 'Remembered Rurality: The Idyllic Places and Troubled Spaces of Jat Sikh Nostalgia', in Pauline McKenzie Aucoin (ed.), *Culture, Meaning and Space: Studies in Place and Practice*, Berghahn Books.

Nandy, Ashis. 1998. 'Introduction: Indian Popular Cinema as a Slum's Eye View of Politics', in Ashis Nandy (ed.), *The Secret Politics of Our Desires: Innocence, Culpability and Popular Indian Cinema*, Zed Books.

Pettigrew, Joyce. 1995. *The Sikhs of the Punjab: Unheard Voices of State and Guerilla Violence*, London: Zed Books.

Rao, Shakuntala. 2007. 'The Globalization of Bollywood: an Ethnography of Non-Elite Audiences in India', *The Communication Review*, vol. 10, pp. 57–76.

Rapport, Nigel and Andrew Dawson (eds). 1998. *Migrants of Identity: Perceptions of Home in a World of Movement*, London: Berg.

Roy, Anjali Gera. 2005. 'Folk's Kool Turn', paper given at M.B. Emeneau Centenary International Conference on South Asian Linguistics; http://www.ciil.org/announcement/MBE_programme/paper/paper9.htm.

Roy, Parama. 1998. *Indian Traffic: Identities in Question in Colonial and Post-Colonial India*, Berkeley: University of California Press.

Rushdie, Salman. 1991. *Imaginary Homelands*, London: Granta.

Safran, William. 1991. 'Diasporas in Modern Societies: Myths of Homeland and Return', *Diaspora*, Spring, pp. 83–99.

Shiva, Vandana. 1989. *The Violence of the Green Revolution: Ecological Degradation and Political Conflict in Punjab*, Dehra Dun: Research Foundation for Science and Ecology.

Tatla, Darshan Singh. 1999. *The Sikh Diaspora: The Search for Statehood*, London: UCL Press.

Uberoi, Patricia. 1998. 'The Diaspora Comes Home: Disciplining Desire in DDLJ', *Contributions to Indian Sociology*, vol. 32, no. 2, pp. 305–36.

Vasudevan, Ravi. 2000. *Making Meaning in Indian Cinema*. New Delhi: Oxford University Press.

Werbner, Pnina. 2002. *Imagined Diasporas among Manchester Muslims: The Public Performance of Pakistani Transnational Identity Politics*. Oxford: James Currey.

6 Bollywood, Tollywood, Dollywood

Re-visiting Cross-border Flows and the Beat of the 1970s in the Context of Globalization

ANURADHA GHOSH

The terms of reference for Hollywood and its other(s) become the focal point of this chapter that wishes to engage with one historical axis, that is the period of the 1970s, and the beat of resistance aesthetics, which finds three diverse expressions in the cinematic productions of Mumbai-based industries referred to in the past decade or so as 'Bollywood', Kolkata-based productions in Tollygunj as 'Tollywood', and Dhaka-based productions in Bangladesh as 'Dollywood'. The issues that are simultaneously thrown up occur in a dialectical bind. The first binary is that of the popular and the canon represented through the alternative cinema movement that had a regional location (primarily the state of West Bengal in terms of its origin) but not necessarily a regional orientation. This, however, changes to what can be termed as the popular as canon in the productions of Bangladesh and Mumbai. The second binary that is operative in cinematic representations is that of the region and the nation in primarily what is defined as national cinema and the nation through the region, in what can be called regional cinema keeping in mind the nature of the form that genres and cycles took, addressing as it did, the phenomena of stardom, the auteur-director, the actor-director in a mode of spectacle-creation that was divided on the debate between fantasy and reality as if it could forge no middle path. It is only in the productions of the late 1980s and 1990s that this rift seems to be getting somewhat bridged by the growth of what Ashis Nandy termed as 'middle cinema',[1] quite pertinently circumventing the twin polarities of intellections on the subject.

The series of questions that are therefore raised in the course of this chapter are as follows:

- What warrants the need to re-visit the beat of the 1970s in the three contexts taken into consideration in the present times?
- What are the conjunctions and disjunctions within the three contexts that help build an argument for a kind of cross-border flow that follows a trajectory that is integrationist and constructivist in nature if one traces people to people movements? Can we use a meta-fictional mode as an axis of critical reflection to 'read' this phenomenon from the point of view of the 'Common Man' as created by R.K. Laxman?[2]
- How do the sociopolitical realities of the three contexts influence the welding together of the three rhythms of resistance to create an aesthetics that is quite opposed to what Hollywood foregrounds and why?

Before taking up the points raised above, it is important to keep in mind the rich texture of debates that inform the body of discourses on the subject of Hollywood and its other(s) at the back of my mind, although I do not take them up directly here. They rather inflect my reflections in a hauntological[3] mode, in terms of a spectre of ideas that keeps revisiting me to question the validity of the 'other(s)' constructed to define a certain 'self', which in this case is 'Hollywood' as a sign signifier indicating a certain practice of film-making.

In the subsequent section, therefore, my aim is to study how the (cinematic) text is welded to the contexts of their production, be it Bollywood, Tollywood, or Dollywood, both on popular terms, and those that comprise the 'New Wave'.

Mapping the Legacy of Social Movements and the Politics of Representation in the Cinema of the 1970s

CONTEXT OF 1970S BENGAL/INDIA AND
INDIA/BANGLADESH

History has strange ways of unfolding itself. The period beat of the 1970s was that of resistance against the rulings of capital globally. The discontent simmering beneath the context had its roots in the underlying economic turmoil that found manifestation in the food movement of the times apart from the ravages of the PL 480 agreement[4] that the country had gone into. Unemployment, under-employment, poverty, malnutrition, illiteracy, and corruption ruled the day. If social movements, spearheaded in the form of armed political uprisings, were the reality of the region of West Bengal, then the issue of anti-Emergency movements on the lines of Lohiaite Socialism rocked the Hindi-speaking heartland; across the border, the situation was initially one of civil war which later became the struggle for complete freedom with India's intervention. If calls for 'total revolution' fail to take off, then it is called often described as civil disobedience, and if the struggle takes a violent turn, then it is called militant insurgency, which may even be ascribed as terrorism, no matter how justified or ill justified the causes championed are. Such was the fate of the call for revolution by the extremist Left that operated as Naxalites trying to imitate the Chinese model of armed struggle to seize state power. Their claim of 'Chiner Chairman amader Chairman', that is, 'China's chairman is our chairman', the central slogan[5] for the urban educated youth, whose abortive attempt at a guerilla warfare, which by sympathizers are euphemistically alluded to as spring thunder over Naxalbari[6], became the catchword of the times despite the hostility that the Indo-China War of 1962 necessarily implied considering the sovereignty of the nation on the whole. If Bengal, Bihar, and the entire coastal belt of Telengana[7] as well as Tebhaga[8] reeled under this upsurge while the communist Parties witnessed internal divisions, by the early 1970s, the socialists under Jai Prakash Narayan started questioning the nature of Congress rule at the centre. Their final resurgence with the call for 'Sampoorna Kranti' or 'Total Revolution' after the declaration of national emergency and call for military rule by Mrs Indira Gandhi on 26 June 1975 (which was lifted on 21 March 1977) sent shockwaves all over northern India which interestingly finds lesser representation[9] in the cinema of the times compared to the Naxal[10] uprising, if one leaves documentaries outside one's consideration. The Janata Party formed in its wake was the first anti-Congress political formation that came to power after Independence.

On the other side of the border too, the cry of liberation grew stronger and guerilla warfare broke out following Sheikh Mujibur Rehman's call for total independence based on the six-point charter placed before General Yahya Khan's military dictat from Islamabad. Re-visiting the times, several scholars across the border have pointed out India's support of East Pakistan's war for independence was nothing but an interference that did not allow the balance of forces to settle into a decisive alignment and leading to the kind of crisis that the nation is still caught in with little or no industry, spiralling agrarian crisis, food deficit, and total economic disorder leading to a dependent economy of the worst kind, parallels of which can be drawn with the ongoing crisis in Latin American nations,[11] reeling under the impact of globalization.

ACTOR AS AUTEUR IN THE POPULAR CANONS OF BOLLYWOOD, TOLLYWOOD, AND DOLLYWOOD

When one considers the Bollywood of the 1970s, one set of discourses emerge as prominent as social anxieties are played out in popular forms in the cinema of the times. Interestingly in most of the genres and cycles that emerge, the aspiration of an India of Nehru's dreams finds a kind of pre-dominance replicating not only the earlier legacy of anti-colonial movements of that people, but also in a way the questions that became prominent through Lohiaite discourses after the declaration of Emergency, if not directly (as the parallel and middle cinema suggests) then indirectly (in popular cinema which was usually referred to then as 'commercial' cinema). In the 'actor as auteur' films of the popular canon from the 1950s to the 1980s, this trend is indicated in the stories woven around either the protagonist as the peripheral character of the tramp as epitomized in the Raj Kapoor productions, the broken romantic dreamer as portrayed by the celebrated figure of Guru Dutt, the jungle-guy[12] figure of Shammi Kapoor, the iron-man image of Dharmendra, culminating with that of the angry young man image of Amitabh Bachchan. 'India's tryst with destiny'[13] and the narrative thereafter is the subject of discourses that are charted through stories that deal with a plethora of genres like romance, action films, crime thrillers, film noir, war films, films with explicit sociopolitical overtones, religious cycles—all dealing either directly or obliquely with the dystopic-utopic bind in a symbolic portrayal of the predicament of the post-colonial nation. In Dollywood however, the story is somewhat different and film personalities like actor Razzak, regarded as the 'King of Bangladeshi cinema',[14] migrated from West Bengal and ruled the silver screen from the 1960s till the present. Paired with actress Shabana, he enjoyed immense popularity, a phenomenon that deserves to be examined separately. Likewise, actress Bobita (Farida Akhter)[15] of Bangladeshi origin was successful in Dollywood, Tollywood, as well as Bollywood.

When one engages with Tollywood productions of the time, particularly in relation to the 'actor as auteur' films of the popular canon from the 1950s to the 1980s, certain interesting features emerge. It is primarily the Uttam-Suchitra *jodi*[16] that dominated the scene and that too within the cycle of romance where mostly Bengali literary classics as well as bestsellers were taken up for making film narratives. Independent scripts too were being made but family drama gained prominence over and above other genres, and for auteurs like Satyajit Ray, this 'wishy-washy sentimentalism'[17] was the malady that he at least tried correcting in his venture of film-making. However, Ritwik Ghatak appropriated melodrama as a form to create what can be called India-specific expressionism for want of a better description that can place his work alongside European masters like Bergman.

THE REGION/NATION DIALECTIC THROUGH THE FRAMES OF BOLLYWOOD/TOLLYWOOD AS THE *'KHWABNAMA'*[18] OF THE 1970S

If the *khwabnama* of the 1970s is traced through the region/nation dialectic as represented through the frames of Bollywood/Tollywood, then the common features that emerge are worth considering. If one first traces the lineages that emerge from the popular as canon or even the populist canon, then certain characteristic features become evident primarily since all populist cinema works on the development of archetypal patterns most acceptable by the people. The notion of populism[19] thrives on certain key assumptions and these can be categorized as follows:

- notion of self-help;
- ideology of individualism;
- anti-intellectualism and mass identity or being a man of the people;
- concept of good leadership;
- pursuit of happiness through restoration of order;
- re-affirmation of institutions of governance as well as ethical objectives;
- reward of 'good' but annihilation of 'evil' (if not literally, then metaphorically).

These categories are quite universal in their application, as despite the cultural specificity of the cinema concerned, the model on which it works is quite similar. Of course, the pattern on which it is evolved is developed as a result of the sociopolitical and economic implications of the context concerned. Despite the transitions through which archetypal patterns defining kinship and allied social ties, values and ideals, as well as institutional ethos undergo, there is a certain predominance of a central archetype derived as it is from the classical Sanskrit epics.[20] The images of the good son, the dutiful wife, the daughter, the daughter-in-law, so on and so forth have their mythic counterparts in ancient legends. Traditional values are transmuted to suit the needs of the times and the issues thereof. In the pre-Independence cinema of the 1930s and 1940s, we see that the purpose of using these archetypes is different as the political context of the said times are different. Films on religious themes during the colonial period had been subversive in intent. Westernization was critiqued as it was seen as an impact of colonialism. Western values were considered inimical to and threatening Indian familial social traditions.

In the phase following Independence, apart from the saga of nation-building and the nostalgic romanticization of the heroic war for Independence, little else seemed to be of interest. The problems of the fledgling nation came to the surface by the 1950s and once the euphoria of Independence was over, the challenges in front of the nation found its way in the cinema of the times leading to the creation of the period beat of the 1970s orchestrating in some ways a kind of resistance aesthetics which even a preliminary classification of the genres and cycles of Hindi language productions from Bollywood would suggest. By adopting a morphological approach to the 'fairy-tale structure' of the popular

Bollywood productions purely on formal lines, the following configuration emerges:

I. Melodrama as Genre
   • Musical melodrama—*Parichay* (directed by Gulzar, 1972).
   • Tragic melodrama—*Anand* (directed by Hrishikesh Mukherjee, 1970), *Mera Naam Joker* (directed by Raj Kapoor, 1970), *Pinjra* (directed by V. Shantaram, 1972).
   • Family melodrama—*Johnny Mera Naam* (directed by Vijay Anand, 1970), *Sachcha Jhutha* (directed by Manmohan Desai, 1970), *Andaz* (directed by Ramesh Sippy, 1971), *Dushman* (directed by Dulal Guha, 1971), *Koshish* (directed by Gulzar, 1972).
   • Romantic melodrama—*Prem Pujari* (directed by Dev Anand, 1970), *Guddi* (directed by Hrishikesh Mukherjee, 1971), *Bobby* (directed by Raj Kapoor, 1973), *Yadon Ki Baraat*[21] (directed by Nasir Hussain, 1973).
   • Buddy melodrama—*Namak Haram* (directed by Hrishikesh Mukherjee, 1973).
II. The Genre of Romance
   • Desire as Attainment—*Daag* (directed by Yash Chopra, 1973), *Swami* (directed by Basu Chatterjee, 1977).
   • Desire as (Ethical) Fulfilment—*Dharam Veer* (directed by Manmohan Desai, 1977).
   • Desire as Anxiety—*Julie* (directed by K.S. Sethumadhavan, 1975).
   • Desire as Horror—*Aur Kaun* (directed by Tulsi and Shyam Ramsay, 1979).
   • Desire as Tryst—*Junoon* (directed by Shyam Benegal, 1978).
   • Desire as Displacement—*Kabhi Kabhie* (directed by Yash Chopra, 1975), *Muqaddar Ka Sikandar* (directed by Prakash Mehra, 1978).
III. The Genre of the Social
   • The Social as Cultural—*Hare Rama Hare Krishna* (directed by Dev Anand, 1971).
   • The Social as Political—*Mere Apne* (directed by Gulzar, 1971), *Aandhi*[22] (directed by Gulzar, 1975), *Amar Akbar Anthony* (directed by Manmohan Desai, 1977).

- The Social as Ethical—*Pakeezah*[23] (directed by Kamal Amrohi, 1971), *Reshma Aur Shera* (directed by Sunil Dutt, 1971), *Tere Mere Sapne* (directed by Vijay Anand, 1971), *Manzilein Aur Bhi Hain* (directed by Mahesh Bhatt, 1973), *Amanush*[24] (directed by Shakti Samanta, 1974), *Mausam* (directed by Gulzar, 1975).

IV. The Religious Genre
- Iconographical—*Jai Santoshi Maa*[25] (directed by Vijay Sharma, 1975).

V. The Genre of Satire
- Satire in a Political Mode—*Kissa Kursi Ka* (directed by Amrit Nahata, 1977).

VI. The Mystery, Suspense, Crime, and Action Thriller
- Intrigue as Personal—*Dhund* (directed by B.R. Chopra, 1973).
- Intrigue as Political—*Zanjeer*[26] (directed by Prakash Mehra, 1973), *Kala Patthar* (directed by Yash Chopra, 1979).
- Intrigue as Social—*Deewar* (directed by Yash Chopra, 1975), *Sholay*[27] (directed by Ramesh Sippy, 1975), *Trishul* (directed by Yash Chopra, 1978).

The above classification leaves outside its purview both middle cinema as well as the art house productions, which were largely auteur-based primarily because of the nature of the engagement here. Compared to what the Bollywood genres and cycles represent, Tollywood productions of the 1970s have the following structure:

I. Melodrama as Genre
- Family Melodrama—*Dadar Kirti* (directed by Tarun Majumdar, 1980).
- Romantic Melodrama—*Bon Palashir Padabali* (directed by Uttam Kumar, 1973).

II. The Genre of Comedy/Children's Cinema
- Pure Comedy—For Children: *Padi Pishir Barmi Baksha* aka *Aunt Padi's Burmese Box* (directed by Arundhati Devi, 1972), *Sonar Kella* aka *The Golden Fortress* (directed by Satyajit Ray, 1974).
- Detective Film—*Joi Baba Felunath* aka *The Elephant God* (directed by Satyajit Ray, 1978).
- Dark Comedy/Satire: *Bilet Pherat* (directed by Chidananda Das Gupta, 1972), *Bancharamer Bagan* aka *The Garden of Bancharam* (directed by Tapan Sinha, 1980).

- Political Comedy (in a fantasy mode): *Hirak Rajar Deshe* aka *The Kingdom of Diamonds* (directed by Satyajit Ray, 1980).

III. The Romance

- Realist love story—*Sansar Simantey* (directed by Tarun Majumdar, 1975).

IV. The Genre of the Social

- The Social as Political—*Jadu Bansha* (directed by Partha Prathim Choudhury, 1974), *Palanka* (directed by Rajen Tarafdar, 1975), *Jhor* aka *The Storm* (directed by Utpal Dutt, 1979).
- The Social as Ethical—*Amanush* (directed by Shakti Samanta, 1974).

V. The Religious Genre

- Mythologicals—*Baba Taraknath* (directed by Sunil Banerjee, 1977).

When one takes the structure of popular cycles and genres in terms of Bollywood and Tollywood productions, one notices an interesting phenomenon. First, although the number of productions of Bollywood is much higher than those in Tollywood, leading naturally to more experimentation with the film form as compared to the regional language productions, it is worth noticing the singular absence of children's cinema in Hindi during the 1970s. Second, the character of melodrama in Bangla is ridden with a kind of sentimental romanticism which is in continuity with pulp literary traditions, whereas the Hindi language productions are far more complex in terms of their structure, tone, and rhythm. Third, the sub-genre of detective films which enjoys a huge popularity in Hollywood like the Alfred Hitchcock productions and in UK, the Sherlock Holmes series, is singularly missing in Bollywood. Those enacted by actor Raj Kumar were often in the role of an agent of state institutions like the CBI in a parody of the FBI, and later, investigative crime fiction thrillers with the 'good' police officer at the centre vis-à-vis the corrupt agents of the state and even the army, are very different from the Pheluda series of Satyajit Ray, which, like Bomkesh Bakshi of Saradindu Bandopadhyay's stories, were popular in both sides of Bengal.

At the symbolic level, the narrative structure of the popular commercial or mainstream cinema in Hindi addressed issues that had national implications. Particularly the idea of the incomplete family, search for father and mother, misrecognition of siblings who were torn apart by force of circumstances, and the idea of happy re-union through trials and tribulations often worked in terms of a displacement of how the political event of the 1947 Partition is negotiated within the cinematic space. The issue of Indian nationalism, despite a secular, integration-ist orientation, often needed a Hindi versus the other(s) in terms of a cultural opposition of the national and the regional where the butts of ridicule were often south Indians, Bengalis, and by the late 1980s, even Biharis, in quite an offensive undertone. Although in the Tollywood productions of the 1970s characterized as popular, there is seemingly no attempt to address the issues that pertain to the anxieties and aspira-tions of the nation at large, there is a distinct anti-colonial thrust in the cultural critique of identity offered in satirical terms in a film like *Bilet Pherot* ('Foreign Returned'), which is quite similar to the kind of critique offered in *Hare Rama Hare Krishna*. This, in fact, follows the rich literary legacy of the two Bengals that suffered the babu culture in its best and worst forms, and therefore, as we shall see later, that post 1971, with the transition of East Pakistan to Bangladesh, there are more than one commonalities that the cinema of the region enjoys across borders rather than within the same national territory in terms of exchanges between the nation and the region. The idea of what comprises the comic, too, is very culture-specific and the main difference between the comic in Bangla is the oblique manner in which it works—subtle and poised through a restraint that can be best described as the traditional clas-sic—whereas in Hindi, the sense of the comic is direct—quite frontal and at times even physical in the way it works. Last, the genre of action films or thrillers is singularly absent in Tollywood and it is only in the past two decades or so that extremely bad imitations of Bollywood are being made, whereas in Dollywood, in the genre of films called 'Muktir Juddho' or war for liberation, some commonalities can be traced with Bollywood but not Tollywood, as the modus operandi which it follows is largely similar. To cite a few examples of films comprising the political genre celebrating primarily the Bhasha Andolan (Language Movement) in which the ringing cry of '*Joy Bangla*' or 'Hail Bengal' as well as those drawing inspiration from the anti-colonial struggles of the past, one must mention Ruhul Amin's *Nijere Haraye Khunji*, or Asadurzamman's *Aguner Poroshmoni*, Subhash Dutta's *Arunodoyer Agnishakshi*, or Masud Parvez's *Ora Egaro Jon*—based on the real-life story of eleven freedom fighters, Tareque and Catherine Masud's *Muktir Gaan*, Tanvir Mokammel's *Rabeya*, re-working Sophocles's *Antigone* as the matrix through which the events of the war were critiqued. *Abar Tora Manush Ho, Shangram, Alor Micchil, Dhire Bohe Meghna* all had the context of 1971 as the central theme. Thus, while Bollywood and Dollywood productions replicate national interests, Tollywood represents the interests of the region vis-à-vis the nation.

THE AUTEUR AS DIRECTOR AND THE ALTERNATIVE CINEMA MOVEMENT AS THE *KHWABNAMA* OF THE 1970S

In this section, how the parallel cinema movement portrays the beat of the 1970s in terms of constructing an aesthetic of resistance would be traced with reference to Bollywood, Tollywood, and Dollywood. If one begins with a kind of contextual understanding of the times, one can trace parallel trajectories of crisis that posed different kinds of challenges to the two young nations on both sides of the border, which is why the 1970s became a metaphor for resistance inspiring generations to look back into that phase of the struggle when the cry of liberation, drawing sustenance from the Tebhaga movement (with slogans like '*langol jar, jomi tar*' meaning 'the land belongs to the tiller') became strongest on both sides of the border inviting state repression of the worst kind after the trauma of 1947. The beginnings of alternative cinema practices both in Tollywood and Dollywood, as well as in the Hindi language productions from Mumbai drew their political inspiration from the idea of liberation thrown up as a theme in terms of a khawabnama in the legacy of social movements of undivided Bengal and, by extension, pre-Partitioned India, although the forms of manifestation, as exemplified in the Naxalbari movement and the Bhasha Andolan or language movement in East Pakistan leading to the creation of Bangladesh, followed different historical contours creating one set of problematic that warrants attention. In the pan-Indian context, the mainstream Hindi language productions that may be considered under the genre of the social or the political, largely left the issue of Emergency unaddressed except for perhaps a fictional affirmation for it as in *Aandhi*. A critical reading of the times was offered by Satyajit Ray in *Hirak Rajar Deshe* in Bangla in a fantasy mode, and interestingly the film, which is in the nature of a spoof, is generally considered to be for children. Regarding the problems confronting the nation like poverty, unemployment, sex trafficking and the like, several films were made like *Uski Roti* (directed by Mani Kaul, 1969), *Samaj Ko Badal Dalo* (directed by Madhusudhana Rao, 1970) and *Garam Hawa* (directed by M.S. Sathyu, 1973), with explicit communist overtones, *Do Boond Pani* (directed by K.A. Abbas, 1971) on the lines of Nehruvian ideas of socialism, *Ek Adhuri Kahani* (directed by Mrinal Sen, 1971) and *Nishant* (directed by Shyam Benegal, 1975) in terms of a critique of the system justifying feudal/capitalist benevolence. Similarly, in Bangladesh, social issues comprised the core of Tareque and Catherine Masud directed films like *Matir Moina*, which bagged the 2002 Cannes award, and *Ontor Jatra*; Tanvir Mokammel's *Lal Salu* attacking religious bigotry; Saidul Anam Tutul's *Adhiar* documenting in a fictional mode the battle of sharecroppers in the post-World War II context apart from the legacy of those that marked the freedom movement. If the spirit of the three tendencies in Bollywood, Tollywood, and Dollywood are compared in analogous terms, then the point of conjunction that emerges can be best defined in what Barrows Dunham describes as 'the thinker's function', which by extension is the function of peoples' movements reflecting certain common characteristics despite the differences in two cultures of resistance:

> The thinker's function is, to contribute our share to the description of reality, to improve (so far as we may) the modes of getting things chosen and done. This is everybody's guarantee of honour in other people's thoughts. It is the sole true objectivity, namely, a bias in favour of mankind.[28]

TRACING THE BEGINNINGS OF THE ALTERNATIVE CINEMA MOVEMENT WITH SPECIAL FOCUS ON WEST BENGAL (INDIA)—THE ANGST OF JANUS-FACED MODERNITY

It is in creating this 'bias in favour of mankind' that the cinema of the 1970s and about the 1970s seems geared, embedded as it is in the matrix of social movements, celebrating an idea of liberation that has its genesis in the anti-colonial resistance aesthetics of pre-Independence days. Despite the kind of skepticism that this movement encountered from some of the best critical minds on the subject of Indian cinema as exemplified in the writings of Vasudev (1995: 137–43) who, while reflecting on the ideologies of underdevelopment in an article with the same title, almost rejects this whole endeavour as it smacked of conformism since it was state-sponsored. But can one wholly dismiss the gains of the same merely for the kind of patronage it had in its nascent state?

The kind of cinema that came into being following *Pather Panchali* ('Song of the Little Road' 1955) by Satyajit Ray and *Nagarik* ('The
Citizen' 1952–3) by Ritwik Ghatak following the production of Nemai
Ghosh's *Chinnamul* ('The Uprooted' 1950), a fictional documentary on
the condition of refugees forced to live on the platforms of the Seal-
dah station following the liberation war in Bangladesh or Mrinal Sen's
Calcutta trilogy a few years down the line portrayed two kinds of realities—the travesty of urban existence and the plight of rural Bengal/India
despite the aura of romance that nature in its moist green benevolence
ushers in. Although the cinema of Satyajit Ray, be it on themes of urban
Bengal or that of the rural, is steeped in an indigenously synthesized
neo-realist vocabulary that Chidananda Das Gupta[29] rightly claims as
belonging to the last votary of the Bengal renaissance,[30] there is a sincere attempt to refract the crises of a Janus-faced modernity, internally
flawed as it was, which was at the heart of existence of the post-colonial
nation as it came into being. In this context, it is worth mentioning
the only cinematic representation of Bollywood on the question of East
Pakistan becoming Bangladesh in 1971 is a documentary film titled *Nine
Months to Freedom: The Story of Bangladesh* (1972) by S. Sukhdev. Quite
in contrast to Ray and Ghatak, the documentary intensity of Mrinal
Sen's works reflects the influence of avantgarde practices of realism. The
kind of cinema practice Sen is involved in has a poster-like ambience
best described by Hood (1993). The classic example of cinema celebrating a non-event is Sen's *Ek Din Pratidin* ('And Quiet Flows the Dawn'
1979) where through the mode of waiting for Chinu her family tries
to come to terms with the fact as to what might be the possible cause
of her not returning home from work as she was a sincere, diligent girl
who knew how to shoulder responsibility and was uncomplaining of the
hardships that the family had been forced to thrust on her living as they
were on her income. The implications of an adult daughter not coming
home are many. Not interested in tracing the cause of her absence or
even giving a plausible justification of the same, Sen makes the audience
bear the brunt of a middle-class morality that could hardly bear to place
their trust on women whose labour they fed on. The social surveillance
that is still in practice creates a claustrophobic environment for women
and the film faithfully depicts the trauma that can be unleashed not
by large forces but simple peering eyes, questioning the whereabouts
of a girl who has not returned home from work for one reason or the

other—an apparent non-event exploited to the fullest into a full-length feature film. Whether it is *Kharij* ('The Case is Closed' 1982), *Kandahar* ('The Ruins' 1983), *Akaler Sandhane* ('In Search of Famine' 1980) or *Oka Oorie Katha* ('The Outsiders' 1977), very few within the Indian cinema spectrum can compete with the uncompromising realism that Sen puts into practice to document the times. Another distinct trait of Sen is his directorial forays into non-Bangla language films which is unique for an Indian auteur who has worked in multiple linguistic and cultural contexts like Hindi, Oriya, and Telugu that did not suffer the fate of Ray's adventures outside Bengal.

If personal morality formed the substance of Ray's engagement with cinema and social conditions that shaped human consciousness for Sen, Ghatak's concern was to create a kind of cinema of poetry[31] using the existential dialectic in an epic portrayal of archetypes that captures within its fold the play of ideas that forms the wharf and woof of life itself. Among the eight films that Ghatak made in a career spanning three decades from 1950 to the early 1970s, apart from *Nagarik* or 'The Citizen', his endeavour had been to portray primarily a sense of loss that emanated from the nostalgia that the Partition of Bengal and the creation of East Pakistan entailed. This crisis, that Ghatak so intensely felt, found a vent through art and several Ghatak scholars have therefore commented on the kind of exilic consciousness that imbued his works. The river acts as a central motif therefore in almost all his films except *Nagarik* as it is the lost world of rivers that he yearned for and to which he poetically turned to find succour in. Enmeshed with the flow of time that a river necessarily embodies was grafted the images of archetypal femininity and most of his narratives, be it *Subarnarekha* (1965), *Komol Gandhar* ('E Flat' 1961), *Meghe Dhaka Tara* ('The Cloud Capped Star' 1960), *Titash Ekti Nadir Naam* ('A River Called Titash' 1973), *Bari Theke Paliye* ('The Runaway' 1959) or *Jukti Takko Aar Gappo* ('Reason, Argument and Story' 1974) was woven metaphorically around this sense of loss that he so acutely felt.

The theme of rupture and fragmentation leading to an alienated existence is the predicament brought forth by modernity and liberation from it was the search that Ghatak embarked upon. In fact, the character Neelkantha in his last film *Jukti Takko Aar Gappo*, representing the blue-throated aspect of Shiva, who saved the universe by drinking the poison that emanated from the churning of oceans in mythical times so that *amrita*[32] for eternal existence can be collected for the use of the gods, has biographical overtones. Ghatak, in order to lay bare the purpose of his quest, acted in the role of the protagonist himself. What he aimed at exemplifying was the bankrupt condition of the Bengali intelligentsia who had little or no social commitment barring people like him, who though inebriated and considered largely as 'broken intellectuals' were driven by an inner need to address the issues confronting the body polity of the nation at large. Hence while the immediate family of his wife Durga and son Satya (performed by Ritaban Ghatak[33] as a child) broke all ties with him for his inordinate capacity to drink, he turned to the streets and collected vagabonds like himself in the form of Nachiketa, an unemployed engineer who looked upon him as elder brother, Bangabala, and Jagannath Pundit who were in search of shelter as they had escaped from the torments of the Pakistani army then stationed in Bangladesh as the people there fought for freedom, to create a family of sorts till at one point in the narrative he comes face to face with history—the urban guerilla fighters who thought they could seize liberation at gun point by fighting against the state. The two kinds of history that almost converge are—ravage-torn Bangladesh of 1971 fighting against the Pakistani army and the Naxalite outfits that worked in close coordination with tribal communities of the forests and the poorest sections of the peasantry and urban working class trying to swerve the ruling machinery of the state off-track by an almost juvenile obduracy[34] in the power of their movement little realizing that the fire had been doused even before a single straw could be set alight to start the prairie[35] burning. It is this pre-occupation with history that made Ghatak see a possible cultural synthesis happening and like Lalan Fakir (1774–1890),[36] who sang the song of freedom of the soul, he prophetically claimed that the time had finally come to sing the song of unity of two the Bengals linked as it were by a consciousness that political divisions can hardly wipe out.

TRACING THE BEGINNINGS OF THE ALTERNATIVE CINEMA MOVEMENT IN EAST PAKISTAN/BANGLADESH: POSITING NATIONAL IDENTITY IN COMPOSITE TERMS

The language movement in East Pakistan/Bangladesh drew its inspiration from the syncretic secular cultural traditions of undivided Bengal. The dominant Bengali Muslim population here without any religious bias whatsoever made literary figures like Rabindranath Tagore, Kazi Nazrul Islam, Atul Prasad[37] the icons of the times as slogans of '*Joy Bangla*' or 'Hail Bengal' rend the air pregnant with the euphoria of another awakening. The activists of the Cultural Front followed the footsteps of the people's army and in the liberated zones were heard the rhythms of '*Amar sonar Bangla, ami tomai bhalobashi*' meaning 'O my golden Bengal, We love you with all our heart' from a Tagore composition and several such tunes glorifying the land, the people, and the culture to mark the moment of celebration of a linguistic victory quite unparalleled in the history of colonization that nations till date have witnessed. From the strange '*panch mishali bhasha*'[38] meaning 'mixed language' that people spoke in was born a Urdu-inflected Bangla, quite distinct from the one spoken on this side of the border, to give shape to the fears, anxieties as well as aspirations of a people who witnessed a division on the lines of religion in 1947 and then language in 1971. Although joint collaborations with the Indian part of Bengal was not a common feature either in the Dhaka film industry nor the Tollygunge studio in Kolkata, Ritwik Ghatak's *Titash Ekti Nadir Naam* based on a novel by the same name by Advaita Mallabarman[39] signalled a new beginning altogether. In 1976, the experiment of joint collaboration was carried forward by Rajen Tarafdar who, too, used primarily a Bangladeshi cast to film *Palonko* or (Bed 1975). Prior to this, the Dhaka film industry had a beginning not quite similar to that of Calcutta, Bombay, Madras, or for that matter Lahore in the early 1930s. The kind of productions that dotted the filmscape like Khwaja Ajmal's *The Last Kiss* or Franz Osten-directed *Light of Asia* (1925), *Throw of Dice—A Romance in India* (1929), and even *Shiraj* (1928)[40] were often made in collaboration with funds from countries in Europe, pandered understandably to populist notions about the Orient, whereby constructions of the untamable exotica, which lay Eastwards not mellowed or pruned by the winds of civilization, as the white world understood it, became the overriding theme that gained currency. Owing to the kind of technology that was available for film production and the heavy investment that it involved, without state support the entire industry was jeopardized as black money circulated for easy multiplication through manipulation of sensibilities on a mass scale. While commenting on the early film scene in Bengal, Kironmoy Raha (1991) points out the reasons behind the poverty of cinema at the time of its inception and traces how certain genres and cycles like the domestic/family drama, mythological narratives, light-hearted comedies were in prominence with little attention paid either to the art form or the social purpose of it all except rampant profiteering.

If Ritwik Ghatak's *Nagarik* and Satyajit Ray's *Pather Panchali* signalled the beginnings of a serious engagement with cinema, in East Pakistan, Abdul Jabbar Khan's[41] *Mukh O Mukhosh* ('The Face and the Mask' 1956) by Eqbal Films, was the first institution laid down for such a purpose. The East Pakistan Film Division Corporation Act was passed in 1957 and implemented in 1958 to address the needs of the emerging new industry, and it was in 1959 that four films: *Matir Pahar* ('The Earthy Hill') and *E Desh Tomar Amar* ('This Country is Your's and Mine') directed by Mahiuddin, *Akash Ar Mati* ('The Sky and the Earth') and *Ashiya* directed by Fateh Lohani were released. In *Akash aar Mati*, a Kolkata-based actor, too, had a role but all these films did not have the success that *Mukh O Mukhosh* enjoyed despite being fraught with many shortcomings as the idea that Dhaka could now have a film industry of its own was far more important to the Bengali Muslim community rather than questions of aesthetic merit. The 1960 production of the first Urdu film in East Pakistan *Jago, Hua Savera* ('The Day Shall Dawn') by A.J. Kardar was significant in more ways than one. Based on the lives of the fishing community of Bangladesh, this film, whose narrative was scripted by the renowned Urdu poet Faiz Ahmed Faiz, attempted to fuse Bangla and Urdu into a kind of mixed language of communication that was found appealing neither to the Bengali-speaking nor the Urdu-speaking community and despite some sequences of merit and the Moscow award it received, according to Chinmoy Matsuddi, the film was internally flawed as those behind its conceptualization lacked the cultural command required to portray existences of those who lived in ways that were not one's own.

The kind of impact Satyajit Ray's *Pather Panchali* had on the film world of Dhaka primarily on Fateh Lohani's *Ashiya* (1960)—the sequences of nature that he tried shooting in the same manner as Ray had done in the long take that he had taken of Apu and Durga running amid a field of *Kash*, trying to catch a glimpse of the great smoking serpent—the train—an emblem of modernity that not only Tollywood but also Bollywood right up to the 1970s, used as a central trope, left much to be desired.

Counter-pointing Cinema of the 1970s and about the
1970s: Cross-border Exchanges and the Contours of
Cinematic Representation in the Context of Globalization

In the final analysis, the kind of resistance aesthetics that emerges as a
result of cross-border exchanges by counter-pointing the cinema of the
1970s and about the 1970s, in order to lay bare the fundamentals of a
cultural politics that is imbued with the aspirations for universal human
emancipation on composite lines through the period beat of Bollywood,
Tollywood, and Dollywood, is traced. Countering the complex fall-out
effect of globalization and the economic implications associated with
it for the people of the developing world, the turbulent decade of the
1970s provides political inspiration for creating a cinema both within
the popular canon and the alternative mode, invoking the struggles of
the times in terms of a nostalgia for a past of heroic resistance against
injustices perpetrated and the investment in the possible outline of a
hopeful legacy that is yet to be born to further the cause of liberation
on individual as well as collective terms. Cinema about the 1970s is
significantly absent in West Bengal and the political genre that came
into being in the wake of the so-called 'spring thunder', has undergone
a transformation not because the context has changed for the better.
Interestingly, it is in Bollywood again that the Bengal of the 1970s finds
representation in present times in films like *Hazaron Khwaishen Aisi*
('In Search of Thousand Dreams' directed by Sudhir Mishra, 2003) and
Hazar Chaurasi ki Maa ('The Mother of the Corpse of 1084' directed
by Govind Nihalani, 1998). The setback that the Left has suffered
throughout the world after the Soviet debacle has made inroads not only
in Party organizations operating within the parliamentary framework
in India but also the sphere of influence that the 'Social Left'[42] so long
exercised in the world at large.

The general vacuum that has apparently been created is being bridged
by documentary filmmakers and video filmmakers following the revolution in camera technology that has made digital filmmaking far more
cost-effective than before leading to an inevitable democratization of
the same. Again films in Indian English, bilingual, and even multilingual productions and the cinematic interventions of the Indian diaspora spread over the world has taken the space of the parallel cinema

movement while the popular cinema of the three contexts under consideration has taken a new turn. The invocation of a political genre to address the crisis that exists in present-day Bangladesh in terms of an inspiration to carry forward the unfinished movement for liberation and the decline of the same in the context of India in the parallel cinema movement and the rise of documentary filmmaking and other experimental modes on similar lines show how social forces operate to influence representational strategies in art. Filmmaking then can hardly be an exception. By focusing on how a period became significant for the cinema of the two nations, as well as a region and a nation through the cinema of the 1970s and about the 1970s indicate a flow of exchanges that has a way of travelling across spaces unhindered as it were, for finally it is an erotics of the art that gives cause for celebration over anything else. After all, it is the phenomenon of voyeurism in cinema that inspires the power it wields uniting in diverse harmonies the symphony of the 1970s in Bollywood, Tollywood, and Dollywood.

Notes

1. See Nandy (1992: 43–76). While analysing 'The Cultural Matrix of the Popular Film', he looks into the demographic composition of the viewing public, their geographical distribution, and thereby, appraises the kinds of entertainments that occupy leisure-time activities, including cinema as the macro axis. Through cinema, he locates the lopsided dominance of debates of art over the commercial in relation to cinema that tends to prioritize one mode of critical discourse with explicit 'middle-class' overtones (p. 48) leading to the outright rejection of cinematic practices that catered to the needs of survival of a working population dwelling in the city and the country in terms of what he later best explains in the introduction titled 'Indian Popular Cinema as a Slum's Eye View of Politics'.

2. The 'Common Man' as a cartoon character created in the *Times of India* to posit a general layman's perspective over primarily political events that were of national importance.

3. Jacques Derrida (1994) who argues that the 'apocalyptic tone in philosophy' (ibid.: 15) was largely a result of the material, historical context of post-World War Europe and the failure of 1968 France, besides several other factors in which even his ideas of 'deconstruction' (ibid.: 15) grew. Foregrounding, what he almost playfully calls a 'hauntological' discourse (ibid. 10), he invokes the central metaphor in Shakespeare's *Hamlet* to question the 'spectrality of the spectre' (ibid.: 17), to establish the need for re-visiting the 'quasi-paternal figure of Marx' (ibid.: 13), and thereby, Marxism. This was occasioned by the circumstances that led to the death/ martyrdom of Chris Hani on 10 April 1993, a communist (to whom he dedicated the

lecture in the October 1993 conference at the University of California, at Riverside's Center for Ideas and Society on 'Whither Marxism? Global Crises in International Perspective'. In fact in the introduction he mentions that it is this death that pushes him to confront as Hamlet did, the ethico-political frames of reflection born from the womb of processes that define social totality.

It was the global context that made Derrida deconstruct himself and thereby the narratives he was caught in and like Marcellus urged Horatio to speak to the ghost, 'Thou art a Scholler; speak to *it* Horatio .... Question *it* (emphasis in the original)' (ibid. qtd. in 175), he questions the sweep and scope of time itself in material terms saying: 'Could one *address oneself in general* (emphasis in the original) if already some ghost did not come back? If he loves justice at least, the "scholar" of the future, the "intellectual" of tomorrow should learn it and from the ghost' (ibid.: 176) in order to return the gift of speech to the past, linked as it is through times present into the future that is yet to be born in almost a Bergsonian sense. I invoke Derrida here as it is his method that informs my critical praxis when I deal with the terminological matrix with reference to Bollywood, Tollywood, Dollywood as Hollywood's other/s which has gained prominence in the oeuvre of discourses reflecting what Lyotard calls the 'post-modern condition' albeit in a completely different sense.

4. Public Law 480 or Food for Peace was commonly referred to as PL 480 whereby the food crises of the 1950s in India was attempted to be solved with the US aid extended to countries that had food grain deficit. This scheme received a lot of counter criticism due to one of its aims of privatizing the food market.

5. Depictions of such slogans on the wall has been used in Mrinal Sen's *Calcutta '71* (1972) and Govind Nihalani's *Hazar Chaurasi Ki Maa* (1998)—based on a novel by Mahashweta Devi in Bangla, *Hajar Churashir Ma*, published in August 1974—has been very aptly used to chronicle the times.

6. A book with the same title *Spring Thunder over Naxalbari—An Anthology of Articles on Naxalbari* published by Arun Kumar Hnesh on behalf of Radical Impression, Kolkata: 1985 delineates the times from the perspective of the movement.

7. Armed guerilla uprising that began in the Punnapra-Vayalar region as well as Telengana under the leadership of the Left from July 1946-October 1951 to address the land question covering 3 million people in 3,000 villages spread over 16,000 square miles which had to be curbed through the intervention of the Indian army according to a propaganda document of the times.

8. 'Tebhaga', as the term suggests, was a demand for two-thirds crop share for the sharecroppers. It was a popular peasant movement that was initiated in North Bengal under the leadership of the Bengal unit of the Kisan Sabha in September 1946.

9. Representations of the JP movement and its evils of Emergency are primarily in the documentary mode except the fictional rendering in *Kissa Kursi Ka* in a vituperative burlesque (directed by Amrit Nahata, 1977). Mrinal Sen's *Mrigaya* ('The Royal Hunt' 1976) too dealt in symbolic terms with the issue of imposing authoritarian rules like the Emergency, equating it with colonial institutions before

the nation's Independence, while Satyajit Ray's *Hirak Rajar Deshe* in Bangla dealt with the issue in oblique terms masking its radical cutting edge by turning it into a children's film based as it is on Tagore's play *Rakta Karabi* or *Red Oleanders*. Anand Patwardhan directed documentaries *Waves of Revolution* (*Kranti ki Tarangein*, 1975) and *Prisoners of Conscience* (1978) fearlessly dealt with the issue both during and after it. Documentaries like the *Thunder of Freedom* (directed by S. Sukhdev, 1976) dealing with Mrs Gandhi's Twenty-Point economic freedom upheld the Emergency like *Aandhi* did in a fictional mode.

10. *The Naxalites*, in Hindi (directed by K.A. Abbas, 1979), *Ningalenne Communistaki* in Malayalam ('You Made Me a Communist', directed by Thoppil Bhasi, 1970), *Mukti Chai* ('Call for Freedom', directed by Utpalendu Chakraborty, 1977) and *Dooratwa* ('Distance', directed by Buddhadeb Dasgupta, 1978) in Bangla.

11. See Anu Mohammad's series titled 'Marxer Punji 3—Muller Rup Ebong Ponner Rahoshyamayata' (Marx's Capital 3—Value and Commodity Fetishism'—translation mine) or Imtiyar Shamim's 'Bajarer Khuda: Bolivia theke Bangladesh' ('Market Hunger: Bolivia to Bangladesh'—translation mine) in the journal *Natun Diganta*, Sirajul Islam Chowdhury (ed.), 7th year, first issue, 2008.

12. '*Chahe koi mujhe jungle kahe*', one of the all-time hit songs in the film *Junglee* (directed by Subodh Mukherji, 1961) falls within a certain gesture of rebellion against the stardoms of Dilip Kumar, Raj Kumar, Manoj Kumar, and Rajesh Khanna representing a certain trajectory.

13. Jawaharlal Nehru's speech on the midnight of India's awakening to the first dawn of freedom. Jawaharlal Nehru, 'Speech on the Granting of Indian Independence, 14 August 1947'.

14. See http://banglamovies.com/news/actor-razzaq-the-king-of-bangla-cinema-233.html.

15. See http://en.wikipedia.org/wiki/Bobita.

16. The term jodi in Hindi means couple or duo. Uttam Kumar and Suchitra Sen were the leading star couple within the romance cycle right from the major hit of *Share Chuattur* ('Seventy-Four and a Half', directed by Nirmal Dey, 1953) right till the late 1960s, whose popularity till date remains unchallenged. Other figures of Bengali cinema do not enjoy the kind of celebrity status as the lead couple does even today.

17. See Satyajit Ray (2005: 6).

18 Illyas, Akhtarul Zaman. *Khwabnama*. (Dhaka: Mowla Brothers, 1996). This novel received the Anando Puroshkar (Anando Awards) in 1996 and has been critically acclaimed as one of the best Partition novels in recent times. The term 'Khwabnama' literally means a charter of dreams.

19. See Anuradha Ghosh (1999).

20. See Vijay Mishra (2002).

21. Also classified as 'vendetta movie'. See Ashish Rajadhyaksha and Paul (1994: 391).

22. The Bengali superstar Suchitra Sen was in the lead role replicating the controversial life of Mrs Indira Gandhi's personal as well as political life in a fictional

mode. The film becomes interesting for the oblique references to the period of Emergency as it tries to draw sympathy rather than anger for the predicament in which she might have been trying to gather some kind of consensus for her by portraying the human dimension to redeem the Satanic overtones, which became part of the anti-Congress propaganda.

23. Falls within the courtesan genre, it uses thematic categories for classification rather than formal ones in genre and cycle studies.

24. Probably one of the first Bangla-Hindi bilingual productions with the megastar Uttam Kumar as protagonist and an all-Bengali cast addressing the root of evil in society as it operates through institutions and negative power play.

25. A little known mother goddess of the Hindu pantheon with Anita Guha as the lead actress had a blockbuster appeal equal to *Sholay* and *Deewar* released the same year.

26. Amitabh Bachchan's persona as the angry young man is foregrounded. The film can both be seen as a 'vendetta movie' with several transitional elements where the search for justice becomes central.

27. The film has attained the status of popular as classic, which has been the subject of various discourses on Indian cinema.

28. Qtd. in Randhir Singh's deliberations in the 2008 Durgabai Deshmukh Memorial Lecture titled 'Indian Politics in the Age of Globalisation', vol. 1, Council for Social Development, New Delhi, 15 July 2008.

29. See Chidananda Dasgupta (2005). In the sections titled 'The Bengal Renaissance and the Tagorean Synthesis' (pp. 3–14) and 'Modernism and Mythicality' (pp. 173–84), Dasgupta tries to establish a certain classical balance in Ray's cinematic style by quoting Ray's comment on Asian cinema and showing how he identified with it himself as 'Calm Without: Fire Within' (p. 184) to place him (rightfully so) in the intellectual legacy of the Bengal enlightenment. But why Ritwik Ghatak never came within the purview of his discourses as well as other Ray scholars remain largely un-interrogated still.

30. 'Satyajit was the last great representative of this (*meaning modernity and renaissance/enlightenment*) movement for the regeneration of India—a movement triggered by the coming of the British through whom modernist Indians found a point of contact with the Western civilization.... The movement was marked by an effort by the middle-class Indian to establish the primacy of rationalism without severing its umbilical cord with ancient tradition', writes Dasgupta in *The Cinema of Satyajit Ray*, 6–7 (phrase in parenthesis—mine). Similar arguments have been foregrounded on several occasions by Amartya Sen in recent times while addressing the issue of nationalism with reference to Mohandas Karamchand Gandhi and Rabindranath Tagore as well as cultural modernity in his observations on the cinema of Satyajit Ray.

31. 'The cinema of poetry' was a phrase used by Pier Paolo Pasolini to distinguish between the cinema of poetry vis-à-vis that of prose while discussing 'insistence' of framings and montage rhythms in pure formalistic terms to describe the technical language of poetry and how it could be appropriated to understand the language of cinema with reference to Antonioni's *Red Desert* and Bertolucci's *Before the Revolution*

in order to delineate the distinctive language of this art form that worked primarily through symbols that are visual in nature. See the full article in Bill Nichols (ed.), 1993: 542–58.

32. Akin to ambrosia or nectar in the Greek tradition.

33. Ritaban Ghatak, son of Ritwik Ghatak.

34. A phrase used in the last syntagmatic unit of the film itself through the persona of Neelkantha. A clarification regarding the comment is warranted at this point. It is Ghatak's personal observation of the Naxalbari uprisings that followed in the wake of an incident of peasant unrest in a small village by the River Tista in North Bengal during the late 1960s and early 1970s under the leadership of Charu Mazumdar that later resulted in the second split within the Indian communist movement leading to the formation of Communist Party of India (Marxist-Leninist) or CPI (ML) from the Communist Party of India (Marxist) or CPIM. The apparent silence of those who spearheaded the movement over the Bangladeshi 'Mukti Andolan' (Movement for Liberation) fought in 1971 made Ghatak critical of the basic thesis behind the battle on the agrarian and industrial labour movement being fought with the support of the urban intelligentsia (particularly the youth) in India around that time. This argument finds its way into the contentious political theme of his last film *Jukti, Takko Aar Gappo*, where he tries to address it using the language of cinema as an alternative that could pose through archetypal motifs, when discourse over the issue failed historically at least.

35. A single spark could set the prairie fire burning was a popular slogan of the Left of the times.

36. Lalan Fakir's birth is shrouded in mystery and regarding his identity (like stories about Kabir's death), there are only speculations as his songs that are in currency till date reflect the syncretic secular tradition of the land, making him one of the natural icons of the language movement.

37. Poets and singers of Bengal of the late nineteenth and early twentieth century who established different stylistic traditions in the cultural and aesthetic landscape of the times.

38. Chinmoy Mutsuddi uses the phrase in *Bangladesher Chalochitre Samajik Angikar* ('Bangladeshi Cinema and Its Social Commitment'—translation mine) p. 30.

39. *Titash Ekti Nadir Naam*, Kolkata: Puthi Ghar, Ashwin 1363 [Bengali year], roughly in the 1950s CE.

40. In these films, the lead role was played by Himanshu Roy and Devika Rani who later founded the Bombay Talkies in 1934.

41. Abdul Jabbar Khan was a man of the theatre like Ritwik Ghatak as the IPTA had a long legacy of spearheading the theatre movement in the subcontinent still under colonial rule. According to Chinmoy Mutsuddi's *Bangladesher Chalochitre Samajik Angikar*, Abdul Jabbar Khan's entry into cinema was in the form of a challenge that he had taken up when in 1953, the Director of the Statistical Bureau of East Pakistan, Dr Abdus Sadiq (Marhum), called a meeting of leading intellectuals and artists of the times to initiate movie-making in the country. The proposal was

uncalled for and despite discussion on several challenges that were pertinently posed, it was Abdul Jabbar Khan who rose to the occasion followed by their venture into Calcutta and Bombay from where armed with an old model of an Aimo camera the shooting of *Mukh O Mukhosh* based on a play titled *Dacoit* written by Khan himself began (pp. 50–1).

42. See Marta Harnecker (2007) and Aijaz Ahmed (2001) where the distinction between the 'Party Left' and the 'Social Left' capable of integrating all progressive movements on race, caste, class, gender, issues in one platform as an offensive against the rulings of global capital with imperialistic hangovers has been quite pertinently traced.

References

Ahmed, Aijaz. 2001. 'Resources of Hope: a Reflection on Our Times', *Frontline*, vol. 18, no. 10, May 12–25.

Dasgupta, Chidananda. 1994 (2005). *The Cinema of Satyajit Ray*, New Delhi: National Book Trust.

Derrida, Jacques. 1993 (1994). *Spectres de Marx* (originally published in French and trans. by Peggy Kamuf), or *Specters of Marx: the State of the Debt, the Work of Mourning, and the New International*, New York & London: Routledge.

Ghosh, Anuradha. 1999. 'Ideological Discourse on Indian Cinema–Bengal of the '60s and '70s: The Genre of Protest', Doctoral dissertation submitted in Centre for Linguistics and English, JNU, September.

Harnecker, Marta. 2007 (first Indian reprint). Janet Duckworth (trans.), *Rebuilding the Left*, New Delhi: Daanish Books.

Hood, John W. 1993. *Chasing the Truth—The Films of Mrinal Sen*, Calcutta: Seagull Books.

Illyas, Akhtarul Zaman. 1996. *Khwabnama*, Dhaka: Mowla Brothers.

Mishra, Vijay. 2002. *Bollywood: Temples of Desire*, London and New York: Routledge.

Nandy, Ashis. 1992. 'An Intelligent Critics Guide to Indian Cinema', in K.S. Singh (ed.), *Visual Anthropology and India—Proceedings of a Seminar*, Calcutta: Anthropological Survey of India.

—————. 1998 (2002 reprint). 'Indian Popular Cinema as a Slum's Eye View of Politics', in Ashis Nandy (ed.), *The Secret Politics of Our Desires—Innocence, Culpability and Indian Popular Cinema*, New Delhi: Oxford University Press.

Nehru, Jawaharlal. 'Speech on the Granting of Indian Independence, 14 August 1947', *Modern History Sourcebook*. Internet History Sourcebook Project. http://www.fordham.edu/halsall/mod/1947nehru1.html; accessed on 3 March 2010; http://en.wikipedia.org/wiki/Tryst_with_destiny.

Nichols, Bill (ed.). 1993. *Movies and Methods—An Anthology*, vol. 1, Calcutta: Seagull Books.

Raha, Kironmoy. 1991. *Bengali Cinema*, Calcutta: Nandan, West Bengal Film Centre.

Rajadhyaksha Ashish and Paul Willeman. 1994. *Encyclopaedia of Indian Cinema*, London: Oxford University Press.

Ray, Satyajit. 2005. *Speaking of Films*, New Delhi: Penguin Books.

Vasudev, Aruna. 1995. 'Ideologies of Underdevelopment', Aruna Vasudev (guest) (ed.), *Indian Horizons*, vol. 44, no. 1.

7 Cinematic Border Crossings in Two Bengals

Cultural Translation as Communalization?

During the last two decades, Bollywood, a misnomer, or at the best an umbrella term, has reconfigured the possibility for the dissemination of South Asian screen media worldwide. This has led to the transnational framing of South Asian screen media once again underlining the need for interrogating the idea of the nation and national culture initiated by a group of scholars like Ashcroft (1989), Bhabha (1990a and b), and Anderson (1991). When we look at South Asian cultural flows in the present, we cannot but feel affinity with scholars like Appadurai (1994), Hall (1995, 1996), and Featherstone (1995) who argued that globalization of the market and media has transformed the old categories of nation and culture and made way for the dialogue of the local and global. Arjun Appadurai (1996) emphasized the 'cultural dimensions of globalization' and the effects of multi-directional media flows upon the social imagination, particularly in the global south. In the same vein, Curtin (2003) argued that due to the rapid spread of screen media through so many different channels originating from various Asian cities, we can no longer think of the global media as an imperial force based in the West controlling the rest of the world, but rather as a more complex matrix linking media capitals. Such transnational media migrations into, out of, and within Asia all serve to indicate that we can no longer talk about only a one-way traffic of media content from the West to Asia (Chadha and Kavoori 2000).

The screen media, especially the film industries of/in South Asia are key sites on which the local, global, and transnational intersect with each other. At the same time, South Asian cinemas, as carriers of national culture and as globalizing agents, are both celebrated and critiqued. Within this context, we can locate here the contemporary scenario of two South Asian national and sub-national/regional cinemas sharing the same vernacular, that is, Bengali. These two cinemas are Bangladeshi cinema and Indian West-Bengali cinema that are produced and circulated from two of the lesser known 'media capitals': Dhaka and Calcutta. This chapter illustrates how to reconsider the transnational function of the 'national' film industries in South Asia in constructing nationhood and identity outside its national borders, but within colonial and postcolonial predicaments. By looking at the recent transformations of the two least studied Asian national cinemas, this analysis will show how slippery and constructed the 'national' of an Asian cinema can be. This analysis will show how globalization impacted and transformed the older transactions between the two Bengali popular film industries in the world. The new relationship between the two national/regional film industries that emerged in the 1990s and the first decade of the twenty-first century is outlined in this chapter. By analysing cinematic movements between Bangladesh and India, this chapter attempts to look at the transnational dimensions of the 'national cinema' of/in Bangladesh. It may be argued that even Asian film industries anchored in a vernacular language and with a large 'captive' audience tied to the vernacular (as it is the case with Bangladesh and West Bengal cinemas) need to be reconsidered as 'transnational' discourses.

This chapter focuses on the connections between Bangladeshi and West-Bengali popular film production and their transnationalization and localization efforts. The remakes of Bangladeshi film melodramas in the West Bengal film industry will be examined as the 'transnationalizing' symptoms of these two cinemas that are linguistically defined. These remakes are unique in the sense that the original and remade films are both in the same language. The history of remakes posits remaking as a translation of films from one language to another, from one culture to another, and from one time to another (Verevis 2006). In many cases, all such translations can be located in one single, remade film (Ganti 2002; Gurana 2006). The West-Bengali films that are remade from Bangladeshi films from the 1920s till the end of the twentieth century, thus pose a problem for researchers: these films share the same language and time with the originals and differ only in terms of culture. More precisely, the remade films are intended for consumption in a different context: contemporary West Bengal. This chapter is therefore an effort to understand the cultural translation happening through such remaking of 'Bangladeshi' films addressing a different, non-Bangladeshi audience and viewing context.

The Genealogy of Two Bengali Film Industries

Both the Bengali film industries based in Dhaka and Calcutta target a distinct population, a Bengali-speaking audience within their national or regional boundaries, and sometimes beyond that. Such a linguistically defined viewing context coupled with 'captive' audiences for Bengali popular films ensured that Bengali film industries continued to survive as a rare species of medium-sized, vernacular film industries amid globalizing forces. Therefore, almost ignoring the Hollywood film industry, which is considered as a major threat to many film industries in the world, the two Bengali cinemas manage to survive. Their success lies in the fact that the two cinemas address a well-identified market sector, a non-English-speaking national/subnational audience, that is, Bengali-speaking Bengali Muslims in postcolonial Bangladesh and Bengali Hindus in West Bengal and eastern India. In other words, the two Bengali cinemas somewhat divided the Bengali population in terms of their national and religious orientations and their films represent these biases in creating a particular spectatorship though sharing a common language.

The effort to use cinema towards constructing particular national-religious identity began with the silent feature films produced in the first Bengali film industry, the Calcutta film industry in the early twentieth century. The Bengali cinema of Calcutta started its journey with a strong commitment to a certain version of colonial modernity. The leaders and crew of the then Calcutta film studios like the New Theatres were working to produce a literary and cultural modernity for the Bengalis and

Indians in the then British India. This was a version of modernity that was espoused by middle-class Bengali Hindu litterateurs and reformers in the late nineteenth-century Calcutta whose combined modernist efforts have been termed as Bengali Renaissance by the later historians.[1] During the early- to mid-twentieth century, a period when the Calcutta film industry served as one of the two major film industries in the then South Asia, this industry mainly produced pro-reform feature films accommodating such notions of cultural modernity propagated by the Bengali Hindu middle-class (Raju, forthcoming 2011). Despite being the base for renowned Indian art cinema filmmakers like Satyajit Ray and Ritwik Ghatak, the Bengali cinema of Calcutta retained its somewhat communalist characteristics. This 'Bengali Hindu' cinema still serves the Bengali-Hindu audiences of West Bengal and neighbouring states in eastern India. The so-called 'Golden Period' of this film industry ended in the 1960s. Bhowmik (1996: 120) has pointed out that during the late-1960s, the annual average production of Calcutta film industry had come down to twenty-eight films from fifty-two films per year produced in the mid-1950s. On the other hand, the Dhaka film industry came into being as a full-fledged production industry only in the 1960s. The first feature film production in Dhaka happened in 1955, more than three decades after Calcutta and other Indian film centres started producing feature films. Its rise as a Bengali film industry, coupled with the ban on the theatrical exhibition of Indian films in East Bengal/Pakistan as decreed during the India-Pakistan war in 1965, have also contributed to the declining Bengali film production in Calcutta since the 1960s. Rajadhyaksha and Willemen (1999: 23–4) also note that there was a loss of revenue for Indian films when the cross-border exchange of films between India and Pakistan was banned.

In the first decade of the Dhaka film industry, that is, between 1966–75, it produced on an average twenty-eight films each year, the same number of films produced by Calcutta in the late 1960s. However, since 1976, the Dhaka industry has seen a dramatic increase in the number of films produced annually. During 1976–83, it produced on an average forty-two films each year including fifty films in 1979. This number has gone up to an average of sixty-seven films each year during 1984–92 (Quader 1993: 211). In the next eight years, during 1996–2003, the Dhaka film industry produced on an average eighty feature films annually.[2] In other words, since the mid-1970s, the annual film production in Dhaka industry has increased at a rate of 25–30 per cent in every five years or so, while the Calcutta industry has seen a sharp decline in the number of productions since the 1960s. While the Calcutta film industry produced forty-six films per year in the 1950s, this number decreased by 35 per cent in the 1960s–1980s and went down to thirty films or less a year (Barnouw and Krishnaswamy 1980: 294). In this way, the Bangladesh popular film industry has turned out to be a vibrant, medium-sized national cinema and the larger and stronger Bengali-language film industry in contemporary South Asia. During the last decade of the twentieth century, it produced around ninety feature films every year, which were shown in around 1,200 theatres all over Bangladesh and also disseminated on VCDs and DVDs among local and diasporic Bangladeshis. Most of these films were genre-based formulaic popular entertainment films produced in the vernacular (Bengali).

As we can see, the Partition of India in 1947 and its after-effects gave rise to the second Bengali film industry in Dhaka that eventually consolidated its position as the producer of a Bengali-Muslim cinema. Especially after Bangladesh became independent in 1971 and middle-class Bengali Muslims seized the nation state here, this cinema strengthened its position as Bengali-Muslim cinema both at the national and transnational level. At the same time, the Calcutta film industry still serves as a Bengali Hindu cinema, though its reach and output got curtailed in the new transnational configurations of nation, region, and religion from the 1960s onwards.

Cinematic Travels: Between Calcutta and Dhaka

Calcutta and Dhaka have 'always shared a love-hate relationship' (Kudaisya 2008: 224). Within such a relationship, cinematic travel happened almost as a one-way traffic, that is, from Calcutta to Dhaka. For example, the first film screening that happened in Dhaka in 1898 in the then East Bengal was organized by a group of film exhibitors who travelled there from Calcutta. Both Hindi and (Calcutta-produced) Bengali films, most of which were melodramas depicting Bengali-Hindu lives, were exhibited in East Bengali film theatres until the 1960s. For example, the Uttam-Suchitra cycle of Bengali melodramatic films of the 1950s–1960s produced in Calcutta, was and is very popular among the Muslim middle class in East Bengal (now Bangladesh). These films are the foremost examples of 'melodramatic Bengali sentimentality' even for Muslim Bengalis and thus dissolved the communal barrier between Hindu and Muslim audiences in both parts of Bengal at least partially during the mid- to late twentieth century. Especially the availability of consumer VCRs since the early 1980s made the circulation of video-taped West-Bengali as well as Hindi film melodramas among Bangladeshi audiences much easier. West-Bengali film melodramas were seen as models for the romance and family drama genres in Bangladesh cinema in the 1960s–1990s. Though Bangladesh cinema appropriated and localized film plots and other elements from Calcutta cinema since film production began in Dhaka in the 1950s, the film industry in Dhaka somewhat positioned itself as the base for a Bengali-Muslim cinema from the 1960s onwards.[3]

In the last decade of the twentieth century, both Dhaka and Calcutta-based Bengali-language film industries, as popular-cultural institutions, are negotiating their roles and functions with globalizing forces and nationalist discourses. The survival and expansion of both these cinemas depend on their partly conflicting and partly dialogic relationship with postcolonial nation-states and their captive audiences, who are greatly affected by the globalization of the media and the economy. Within the global/local interface, a reverse cultural flow (that is, the travel of Bengali cinema from Dhaka to Calcutta) has been taking place in the recent years. In the last one decade or so, a number of Bangladeshi 'Bengali-Muslim' popular films have been remade in the Calcutta film industry for Indian, Bengali-Hindu audiences.

The Bangladeshi film texts that got remade in Calcutta are the 'social' films, sentimental family dramas supposedly addressed to female viewers. The Dhaka film industry that borrowed from Calcutta-produced Bengali social films of the 1950s–1960s, now started exporting such films for being remade in Calcutta. The social films became the major genre of Dhaka film industry in the semi-traditional social backdrop of East Pakistan in the 1960s' and Bangladesh in the 1970s, where Bengali-Muslim identity took a concrete shape. These Bangladeshi socials, following their South Asian, especially the Calcutta 'models', would portray males and females as simple and unproblematic iconic figures within a moral universe in which the conflict between good and evil was clear-cut and easily solvable. Obviously, all these happened within a 'Bengali-Muslim' world. Later, the social films met the challenge of addressing the complexities of gender and class relationships in a rapidly modernizing and commercializing 'national' society of Bangladesh between the 1980s and the 1990s. In these films, the central characters were no longer idealist rural-based male figures traumatized by the process of industrialization matched with a couple of all-sacrificing and mostly silent female figures as propagated and prevalent in the 'social' films of the 1960s–1970s. Rather, the protagonists were now more into facing the challenges of urbanization and modernization in a globalizing Bangladesh. Social transformations and the new media scenario gave rise to at least two sub-genres of social films: social action films with a heightened level of bodily actions and semi-conventional social films.

The semi-conventional socials resemble the Bangladeshi socials of the 1960s–1970s. Though this genre does not represent the major trend of textual production in the Dhaka film industry during the last decade of the twentieth century, few of these socials became record money-spinners in Bangladesh and were subsequently remade in Calcutta. These films create a simplified resistance to global modernity and popular culture through an innocent plot and a host of easily recognizable morally biased, Bengali-Muslim characters. Below, two such Bangladeshi socials that were remade and circulated in West Bengal in the last decade have been analysed.

FATHER AS SERVANT AND CHEERS FOR THE IN-LAWS: FAMILIES AS COMMUNITIES DEVASTATED BY EVIL IMMIGRANTS

Two popular Bangladeshi film melodramas: *Father as Servant* (1997) and *Cheers for the In-laws* (2001) and their Calcutta remakes made in 1998 and 2002, respectively have been analysed. When one watches *Father* and *Cheers*, he/she will be surprised to note the similarity of the diegetic world that these two films (and their remakes) represent. First of all, these socials, following other exemplary South Asian family-drama films, are also centred in an extended bourgeois household. The supremacy of the traditional patriarchal family and the collision between traditional values and emerging modern identities within a modernizing and commercializing Bangladesh/India is the key theme of the films. Both the films visualize and sometimes verbalize (through dialogues) the importance of traditional patriarchal family values and roles (for example, the absoluteness of parent-children relationship, supremacy of the father in the family, women as homemakers, men as bread-earners). One can feel that national, cultural, and religious 'traditions' are presented against the palpable fear of/against modern/Western forces as well as to empathize with the woes of the ordinary population in contemporary Bangladesh and West Bengal. Thus, both *Father* and *Cheers* signify not only the conflict between tradition and modernity, as melodramas do in most contexts, but also convey the anxiety of the ordinary Bangladeshis or Indians facing Westernization and globalization of the economy and culture. This anxiety is translated in the efforts of these melodramas in keeping the well-knit traditional families intact in contemporary South Asia.

Second, the admittance (or denial of entry) of new members in the family is the key issue of the two films. These can be read as narratives of immigration and denied access. Both the films deal with existing or would-be sons- and daughter-in-law who face problems in gaining entry into the family or are simply kept in waiting to be accepted as legitimate members of the family. *The Cheers* elaborately deals with the process of earning legitimacy for a son-in-law. The greater part of the film narra-tive is centred on the antagonism between the new son-in-law and his mother-in-law who does not want to accept him and, thus, to welcome him 'in' the family. Mother-in-law makes numerous attempts to prove that the son-in-law (who is a 'mere motor mechanic') is evil, but her own evil plans become exposed at the end and she has to admit the motor-mechanic as her son-in-law. It is also revealed that he is actually an engineering graduate of Boston University masquerading as a motor mechanic! *The Father* also depicts the antagonistic relationship between a daughter-in-law and her parents-in-law. Interestingly though the daughter-in-law is already 'in' the family, she has been portrayed not only as an evil person but also as an 'outsider' in the family, who collaborates with her evil mother and destroys the lives of her parents-in-law.

In this way, the son- or daughter-in-law are constructed as intruders, or even evil intruders in both *Father* and *Cheers*, because like many other Asian film melodramas these films share a certain tendency of com-munalizing the family, or defining the family as a 'community'. Here an individual is not independent; rather he or she is interdependent as a 'member' of an extended family. So he/she should not rush to fulfil only his own will and desires. Rather he/she always needs to consider how he/she can contribute to the family and how he/she can be a worthy 'part' of the family, almost in the same manner somebody 'should' aspire to become a 'good' citizen in a modern nation-state. Therefore, the granting of membership in the family to 'outsiders' like the son- or daughter-in-law is not easy. Since they are not members-by-birth like sons or daughters, they have to earn their membership by proving that they are suitable for the family. These characters may be termed as 'immigrants' to these well-knit families who are viewed as endangering the status quo by their mere presence. This may remind us of the plight of the legal or illegal immigrants, the citizens-in-waiting in places like the US, the UK, Australia or Canada, where an Indian IT professional may earn citizenship by proving his worth, but less qualified immigrants in need may be denied access even after they have gone through many hurdles.

FATHER AND *CHEERS*: THE REMAKES AS THE SITE FOR PRODUCING THE LOCAL

Though no research has been done so far on the remakes in Bengali cinema, most studies of remakes view them as hybrid texts, connected to various intertextual relationships. These studies analyse remakes as cross-cultural interpretations by focusing primarily on the issues of narrative, genre, and intertextuality (Horton and McDougal 1998; Aufderheide 1998; Nayar 1997). However, such a textual approach to remakes may be considered as a point of departure, raising the following questions: what are the functions of a 'cross-cultural' remake like *Father* or *Cheers* in contemporary South Asia? What are the relationships between Bangladeshi originals and their Indian remakes? And how do the remade Bangladeshi films address the audience in West Bengal?

The process of cultural translation of Bangladeshi films may be located in the Indian remakes. The manner in which the two versions of a particular film appeal to two distinct socially, politically, and economically constructed audience needs to be understood. It may be argued that the relationship between the text and audience changes in the process of remaking Bangladeshi texts in India because the remade versions are addressed to a different ('Indian, Bengali-Hindu') audience than the ('Bangladeshi') audience assumed for the original one. In this chapter, the remade Bangladeshi films are deconstructed as sites on which the state-nationalist agenda, religion, and Western/global modernity contest and complement each other and the identities for the West-Bengali film audiences are redefined accordingly.

In this context, the concerns are: how do these remakes and originals differ to defining the local? And more importantly, when going through a process of cultural translation, how do these texts construct different versions of national, cultural, and religious identities for the audiences of Bangladesh and West Bengal? How can the local be produced in cinema? Srinivas (2005: 290) has offered a hypothesis in this regard especially in relation to Telugu cinema:

> The local is produced by constructing a particular spectatorial position that is misrecognized or conveniently named as the 'Telugu'. ... [T]he local is not produced by historical, political and other contextual references at the level of theme or story alone, but also by the deployment of a variety of cinematic techniques that add up to a particular *mode of address*. Telugu films address me as someone who belongs to a particular context ... .

Taking a cue from Srinivas, the remakes of Bangladeshi film melodramas in relation to their new context of production and reception, that is, in an Indian, Bengali, Hindu context, can be reconstructed. These national, religious, and regional parameters certainly transform the remakes to a great degree. These transformations are aimed at mobilizing the local and creating a mode of address that is known to Bengali-Hindu audiences of popular film melodrama of/in West Bengal.

Cultural Translation of Bangladeshi Film Melodramas for West-Bengali Audiences: Towards Communalization?

The directors and producers of popular films in the Calcutta film industry utilize various strategies of cultural translation in order to turn Bangladeshi films into Indian-Bengali films, especially to develop a mode of address familiar to the West-Bengali film audience. These tools and techniques localize the text for the Indian/West-Bengali reception as well as create a different spectator (Indian, Hindu) for such films.

When studying the remaking of Hollywood films in Bombay, Ganti (2002: 282) points out that the directors and producers of the Hindi film industry work on a 'difference-producing set of relations' between the filmmakers and the audience when deciding for or against the '(H)Indianization' of certain Hollywood films for Indian audiences. Taking this further, it may be argued that the West-Bengali film industry

when remaking certain Bangladeshi films, 'Indianize' these films producing differences not only between the remakes and the original films,
but also developing differences between the film viewers' relationships as
created by the original and the remake. Then, at the textual level, these
films construct and disseminate a particular model of the spectator in
globalizing Bangladesh and India: a Bangladeshi Bengali Muslim or an
Indian, West-Bengali, Bengali Hindu.

The means used to construct such differences through cultural translation in the remakes can be located both in diegetic and non-diegetic
devices. Among the diegetic devices, the transformations brought in
the characters and in the film narratives as major tools may be located.
The extradiegetic strategies include the creation of localized cinematic
spectacles by using the star persona of well-known Indian/West-Bengali
origin and by composing 'original' song-and-dance numbers for the
remakes.

Communalization of Characters

The protagonists in the remakes are identified by 'Indian', Hindu names,
especially to clarify their religious affiliations. For example, Bengali
Muslims Arman Chowdhury and Dilruba Chowdhury became Achintya
Roy and Binodini Roy to denote Bengali Hindus in the remade *Cheers*.
All other characters are renamed through suitable Bengali-Hindu names,
except one 'Mr Mazumdar', a name that could mean either a Muslim
or a Hindu. Similarly, all the characters of *Father* were renamed with
appropriate Bengali Hindu names (for example, Rakibuddin Ahmed
became Rajnarayan Datta, and so on). Again one name, the name of
Rajnarayan's daughter remained 'Khushi', a Bengali name that is in use
by both Muslims and Hindus.

In order to be recognized as 'Indians', the protagonists in both the
remade films used the dialects and slang of West-Bengali origin. Hindi
popular cinema as an 'all-Indian lingua franca' was evoked by making
references to Hindi film stars in both the films. Stars like Dilip Kumar
or Sonali Bendre were evoked in the remade *Cheers*, while Padmini
Kolhapuri was mentioned in the remake of *Father*.

Costumes were utilized as the markers of religious and regional
affiliation in the remakes. Such signs were used to indicate that all the
characters are avowedly Hindus living in contemporary West Bengal.

In the remade *Cheers*, Bibha a widow who takes refuge in Achintya and Binodini Roy's house always wears a white cotton sari, a common dress code prescribed for Hindu widows in India. Binodini Roy, the 'modern' mother-in-law in conflict with her 'traditional' son-in-law, always put on *sindur* (vermillion) in the parting of her hair, a supposedly essential mark of identification for married Hindu women. The same 'red lead' is worn by the married women characters in the remake of *Father* too. In this film, Rajnaryan, the father, always wears a white dhoti, a costume commonly used by traditional Hindu men in West Bengal.

Communalizing the Narrative

Ganti (2002: 293) points out that the addition of subplots, such as romantic, comic, or dramatic, has always been seen as necessary when Hollywood films are remade in Bollywood. Turkish scriptwriter Bulent Oran noted way back in the 1970s that remaking Hollywood films for the Turkish audience meant facing the challenge of cross-cultural adaptations:

> Remaking a movie ... appears to be very easy. In fact, that is the most difficult and risky [of all the scenarios]. The reason for this is the difference between the sensations, worldview and understanding. (1973: 17, cited in Gurana 2006: 244).

The Calcutta remakes of *Cheers* and *Father* brought minor changes, especially creating new subplots and characters to make the narrative 'Indian' and include 'sensations, worldview and understanding' of/for West-Bengali film spectatorship. Religion played an important role in producing the local in the remakes. For example, in the original *Cheers*, Dilruba's sister Rehana takes refuge in her parental home as a widow, later whose son Badhon marries her cousin Prema (that is, Dilruba's daughter) and fights with Dilruba to gain entry as a legitimate son-in-law. In the remake, the character Rehana, renamed as Bibha, is not shown as Binodini's sister but as an acquaintance in need of shelter. This change was crucially needed for localizing the film, because cousins cannot marry as per Hindu customs, but it is normally allowed by Muslims. In the same vein, though the protagonists in Bangladeshi *Cheers*, Badhon and Prema, visit a Muslim shrine, in the remake, the 'Indian' protagonists, Soumya and Ruma, predictably go to pray in a Hindu temple.

Subplots and characters were added in the remakes to make the narrative denote a rigid patriarchal society. The degree of evil caused by evil women was maximized by bringing in the mother of the evil daughter-in-law in the remade *Father*, a character that was not in the original. Similarly, in the remade *Cheers*, Binodini strikes the helpless widow Bibha's palm with a heated rod when she accuses Bibha of stealing. Such a physical punishment with a vivid close-up is not present in the original film.

Interestingly, the presence of East-Bengalis as a marginal community in contemporary West Bengal has been acknowledged in the remakes. For example, the scenes of the sweetmeat shop are added in the remade *Cheers* where Soumya and Ruma go to buy local delicacies (a subplot that was not in the original film). This shop is named as 'Dhaka Sweet Store' in a bid to produce another difference as well as to construct the local: a character in the remake of *Cheers* talks in East-Bengali dialect. This dialect, as a 'lesser' version of standard Bengali, is a popular stereotype used to denote the East-Bengali refugee as the 'other' in West Bengal. This insertion also signifies that the Indian, West-Bengali identity as it is constructed in and by these films, is not homogeneous and unified.

Stars and Spectacles as Vehicles for Cultural Translation

In both *Cheers* and *Father*, West-Bengali actors were cast in all the characters, except one, which was played by Razzaque, the well-known Bangladeshi film star. This was in the remake of *Father*, the character of the father, Rajnarayan Datta, a character whom Razzaque as scriptwriter had imagined for himself. Thus, this can be seen as the only compromise that the West-Bengali film crew agreed to make when casting the actors.

However, the most important cast, the hero and the heroine, were film stars of the Calcutta film industry. Actually the same star duo, Prasenjit and Rituparna acted as the romantic couple in both the Indian remakes. They have been projected as 'spectacles' in the remade films. Especially new song-and-dance numbers have been composed to make the optimum use of their star persona on screen. Other than these principal characters, supporting actors were also of West-Bengali fame. A well known comedian of West-Bengali cinema played a comic character that was added in the remake of *Father*. This character was apparently added only to present the comedian to the West-Bengali audience. The same actor also performed in a comic role as Binodini's servant who speaks in the East-Bengali dialect in the remake of *Cheers*. Making a narrative detour from the original, his character was also given a larger treatment by attaching him to a romance subplot. We can also locate the presence of Soumitra Chatterjee, the legendary actor of the Calcutta film industry in the remake of *Father*. His onscreen presence in a minor role can be seen as balancing Razzaque's larger role in the film. Since all of these film stars and actors are well-known icons of West-Bengali film industry, their mere presence and trademark mannerisms made the remakes look very 'Indian', and the films, thus, positioned them as 'Indian films' for their audiences.

Conclusion

In this chapter, the focus lay on the trend of remaking Bangladeshi popular film melodramas in the Calcutta film industry in the last decade of the twentieth century. Two such remakes were closely studied as cases of an extraordinary transaction between two cross-border Bengali cinemas. These films can be seen as examples of how national cinemas in today's globalizing Asia are negotiating the national and the transnational. The two social films *Father as Servant* and *Cheers for the In-laws*, which were analysed above, illustrate the role of remakes in constructing the particular viewing context and spectatorship for West-Bengali popular cinema and how the remade texts create an Indian, Hindu, Bengali subjectivity.

The above discussion on remaking Bangladeshi films in an Indian context reminds us that the composition of any text, as 'original' or a remake, is largely dependent on its conditions of production and circulation. The film text is essentially connected with its constructed 'local' audiences. Drawing upon Appadurai, locality is taken as 'relational and contextual ... constituted by a series of links between the sense of social immediacy, the technologies of interactivity, and the relativity of contexts' (1996: 178). In that case, the distinction between the originals and the remakes is not as sharp as we tend to assume; rather one can locate the production of the local in both versions.

Notes

1. For details on the relationship between film industry and colonial modernity in early twentieth-century Bengal, see Raju (2012).

2. Calculated from the data presented in the annual reviews on Bangladesh film industry published in various Bangladeshi magazines and newspapers of this period. See, *Jai Jai Din* 20.12 (30 December 2003): 27, 19.12 (31 December 2002): 35, 14.13 (30 December 1997): 29 and 13.13 (31 December 1996): 39, *Weekly 2000* 4.33 (4 January 2002): 78, *Daily Banglabazar* (30 December 1999): 16 and *Anandabhuban* 3.16 (1 January 1999): 17.

3. For details on the development of Dhaka film industry as a Bengali-Muslim cinema, Raju (2012).

References

Anderson, B. 1991. *Imagined Communities*. London: Verso.

Appadurai, Arjun. 1994. 'Disjuncture and Difference in the Global Cultural Economy', in Patrick Williams and Laura Chrisman (eds), *Colonial Discourse and Postcolonial Theory*, New York: Columbia University Press.

———. 1996. *Modernity at Large: Cultural Dimensions of Globalization*, Minneapolis and London: University of Minnesota Press.

Ashcroft, Bill, Gareth Griffiths, and Helen Tiffin. 1989. *The Empire Writes Back*, London: Routledge.

Athique, Adrian M. 2006. 'The Global Dispersal of Media: Locating Non-Resident Audiences for Indian Films', in T.J.M. Holden and Timothy Scrase (eds), *Medi@sia: Global Media/tion in and out of Context*, London: Routledge.

Aufderheide, Patricia. 1998. 'Made in Hong Kong: Translation and Transmutation', in Andrew Horton and Stuart Y. McDougal (eds), *Play It Again Sam: Retakes on Remakes*, Berkeley: University of California Press.

Barnouw, E. and S. Krishnaswamy. 1980. *Indian Film*, New York: Oxford University Press.

Bhabha, Homi. 1990a. 'Introduction: Narrating the Nation', in Homi Bhabha (ed.), *Nation and Narration*, London: Routledge.

———. 1990b. 'DissemiNation: Time, Narrative, and the Margins of the Modern Nation', in Homi Bhabha (ed.), *Nation and Narration*, London: Routledge.

Bhowmik, Someswar. 1996. *Indian Cinema: An Economic Report*, Calcutta: Papyrus.

Chadha, K. and A. Kavoori. 2000. 'Media Imperialism Revisited: Some Findings from the Asian Case', *Media, Culture & Society*, vol. 22.

Curtin, Michael. 2003. 'Media Capital: towards the Study of Spatial Flows', *International Journal of Cultural Studies*, vol. 6, no. 2.

Featherstone, M. 1995. *Undoing Culture: Globalization, Postmodernism and Identity*, Thousand Oaks, CA: Sage.

Ganguly-Scrase, Ruchira and Timothy Scrase. 2006. 'Constructing Middle Class Culture: Globalization, Modernity and Indian Media', in T.J.M. Holden and Timothy Scrase (eds), *Medi@sia*, London: Routledge.

Ganti, Tejaswaini. 2002. 'And Yet My Heart Is Still Indian': The Bombay Film Industry and the (H)Indianization of Hollywood', in Faye Ginsberg, Lila Abu-Lughod, and Brian Larkin (eds), *Media Worlds: Anthropology on New Terrain*, Berkeley: University of California Press.

Gurana, Ahmet. 2006. 'Translating Modernity: Remakes in Turkish Cinema', in Dimitris Eleftheriotis and Gary Needham (eds), *Asian Cinemas: A Reader and Guide*, Edinburgh: Edinburgh University Press.

Hall, S. 1995. 'New Cultures for Old', *A Place in the World?*, D. Massey and P. Jess (eds), New York: Oxford University Press.

Hall, S., and P. du Gay (eds). 1996. *Questions of Cultural Identity*, London: Sage.

Hall, Stuart. 2000. 'Cultural Identity and Cinematic Representation', in Robert Stam and Toby Miller (eds), *Film and Theory: An Anthology*, Oxford: Blackwell Publishers.

Horton, Andrew and Stuart Y. McDougal (eds). 1998. *Play It Again Sam: Retakes on Remakes*, Berkeley: University of California Press.

Kudaisya, Gyanesh. 2008. 'Capitol Landscapes': The Imprint of Partition on South Asian Capital Cities', in Tai Yong Tan and Gyanesh Kudaisya (eds), *Partition and Post-Colonial South Asia: A Reader*, vol. 3, London: Routledge.

Quader, Mirja Tarequl. 1993. Bangladesh Film Industry. Dhaka: Bangla Academy.

Rajadhyaksha, A. and P. Willemen. 1999. *Encyclopaedia of Indian Cinema*, London: BFI.

Raju, Z.H. (2012). *Bangladesh Cinema and National Identity: in Search of the Modern?*, London: Routledge.

Sonwalkar, P. 2001. 'India: Makings of Little Media/Cultural Imperialism?', *Gazette*, vol. 63, no. 6.

Srinivas, S.V. 2005. '*Kung Fu Hustle*: A Note on the Local', *Inter-Asia Cultural Studies*, vol. 6, no. 2.

Verevis, Constantine. 2006. *Film Remakes*. Edinburgh: Edinburgh University Press.

Part 3

8   Region, Language, and Indian Cinema

Mysore and Kannada Language Cinema of the 1950s

M.K. RAGHAVENDRA

The states in India were constituted on the basis of the spoken language in 1956 and the cinemas in languages other than Hindi usually address the identity of people in different states or regions apparently determined by language. Tamil cinema, for instance, addresses the regional identity of the people of Tamil Nadu and Telugu cinema the identity of those in the state of Andhra Pradesh. An interesting question here is the nature of the identity addressed by a language cinema before linguistic reorganization.

The following is an inquiry into how the prospect of linguistic reorganization was registered by Kannada cinema in the 1950s, before the different Kannada-speaking areas were amalgamated into a single state and how Kannada cinema addressed the identity of the citizens of the former princely state of Mysore. This inquiry cannot evidently be undertaken without an understanding of other factors. Among these factors are the tendencies of national cinema and regional cinemas within India and the history of Mysore state before Independence and immediately after it.

Regional Cinema and Hindi Cinema

Indian cinema has attracted much attention globally as a body to have withstood the commercial onslaught of Hollywood but, for some reason, the popular variety is considered synonymous with 'Bollywood' or Hindi cinema from the city of Mumbai, the former Bombay. Only around a third of the cinema made in India is in Hindi and it has been suggested[1] that the 'cinemas of India' is a more appropriate way to regard the body as a whole because of the varieties of film that 'Indian cinema' has traditionally included.

There are different ways in which Indian cinema can be categorized and if one of the earliest was to regard it in terms of its commercial appeal ('popular', 'art', and 'middle' cinemas), it is also possible to identify the categories on the basis of the regional audiences they address. Such identification is useful when our interest is in understanding the preoccupations of an audience by interpreting the respective regional language cinema and it is apparent that only 'popular' kinds of cinemas address sizable audiences. While 'Bollywood' has as its constituency audiences dispersed across the length and breadth of India including Indians from the diaspora, the regional cinemas address local constituencies based on the languages they are made in. Hence, while Hindi cinema may be said to be pan-Indian, articulating 'national' concerns and addressing the 'Indian' identity, popular films made in the regional languages articulate different concerns and address local identities within India.

The idiom of Hindi cinema, while being responsive to the spectator's needs, tries to avoid 'local' influences within India to keep its reach widespread.[2] It caters to the 'lowest common denominator' across a larger space, and therefore, eschews much of the vibrancy and the audacity of a localized cultural form. To illustrate, a tradition of performance like the *nautanki* willingly takes chances with regard to 'sensitive' issues. Religious tales told in the nautanki have a secular colouring. Even in as sacred a play as *Raja Harishchandra*, when the noble Queen Taramati begs money for the cremation of her dead son, she dances, kicking her heels and swinging her hips. In a religious tale, Sita sings of her tragic plight while casting 'come hither' glances. Such boldness is unimaginable in the Hindi film—when it deals with sacred subject matter (Gargi 1991: 39). Students of theatre have also commented upon the lewdly non-religious note of *tamasha* performances while dealing with Krishna and the milkmaids and such impiety is rare in cinema. The Hindi film is apparently more accommodative and intended to appeal to people spread over a wider territory without causing annoyance.

The 'catholicity' of the mainstream Hindi film has received attention and has been explained in terms of its all-India appeal. Different regional cinemas have different appearances and are less bland than the mainstream Hindi film and this suggests that they give expression to entirely different experiences. If the regional cinemas address local experience in a way that Hindi cinema is unable to because of its pan-Indian reach, interpreting them has still not engaged the film scholar adequately so far. Studying them could be useful in a different way from studying Hindi cinema.

Hindi Cinema of the 1950s

It has been argued by film scholars (Chakravarty 1998; Prasad 1999) that the Hindi film played an important role in the 1950s to take issues like Nehru's modernization project to the people. They have found evidence that Hindi cinema was, consequently, also engaged in defining the 'Nation' on behalf of the state. In examining Indian cinema after 1947, they postulate that the resources of the independent nation-state were deployed to define a homogeneous 'Indian' culture and critically examine how cinema became useful. Cinema apparently served political purposes in India because it was already bridging cultural differences and producing a homogeneous mass culture for an undifferentiated audience in the period before Independence. What this means to the cinema of the 1950s is the proliferation of motifs like the following (Raghavendra 2008):

- The police and the judiciary—as emblems of the independent state—become treated as sacred institutions which is not so before 1947. They could be made fun of before 1947. For instance, surrendering to the police becomes an admission of moral guilt as in *Footpath* (1953). To show that justice is fair, the judge himself stands trial in the courtroom (*Awaara*, 1951).
- The city—as represented by Bombay—becomes an important locale in the 1950s' cinema and becomes an emblem of national optimism because of its association with the modern (*Aar Paar*, 1954; *Shri 420*, 1955; *Baazi*, 1951).

- The attitude towards the 'modern' is always ambivalent. As instances, good modernity is often represented by the construction engineer (*Aah*, 1953) and the doctor (*Dil Ek Mandir*, 1963; *Chirag Kahan Roshni Kahan*, 1959) and bad modernity by gamblers (as in *Shri 420, Baazi*), the club dancer, and the night-club (*Baazi*).
- Land reform and agrarian issues are frequently brought into focus as in *Mother India* (1957).
- The conflict between tradition and modernity is presented as the conflict between the village and the city as in *Naya Daur* (1957). It is also represented by the love of a club-dancer and a village woman for the hero and the hero being united with the village woman as in *Baazi*.
- The sacred 'mother' becomes a way of representing the nation or the land (*Awaara, Mother India*).
- The modern woman (as in *Andaz*, 1949) becomes a way of dealing with the issue of modernization.
- The lawyer becomes a way of representing the ruling class because of many Congressmen being lawyers (*Mahal*, 1949; *Amar*, 1954).

Within Hindi cinema itself, as has not been noticed, is the tendency of Madras-based and Bombay-based productions to contain conflicting discourses with regard to the nation because the Madras-based productions were often remakes of successful Tamil/Telugu films, with very different purposes.

Regional Cinema and the Nation

The motifs just described pertain to mainstream Hindi cinema although some regional cinema exhibits it as well, especially Tamil cinema. Madras, like Bombay, was a territory under the direct control of the British before 1947 and Independence could also mean to Tamil cinema what it meant to the Hindi film. There is, nonetheless, a fundamental difference between Hindi and Tamil regional cinema. *Parasakhti* (1952), the well-known film by Krishnan-Panju, which was an instrument of political propaganda by the DMK Party, includes all the standard devices such as lampooning of the government in Madras and criticism of religious exploitation. At the conclusion of the film, the hero Gunasekharan is produced in court where he indicts the whole organized society. But the interesting point here is that everyone accused in court lowers his gaze as if in acknowledgement of his/her guilt. Although *Parasakhti* is nominally set in the pre-Independence era, it portrays the court as Hindi films portray it after 1947—as a sacred site in which the truth must prevail. The colonial courtroom did not have the moral sanctity of a courtroom in independent India. *Parasakhti* demonstrates that a Tamil film can be both respectful *and* scornful of the independent nation and its institutions—in a way not true of the Hindi films of the same period. This has, by and large, been the tendency of regional cinema, which has to address both the 'Indian' identity and the local identity within India, which in times of regional turmoil might even clash with the national one. Tamil films serving the DMK cause are therefore beset by a contradiction in as much as they affirm the independent nation while promoting clashing local issues (such as the DMK-inspired satirizing of 'independence' and 'progress' under Congress rule).

The contradictory discourse present in many regional films is also carried forward into their Hindi remakes. S.M. Sreeramulu Naidu's *Azad* (1955) is based on the director's own Tamil film *Malaikallan* (1954), which was also employed as an instrument of regional political propaganda by the DMK Party. The hero of *Azad* is a vigilante and when the villain kidnaps the heroine with the intention of forcing her into marriage, the vigilante hero intervenes. The police, who regard the vigilante as a 'bandit' initially, also change their minds when they understand his good intentions. *Azad* perhaps gives us the first comic portrayal of the police after 1947, only the inspector redeeming himself in the final battle with the villains. Also pertinent is the uncharacteristic notion of 'vigilante justice' in the film. The notion gains ground when the state is either beleaguered or morally discredited and only in the 1980s is vigilante justice widely promoted in Hindi cinema. *Azad* may be a Hindi film with major Hindi stars but its discourse is frequently contrary to the tendencies of the times and this is due to its origins in regional cinema, namely, the propagandist DMK film.

As far as Kannada cinema is concerned, the films of the 1950s exhibit virtually none of the motifs of the Hindi cinema contemporary to it. The mythological, the saint film, and the folklore film dominate Kannada cinema in the period with films like *Jaganmohini* (1951), *Bedara Kannappa* (1954), *Mahakavi Kalidasa* (1955), and *Bhakta Vijaya* (1956). The mythological had, by and large, left Hindi cinema around

1942–3 and Kannada cinema's attachment to it in the 1950s is unusual. In any case, based on a comparison between Hindi, Tamil, and Kannada cinema, one could conclude that the winds of Independence apparently had a stronger effect upon Tamil than Kannada cinema, although both were nominally 'regional cinemas' within India. To understand the unique position of Kannada cinema, it will be useful to look at the history of Mysore state before and after Independence briefly. Kannada cinema's constituency in the 1950s was concentrated in the erstwhile state of Mysore or 'old Mysore' as we refer to it today and understanding old Mysore in the 1950s may assist in helping us interpret some of the Kannada cinema of the period.

Mysore State and Independence

Before we look at Mysore state in the 1950s it is necessary to understand that indirect rule of the British through the princely states had a very different logic from direct rule. This meant that local politics and political movements in Mysore developed differently from the way they did in British India. Since the Mysore rulers belonged to a minority caste group with few affiliations, they were reluctant to intrude upon the prerogatives of the dominant elements of the land and exercised absolute authority only around the cities and towns. Consequently, there was a discontinuity between state-level political arena and the political arenas at the village and local levels. At the same time, the tendency of the British had been to keep the princely states insulated from political change in the British provinces and to allow well-administered states like Mysore a high degree of autonomy. Consequently, there was another discontinuity between state-level and national-level political arenas and it was difficult for local activists to draw upon the resources offered by Indian nationalism from outside the state borders (Manor 1977: 1). There was, in effect, a lack of integration between the three political arenas (national, state level, and local) because of the twin discontinuities.

Political activity in the name of the Congress developed in Mysore in fits and starts. By the 1930s the Congress in Mysore found itself dominated by Brahmins from the urban areas while the only other political force in the state was the People's Federation, an organization founded to give non-Brahmins a voice in the state and which enjoyed the patronage of the landed elite. As late as March 1937, the People's Federation routed the Mysore Congress in the elections to the Legislative Council and the Representative Assembly—despite the Mysore Congress fighting the elections with All India Congress Committee (AICC) support. But later the same year, after correctly reading the political climate and seeing this as essential in its own interests, the People's Federation decisively merged with the Mysore Congress. This move strengthened the Mysore Congress considerably and the party now hoped to gain further strength through the AICC's support.

But the AICC was decidedly two-faced in its relationship with the Mysore Congress. The difficulty was perhaps its maintaining a good relationship with the rulers in Mysore. One of the strategies of the Congress at the national level was to hold up the better governed princely states as evidence that good governance was possible without the British and this tended to strengthen the Congress' relationship with Mysore rulers. Consequently, the Mysore Congress was persuaded by the AICC to restrict itself to a constructive work programme. After the merger of the People's Federation with the Mysore Congress, there was unrest in Bangalore and six persons were killed in police firing. A representative was therefore dispatched to Calcutta to an AICC meeting where a resolution was passed condemning the 'ruthless policy of repression of the Mysore government'. Within a fortnight, however, Gandhi attacked the AICC resolution in an article in the *Harijan* where he reiterated that the Congress in Mysore should restrict itself to 'constructive work' and the Dewan Sir Mirza Ismail had Gandhi's article translated and read out in hundreds of villages (ibid.: 105–7). It appeared that the Central leaders were not particularly concerned with bringing freedom to Mysore.

These facts may appear extraneous to the subject on hand but it is necessary to understand that political activism in Mysore was far behind what it was in the presidencies ruled directly by the British. When the Quit India movement began in 1942, there was a spontaneous upsurge among students in the cities to Gandhi's call while the Mysore Congress had actually fallen behind and it even abstained from the Quit India agitation (ibid.: 138–9), which had taken a life of its own without its leadership. It may be generally observed that between 1942 and 1947, the younger nationalists tended to look to the national leadership rather than the leaders of the Mysore Congress whom they did not altogether trust although the Mysore Congress did eventually take over the reigns of leadership.

Mysore in the 1950s and Linguistic Reorganization

The Congress leadership in Mysore was not brought into prominence through mass mobilization and was therefore, largely, an elite body with its influence founded on group loyalties and patronage. Mass mobilization implies appealing to the lowest level, resulting in competition for the same support base and therefore, the growth of a multi-party system. The absence of mass mobilization in Mysore meant one-party rule and the party itself was largely constituted as earlier, finding its bases in patronage and group loyalties. This also meant that the single party had no clear ideology or a programme to offer but proceeded by trying to offend as few supporters as possible and building a consensus. Also, when dissidence developed due to dissatisfaction, it developed within the Congress rather than as opposition to it. It was because of the squabbling within the party that Nehru visited the state in January 1951 to urge Congressmen to mend their differences (ibid.: 168–75). Alongside, although the huge party enrolments of the Congress brought influential people at the local level in non-urban areas into politics, the lack of integration between the state level and the national level political arenas continued. We may, therefore, hypothesize that Mysore state was relatively slow in integrating with the national mainstream in the 1950s although this does not mean the existence of strong regional loyalties to Mysore state.

The other factor of importance here is the relationship between Mysore and the other Kannada-speaking areas outside. The national leadership, as already explained, had been lukewarm to the Mysore Congress because of its own affinity to the princely rulers. This was very different from the situation in the other Kannada-speaking areas. As part of the Kannada-speaking area of India, Mysore had been placed under the jurisdiction of the Karnataka Provincial Congress Committee (KPCC), centred mainly in the area coming under the Bombay Presidency, an area left undeveloped by the Bombay government because it was a linguistic minority region. During the civil disobedience movements in British India in the 1930s, the KPCC cultivated its contacts in Mysore to obtain money and manpower but did not reciprocate with financial aid to the Congress in Mysore. Not surprisingly, Mysore Congressmen felt they were being used by the Karnataka Congressmen. Relations between the two worsened after 1935 when the KPCC placed itself in the camp of those opposing AICC aid to the nationalist organizations in the princely states (ibid.: 81–2). Mysore Congressmen were also more drawn to Madras than to Bombay-Karnataka because popular newspapers bringing news of British India to Mysore came from Madras. Transportation to Madras was better than the transportation to Hubli Dharwar and Gandhi also tended to be accompanied on his visits to Mysore by leaders from Madras.

Since the Kannada-speaking areas outside Mysore suffered the most because of their linguistic minority status, it was outside Mysore that the movement for unification of Kannada areas began. The Karnataka Vidyavardhaka Sangh, for instance, was founded in Dharwad in 1890 by R.H. Deshpande and the important personages of the Ekikarana movement like Aluru Venkata Rao came from northern Kannada-speaking region outside Mysore state. Mysore itself did not stand to gain materially through the unification of the Kannada areas because it was the most prosperous of the regions. When the linguistic reorganization of the states was considered in the 1950s, the government agreed to the creation of Andhra Pradesh because everyone was for it. When it came to the unification of the Kannada-speaking regions, however, the required consensus proved elusive for want of agreement of a majority of the people including the people of the erstwhile Mysore state (Muthanna 1980: 89). Those opposing the linguistic reorganization of Mysore into a new state felt that their interests, both cultural and administrative, would suffer in the enlarged state. Mysore state had the smallest incidence of landlessness in south India and this was hardly true of the other Kannada regions. Another important consideration was the prospect of demographic realignment. The largest single community—Vokkaliga— would lose its political influence with the integration of Lingayat majority regions with Mysore.[3] As a result of the ambivalence in the stand taken by Mysore, the linguistic reorganization of the Telugu regions into a single Andhra Pradesh was conceded in 1953 after Potti Sriramulu's death in 1952 but that of the Kannada regions was put off once again. The ambivalent position taken by Mysore state with regard to reorganization apparently persisted until Chief Minister K. Hanumanthiah's statement in late 1953 dispelled the idea that Mysore was not in favour of reorganization (Diwkar 1968: 950–9). Reorganization was a key issue between 1953 and 1956 with the state gradually reconciling itself to its prospect because of the pressure applied (largely) from outside through agitations and protests.

Interpreting Kannada Cinema

Interpretation of cinema depends largely on the detection of representational anomalies. For instance, the motifs pertaining to the modern nation (courtroom, the city and its attractions/dangers), which also find a place in Tamil films of the 1950s are not seen in Kannada cinema of the same period. This can be justifiably interpreted as Mysore state being less integrated with the nation than the Madras Presidency because of princely rule before 1947.

A key factor to be considered in interpreting a body of popular cinema is whether certain motifs are repeated at certain times. It is generally conceded that popular culture is co-authored by both the creator-author and the consumer-author and the involvement of the audience in the creation of popular cinema is apparent. The audience decides what films are successful and the filmmaker, in seeking success must address their immediate concerns. There is, consequently, a natural selection of stories and motifs in popular cinema depending largely on their pertinence. The popularity of a motif in a short period of two to three years may therefore be a reliable indication of its pertinence and merits interpretation.

Interpretation of popular cinema often presumes that films may talk indirectly. Fantasies and mythologicals then have covert significances that need to be dug out. As an instance, Zhang Yimou's *Hero* (2002), a martial arts fantasy, apparently set in ancient China is widely interpreted as a defence of dictatorship in China today.[4] Historical films are themselves seen as dealing with present concerns—though projected into the past. If films need to be pertinent even while being fantasies, historical films or mythologicals, their methods may be allegorical. Three Kannada mythologicals in the period from 1954 to 1956 exhibit the same motifs although they do not deal with the same events and this leads us to interpret them as allegories. The films are H.L.N. Simha's *Bedara Kannappa*, K.R. Seetharama Sastry's *Mahakavi Kalidasa*, and Aroor Pattabhi's *Bhakta Vijaya*. What follows is an examination of the three films and the interpretation of a key motif appearing in them. It is necessary to describe the films briefly in order to identify the common motif.

Bedara Kannappa, which is based on a folk tale involving a tribal saint from Srikalahasti, begins in heaven with a *gandharva* (a heavenly being) accidentally killing a peacock and being cursed by the God of wealth

Kubera to be reborn on earth as a lowly hunter. The young gandharva (Rajkumar) appeals to Shiva, who regrets his inability to undo the curse, but advises the gandharva to make use of the opportunity provided by the curse to bring righteousness to the world. The gandharva agrees and he and his wife (Pandari Bai) are therefore planted on Earth as infants, to be adopted by a tribe of hunters and given the names Dinna and Neela. The two grow up to adulthood and their marriage is duly solemnized by the tribe. Dinna has however grown up to be an impetuous young man and he soon quarrels with some other tribals and is cast out with Neela by his adoptive father, the tribal chieftain. Dinna, although made to undergo hardship, remains proud and a fierce unbeliever until God Shiva appears as a mendicant to relieve him of his troubles. Dinna then understands his errors and becomes a devotee. Providing comic relief in the story are a cunning Brahmin (G.V. Iyer), his good-hearted wife and son (Narasimharaju), and two courtesans, a mother and daughter. Much of the story of *Bedara Kannappa* is true to the original legend. Dinna offers meat to the deity and, while he is castigated for it by the Brahmin priest, Shiva recognizes his devotion. Dinna cuts out both his eyes and offers them to the *linga* (sacred stone phallus) when he finds the eyes on it bleeding. Shiva restores his eyesight when he recognizes Dinna's devotion and the story ends happily and he is called Kannappa. The story is fairly true to the original legend but very significant are the changes instituted.

The scheming Brahmin is a characteristic presence in many saint films (for example, *Sant Tukaram*, 1936) because the Bhakti movement was itself a reaction to the Brahmin domination of religion. But more significantly, the gandharva in the prologue is dressed like a prince, with Kubera and the other gods as higher ranking kings or princes attending Shiva's court. His 'princely pride' is also carried over when he is reborn although the story is about his losing it. The original legend itself is silent about Kannappa's pride and the film introduces it with a purpose. Another factor to be noted is that while Dinna is born a tribal, there is no more mention of the tribe once he is cast out of it. His dealings thereafter are entirely with mainstream society complete with its caste and class hierarchies. Dinna's devotion being acknowledged by God Shiva at the conclusion sees him neither going back to his tribe nor ascending to heaven. He is simply gathered into society and Dinna and Neela may be said to gain a community. This is given emphasis when the film does not end as popular films in India usually do—with a family reunion or a happy meeting of separated lovers but with the two joining the social mainstream. The Gowda who is nominally the chieftain is not dressed as a prince/king but simply as a landowner is portrayed in popular films. Perhaps this is done because the true stature of Kannappa is that of a prince and having another prince/king in the concluding scenes might be confusing. As presented in the film, Kannappa is not the social inferior of the Gowda because he is actually a prince, although there are 'kings' above him outside the community.

The second film, *Mahakavi Kalidasa*, also relies on a legend—the legend of Kalidasa who authored the Sanskrit classic *Shakuntala*. In the legend, an arrogant princess is tricked into marrying an ignorant rustic by making her believe that he is learned. When the rustic is cast out, he seeks the blessings of the goddess who blesses him with great scholarship. In the film, the rustic is actually an aristocratic young man (Honnappa Bhagavatar) who is cursed with ignorance by his guru for showing him disrespect and he becomes a cowherd. Here the princess does not cast out her husband but he forgets her when he is blessed with scholarship by the goddess. The princess nonetheless follows him to the court of Vikramaditya in Ujjain and both of them eventually become ordinary subjects of King Vikramaditya. There is also a twist in the story when Kalidasa's father-in-law intends to install him as his own kingly successor but Kalidasa prefers to remain an ordinary subject in Ujjain to being a king in his own land and the general sense is that it is the community in Ujjain presided over by Vikramaditya where he and his wife the princess rightly belong. The film also includes the motif of scheming Brahmins out to undermine Kalidasa in Vikramaditya's court.

The third film, *Bhakta Vijaya*, by Aroor Pattabhi is also about a proud aristocrat cursed with poverty. In this film, Santhoba (Rajkumar) is a landowner who is cursed by a poor tenant's wife when he tries to evict them for remaining behind in their payments. Santhoba also conducts himself arrogantly with Saint Tukaram but understands his errors and gives away his wealth. Joined by his wife, he thereafter becomes a mendicant and undergoes suffering, to be helped by God Pandurang in human form. The film concludes with Pandurang appearing to Santhoba and joining Tukaram's community of devotees. In this film as well, there is the motif of the self-serving Brahmin with the good-hearted wife who come into contact with Santhoba although the Brahmin does him no harm. The film has aspects in common with the other two films and one of these is the representation of the proud Santhoba as a princely personage, wearing jewellery, riding on horseback, and living in a palace.

The three films appear to conform to a single pattern. If we were to identify the common motifs in them, we could say they were about an arrogant prince and/or princess who suffer hardship and poverty because of a curse but overcome it by appealing to the divine. In all three films there is the sense of a community gained, a community not presided over by the protagonists but by a benevolent authority to which the protagonist submits. In *Bedara Kannappa* and *Bhakta Vijaya*, the community is one of devotees and the authority divine, while in *Mahakavi Kalidasa*, the community is in Ujjain and presided over by King Vikramadhitya. In all three films, the wife joins her husband but the films do not achieve closure through the family reunion, as is more common. All three films feature self-serving Brahmins but their presence can be explained as characteristic of the saint film in which Brahmin villains tend to exist only to provide convincing obstacles to saintly people.

The fact that the stories of at least two of the films have been deliberately altered suggests that the changes are intended to have them fit a model that would make them pertinent to the times. It is significant that the story of Kalidasa was retold as *Kavirathna Kalidas* (1983) with Kalidasa initially being an ignorant rustic and not an aristocrat. As indicated earlier, for a fantasy or a mythological to be made 'pertinent' its approach must be allegorical. It is now argued by Jameson (1987) that the distinction between the 'public' and the 'private' that characterizes the First World/developed countries has not yet emerged in the newly independent nations of Africa, South America, and Asia and 'private stories', therefore, have public connotations. Since a popular text must have common connotations for the community it is addressing and the community is usually national, the text is a 'national allegory'. In the case of Kannada cinema, which addresses both the regional and the national identity, we may surmise that the allegory pertains to the region and/or the nation.

Coming to the actual interpretation of the common motif identified in the three films, the motif of the prince should perhaps be considered in the light of Mysore being a former princely state and the habits cultivated under monarchy may persist for a while. 'King' and 'Country' are synonymous to subjects in a monarchy and this suggests the prince's/princess' predicament in the three films has parallels with the predicament of Mysore state in the period 1954–6. The fact that the prince and the princess share the suffering substantiates that this is a 'royal predicament' rather than the privation forced upon an individual. If this interpretation is conceded, the 'curse' of poverty and hardship finds correspondence in the apprehensions of prosperous Old Mysore when faced with the prospect of integration with areas, which were much poorer and relatively undeveloped. The fact that it was a 'curse' with no remedy suggests that the people of Old Mysore (the constituency addressed by the film) gradually came to realize that they had no option but to submit. The only solace was perhaps that there was a 'higher' benevolent monarch/authority (perhaps in Delhi) ensuring that the dispensation would not be without recourse. By showing that in the process of dealing with the curse, the prince also gains a larger community, the films seem to appeal to the attractions of an integrated Kannada community.

Conclusion

Given the discourse identified in the three films, there is evidence that Kannada cinema in the mid-1950s did not address the Kannada identity but the one belonging exclusively to 'Old Mysore'. Since then, however, it is certain that the range of Kannada cinema's address has widened considerably but it still cannot be asserted that it is pan-Kannadiga. The language/dialect employed in Kannada cinema is still that of Mysore. The lack of visibility of Kannada film stars as state-level politicians as opposed to their strong presence in the neighbouring states suggests that Kannada cinema is still not as inclusive as its Telugu and Tamil counterparts. While the required data may be elusive, it would be of great interest to find the geographical areas where Kannada cinema is consumed today and the true extent of its consumption in these areas— so that one can understand the relationship between Kannada cinema and the Kannadiga identity today. This in turn may help us understand many things about the changing constitution of the identity since the linguistic reorganization of 1956.

Notes

1. For instance, see Thoraval 2001.
2. Hindi cinema has perhaps roughly the same relationship to the regional cinemas as classical literature (and myth) in India has to 'folklore'. Ramanujan notes how folklore 'domesticates' classical literature when it draws from it. See Ramanujan (1986: 65–6).
3. It is no coincidence that all the chief ministers after the reorganization and up to 1973 were Lingayats.
4. Sharon Hom and Hu Ping, 'Viewing Hero: a Conversation about History, Art and Responsibility', http://www.hrichina.org/public/PDFs/CRF.2.2005/2.2005-RF-Hero.pdf

References

Chakravarty, Sumita S. 1998. *National Identity in Indian Popular Cinema*, New Delhi: Oxford University Press.

Diwkar, R.R. (ed.). 1968. *Karnataka through the Ages: from Prehistoric Times to the Day of the Independence of India*, Bangalore: Government of Mysore.

Gargi, Balwant. 1991. *Folk Theatre of India*, Calcutta: Rupa and Co.

Jameson, Frederic. 1987. 'Third World Literature in the Age of Multi-national Capitalism', in C. Koelb and V. Lokke (eds), *The Current in Criticism*, West Lafayette: Purdue University Press.

Manor, James. 1977. *Political Change in an Indian State: Mysore 1917–1955*, Delhi: Manohar.

Muthanna, M. 1980. *History of Modern Karnataka*, New Delhi: Sterling.

Prasad, M. Madhava. 1999. *Ideology of the Hindi Film*, New Delhi: Oxford University Press.

Raghavendra, M.K. 2008. *Seduced by the Familiar: Narration and Meaning in Indian Popular Cinema*, New Delhi: Oxford University Press.

Ramanujan, A.K. 1986. 'Two Realms of Kannada Folklore', in Stuart Blackburn and A.K. Ramanujan (eds), *Another Harmony: New Essays on the Folklore of India*, Delhi: Oxford University Press.

Thoraval, Yves. 2001. *The Cinemas of India*, Chennai: Macmillan India.

9   Modernity and Male Anxieties in Early Malayalam Cinema

MEENA T. PILLAI

Cinema offered Indian societies a mirror by which they could look into and find a visual form for the material and cultural shifts that displaced and transformed the earlier social life during the process of their transition into modernity. Regional cinemas in India have had a great role in imagining and embodying cultural and social identities as part of the project of this modernity. As national/sub-national narratives, they have functioned as part of the ideological state apparatus in creating a sense of belonging that shapes the contours of a linguistic or cultural community, constructing common identities and acculturating men and women to function within symbolic boundaries. Thus regional cinemas in India have been instrumental in crystallizing social formations with clearly demarcated structures and meticulously codified social relations.

Keralam, with its erstwhile tradition of matrilineal forms of kinship pattern, has evolved into one of the most advanced states of India in terms of social development indicators. Yet in 1933, its unique form of matrilineal kinship became the first kinship system in the world to be legally abolished. In 1928, the first Malayalam silent movie *Vigathakumaran* was produced. Since then to the first talkies *Balan* (1938) and *Jnanambika* (1940), Malayalam cinema shows a curious fascination with the erasure of the mother and the trope of the stepmother.

Even when cinemas from all over India sought to install 'motherhood' as the epitome of the 'Indian woman', early Malayalam cinema is permeated with negative stereotypes of the mother, based on formulaic misogynist myths like those of Parasurama and Poothana. This served to situate the sign 'Malayali woman' in a liminal narrative and cinematographic space and thus laid the foundation for the future tokenization and marginalization of the images of the women on the celluloid in Keralam.

This chapter seeks to study the emergent discourse of cinema in Keralam in the 1930s and 1940s and explicate how it has sought, in varying degrees, to consolidate and reinforce the 'patrifocal' ideologies of a society that was continually struggling to efface a matrilineal past by pegging down with a vigour, infused by colonial modernity, the contours of a normative, 'native' femininity.

Keralam, with its long coastline and strategic location was a land where traders, missionaries, refugees, and travellers arrived and mingled and where 'modernity' in the sense of re-viewing 'tradition' would not be a misnomer from as early as the first century AD when St Thomas is believed to have spread Christianity here. As Logan says,

> Whether St. Thomas the Apostle visited the Malabar Coast about this time and founded the Christian Church, which certainly from a early period down to the present day has existed there, is likely ever to remain a subject of controversy. But it will be seen that, had he been so minded, he would have found in these annual pepper fleets every facility for effecting his journey to Malabar. (2004: 252)

And again,

> The Malabar Coast with its Christian settlers must have been one of the chief centres whence European influences spread throughout the land, so it is not to be wondered at that Vedantism at the hands of its expounder, the 'gracious teacher'—*Sankaracharyar*—spread from Malabar over the whole of India. (2004: 255)

Jewish and Roman settlers, Chinese travellers, Persian traders, and after Vasco Da Gama's historic landing at Kappad in 1498 the Portuguese, the Dutch, the French, and finally, the English sought Keralam. The arrival of modernity in Keralam is a much more natural, eager, and complicitous process than in the rest of India, facilitated as it was by long-standing trade and commerce with the West and a culture open and malleable to the influences of global migration, religious syncretization, and the flow of capital. Thus, compared to the rest of India, the arrival of modernity was a more long-drawn out process in Keralam. Probably because of this long-drawn exposure and influence of the West, Keralam tends to show traits of 'societal modernization' based on the doctrine of progress under the aegis of colonialism rather than traits of 'cultural modernity' with its tilt towards the 'aesthetic self'. The former envisages a break with tradition while the latter tradition 'haunts and instructs' the new. Thus, modernity in Keralam, at least to some extent signals a willingness and an urge to break out of the continuum of tradition.

The ideas of Max Weber seem to have great relevance as far as Kerala modernity is concerned. Weber argues that the reason why the occidental and the oriental cultures are so different is mainly because of religion. Protestantism influenced the development of capitalism, bureaucracy, and a rational legal state in the West. Therefore, in contrast to Marx, Weber argued that religion also shaped human institutions and not material causes alone. In Keralam, the Christian missionary zeal in all walks of life as also the influence and conversion to Christianity of large sections of people created a shift in harnessing human effort into employing a rationale for economic gain. Thus, enterprise, especially an economic enterprise became a marked trait of the Malayali. Therefore, the spread of Christianity did accelerate and strengthen the pace of the social movement here to a capitalist economy. In contrast, many other parts of India show signs of domination by strong Hindu religious beliefs, which, according to Weber, slows down the pace in the development of capitalism. Modernity in Keralam seems less tradition-bound than elsewhere in the country. Therefore, it can be argued that Keralam does offer a great scope for the notion of an alternative Indian modernity emphasizing ethnic, ideological, religious differences, the role of the family and kinship patterns, legal forms of property and administration. In face of the homogenizing, universal, convergent model of modernity, it interrogates and problematizes the 'universalist' model of colonial modernity that one keeps referring to in countries like India.

Today, Kerala's high social development indices have given rise to the 'myth of Malayali women' as enjoying a higher status than their counterparts elsewhere in the country especially in view of the fact of high female literacy in the state. This myth has been augmented and nurtured by evidence that matrilineal forms of kinship patterns were prevalent among certain communities in Keralam. However, what is to be taken into consideration here is that between 1896 and 1976 as many as twenty legislations were enacted in the erstwhile states of Travancore, Cochin, and Malabar, and later on in the current state of Keralam (which was an amalgamation of the earlier princely states), in order to gradually revoke the legal framework of matriliny (Eapen and Kodoth 2001).

> These legislations sought to radically change the structure and practices of families through changes in marriage, inheritance and succession patterns that were largely patrifocal and aimed at weakening women's access and control over inherited resources while at the same time curtailing their power over their own lives. Thus the seeming idealization and nostalgic glorification of Kerala's matrilineal past today is a sham that needs to be critiqued from the point of the conjuncture of woman, modern and Malayaliness, thus problematising and pitting the Malayali modern vis-à-vis the Indian national modern. The process of carving out of a national subject being worked out in Keralam in the early 20th century was in numerous ways different from that in many other parts of India. (Pillai 2010: 4)

Before the British colonial rule, households in many parts of Keralam were sufficiently flexible and adaptable to changes in political, economic, and personal factors. With sufficient social mobility, no overtly rigid systems or customs pertaining to descent, succession, or inheritance were prevalent. However, it was only by the mid-nineteenth century that 'colonial jurists and judges identified co-residence and the impartibility of property as the main organizational principle of the matrilineal households. In the pre-colonial period, none of these identities surface as crucial indices, along which households were organized' (Arunima 2003: 36)

Matriliny itself, not as a well-defined or monolithic pattern of kinship system, had in the course of the eighteenth and nineteenth century become an ambivalent and fluid set of amorphous practices and relations echoing and reflecting the hegemonic power system existent in the society in which it was located. Colonial rule vested the eldest male with all legal powers to be the head of the *tharavadu* (the house of the matrilineal joint family). Thus, women were relegated to being mere dependents from their earlier position of power. One of the most crucial issues debated around matriliny was the practice of *sambandham* or marriage of a hypergamous sexual nature entered into by Nair womenfolk. The reformers of the late nineteenth century, imbibing Victorian moral standards viewed matriliny as immoral, unnatural, and barbaric. Thus, they believed that the polyandrous and 'promiscuous' Nair women could only reproduce 'unnatural families'. By the late nineteenth century, there were vociferous demands in courts for the natural right of the father over his children and above the legal authorities of the *karanavar* (the eldest male of the tharavadu). 'Significantly, such debates never extended to examining questions of mother-right. The mother (woman) was increasingly seen as a mere conduit for the continuation of the "*tharavadu*", and the household a matrilineal variant of patriarchy' (Arunima 2003: 192).

These debates and conflicts also point to an internal conflict among certain sections of Malayali men—their negotiations with a new kind of modernity, an aesthetic modernity that made them aware of the 'self', of their identity as being part of larger identities of caste and the nation. In order to belong to these larger groups, an attack and decapitation of the mother-centred family form became imperative.

Early Malayalam cinema provides very useful insights into the construction of the Malayali modern whose logic runs counter to that of the 'Indian modern' and traces a different trajectory to modernity albeit played out on the woman as in the larger national context but from an entirely different angle. Reforms impelled by the fear that the Malayali models of conjugality, domesticity, and motherhood were far from modern and were in fact anti-modern, unsettled large sections of Nair reformers of Keralam. Along with this was also a palpable anxiety of being left out of the larger ideological project of nation-building. A shame that their women conformed to what by then was an 'immoral' and 'barbarous' system of polyandrous and polygamous conjugal relations made them want to disown and hide their exogamous matrilineal lineage. Thus, if the spiritual essence of the home and motherhood became celebrated in the national context, this became for many in Keralam a 'licentious' past that had to be systematically buried.

It is interesting to note that in a matrilineal society where women could enter into hypergamous sexual relations, early Malayalam cinema portrayed female chastity as being the natural correlative of male valour. Early films such as *Jnanambika* (1940), *Nirmala* (1948), *Prasanna* (1950), *Chandrika* (1950), *Nallathanka* (1950)—all eponymous titles of the heroine in the respective story, seem to guarantee the predominance of the image of the woman on screen.

> The heroine of the period is a romantic ideal, with fluttering eyelids and timid gait, treated with loving reverence by the camera. But it is her essential submissiveness, and coy charm which she offers at the altar of her male ego ideal that

earns her this halo of romantic reverence. In retrospect we can see in these films the first effort, however unconscious, to give shape to the 'myth of the Malayali woman' where the myth is as much a public dream as an oral culture trying to find new fables in order to represent itself in a visual medium in tune to hegemonic social structures. (Pillai 2010: 11)

In all of the early Malayalam cinema women characters are mere stereotypes which seem to legitimize the gender hierarchies existing in society even in those times.

> It is interesting to note here that the mother image as in *Mother India* which catapulted Nargis to fame and served as one of the prime symbols of national integration in India, is not central to Malayalam cinemas as it has been in Hindi. Mehboob Khan's *Mother India* was released in 1957 and its tremendous popularity helped Nargis become an icon that represented India. This film, in a sense, installed motherhood as the epitome of the Indian woman, symbolizing her dignity, purity and suffering. In contrast the mother image in Malayalam from the time of the first talkie has been torn by the negative and positive stereotypes. In fact Malayalam cinema seems more preoccupied with the theme of the stepmother—a stereotype embodying greed, selfishness and moral degeneracy. (Pillai 2010: 12)

Myths are stolen languages according to Barthes (1972). Most of the early films in Malayalam from *Balan* (1938) onwards have used the myths of Poothana and Soorpanaka, which are premised on the notion of man's power to punish as also woman's powerlessness before the punishment man inflicts. However, these punishments are meted out only when she transgresses the laws of the symbolic order. These myths help to situate the sign woman appearing in these films as already laden with a certain meaning.

> The contemporary reality of women's oppression and the conflicting issues confronting women are all impoverished and tamed by the connotative denotedness of myths. Thus the contingency of real women's experience is hollowed out, drained and the very process of signification appropriated or distorted. But the most subterfugous aspect of myth is that it effaces itself, and even as it steals meaning looks innocent on the surface, thus performing a vanishing trick in the last act of its kleptomaniacal exercise. (Pillai 2010: 12)

Thus, in *Jnanmbika* (1950), adapted from a novel by C. Madhavan Pillai, the director, S. Nottani, creates the character of a stepmother Rajamani who is not only cruel to her stepdaughter but also unchaste, cheating on her husband Rajasekharan. Rajamani, as a woman who transgresses, has to be punished for her crimes. Thus, like Soorpanaka her overarching ambition and desire are punished by Raveendran, the anti-hero. Here the Soorpanaka myth becomes an eternal referent which establishes that there are fallen women who desire too much and they are to be punished. As Barthes says,

> On the surface of language something has stopped moving; the use of the signification is here, hiding behind the fact, and conferring on it a notifying look; but at the same time, the fact paralyses the intention, gives it something like a malaise producing immobility, in order to make it innocent, it freezes it. This is because myth is speech stolen and restored. Only, speech which is restored is no longer quite that which was stolen: when it was brought back, it was not put exactly in its place. It is this brief act of larceny, this moment taken for surreptitious faking, which gives mythical speech its benumbed look. (1972: 125)

Malayalam cinema might never have been overtly mythical. Nevertheless, as far as the women's representations are concerned, there are paradoxically enough attempts to conform to the *pathivratha* myth, thus making women's oppression seem universal and 'natural' and propelling the audience to read images that are constitutive of reality as an obvious reflection of reality.

Early Malayalam cinema has used the myth of Poothana, the 'she-devil' as stepmother who rubs poison on her breasts before suckling the little Krishna. But the Lord feeds on innocently until he draws the very life out of Poothana. Poothana has also occupied a significant amount of space in the aesthetic realm of the performing arts of Keralam like Kathakali, Nangiarkoothu, and Krishnanattam, thus displaying a predominantly misogynist trait in the Malayali psyche. The very evolution of the land of Keralam has a misogynous myth at its root. It is believed that this land surfaced from the ocean, when sage Parasurama threw his axe (parasu) into the ocean. Parasurama is himself one of the Dasavatara (ten incarnations of Lord Vishnu) and, according to mythology, decapitated his own mother, Renuka, at the behest of his father sage Jamadagni for neglecting her wifely duties. Thus, the negative stereotype of the mother that permeated early Malayalam films like *Balan, Jnanambika, Jeevithanauka,* and *Nallathanka,* based on formulaic myths such as those of Poothana and Parasurama served to situate the sign 'Woman' in a liminal narrative and cinematographic space and laid the cornerstone of future tokenization and marginalization of images of women. This point becomes extremely significant when viewed in the context of the fact that this was a time when other regional cinemas all over India were passionately embracing the devotional and mythical.

Malayalam cinema however, right from its inception chose to invest in contemporary social reality than mythical or puranic stories. But while apparently rooted in social realism it abounded in stereotypes at the level of characterization. This was especially true of women characters who were either virtue or vice incarnate. Malayalam cinema, right from its early years rejected the devotional trend in other regional cinemas in India and exhibited a leaning towards more socially realistic films that depicted rural themes, feudal tensions, and the evils of class and caste, significantly silent over gender issues in a fast changing social milieu.

> While it proves modernist in discarding the retelling of devotional stories from epics, puranas and mythologies, it is curiously conformist in its portrayal of women as mere stereotypes, acting out roles positive or negative as already drawn out in traditional myths and symbols. Women thus subjected to the new rigorous gaze of the camera are forced to classify themselves under one of the two signs of the new discourse—the spiritual essence of femininity or its crass materialistic embodiment. Thus in the new discourse of cinema in Malayalam we see how ambivalently women are located as stylized representations amidst realistic portrayals of ordinary men and objects. Early Malayalam cinema is seen to create a shift in taste attempting to shape an aesthetic pleasure from an 'objective' and 'realistic' representation of 'reality', while as far as women are concerned 'naturalising' stereotypes seem to be the norm. What evolves and matures in Malayalam cinema across the decades in varying degrees is this dichotomy of representation of male character subjects and female character subjects. Interrogating and analysing these double strategies of representation reveal the tangled mass of gender issues that cinema so skilfully hides and reveals in the process of creating the myth of the veracity of cinematic representation. So a study of representation in early Malayalam cinema as posing both political and epistemological problems makes one aware of a gross misrepresentation and tokenization of the female subject in the very process of attempting to represent the woman. The new discourse of cinema naively believed to 'represent' hitherto marginalized groups and voices was in fact hand in glove with the hegemony of 'representational realism', which distorts and misrepresents, assimilates and appropriates, in the name of mimesis. Thus, early Malayalam cinema fails to represent the heterogeneity of women's experience and identity in Keralam. But paradoxically enough without 'really' representing the reality of women's life or situations this cinema did shape at least to some extent the contours of the 'feminine' in Kerala society. (Pillai 2010: 14)

Early Malayalam cinema is not unduly influenced by either the nation-alist struggle for Indian independence or the exigencies of imagining the nation.

> Yet the gendered politics of the transactions of Indian nationalism surfaces in Malayalam cinema too with a characteristic regional flavour and ethos. The gen-dered subjectivity of the woman constructed in Malayalam cinema is premised not on the concept of nationalist identity politics but on the particularity of Malayali identity. Malayalam cinema, during its nascent stages, was inordinately influenced by Tamil, but later on it learnt to deploy popular folk idioms to garner popularity. This could be the reason why, as mentioned earlier, the mother figure which literalized the nation and acted as a trope for the motherland elsewhere in the country, never enjoyed great popularity in Keralam. The mythic status of motherhood did not seem to hold any undue fascination for the Malayali audi-ence. Paradoxically enough this comes in a society, which was predominantly matrilineal. The liminality of the figure of matriarch could also be in part due to an attempt to inscribe humanist and masculinist myths of power into the discourse of cinema. (Pillai 2010: 15)

The critique of matriliny in Keralam was part of the political and cultural logic of colonial modernity. However, Keralam's access to the modern especially in terms of the 'woman', question becomes prob-lematic. Chatterjee's (1993) famous argument that Indian nationalism resolved this question by attempting to remodel modernity in tune with the nationalist project does not hold water in Keralam. The dichoto-mization of the spiritual and the material, of the home and the world, privileging the former and thus emphasizing the spiritual superiority of the colonized, would become a doomed project in Keralam given the shame of—what was perceived in those times to be—a tainted matrilin-eal past. Therefore, the home and the domestic had to be cast as a space that needed a male logic, which would help create order and restore har-mony. This necessitated discourses that would not valorize tradition, but instead seek to work tacitly with colonial modernity to entomb a kinship practice that defied the new male order. In a sense, this led to an ironic situation—for, on one hand, the Malayali could not identify and align with the national modern, neither was it possible to dissociate himself from the colonial modern. That many women of Keralam, following patterns of polygamous marriage, would not qualify for the high ideals of the traditional 'Indian woman' account for the liminality of the 'mother' in early Malayalam cinema and the presence of the loud, greedy, vulgar, scheming, and potentially disruptive 'anti-mother' or stepmother. Thus invoking 'Indian tradition' was not something that could be resorted to by the new discourse of cinema in Keralam. Such discourses would also eventually aid the new patriarchy in warding off questions of women's freedom and agency, thus laying the foundations of women's future tokenization as citizens here.

References

Arunima, G. 2003. *There Comes Papa: Colonialism and the Transformation of Matriliny in Kerala, Malabar c. 1850–1940*, New Delhi: Orient Longman.

Barthes, Roland Barthes. 1972. *Mythologies*, Annette Lavers (trans.), London: Vintage.

Chatterjee, Partha. 1993. *The Nation and Its Fragments*, Princeton: Princeton University Press.

Eapen, Mridul and Praveena Kodoth. 2001. *Demystifying the 'High Status' of Women in Kerala: An Attempt to Understand the Contradictions in Social Development*, Thiruvananthapuram: Centre for Development Studies.

Logan, William. (1887) 2004. *Malabar Manual*, vol. 1, New Delhi: Asian Educational Services.

Pillai, Meena T. 2010. *Women in Malayalam Cinema: Naturalising Gender Hierarchies*, New Delhi: Orient Blackswan.

Vijayakrishnan. 2004. *Malayalam Cinemayude Katha*, Kozhikkode: Mathrubhumi Books.

Weber, Max. 1958. *The Protestant Ethic and the Spirit of Capitalism*, Talcott Parsons (trans.), New York: Scribner's.

10 Cinema in Motion

Tracking Tamil Cinema's Assemblage

VIJAY DEVADAS AND SELVARAJ VELAYUTHAM

On Assemblage

In her book *The Evolution of Film: Rethinking Film Studies*, Harbord argues that 'whether gentle or savage, the discourse of film studies bifurcates into oppositional camps where either position is known in advance: either text or context, formalist analysis or interpretive analysis, film or theory, must take priority. The extant of schema of binary thought maps out the possibilities, yet the cartography ceases to serve us' (2007: 19). Similarly, the Indian film scholar Singh (2003) had earlier asserted that approaches to cinema must be reconsidered given that cinema 'has become radically dispersed', in terms of contexts of appearance (airplane screens, computer screens, multiplex halls), fluidity of movement between different media technologies (online movie portals, television, and DVDs), and the superfluous integration with other commodity forms (for instance, the seamless integration of animated films, game art, and comic book spin offs). Further to this, one might also ask in what ways do people engage with films 'within diverse modes of sociality, forms of experience and ways of being in the world' (ibid.). How do their own conditions, contexts, histories, entangle with films and cinema? The shifts and changes that have come to bear on cinema testify to the point that cinema 'has completely changed its shape, form, and mode of dispersal' (ibid.). And this dispersal demands that 'we shift "cinema" from its conception as a purely textual object to being a socially embedded set of practices. This is a shift away from the fictionality of cinema as a formal "text" towards its *fictive* quality, its being "made up" as a form on the terrain of life, labour, and language' (ibid.).

We wish to suggest that the questions that Singh raises can be addressed by shifting the view of film and cinema as something to be analysed for meanings and representations to one that approaches it as cartography or as an event; something experienced as a dynamic exchange, as activities, in motion; in short, as an *assemblage*, after Deleuze and Guattari (1987). An assemblage refers to any number of 'things' compiled into a single context and this compilation, the assemblage, can produce any number of effects. Deleuze and Guattari's discussion of the book provides a number of insights into this loosely defined term:

> In a book, as in all things, there are lines of articulation or segmentarity, strata and territories; but also lines of flight, movements of deterritorialization and destratification. Comparative rates of flow on these lines produce phenomena of relative slowness and viscosity, or, on the contrary, of acceleration and rupture. All this, lines and measurable speeds constitutes an *assemblage*. A book is an assemblage of this kind, and as such is unattributable. It is a multiplicity—but we don't know yet what the multiple entails when it is no longer attributed, that is, after it has been elevated to the status of the substantive. (1987: 3–4)

What this means for film studies and our study of Tamil cinema, as Kennedy suggests, is that 'we need to rethink a post-semiotic space, a post-linguistic space, which provides new ways of understanding the screen experience as a complex web of inter-relationalities ... [it] is never purely visual, but also tactile, sensory, material and embodied' (2000: 3). This is precisely why Velayutham points out that 'academic scholarship [on Indian cinema] has tended to overlook the relationship between the various cinemas of India, and the role and contribution of regional cinemas to Indian cinema as a whole' (2008a: 5). These other tactile, sensory, material, and embodied inter-relationalities remain obscured. Velayutham's lament, we argue, draws from the sentiments expressed by Grosz where she points out that it is 'no longer appropriate to [just] ask what a text means, what it says, what is the structure of its interiority, how to interpret or decipher it. Instead, one must [also] ask what it does, how it connects with other things' (1994: 199). Grosz's emphasis on connectivity ruptures the binaries of text-context, formalist-interpretive, and film theory and as in Deleuze and Guattari's assemblage, shifts the focus to what a film does and how it connects with people and things. What the notion of assemblage offers, specifically in terms of exploring Tamil cinema, is a conceptual tool for thinking about cinema's complex entanglement with different modes of sociality, its relationship to the production and consumption of other commodity forms, the ways in which it 'blocks, or makes possible other worlds' (Fuller 2005: 1) and calls on us to 'attend to the ways in which people position or embody themselves (or are marked) as bearers of identity within particular social and institutional networks' (Singh 2003). More importantly, in thinking about Tamil cinema as an assemblage, we are attuned and attentive to the various connections that it has with other cinematic and non-cinematic moments to elucidate the dynamism of conceiving Tamil cinema as 'cinema in motion'.

This chapter then seeks to develop the notion of 'cinema in motion' through the example of Tamil cinema by shoring up the various travels, connections and disconnections, rhythms and codes, politics, predispositions, and drives that this cinema has with other cinemas within India, with particular forms of representations, and the 'vital structuring principles in popular culture in India' (Mankekar 1999: 18), with practices of viewing, recent shifts in the domains of production, distribution and exhibition, and with audiences both within India and the larger Tamil diaspora (Velayutham 2008b). The list of connections and travels that we have alluded to is by no means exhaustive for there are various other linkages that inform Tamil cinema, such as the impact of digital technologies and new media platforms and various forms of popular culture (television, theatre, music) amongst others. Using the Deleuzian concept of assemblage as the model for the complex clustering of technological, historical, and physical processes, we wish to draw up an assemblage of Tamil cinema that moves from a representational and linear understanding that dominates discussions on Tamil cinema (Baskaran 1996), to one that emphasizes how it interacts with or carries out interactions with other media systems, popular culture, bodies, institutions, forms of lives, communities (defined by gender, caste, class, ethnicity, and nationality), and urban and industrial developments (Velayutham 2008 and 2008a).

In what follows, we reconstruct three different fragments that constitute one such assemblage: the first is a framing of the early history Tamil cinema to emphasize the ways in which this cinema is closely linked to other cinema histories, Indian film industries, commodities, and forms of sociality; the second is an exploration of the texts produced during the upsurge of ethno-nationalist Tamil cinema to explore the blockages and boundary-crossing imperatives mediated across the structuring principles of nation and nationalism; and the third is a mediation on the audience to shore up the contingency of viewing and the various ways cinema is implicated within specific modes of sociality. An examination of these selected fragments of Tamil cinema allows us to see how Tamil cinema mixes, interrelates, to produce patterns, blockages, and potentials. It is in these terms for example that we can argue that the regional cinema tag that has been bestowed on Tamil cinema can be challenged by looking at, for instance, the ways in which Tamil cinema has connected with the issue of nation and nationalism. It is also in these terms that we can rethink the often-heard argument of the hegemony of Bollywood cinema as national cinema by exploring the connections that Tamil cinema has with this national cultural industry.

Fragment One—Early History of Tamil Cinema

The year 1916 is often marked as the birth of Tamil cinema with the establishment of the first studio in Madras, the India Film Company, and the release of the first South Indian feature film, *Keechaka Vadham* (The Destruction of Keechakan), produced by R. Nataraja Mudaliar.[1] But cinema arrived in Tamil Nadu well before this, in 1897 to be precise, at the Victoria Public Hall, when 'an Englishman named M. Edwards' screened *Arrival of the Train* and *Leaving the Factory*. And cinema did not arrive alone, as an isolated machine of modernity. Rather, it was part and parcel of a larger assemblage of machines and commodities that marked 'the mechanical reproduction of the works of art'. In Benjamin's (1968) sense: it marks both the coming of modernization and the democratization of art. Cinema, from its inception in Tamil Nadu was entangled with the changing sociality of this region, with the larger project of modernization and industrialization. This was the time when 'daily newspapers in Tamil, beginning with *Swadesamithran* (Friend of Self Rule) in 1899, had been launched. In Madras city, a motor car could be occasionally sighted .... Just two years earlier, trams had been introduced ... some affluent households and companies had telephones. People were getting used to the marvel of listening to recorded music from ... the gramophone' (Baskaran 1996: 2), which would become intimately connected to cinema. In that sense, cinema arrived in Tamil Nadu in connection with other commodity forms, a differing sociality and the powerful discourse of industrialization, marked as the quintessential manifestation of modernity. The choice of Victoria Hall is significant as it was then consecrated as the Town Hall for the town of Madras, a decision that was made in March 1882 at a meeting of leading citizens (Ramakrishnan 2006). More crucially, cinema was intimately entangled with the project of capital accumulation, a connection that was not lost on Major Warwick who 'built the first cinema house in South India, Electric Theatre in 1900 on Mount Road in Madras' (ibid.). Warwick's choice of Mount Road was astute: it was and still remains the main arterial road in Chennai, stretching 15 km and running diagonal across the city; the theatre itself had ante-rooms that had a bar and a billiards table, and 'across the way from the Electric was Misquith & Co which a man called Cohen had acquired *circa* 1907 from the founders. The hall on its first floor he called the Lyric and used it to organise entertainments' (Anon 2007). The Lyric, boasted a variety of events, including plays in English, Western classical music concerts, and ballroom dances. And silent films were also screened as an additional attraction. In that sense, films were appended or attached to other cultural industries and performances. It was not the main attraction. While it is difficult to ascertain Cohen's motivations other than perhaps as business acumen, it is clear that Electric Theatre spanned the development of other entertainment venues and forms. Cinema in that sense was part of a larger entertainment-industrial complex. And from the connections that we can draw, it is also clear that the clientele targeted was not the local population. Rather it was the colonizer's community that was the target. After all, this was the favourite haunt of the British community in Madras who could afford to pay for the entertainment. That said, cinema was not solely for the colonizers: as Sivathamby notes, the coming of cinema as a site where a large gathering of people assembled, helped break down caste hierarchies and fostered a sense of collective solidarity. In the words of Sivathamby (1981: 18), for the time 'all Tamils sat under the same roof'. However, cinema still remained the purview of those in the city and it was a draughtsman, Swamikannu Vincent who 'worked for the Railways in Tiruchi, who [between 1905–9] introduced this newfangled entertainment medium to the interior of the Madras presidency' (Baskaran 1996: 3). Around the same time, 'R. Venkiah who owned a photographic studio on Mount Road' bought a chrono megaphone, 'which was a film projector attached to a gramophone. A gramophone record could be played as the film was screened .... With this equipment, he screened [two] ... short films ... These films were each only 500 feet long, to match the duration of the gramophone' (Baskaran 1996: 3). The chrono megaphone that Venkiah bought was initially imported by a British company to celebrate the event of King George the Fifth's visit in 1909, where the major attraction was the screening of short films accompanied by sound. Venkiah later on went to build Gaiety in 1914, the first cinema house in Madras built by an Indian. Gaiety is located to the rear of Electric Theatre, which was closed down two years after opening as the property was acquired by the government to develop the Mount Road Post Office. Venkiah then went on to build the Crown in Mint Street in 1916 and the Globe (later Roxy) in Purasawalkam in 1917/1918, both of which were close to the Chennai Railway Station and Chennai Central.

Our reading of this initial history suggests that cinema arrived in Tamil Nadu in and amongst other industrial developments, as a commodity in and amongst other commodities, as 'implicated within diverse modes of sociality' (Singh 2003). While the first two, as technology and commodity 'have a certain logic to them, ... the last as a form of experience is perhaps the hardest to grasp' (ibid.). We will discuss the last in the final section where we explore the reception of cinema amongst those of the Indian diaspora to Singapore.

Cinema's appearance and development in Tamil Nadu coincided with the general ethos of modernization and industrialization: the railway for instance ensured that cinema reached the interiority while the gramophone and the printing press (magazines, daily newspapers) set the stage for a much more fluid relationship to the technology and commodity of cinema. After all, the mechanical reproduction of art had become part of the social present. The coming of the gramophone had a democratizing impact in that it made possible the recording and mechanical multiplication of Carnatic music, historically a form of art for the privileged (kings and landlords) (see Hughes 2007). And now 'the common man has the opportunity to savour it [recoded classical music] for the first time' (Baskaran 1996: 40). This, coupled with the developed status of company dramas—itself a mutation of traditional Tamil theatre—that operated on a commercial basis with professional actors had produced a mass entertainment sensibility into which cinema connected. Cinema also linked up with other commodity forms such as the gramophone, bars (and all that comes with it), forms of retails, Western classical music concerts, English plays, and other colonial forms of expressions as well as with traditional theater and the company drama, 'which contributed to the basic of film music' (Baskaran 1996: 40). While Carnatic music was the mainstay of the drama companies, which explain their take up in early talkies in Tamil cinema,

> they introduced a new strain of music into Tamil Nadu, ... drama music, a kind of Hindustani music appropriated from Marathi drama companies which toured Tamil Nadu at the beginning of the century. Through this strain, Hindustani ragas were assimilated.... Another influence on drama and cinema music came from Parsi drama companies which toured the Madras presidency in the 1930s. They introduced a mixture of Carnatic and Hindustani music called Parsi tunes which eventually found their way into cinema. (Baskaran 1996: 40–41)

Further to this, cinema circulated differently within the lives of the people (both colonizer and colonized). So even though as Sivathamby argues that cinema in Tamil Nadu can be conceived as a democratizing public space, in tent cinemas for instance, there were usually three classes of tickets: the floor, bench, and chair. The floor-ticket purchaser sat on sand to watch the movie, but he enjoyed certain advantages that other patrons did not. He could sit as he pleased, or he could turn over and take a short nap when the narrative was particularly dull, and roll back again when the action was again to his liking—luxuries which the upper class could never indulge in. This difference produced through the prism of purchasing power reinscribed another form of division within cinema.

In addition to such crossovers, there was also a great deal of synergy (sharing of technological knowledge and expertise) between various cinematic enterprises that sprung across the Indian subcontinent. During the screening of silent films title cards or 'inter-titles' as they were known, were used to convey the story and dialogue. As the Tamil film historian Randor Guy (1997) notes, these inter-titles were written in more than one language, which meant that films made in Madras were also screened all over India with the respective language inter-titles.

Moreover, 'during the silent film era, films made in Madras were also screened in other parts of India. Film producers, technicians, engineers, and other specialists came from Bombay and Calcutta to work in Madras and vice versa' (Velayutham 2008: 5). The crossover that were dominant during the silent era continued into the early period of Tamil talkies, which were often shot in Bombay, Pune, or Calcutta where studio floors were hired and made by directors and technicians who did not know Tamil. With the arrival of sound, again if we browse through the Indian filmography, we can discover that dubbing and remaking of films were an integral part of Indian cinema history. Films made in Hindi were dubbed or remade into Bengali, Marathi, Tamil, Telugu, and Malayalam, and vice versa. It is worth noting that Tamil film studios such as Vijaya, Prasad, and AVM for example have continued to produce Hindi films since the 1950s to the present (Thoraval 2000). Artists (production and acting) have been working across the various cinemas on a regular basis. For instance, Tamil actors Vyjayanthimala, Sridevi, Kamal Hassan, and Madhavan have had huge success in Bollywood. In addition, Tamil cinema has also attracted, especially, female actors from other cinemas past and present such as Bhanumati from Andhra Pradesh, the Padmini sisters from Kerala, Saroja Devi from Karnataka, and Simran, Sneha, Reema Sen, Sonia Agarwal, and Aishwarya Rai from other parts of India. These synergies have helped to enhance and invigorate various aspects of the cinemas of India. In recent times, Tamil cinema directors such as Mani Ratnam, Ram Gopal Varma, and Shankar have been working in Hindi, Malayalam, and Telugu films. It is worth noting that Mani Ratnam's award-winning Tamil films such as *Nayagan* (1987), *Roja* (1992), *Bombay* (1995), and *Aayitha Ezhuthu* (2004) that were remade in Hindi have had huge success nationally. Further to this, Indian film music composers like A.R. Rahman and most of the playback singers work across the film industries. Overall, it can be argued that the various film industries in India are not just self-contained production sites but are fluid and versatile in the ways they attract new talents. And these industries have been mutually benefiting from one another.

In that sense, Tamil cinema from its inception has always been historically intertwined with other locations of production in India. Given its multifarious connections, it can be argued that Tamil cinema is a form of contagion, shifting, mutating, and connecting with other cinematic forms, expertise and styles, commodities, cultural practices, and diverse socialities in different ways, producing different intensities and trajectories that are highly complex and multifaceted. In short, it reinforces the proposition calling for a conception of Tamil cinema as 'cinema in motion'.

Fragment Two—Ethno-Nationalist Tamil Cinema

Discussions on the ethno-nationalism of Tamil cinema or more precisely the relationship between cinema and politics have been extensively done (Baskaran 1981; Devadas and Velayutham 2008; Dickey 1993; Hardgrave 1970, 1971, 1973 and 1975; Hardgrave and Neidhart 1975; Pandian 1992 and 2000; Sivathamby 1981). Collectively, these scholars emphasize the symbiotic relationship between cinema and politics by focusing on the representational politics of key Tamil films, stars, and 'how these texts circulate in diverse sociocultural contexts and get hinged to various meanings' (Punathambekar and Kavoori 2008: 8). The argument here is that there emerged a number of films that marked the entry of what Thoraval (2000: 318) calls 'an ethno-linguistic "nationalism", anti-Hindi and anti-north (India), and as its corollary, the putting forward, in literature and on the screen, of the glories, languages and culture of the ancient "Dravidians"'.

Films such as *Ambikapathy* (1937) and *Kambar* (1938) for instance sought to open up a representational space within cinema for the dissemination of a sense of Tamil cultural nationalism. The release of these films coincided with the radicalization of the Dravidian ideology in the 1930s, particularly after the 'the introduction of compulsory Hindustani in 1938' (Barnett 1976: 52), which saw the Dravidian movement engage in agitation politics against the Congress Party, which it had been supporting to date. The antagonism surrounding the compulsory introduction of Hindi as national language, marked the beginning of the affirmation of Tamil identity 'rooted in the Tamil literary movement of the early nineteenth century' (Chadda 1997: 71). Such a political position, one that strongly affirms Tamil nationalism as a separatist discourse and as antithetical to the idea of a singular nation is well played out in the two films through the figure of Kambar, the eleventh-century Tamil poet who authored the Tamil version of the Ramayana. The appeal to the spectre of Kambar in both films must be read as attempts to prise open the hegemony of Hindi and at the same time affirm the ideology and political thrust of the Dravidian movement. *Kambar* was released at the same time that anti-Hinduism agitation took hold in Tamil Nadu over the central government's decision to introduce 'Hindustani in certain schools as a compulsory subject' (Barnett 1976: 51) and the 'the hope for rejuvenation of the Dravidian movement' (ibid.: 65) begun to have a firm grip on Tamil Nadu politics. The cinematic representation of Dravidianism played out through such films while not as dominant as those affirming the nationalist struggle marked 'the cinema of Madras...by two contradictory tendencies' (Thoraval 2000: 318). The latter tendency, of turning inward into an unproblematic, uncontaminated, and unchallenged notion of Dravidianism based on linguistic and cultural differences became key categories that were mobilized during the period of the DMK (Dravida Munnetra Kazhagam [Dravidian Progress Federation]) and later AIADMK (All-India Anna DMK) stranglehold of Tamil cinema. The use of cinema for political purposes, namely, the construction of an imagined community-based on linguistic homogeneity was one of the central themes that preoccupied postcolonial Tamil cinema. There is quite an extensive catalogues of films that demonstrate that the postcolonial rendition of the idea of the nation, as reflected through Tamil cinema, intervenes into a specifically ordered version of Indian nationalism and problematizes the notion of a national cinema.

Beyond the representational politics affirming Tamil nationalism, the success of the cinema-politics nexus is connected to the larger revivalism of Tamil culture in the arts during the colonial period, specifically literature 'in the latter half of the nineteenth century ... [which] created tremendous interest in the language', to the founding in 1880 of the Tamil magazine *Swadesamithran* which 'became a daily in 1899 ... [to the circulation of] around sixty periodicals in Tamil ... in the next two decades' (Baskaran 1996: 19). Other developments which were part of this revivalism included 'the rediscovery and publication of Tamil classics of the Sangam period ... [the publication of] V. Kanagasabai Pillai's *Tamils 1800 Years Ago* ... Somasundara Barathi's *Tamil Classics and Thamizhagam* [Tamil Home] ... and M. Srinivas Ayyengar's *Tamil Studies*' (ibid.: 19–20). The climate of Tamil revivalism entered cinema mainly through the use of dialogue-writers, 'who wrote flowery lines in chaste Tamil, studded with literary allusions' (ibid.: 19–20). One dialogue writer Illangovan 'is identified with a group of Tamil writers associated with the Tamil magazine *Manikodi* [Gem Necklace] who were committed to striving towards excellence in literature and other arts in Tamil Nadu and who recognized the possibilities of film as a medium' (ibid.: 19–20).

While drawing on this larger revivalism history as articulated in various media outlets (stage, plays, magazines, periodicals, literature, and poetry), the DMK's use of cinema for political propaganda strategically reappropriated the form of dialogue in political rallies into cinema. As Baskaran notes, the strategic use of dialogue took form at a particular time, 'when writers began using dialogue to echo the ideas of the Dravidian movement ... [and] reached its apogee when some leaders of the Dravidian movement entered the film industry as dialogue writers and used films for propaganda purposes, as C.N. Annadurai did with *Velaikari* [Servant Maid, 1949]... M. Karunanidhi ... with the film *Marudanattu Ilavarasi* [Princesses of Madura Country, 1950] [and later] *Parasakthi*' (1996: 64–5). In addition, the use of dialogue did not obey normative cinematic conventions of film dialogue in that the leaders of the political party who scripted the dialogue wrote speeches 'that was meant for crowds at a political rally [but which] was delivered to the film audience' (Baskaran 1996: 67). The imposition of political oratory as cinematic dialogue was strategic insofar as it opened the possibility of exploiting film, converting it into 'a public address system ... where characters address not their fellow characters in the film but the camera—in other words, the audience' (ibid.: 67). The use of long dialogues that profess the achievements of the Dravidian culture, the plight of the poor and the untouchables and the urgent needs for social reform and justice exemplifies the way in which cinematic dialogue is reappropriated for political purposes. In addition to reappropriating dialogue for political purposes, the DMK engaged in a politics of subterfuge as a means of combating the Congress-led censorship regulation deterring the use of cinema for political purposes through the coding 'of double meanings in dialogue' (Hardgrave 1973: 294). The explicit and exemplary instance of this occurred through the production of the 'character called Anna'—the Tamil word for elder brother and the popular name for Annadurai—who appeared in almost all the DMK films as a wise and sympathetic counsellor. In a historical film, for example, the dialogue might go, 'Anna, you are going to rule one day,' at which the audience would break into wild applause (ibid.: 294). Another example

of the turn to subterfuge that Hardgrave cites can be seen in the historical film *Kanchee Talaivar* (Leader of Kanchee, 1963) which narrates the
story of a 'Pallava king whose capital was the city of Kanchee (Kancheep-
uram). Not without coincidence, Annadurai was from Kanchee, and he
was known as Kanchee Talaivar ... The censors demanded a change of
title, but, after all, [since] it did refer to a Pallava kingdom ... the DMK
got the title' (1973: 294). The reappropriation of cinematic protocols
for political communication, specifically a brand of politics that was
divorced from that advanced by the postcolonial nation-state, serves to
further demonstrate the ways in which Tamil politics and cinema interrupts the national cinema's project of discursively constructing a sense of
a national people through cinema.

What appears at this moment in Tamil cinema with the ethno-
nationalist turn is a connection with a longer history of ethno-
nationalism expressed through other mediatized and non-mediatized
modes of representation and inscription (plays, literature, magazines),
a connection with, and reappropriation of political strategies of
communication, and with other modes of sociality, specifically the
hegemony of a specific form of nationalism. The connection that Tamil
cinema forged at this time is quite different from the connections that
marked earlier Tamil cinema in that here, the representational politics,
the link with other commodities and technologies and a sociality built
on Dravidian nationalism, served to block the forging of a unified postcolonial nationalism under the auspice of a north-Indian majoritarian
discourse and to challenge the idea of a national cinema articulated
through the optic of Bombay cinema.

Fragment Three—Sensory Experience of the Exhibition Space

In the third fragment we wish to discuss what Rai (2009) calls the
'sensory experience of the exhibition space'. In keeping with our opening
point that the task is to ask what a film does and how it connects with
things, how is film entangled with and 'within diverse modes of sociality,
forms of experience and ways of being in the world' (Singh 2003), we
wish to discuss three narratives briefly and weave them into each other
to exemplify the intricate and complex ways Tamil cinema connects
with human bodies, lives, experiences, and different social worlds. The

excerpts from these three narratives are part of a larger ethnographic study in progress examining the consumption and reception of Tamil cinema amongst those of the Indian diaspora to Singapore.

Here is the first narrative from Mala, a 62-year-old woman, who is part of the second generation Indian diaspora to the then Malaya. Mala was educated in Tamil in an estate, or plantation school until primary six. She now lives in Singapore, having moved here from the estate near Batu Caves in 1967. She married in 1968 at the age of 21 and has three children. This is how she describes her cinematic experience in Tamil, which we have translated here:

> ... when we were in the estates, they [the estate owners and bureaucrats] used to show a film once a month, sometimes once every two months. They would bring along a white screen-cloth and projector and we [the estate community] would set up our mats on the ground, and get our munchies ready for the show. This was a big night for the estate; and everyone came with his or her families, mats, gunnysacks, blankets, and food. When the sun set, the show would begin, and usually, I would fall asleep soon after the samples were shown, and after I had my share of the kachangs [peanuts] and before the actual film begun because I was usually tired from having to work in the oil palm plantation the whole day. But the film was not important; it was the experience of the day that mattered. I never went to a theatre until I came to Singapore in 1967. Once a month my husband's siblings and I would go to the Taj Theatre in Geylang. The Taj used to show Tamil, Hindi and English shows. We will only go on days that Krishnan, my brother was working. He was the ticket seller and would smuggle us in for free. I watched lots of films there, MGR and Sivaji films. The first Hindi film I saw was *Sangam* [Confluence], at the Garrick Theatre, also in Geylang. Sangam had Raj Kapoor and Vyjayantimala and I loved the song '*Dost dost na raha*' [My Friend Was No More My Friend]. [Mala breaks into the song]. I didn't understand Hindi, and the subtitles were in English or Malay and I didn't know either but it didn't matter. I followed the film through the actions: in fact I watched *Sangam* thrice. Like the estate days, it didn't matter what film was on, it was the fun of going to the theatre, getting away from housework which I had to do!

The second narrative comes from Das, one of Mala's sons—a third-generation Indian diaspora born in Singapore. He reflected:

> My first experience of Tamil cinema was through television, on the state-owned Channel 8, screened over two parts and two nights—Thursday and Friday—from around 9 p.m. This was around the early 1980s when there was only four hours of programming commencing from around 6–10 p.m. on Channel 5 (English/Malay) and Channel 8 (Chinese/Tamil) of which Malay and Tamil only had an hour each. When Tamil films were on television and screened over two parts,

I normally missed part one on Thursday since Friday was a school day, and so my entry into the films were mostly after the Intermission. Friday night Tamil films on television was rather special, not only because I got to stay up late but also because it was a night filled with special nibbles, made by Mum or bought from the nearby hawker centre. And most of the time we had relatives from Malaysia who were working in Singapore staying with us. Before the film started we prepared the hall by removing all the furniture and spreading mattresses across the floor so that everyone could lie down and watch the films. The lights were turned off, and before the second part begun, we, the kids, were given a synopsis of part one since the adults did not want to be disturbed with questions during the film. Most of the adults never made it to the end of the film, and were usually snoring by the end of it. They either had work the next day or had been to work. Amidst their snoring I kept awake with my brother and sister, nibbling and trying to follow the film. This was hard since there was no English or Malay subtitles and I was never schooled in Tamil and mainly spoke Malayalam at home. But that didn't matter. It wasn't the film that we were interested in; it was the late-night extended family get together that was important.

The third narrative is from Kumar, also a third-generation Singaporean-Indian:

The first Tamil film I watched at a theatre was in the late 1970s and it was *Aval Oru Thodarkathai* (She is a Continuing Story, 1974) at the Hoover Theatre at Balestiar Road. I went there with my mum and Srinivas, an astrologer from India, who had become a family friend. We used to call him uncle. Srinivas had come to Singapore on a tourist visa on the ship *Chithambaram* to seek his fortune and had been door knocking in our block of flats, singling out Indian homes, which were quite easily identifiable because they had mango leaves tied to the top of the door. When I recollect this, I can't help think that Srinivas, who had come up with the idea of going to the cinema did so because he fancied mum. Dad was not around at that time since he worked offshore in the oil and gas industry and was away for months at end. The film we watched was very erotic; I don't think it was suitable for kids. The film was about a Brahmin girl who is sexually assaulted, raped, by a man who gives her a lift on a rainy day. That day changes her whole life and she attempts at getting her life back to normalcy, her loneliness, silence and things like that. I cried at the movie; perhaps because she reminded me of my mum—she was a silent, domesticated, lonely woman; perhaps that is why Srinivas thought this was the ideal movie.

Between a plantation economy setting to a post-war, newly independent Singapore to a much more embodied response these three narratives exemplify the various, multifaceted and complex ways that Tamil cinema connects with those of the diaspora across different generations. The cinematic experience is mediated variously, through the plantation economy context where going to the cinema meant constructing a cinema space: finding clear, even ground, bringing your own seating, food, and blankets; it is also mediated by a master-slave dialectic since most of the people in the plantation were (historically) part of the indenture and kangani system which brought them to colonial Malaya, and the films that were shown on the estate were at the directive of the colonial masters, and later, the postcolonial local bureaucrats. As recollected by M. Palani who was interviewed for *Malaysiakini* for the special 2000 *Merdeka* issue, "'... we were all working at the plantation and had a white man as our boss," .... He added that while their wages were low, their "boss" had provided them with squatter homes to live in and the weekly Tamil cinema shows for entertainment' (Kabilan 2000). Cinema for Palani compensated for his low wage and is integrated into a circuit of labour exchange: cinema is now part of wage labour. At the same time, such a reconstitution of cinema into the plantation workers' lives tells us that cinema also provided the outlet from the mundane everyday existence of plantation workers. In that sense, for both Mala and Palani, who are separated by one generation, cinema nevertheless functions similarly: it ruptures the harsh condition of plantation labour exploitation; it disconnects them momentarily from the quotidian rhythm of plantation life. For Das, Tamil cinema is mediated quite differently, this time through the technology of television, across two days, one of which is regulated by the demands of schooling; but like Mala and Palani, cinema is also for Das about escapism from the routine of everyday life, a chance to stay up late, have munchies that are not usually part of the daily diet. In comparison to these two narratives, Kumar's recollection of his first encounter with cinema takes on a completely different trajectory: here cinema is implicated in an intimate recollection of relationships, conditions of domesticity, possible transgression of marital vows and infidelity, and the possible exploitation of specific conditions Kumar's mum finds herself. This is a much more embodied, intimate relationship to cinema.

What the above cases underscore is that Tamil cinema moves in and out of the lives of those of the diaspora differently; it is contingent upon 'the sensory exhibition space' (Rai 2009), the context of viewing, the forms of life the viewer is entangled in, their modes of being in the world, and so on. To cite Singh (2003), Tamil cinema as a 'cinematic "machine" ... produces concepts, percepts, affects, forms of life, and modes of being-in-world.' Conceiving Tamil cinema as a machine in the Deleuzian sense—'a machine may be defined as a system of interruptions or breaks' (1987: 36)— not only calls on us to locate cinema as part of a larger assemblage of things, objects, subjects, discourses, but also calls us on us to situate the reception of cinema within specific life worlds such that as we interrogate the ontological status of films, we are attuned to the complexities of circulation and the hierarchies of the consumption of cinema.

Conclusion

Let us end with a brief summary of the key propositions we have made here. We have attempted to track Tamil cinema's assemblage by looking at three different fragments—early Tamil cinema, ethno-nationalist cinema, and the reception of this cinema amongst those of the Indian diaspora in Singapore—to show that Tamil cinema is not a static cultural artefact; quite the contrary, it is a mobile machine that connects with other technologies, commodities, and people outside of its linguistic territory. It is also a machine that connects with other cinematic machines such as Bombay cinema, Bollywood, and Telugu cinema, and film industries, and other non-cinematic machines such as plays, press, cottage industries, plantation economy, and the like. At the same time, we have also shown that the machine that is Tamil cinema also blocks and interrupts, as seen most clearly during the rampant phase of ethno-nationalist cinema when Tamil cinema vehemently rejected the discourse of nation and nationalism and also put into question the status of Bombay cinema as national cinema. Indeed the connections and blockages between Tamil and other Indian language cinemas is a striking feature of Tamil cinema. For instance, most of the female lead actors in Tamil cinema are not native Tamil speakers and are drawn from all over India but the male lead have resolutely been played by a Tamil (perhaps an attempted subversion of the north-south Indian hegemony?). In Tamil films, quite often we also find deliberate and instructive references to Tamilness or Tamil identity through the dialogue or songs working as an interruptive device to articulate the uniqueness of this film industry. Finally, we explored the reception of Tamil cinema amongst those of the Indian diaspora across generations to demonstrate that cinema is entangled in complex and diverse modes of sociality; it connects and interacts with bodies, forms of lives, and communities in different ways. The connections and breaks that we have canvassed, which is only part of a larger assemblage, attempts to echo Jonathan Beller's observation that '"cinema" refers not only to what one sees on screen or even to the institutions and apparatuses that generate film but to that totality of relations that generates the myriad appearances of the world' (2006: 14). It is in this sense that we argue for a conceptualization of Tamil cinema as 'cinema in motion' such that we can draw links, connections, and disconnections between disparate elements, objects, and subjects with and through this cinema. In short, through this tracking of three fragments of Tamil cinema, we wish to emphasize Tamil cinema 'as a form of contagion, endlessly mutating and spreading', connecting with other cinematic forms, 'human bodies, organizational structures, and energies' (Rai 2009) in complex and multifarious ways.

Note

1. We are indebted to the work of the two well-known Tamil film historians Theodore Baskaran and Randor Guy. In Baskaran's (1981 and 1996) and Guy's (1997) works, the only English publications available on the history of Tamil cinema, the authors offer an excellent account of the arrival of cinema to the Madras Presidency at the turn of the twentieth century, the early pioneers of the film industry, who were instrumental in setting up production companies and studios, biographies of directors, producers, and actors, and synopsis of major films over the years (see also Velayutham 2008). Though there are other works on the history of Tamil cinema, these are mostly written in Tamil and have not been translated into other languages.

References

Anon. 2007. 'Madras's first cinema theatre', *The Hindu*, 16 July, http://www.hindu.com/mp/2007/07/16/stories/2007071650970500.htm; accessed on 10 January 2009.

Barnett, M.R. 1976. *The Politics of Cultural Nationalism in South India.* Princeton: Princeton University Press.

Baskaran, T. 1981. *The Message Bearers: Nationalist Politics and the Entertainment Media in South India 1880–1945*, Madras: Cre-A.

————. 1996. *The Eye of the Serpent: An Introduction to Tamil Cinema,* Madras: East West Books.

Beller, J. 2006. *Cinematic Mode of Production: Attention Economy and the Society of Spectacle*, Hanover: Dartmouth College Press.

Benjamin, W. 1968. *Illuminations*, Harry Zohn (trans.), Hannah Arendt (ed.), New York: Schocken Books.

Chadda, M. 1997. *Ethnicity, Security and Separatism in India*, New York: Columbia University Press.

Deleuze, G. and F. Guattari. 1987. *A Thousand Plateaus: Capitalism and Schizophrenia*, Brian Massumi (trans.), Minneapolis: University of Minnesota Press.

Devadas, V. 'Rethinking Transnational Cinema: The Case of Tamil Cinema', *Senses of Cinema*, no. 41 (October–December 2006). http://archive.sensesofcinema.com/contents/06/41/transnational-tamil-cinema.html

Devadas, V. and S. Velayutham. 2008. 'Encounters with "India": (Ethno)-Nationalism in Tamil Cinema', in Selvaraj Velayutham (ed.), *Tamil Cinema: The Cultural Politics of India's Other Film Industry*, London: Routledge.

Dickey, S. 1993. *Cinema and the Urban Poor in South India*, Cambridge: Cambridge University Press.

Fuller, M. 2005. *Media Ecologies: Materialist Energies in Art and Technoculture*, Cambridge: MIT Press.

Grosz, E. 1994. 'A Thousand Tiny Sexes: Feminism and Rhizomatics', in Constantin V. Boundas and Dorothea Olkowski (eds), *Gilles Deleuze and the Theater of Philosophy*, New York: Routledge,

Guy, Randor 1997. *Starlight, Starbright—The Early Tamil Cinema*, Chennai: AMRA Publishers.

Harbord, J. 2007. *The Evolution of Film: Rethinking Film Studies*, Cambridge: Polity Press.

Hardgrave, R.L. 1970. 'Film and Society in Tamil Nadu', *Monthly Public Opinion Surveys of the Indian Institute of Public Opinion*, vol. 15.

———. 1971. 'The Celluloid God: MGR and the Tamil Film', *South Asian Review*, vol. 4.

———. 1973. 'Politics and the Film in Tamil Nadu: The Stars and the DMK', *Asian Survey*, vol. 13.

———. 1975. *When Stars Displace the Gods: the Folk Culture of Cinema in Tamil Nadu*, Center for Asian Studies Press: University of Texas at Austin.

Hardgrave, R.L. and A.C. Neidhart. 1975. 'Film and Political Consciousness in Tamil Nadu', *Economic and Political Weekly*, vol. 10.

Hughes, S. 2007. 'Music in the Age of Mechanical Reproduction: Drama, Gramophone and the Beginnings of Tamil Cinema', *The Journal of Asian Studies*, vol. 66, no. 1.

Kaali, S. 2000. 'Narrating Seduction: Vicissitudes of the Sexed Subject in Tamil Nativity Film', in Ravi S. Vasudevan (ed.), *Making Meaning in Indian Cinema*, New Delhi: Oxford University Press.

Kabilan, K. 2000. 'Independence for Indians', *Malaysiakini: Merdeka Special*, 31 August, http://www.geocities.com/sounvx/ind_indians.htm; accessed on 10 January 2009.

Kennedy, B. 2000. *Deleuze and Cinema: The Aesthetics of Sensation*, Edinburgh: Edinburgh University Press.

Mankekar, P. 1999. *Screening Culture, Viewing Politics: An Ethnography of Television, Womanhood, and the Nation in Postcolonial India*, Durham and London: Duke University Press.

Pandian, M.S.S. 1992. *The Image Trap: M.G. Ramachandran in Film and Politics*, New Delhi: Newbury Park.

—————. 1996. 'Tamil Cultural Elites and Cinema: Outline of an Argument', *Economic and Political Weekly*, 13 April.

—————. 2000. 'Parasakthi: Life and Times of a DMK Film', in Ravi Vasudevan (ed.), *Making Meaning in Indian Cinema*, New Delhi: Oxford University Press.

Punathambekar, A. and A. Kavoori, 2008. 'Introduction: Going Bollywood', in Ashwin Punathambekar and Anandam Kavoori (eds), *Going Bollywood*, New York and London: New York University Press.

Rai, A. 2009. *Untimely Bollywood: Globalization and India's New Media Assemblage*, Durham: Duke University Press.

Ramakrishnan, T. 2006. 'Victoria Public Hall Likely To Get New Life', *The Hindu*, 18 July, http://www.hindu.com/2006/07/18/stories/2006071803400200.htm; accessed on 10 January 2009.

Singh, B. 2003. 'The Problem', *Seminar*, vol. 525, http://www.india-seminar.com/2003/525/525%20the%20problem.htm; accessed on 10 January 2009.

Sivathamby, K. 1981. *Tamil Film as a Medium of Political Communication*, Madras: New Century Books.

Thoraval, Y. 2000. *The Cinemas of India*, New Delhi: Macmillan India Limited.

Vasudevan, R. 2003. 'Cinema in Urban Space', *Seminar*, vol. 525, http://www.india-seminar.com/2003/525/525%20ravi%20vasudevan.htm; accessed on 10 January 2009.

Velayutham, S. (ed.). 2008. *Tamil Cinema: the Cultural Politics of India's Other Film Industry*, London and New York: Routledge.

—————. 2008a. 'Introduction: the Cultural History and Politics of South Indian Tamil Cinema', in Selvaraj Velayutham (ed.), *Tamil Cinema: the Cultural Politics of India's Other Film Industry*, London and New York: Routledge.

—————. 2008b. 'The Diaspora and the Global Circulation of Tamil Cinema', *Tamil Cinema: The Cultural Politics of India's Other Film Industry*.

11   Migrant, Diaspora, NRI

Bhojpuri Cinema and the
'Local in the Global'

D. PARTHASARATHY

The rise to prominence of Bhojpuri cinema around the beginning of this decade has captured the attention of the media in India no less around the world and has sparked scholarly interest in this cultural phenomenon, particularly from the field of film studies and cultural studies.[1] Occurring against the backdrop of a globalizing Bollywood in more senses than one, the fast increasing popularity and market share of Bhojpuri films,[2] and Bhojpuri cultural production in general, has been interpreted by the media as well as by media analysts and scholars in different ways. Two major reasons are often cited for the sudden and quite meteoric rise of Bhojpuri cinema. The first explanation sees Bhojpuri cinema carving an identity of its own as a response to the changing aesthetics, story lines, themes, and language of mainstream Bollywood cinema in the context of globalization. Here big- and small-budget Bombay cinema is viewed as mainly catering to the tastes and sensibilities of what has been termed as a multiplex audience, as well as the NRI (non-resident Indian) audience in North America, Europe, and Australia. The second explanation derives from the converse of this—that the emergence of the Bhojpuri film industry is a consequence of Bombay cinema's failure to consider the cinematic and cultural needs of a large section of the Bhojpuri-speaking audience of Hindi cinema.[3] The entry point for this discussion being a spatial analysis of globalization and its effects on cities in India, this chapter seeks to critically analyse the above arguments and also attempts to go beyond such points of view in contributing to a better understanding of transnational and translocal urbanism, social process, and cultural formations.

The epistemological and theoretical location of the arguments and analyses presented in this chapter is not the field of cultural studies, but is rather the field of debate between proponents of the global cities discourse and those critiquing it from the transnational urbanism perspective.[4] The major objective of this chapter is therefore not one of understanding the rise of Bhojpuri cultural production, but to understand the implications of this rise for our understanding of globalization and urbanisms, of transnational and translocal flows, processes, and practices that link cultural formations and population migrations. In researching post-industrial spatial and social restructuring in the city of Mumbai, and in trying to understand spatially-oriented politics and the politics of space and land use, Bhojpuri cinema and the spaces of Bhojpuri cultural performances emerged as key moments and issues for study. At a theoretical level, a critique of Western Marxist and non-Marxist approaches to globalization and cities may lead one to sympathetically adopt the transnational urbanism approach in understanding Mumbai and Asian cities in general (Parthasarathy 2003). This involved (a) a necessarily more complicated approach to issues of class, community, ethnicity, and nation, (b) a more de-centred and dialectical approach to globalization, and (c) an understanding of the multiple levels and forms of population flows and the relationship of migrant/diasporic populations to the state and to capital.

This chapter then argues that the rise of the Bhojpuri film industry can be better understood through an application and extension of the approaches current in the literature on transnational urbanism. Analysing various forms of linkages between different strands of the diaspora and migrants within and outside India, the chapter generates an understanding of diverse forms of 'local in the global' as a significant outcome of transnational urbanism. The 'naming' of three distinct groups in the discourse on migration within/from India—migrants, diaspora, and NRIs—their relation to India, their recognition and status accorded by the Indian state, their skill levels and professional accomplishments, their linkages to local and global capital, and their location within transnational spaces—all these are seen to be implicated in the creation of new transnational cultural spaces within which Bollywood and Bhojpuri cinema find and create their audiences.

The next section briefly outlines the rise of Bhojpuri cultural production, especially Bhojpuri cinema and reviews the reasons given by media analysts and scholars for its increased popularity and its global spread. This is followed by a concise sketch of the spatial politics of Bhojpuri cultural production in the city of Mumbai which is evaluated against the backdrop of large-scale restructuring of land use and nativist/anti-migrant political movements. A critique of popular views on the emergence of the Bhojpuri film industry is then presented, which also links to the literature and approaches of transnational urbanism and the sociology of transnational flows. The final section weaves the different strands of analysis together and makes concluding arguments linking Bhojpuri cinema and transnational urban processes with certain liberatory aspects of globalization.

Rise of Bhojpuri Cinema

Bhojpuri, along with other major dialects of Hindi, as well as other dialects and languages belonging to the Magadhan branch of the Indo-Aryan family of languages were part of Hindi cinema till the 1960s in the form of dialogues spoken by some characters in the movies and in the lyrics used in Bollywood films, until these gradually yielded place to Urdu-Hindustani, *Bambaiya* Hindi, and other standard forms of spoken and written Hindi. There were also occasional films made in Bhojpuri up until the 1980s, when a few films began to be made each year. It is however only in the early years of this decade that the industry actually took off and it was the massive box office success of a few movies in 2005 that made the Indian and international media take notice of the boom in Bhojpuri films and that they had an identity of their own. Initially made on modest budgets and released in single-hall older theatres in cities, towns, and villages, Bhojpuri cinema has now become big in terms of scale, as are big-budget films made with the participation of big Bollywood producers and financiers, mainstream directors, and big Bollywood stars. Shooting locales have also shifted to popular destinations such as London and Switzerland, even as Bhojpuri film actors and playback singers have become stars in their own right. The Bhojpuri film industry has both paralleled and spawned a Bhojpuri music industry, expanding the sphere of cultural production and giving a new lease of life to older theatres unable to compete with multiplexes located in malls in major Indian cities as well as smaller towns. Bhojpuri films and music cater not only to the migrants from eastern Uttar Pradesh and Bihar in Indian metropolises, but also to the rural and small town populations in north India, extending to non-Bhojpuri-speaking regions of Punjab, Madhya Pradesh, and Rajasthan. Further, Bhojpuri has gone global catering to the diaspora in Fiji, Surinam, Mauritius, and Trinidad with traditional links to Hindi, Bhojpuri, and to north Indian cultures. Big-budget Hollywood movies starting with *Spiderman III* are being dubbed in Bhojpuri along with other major Indian languages. Several older and more recent Bollywood hits have been remade or dubbed in Bhojpuri with varying degrees of success. Bhojpuri TV channels whose mainstay is Bhojpuri cinema and music have started and Bhojpuri film-based events such as film award ceremonies and stage shows have become popular.

While a few of the Bhojpuri films have been box-office hits, in big cities such as Mumbai and Delhi, a majority of them do well in the cities, towns, and rural hinterlands of north India. Parallel to this, Bollywood films have increasingly found their markets among the multiplex audiences of big cities and among NRI audiences abroad, even as their market share in north Indian towns and rural hinterlands have declined. This is usually explained by media columnists and analysts and by scholars as being a consequence of a shift in themes, aesthetics, and sensibilities of Bollywood cinema towards a more cosmopolitan and upper middle-class audience in India and abroad.[5] The infrastructural base of cinema in big cities is partly blamed on this as the decline of single-hall theatres and the emergence of multiplexes have made the cinema-going experience an expensive one and out of the reach of the majority of the lower middle-class and the poor.

A substantial number of Bollywood films are also targeted at what is referred to as the NRI audience in terms of locations, themes, and aesthetics. Mass audiences are no longer able to identify with protagonists and key characters in Bollywood cinema, who belong to a strata of society very different from that of the majority. Nor are mass audiences able to relate to cinematic themes including those of small-budget movies targeted at niche urban audiences. This is reflected not only in the declining viewership for Hindi films in the so-called Hindi heartland but also in the fact that some Hindi films dubbed in Bhojpuri keeping in mind metropolitan/cosmopolitan audiences have done badly. For instance, a film like *Namak Halal* which originally also had a sprinkling of Bhojpuri dialogues, was a big hit in its dubbed version, while *Darr*, which featured an urban psychopath flopped. On the other hand, Bhojpuri cinematic themes are still focused on what used to be the major themes in Bollywood cinema—the travails of rural urban migrants, feudal exploitation in villages and vigilante justice, social reform, and issues of family, kinship, and marriage. The language used in dialogues and lyrics in Bollywood cinema has also undergone a change with a shift towards more standard forms of Hindi, Bambaiya Hindi, and even generous sprinklings of English. Media reports estimate that the audience for Bhojpuri films is around 200 million spread across north India, in Mumbai and Delhi, and diasporic markets in the Caribbean and in Indian Ocean and Pacific/Oceania islands. There are signs that with more money flowing into the industry, Bhojpuri cinema is now targeting urban upper middle class audiences in India as well as the diaspora in North America and Europe where DVD (Digital Versatile Disc) sales of Bhojpuri films are on the rise. Despite the spatial spread of audience for Bhojpuri films however, its production is still concentrated in the city of Mumbai. The next section addresses the issues of spatial politics of Bhojpuri cultural production seen against the background of a nativist/chauvinist political discourse.

Bhojpuri Cinema and Mumbai: The Spatial Politics of Production and Exhibition

It is while researching on the politics of space and land use restructuring in Mumbai and the public discourse on this issue (Parthasarathy 2003) that issues surrounding Bhojpuri cinema came up in the forefront. Nativist political parties[6] in the city, as well as elite urban planning discourse[7] have targeted migrants from the north for many of the city's civic and economic problems. These have taken the shape of strong anti-north Indian sentiments which have in turn led to policy and planning biases. Such sentiments have also been expressed in the form of violence with north Indian migrants from Uttar Pradesh and Bihar being the victims of violent acts perpetrated by agents of the nativist parties. Businesses owned by north Indian migrants and businesses linked to north Indian economic and cultural activities were also targeted and it is thus that cinema halls showing Bhojpuri films were subjected to arson and property destruction. In the ensuing public and political debate, it emerged that many of these cinema halls were actually owned by native Marathi-speaking individuals and that these halls had actually gained a new lease of life as they were on a decline unable to compete with the new multiplexes and unable to pay the same revenue shares from film screening as the multiplex theatres.

The emergence of multiplexes as major venues for film screening in the city began in the late 1990s in response to large-scale land use restructuring partly due to new planning initiatives and partly due to the deindustrialization of the city's economy—the latter linked to large-scale closure of the city's textile mills and resulting in huge amounts of prime real estate becoming available. The malls which came up on many of these defunct textile mills usually had multiplex theatres along with other entertainment centres. At the same time, the entry of big producers and cash-rich Indian business families into the film exhibition business combined with the entry of foreign capital into this sector fuelled the multiplex rush. Some of the single screen cinemas were also converted into multiplexes as a result of this process, but several older cinemas held on for cultural, political, and economic reasons. This had two implications for cinema exhibition and viewing. First, only Hollywood films and big-budget Bombay films, or films made on smaller budgets but appealing to niche urban upper middle-class audiences could be exhibited in multiplex theatres, as theatre rentals for film screening were higher than the rentals for the older single screen theatres. The corporatization of the film industry and a shift in the economics of film distribution meant that theatres were forced into revenue sharing contracts superseding the earlier system of theatre rentals. This worked against the single-screen cinemas, who could not afford the volatility and unpredictability of income flows in the new system of revenue sharing. Second, the multiplexes were part of a new economics whose emphasis was on profit maximization using real estate with little operating and input costs. This led to specific mall and multiplex designs in prime real estate areas which escalated the cost of a cinematic experience for all, but particularly making it unaffordable for the lower middle class and the poor.

The shifts in the built environment for cinema consumption had significant political and cultural consequences for a population for whom films are among the cheapest sources of entertainment. A major impact was on films other than those targeted at a multiplex audience, especially Marathi films. Marathi films generally being made on smaller budgets, with a smaller share of the audience pool in a cosmopolitan city like Mumbai and having no audience outside the state, could simply not afford to screen their films in multiplexes despite a more favourable tax and subsidy regime. Marathi cinema in general has been in a state of decline for some time owing to the higher profitability and reach of Mumbai-based Bollywood produced Hindi films. All this generated some resentment used to fuel nativist and anti-immigrant sentiments among the Marathi-speaking population. In addition, the geography of cinema viewing was affected not only by the emergence of multiplexes and the decline of single-screen cinemas, but also by population movements within and outside the city owing to sectoral shifts in the economy away from the manufacturing sector and especially population movements influenced by the retrenchment of textile mill workers. Owing to a combination of factors, the single-screen cinema halls came to be located in areas with a predominantly north Indian population, in or near slums and blighted areas. It therefore made more sense for these halls to show films which appealed to the local audience—which ruled out both the multiplex films and Marathi films. As these theatres began to exhibit Bhojpuri films, it again became a source of anger among nativist groups towards the north Indian immigrant population.

Two issues need emphasizing at this point. While issues of a Bollywood turn toward multiplex audiences in India and the non-resident Indian audiences abroad may well be an explanation for the rise of Bhojpuri cinema targeting those excluded by Bollywood, it should not be forgotten that *Bhojywood* was and continues to be a part of Bollywood. While new actors and directors have entered cinema thanks to Bhojpuri cinema, a majority of financiers, producers, technicians, and increasingly actors are sourced from Bollywood. The production equipment and infrastructure are shared with Bollywood films. It is interesting to note that the attacks on north Indians and Bhojpuri cinema became so virulent that there was even talk of the Bhojpuri film industry shifting to Patna. However, because of the strong infrastructure and technical expertise in Mumbai, this is largely seen as unfeasible. Second, the economics of space and the built environment in Mumbai played no small a part in the increasing popularity of Bhojpuri cinema, which even as it spread to the Hindi heartland and abroad, used the Mumbai Bhojpuri audience as a springboard success. To properly understand and appreciate the increasing market share of Bhojpuri cinema and its spread to distant corners of the country and markets abroad, one must then go beyond the standard explanations. Focusing solely on factors such as thematic departures of Bollywood films and the presence of a Bhojpuri diaspora lead us to analytical pitfalls and provides us a distorted understanding of globalization and its impacts on native and diasporic populations and the relationship between them. In the section that follows certain alternate hypotheses and questions regarding the rise and spread of the Bhojpuri industry will be raised. In the process, 'transnational urbanism' perspective will be presented as a lens to better comprehend transcultural and transnational processes.

The Bhojpuri Film Audience and Transnational Urbanism

Though the analysis in the above section is specific to Mumbai, similar kinds of spatial restructuring, sectoral shifts, and population movements in other cities have affected the economics of film exhibition and viewing in similar ways. Across India's major cities north of the Vindhyas, the paths of multiplexes and single-screen cinema halls have diverged with significant implications for Bhojpuri cinema. Urban spatial economics is clearly linked to the rise of Bhojpuri cinema along with factors relating to thematic, aesthetic, idiomatic, linguistic, and stylistic turns in Bollywood films. However, arguments relating to the emergence of a Bhojpuri community—itself linked to an expansion of literacy, media, and communication, and emancipatory political changes and upsurges from below in Bihar and Uttar Pradesh—seem inadequate to explain the spread of Bhojpuri films and their popularity in spaces beyond these two states as well as outside India.[8]

Scholars have identified migration flows to cities like Mumbai with population in the Bhojpuri-speaking region creating a 'new public sphere',[9] which affects the 'production, circulation and consumption of the rural in urban spaces through Bhojpuri cultural production'

(Hardy 2008). Temporary migration, the maintenance of economic and cultural links, and communication with the place of origin has 'great cultural significance' as Tripathy (2007: 146) points out. Lal and Rajan take note of the 'extraordinarily expansive reach' (2007: 91) of Bhojpuri 'with audiences beyond the Hindi heartland in Indian metropolises and much further in the far-flung Indian diaspora in Fiji, Trinidad, Guyana, Mauritius, and elsewhere' (2007: 91). Both Tripathy, and Lal and Rajan project a positive image of the global spread of Bhojpuri cinema investing it even with an 'alternative conception of cosmopolitanism, its world of constant flux—the histories of which are etched in varying phenomena, from the historic importance since antiquity of the Gangetic plains in the development of an Indian civilization to the great migrations of Bhojpuri-speaking people in the nineteenth and twentieth centuries' (Lal and Rajan 2007: 91). Themes relating to migration and diaspora are not only common in Bhojpuri films, but also in media and scholarly analysis of the reach of Bhojpuri cinema. In keeping with much of conventional scholarship which accepts unquestioningly nations and nation-states as categories of analysis and study, the term 'migrant' is used when referring to movement of people within the boundaries of a nation-state and the term 'diaspora' when referring to movement across regions which are now different nations but which earlier were part of the same empire. Moreover, when referring to skilled middle-class professional migrants especially to North America and Europe both scholars and media have a tendency to refer to the diaspora as NRIs—whether used in a merely descriptive, laudatory, or derogatory sense.

The different discourses surrounding the migrant, the diaspora, and the NRI is as much a reflection of the location of diverse mobile populations in specific time-spaces as it is an indication of how markets and the state recognize and interpellate the different groups. In linking the migration of Bhojpuri-speaking people within and outside the country to the spread of Bhojpuri cultural production, scholars often overtly or covertly assume/argue for a differentiation of the Bhojpuri population with other migrant diaspora who are seen as being different in terms of class, language, ethnicity, skills, sophistication, and so on. Media analysis of Bhojpuri vis-à-vis Hindi films frequently touch upon the differences in sophistication, style, aesthetics, IQ (intelligence quotient) levels of audiences, coarseness of language, obscene dialogues, and so on. State policy and attitude towards the diaspora and internal migrants have further lent legitimacy to such differential perceptions. Against this, how valid is the assumption by scholars of the creation of a new Bhojpuri public sphere or a Bhojpuri community? Would it be a valid exercise to conceive of the emergence of an imagined Bhojpuri community with increased access to print, electronic, and other media and communication networks being activated? Is the global spread of Bhojpuri cinema premised on the existence of a Bhojpuri speech community?

Such a premise would be difficult to sustain given that in countries like Trinidad, Bhojpuri as a lingua franca has long been dead. Jayaram points out that Trinidad Indians, in fact, appreciate Indian origin cultural products quite devoid of their linguistic meanings owing to lack of language ability (Jayaram 2004). In other countries such as Mauritius as well, spoken Bhojpuri is actually a Creole version. In Fiji, Fijian Hindustani or Fijian Hindi is distinct from Bhojpuri. In addition, the popularity of Bhojpuri films in states like Punjab, Madhya Pradesh, and Rajasthan cannot be explained solely in terms of the existence of Bihari migrants in these states. In Maharashtra, Uttar Pradesh, and Bihar, Bhojpuri cinema is also popular among Urdu-speaking Muslims who also play a big role in film production. If language alone does not quite explain the popularity and reach of Bhojpuri cinema neither can we attribute it entirely to unique themes. During the 1980s and 1990s, there was a parallel Hindi film sector which catered mainly to the rural masses and rural migrants in cities by addressing the same themes as those found in Bhojpuri films. Why did this not sustain and was instead replaced by Bhojpuri cinema, especially as such films would have had a greater and more varied audience than Bhojpuri films, appealing both to Bhojpuri and non-Bhojpuri audiences? Arguing that Bhojpuri films are popular among non-Bhojpuris for their themes would not help in supporting the imagined community argument.

Unlike some cultural studies scholars who emphasize discontinuities,[10] in this case it is essential that we look at continuities to make sense of such issues. Despite the social and economic backwardness that contrasts with the dynamism and global thrust of Bhojpuri cinema, Bhojpuri-speaking people have had exposure and links to Bollywood through migration and an active presence in Bombay's economy. Especially with respect to filmmaking, Bhojpuris unlike others from the north Indian heartland had cultural and social capital when it came to film production. It is this continuity that is theoretically important rather than the discontinuities in themes, production values, and aesthetics. Migration—seasonal, temporary, and permanent—to cities within India and past migration in the form of indentured labour do matter. However, to understand and make sense of the rise to prominence and spread of Bhojpuri cinema and comprehend its implications in the context of global flow of cultural goods and forms, it is essential that we locate the issue of migration whether internal or international in its proper context. While it is important to analyse the rise of Bhojpuri cinema from a cultural studies perspective, this chapter argues that the insights the phenomenon offers to urban studies scholars is equally important. Recognizing global flows as being multidirectional, some urban studies scholars[11] have begun to critique older global cities approaches, and those theoretical premises which explain urban phenomena in the context of globalization purely in terms of capital flows and their consequences. This has led to the emergence of the transnational urbanism perspective (Smith 2001), which together with scholars from sociology, anthropology, and geography, propose an alternative way of explaining global, transnational, and transcultural flows, an alternate approach that recognizes agency to a greater degree and offers a more complex analysis of globalization and urbanism.

A key insight of the transnational urbanism perspective has been to repudiate the idea of the 'local' as simply being the 'other' of the global.[12] The fact that different types of migration have been used as key explanatory factors for the national and global thrust of Bhojpuri cinema, requires that we address this issue and explore how this can be utilized to better understand global flows and the urban-rural relationship. When Lal and Rajan project Bhojpuri films as offering an 'alternative cosmopolitanism', are they referring to an industry which has roots in and close links with a globalizing Bollywood? If Bhojywood is the 'other' of Bollywood as scholars and the media seem to believe, and if Bollywood itself is the local 'other' of the 'global' Hollywood, is Bhojpuri cinema then the 'other' of a local 'other'? The Bollywood turn towards NRIs has been explained as one reason for the popularity of Bhojpuri films. Where do we then locate NRIs as an audience? Are they the 'other' of the global, but located within the global? Over the last few years, the proportion of skilled Bhojpuri-speaking professionals migrating for education and work to the US and Europe has gone up, even as there has been an increased professional class emerging from

Uttar Pradesh and Bihar via the IITs (Indian Institutes of Technology), other professional education schools, and the civil services. They have played no small a measure in the expanding an already large online presence of Bhojpuri speakers and Bhojpuri cultural products. Against this, would we still regard Bhojpuri cultural production as local, as the local 'other' of the global? Given that cities like Mumbai and Delhi are enmeshed in complex networks with rural hinterlands involving flow of people, capital, culture, ideas, and power, can we still talk of local and global in mutually exclusive terms? Or does it make more sense to talk of transnational and translocal urbanism and approach such issues from the perspective of a sociology or anthropology of transcultural flows? What sense does it make to conceptualize the Hindi heartland as being the marginalized or subaltern 'other' of Mumbai, when Bhojpuri cinema would be impossible without Mumbai and Bollywood? Given the popularity of Bhojpuri films among non-Bhojpuri audiences in India, where does one locate the cinema as against Bollywood and Hollywood, especially in the context of Bollywood and Hollywood addressing Bhojpuri and other vernacular audiences in India through dubbed films?

The audience for Bhojpuri films is clearly disparate, mobile, occupying different spaces. They live in a variety of urban and rural spaces. Both state and capital collude to create a fiction of transnational cultural practices and the nation-state as being mutually exclusive entities, evident in discourses and policies on globalization and migration. Scholars seem to accept this fiction unquestioningly by giving academic sanction to particular conceptualizations of the NRI, the diaspora, and the migrant, and their role in particular trajectories of transnational cultural flows especially in discussions of Hollywood, Bollywood, and now Bhojpuri cinema. Could this be a consequence of a type of cultural theorizing (which is) 'derived from a politico-economic model' that is 'preoccupied with the global spread of the cultural condition of post-modernity'?[13] Would it be more convincing and compelling instead to study the spread of Bhojpuri cinema by seeking to unravel the complex networks and relationships that link classes, communities, and politico-economic entities (including regions and cities) by using a transnational urbanism approach? Such an approach as Smith argues avoids the analytical pitfalls of approaching rural and urban, global, and local as discrete entities and instead seeks to comprehend the flows, relations, and tensions between them and their consequent mutual influences and transformations. Seen in the context of 'criss-crossing transnational circuits of communication and cross-cutting local, translocal, and transnational social practices that "come together" in particular places, at particular times' (Smith 2001: 5), Bhojpuri cinema emerges as a marker of transnational urbanism, of a particular moment in history, which is itself a concatenation of a set of moments and events in history which links the local and the global in multiple ways.

Conclusion: Bhojpuri Cultural Production and the Question of Identity

A purely culturalist reading of the rise of Bhojpuri cinema, even one that incorporates notions of power is inadequate both to achieve an understanding of the complexities resident in the phenomenon as well as in deriving larger insights from the exercise. This chapter proposes a more overtly political agenda in the popularity and expanded reach of Bhojpuri cinema—a perspective that is shared with other scholars working on aspects of Indian Caribbean culture such as chutney music.[14] Tripathy, as well as Lal and Rajan, link Bhojpuri cinema to the social churning in Uttar Pradesh and Bihar, especially the rise to power of middle and lower castes. However, their larger point is more to do with language communities and Bhojpuri cinema as resistance to Bollywood and Hollywood than with issues of politics and identity viewed in a more disaggregated way. Scholars working on chutney music and other aspects of India derived cultural elements in the Caribbean and have pointed to the importance of these for local identity formation and for inter-ethnic political struggles. Both in the West Indies and in the case of other countries like Fiji, there is an abundance of literature documenting the influence of ethnicity and race in political movements, struggles, and conflicts.

Going with such perspectives, this chapter proposes that the spread of Bhojpuri cinema can be better understood not in terms of the emergence of a Bhojpuri community or even a Bhojpuri audience, but in terms of the individual and quite discrete forms of significance that Bhojpuri cinema and cultural products have for groups living in different trans-national spaces. With the death of Trinidad Bhojpuri as a lingua franca, and the failure of Hindi revivalism in the country, cultural products provide markers of ethnicity and differentiation, inculcate pride, and help develop historicity—crucial in political struggles involving ethnic groups. Similar arguments may be made about Fiji. In the case of cities like Mumbai—and their extensions in Bihar and Uttar Pradesh— Bhojpuri cultural products are useful also in political struggles with nativist sentiments. It may be argued that while language and culture are important, they are marginal and substitutable by other cultural elements in struggles for mobility and empowerment. At the same time, it is also vital that we understand this specific moment in history when the rise and spread of Bhojpuri cinema becomes possible.

This is where it is crucial that we focus on continuities rather than discontinuities. At the global, national, and sub-national levels, scholars as well as activists have been too preoccupied with understanding the impact of global cultural forms on other cultures. Of late, there has also been interest in studying cultural flows in the reverse direction, as well as identifying multiple dominant centres from which flows occur. However, not much research has been done on the liberatory potential of global flows, wherein sub-national or sub-regional cultures gain an opportunity to practice their cultures and display/make use of their identities under conditions of globalization. Across the world, including in Western contexts and irrespective of where people live, once individuals and groups embrace and accept globalization as a reality, accept their status as global citizens, it also frees them, liberates them, and gives them greater confidence to allow identities other than their nationality to surface. The adoption or adding of one more identity, even privileging one over others, may or may not be linked to processes of formation of imagined and real communities. For Bhojpuri professionals in the US, for Indo-Trinidadians, and Indo-Fijians, for Urdu-speaking Muslim migrants from Uttar Pradesh in Mumbai, for Maithili or Rajasthani speakers in central and western India, and for Bhojpuri speakers across India—Bhojpuri cultural production has meaning in their everyday lives and political struggles. These could be in the form of livelihoods, as a source of pride and self-esteem, as a simple provider of entertainment which at the same time is a marker of identity, or just an indicator of one's roots. Rather than constituting a community, Bhojpuri cinema may be better understood as an outcome of what Schein (1998) refers to as 'deterritorialized nationalisms, loosed from their moorings in the bounded unit of the territorial state and coalescing at both local and translocal levels'. The challenge for scholars is to understand and make sense of 'multiple locals in multiple globals', using the metaphor of transnational urbanism, rejecting simplistic views of globalization's impact 'from above' and instead address the innumerable micro and meso practices of culture and politics that can be observed in different time spaces across the world.

Notes

1. Tripathy (2007). A two-day seminar on 'Bhojpuri cinema in comparative perspective' was organized by Asian Research Development Institute (ARDI), Patna.
2. See Sahi (2008); references in Tripathy (2007) and Tewary (2005).
3. These are summarized in Tripathy (2007) and can also be found in most media reports on Bhojpuri cinema since 2005.
4. For an overview of this debate, see Smith (2001).
5. Summarized in Tripathy (2007) and Tewary (2005).
6. The Shiv Sena and the Maharashtra Navnirman Sena.
7. See Parthasarathy (2003) for an analysis of this.
8. Tripathy (2007) supports such arguments, as do Lal and Rajan (2007).
9. Lal and Rajan (2007).
10. Tripathy (2007) makes use of this argument.
11. For instance, Smith (2001).
12. For a discussion, see ibid. pp. 23–47.
13. Ibid., p. 24.
14. Manuel (1998), and Balliger (2005).

References

Balliger, Robin. 2005. 'Chutney Soka Music in Trinidad: Indian Ethno-Nationalist Expression in Transnational Perspective', in Christine G.T. Ho and Keith Nurse (eds), *Globalization, Diaspora and Caribbean Popular Culture*, Kingston and Miami: Ian Randle Publishers.

Hardy, Kathryn. 2008. 'Screening the Village: the Production, Circulation, and Consumption of the Rural in Urban Spaces through Bhojpuri Cultural Production,' paper presented at the 37th Annual Conference on South Asia, University of Wisconsin, Madison, October.

Jayaram, N. 2004. 'The Dynamics of Language in Indian Diaspora: The Case of Bhojpuri/Hindi in Trinidad', in N. Jayaram, S.L. Sharma, and Yogesh Atal (eds), *The Indian Diaspora: Dynamics of Migration*, New Delhi: Sage.

Lal, Vinay and Gita Rajan. 2007. 'Ethnographies of the Popular and the Public Sphere in India', *South Asian Popular Culture*, vol. 5, no. 2.

Manuel, Peter. 1998. 'Chutney and Indo-Trinidadian Cultural Identity', *Popular Music*, vol. 17, no. 1.

Parthasarathy, D. 2003. 'Urban Transformation, Civic Exclusion and Elite Discourse', *City: A Quarterly on Urban Issues*, vol. 4.

Sahi, Ajit, 2008, 'The Revenge of the Bhojpuria', *Tehelka Magazine*, vol. 5, no. 10 (15 March).

Schein, Louisa. 1998. 'Importing Miao Brethren to Hmong America: A Not So Stateless Transnationalism', in Pheng Cheah and Bruce Robbins (eds), *Cosmopolitics: Thinking and Feeling beyond the Nation*, Minneapolis: University of Minnesota Press.

Smith, Michael Peter. 2001. *Transnational Urbanism: Locating Globalization*, MA: Blackwell Publishing.

Tewary, Amarnath. 2005. 'Move over Bollywood, Here's Bhojpuri,' news.bbc.co.uk/1/hi/world/south_asia/4512812.stm.

Tripathy, Ratnakar. 2007. 'Bhojpuri Cinema: Regional Resonances in the Hindi heartland', *South Asian Popular Culture*, vol. 5, no. 2.

12   *Welcome to Sajjanpur*

Theatre and Transnational Hindi Cinema

NANDI BHATIA

Are there possibilities of a revolutionary countercinema in Bombay cinema...?
(Mishra 2002: 33)

The title of this chapter, at one level, functions as a metaphor for popular
Hindi cinema's return from metropolitan spaces to local places, such as
the fictionalized village Sajjanpur in Shyam Benegal's recent film *Welcome to Sajjanpur* (2008).[1] At another level, it literally indicates Hindi
cinema's return to the local through the representation of theatrical forms
that exist on the cultural margins. Since 2006, at least five films—*Khosla
ka Ghosla* (2006), *Maan Gaye Mughall-e-Azam* (2008), *Halla Bol* (2008)
Aaja Nachle (2007), and *Welcome to Sajjanpur*—have represented theatre
as an agent of social change, activism, and political intervention. What
does such attention to a form that is local, ephemeral, and marginalized
from the global circuits of production, consumption, and circulation
enjoyed by print and cinema, signal? And what implications does it have
on the political arguments of these films and ultimately for theatre? It

* I gratefully thank Teresa Hubel, Anjali Gera-Roy, and D. Parthasarathy for
their critical input on this chapter.

may be argued that the current inclusion of local theatrical forms—popular and street theatre, for example—in Hindi cinema, serves several functions. At one level, it constitutes a representational shift from early post-Independence cinema's ideological investment in nation-building through the revival of the nation's traditional forms and cultural practices (as in *Teesri Kasam*, 1966). By contrast, the current focus on local theatrical engagements constitutes an interrogation of the nation, its political corruption, and underworld politics, and represents an acknowledgement, on the part of cinema, of the political potential of theatre.

In the last couple of decades, Bollywood, in the interest of expanding its diasporic viewership that generates cultural capital, forges transnational communities, and ensures economically lucrative markets as compared to India,[2] has relied on a formula that represents India as largely middle-class, upwardly mobile, and modern, suggesting that despite its 'traditional' value systems, the society is a part of the larger global family. India's 'modernity' is demonstrated through characters who speak English or Hinglish (a mix of English and Hindi), which is the norm in India's metropolitan cities, through fantasies that render 'the holiday in Switzerland and the designer titles' as 'the reality of upper-middle-class life' (Vohra 2008: 46), and through plots that celebrate the fruits of multinational capital. As a result, Bollywood has obscured the diversity of India, wiped out its villages, except to show them in terms of an idyllic and 'pristine' India where all is well and where the lush Punjab fields as in *Dilwale Dulhania Le Jayenge* (which remains the longest running film in India in the history of Indian cinema and has enjoyed a huge popularity in the diaspora) fulfil the non-resident Indian's (NRI's) nostalgia for the (real and imagined) homes that they left behind. The downside of this 'global' Bollywood is its compromise of what one might call the ordinary and the small. Seen as markers of those trailing behind in modernity and Westernization, local dialects, the rural, the folk, and the small are regarded as subjects fit for regional film industries such as Bhojpuri cinema, in which the 'folk allure is significant' as is the 'world of fairs and festivals, the *nautanki*, acrobats' performances, travelling musicians, courtesans, and drama troupes'.[3] Bhojpuri cinema, in the words of journalist and director Dhananjay from Bihar, is seen as providing 'a space for those left behind in the Indian elite's embrace of modernity and Westernization.'[4] Bringing attention to theatrical practices ranging from proscenium performances to folk, street, and activist theatre, in unknown places that lie on the fringes of metropolitan cities where characters speak in dialects different from the staple language of dominant cinema, the above-mentioned five films represent an undertaking that highlights the nation's diverse theatrical traditions that have the potential to showcase the economic and political effects of globalization on localities that do not figure in the celebratory narratives about the upwardly mobile populace of the nation.

The films under discussion are 'commercial'[5] Hindi films that either resemble or, as in the case of *Welcome to Sajjanpur*, have emerged from the 'new' or parallel cinema movement that was initiated by city-bred, middle class and often English-educated intellectuals who sometimes worked 'independently and outside Bombay' and promoted a realist cinema that would communicate 'an "authentic" national consciousness' (Chakravarty 1994: 86) by delineating the 'reality' of India and its cultural-political landscapes. It had its source in the 'idealist' phase of post-Independence India that saw realism as 'the masquerading conscience of the Indian intelligentsia in their assumed (though not uncontested) role of national leadership during the fifties' (ibid.: 81). Usually made on low budgets, the films were largely ethnographic and sought to 'cinematize important areas of Indian reality' through the 'use of understatement' that involves 'a slow meditative camera that weighs the meaning of the most mundane event, avoiding the flashy exuberance normally associated with popular films' (Gokulsing and Dissanayake 2004: 34). Often made in regional languages, they consequently did not receive the 'pan-Indian exposure' received by popular cinema (ibid.: 32). Though they won international and national awards and were screened at international festivals, the films had limited circulation and box-office success. Directors belonging to this neo-realistic parallel cinema movement include Satyajit Ray, Ritwik Ghatak, Mrinal Sen, Adoor Gopalakrishnan, Aravindan, Kumar Shahani, Mani Kaul, Buddhadeb Dasgupta, Aparna Sen, Gautam Ghose, Shyam Benegal, Govind Nihalani, Shaji Karun, Vijaya Mehta, and Ketan Mehta, among others (ibid.: 34).

With subjects similar to those tackled by parallel cinema—which are presented by actors who come from theatre backgrounds and often act in non-mainstream films—and represented through cinematic frames that move beyond the neo-realism of parallel cinema to integrate features such as songs and melodramatic situations, the films under discussion are positioned between parallel cinema and Bollywood. They can be characterized as experiments in agitprop theatre, experiments that imagine theatrical forms not merely as decorative tools of entertainment or as reified national treasures, but as living cultural practices that capture the pulse of society and its people. With the exception of *Aaja Nachle*, which had a big launch in North America as it marked the return of Madhuri Dixit to cinema after her relocation to the USA, these films have not had the benefit of blockbuster status that transnational Hindi cinema, made under banners such as Yash Raj films, enjoys in the diaspora.[6] Yet they have migrated to diasporic locations through the DVD industry and circulate amongst interested viewers through the Indian market circuit, cinema halls, and onsite and online video stores. A brief summary of the films is given below as the backdrop to an analytical study of this genre of films.

Shyam Benegal's *Welcome to Sajjanpur* (2008) is set in a village called Sajjanpur that showcases a street play against land seizure in the capitalistic drive towards constructing a shopping mall. The main story is about the only village graduate (played by Shreyas Talpade) who becomes a letter writer for lack of more gainful employment and in the process of writing letters for people becomes privy to their most private stories—stories that form the basis of the novel that he ultimately produces. However, the small moment where he is threatened for scripting the street play against a shopping mall is important for showing the interest that the play generates in the subject. *Halla Bol*, which is the story of a street theatre actor turned film-star and his commitment to fight against those involved in the brutal murder of a young woman (reminiscent of the Jessica Lal murder case) that he inadvertently witnesses, has as its central plot the role of street theatre in ultimately aiding his determination to expose the murderers.[7] Despite being a famous film star, the hero (played by Ajay Devgan) finally resorts to organizing collective protest by raising the issue through a street play. *Maan Gaye Mughall-e-Azam*, a patriotic comedy, with its uncanny anticipation of the 26 November 2008 bomb blasts in Mumbai, is about the role of a group of theatre actors, who, discouraged by marginalization from national theatre institutions, paucity of funds, and routine threats from local goons, collectively decide to join the nationalist cause against terrorism in the country and use their talents in cleverly exposing a terrorist plot. *Khosla ka Ghosla* solicits the help of a theatre group for restoring a piece of seized land to its rightful owner, after all avenues, including the police, NGOs, and local dons, are closed off. In *Aaja Nachle*, the main protagonist (played by Madhuri Dixit), upon her return to India from the US, is horrified to find that the theatre in her hometown where she danced and performed is being brought down so that a shopping mall can be built in its place. Gradually, she mobilizes the town and successfully sets about the task of reviving the theatre and convincing the local MP, opposition leaders, and the people to save the theatre. Once the theatre is saved, she leaves for the US satisfied at having accomplished her mission. During the course of rehearsing and the performance, the theatre also acts as a catalyst for saving a failing marriage, facilitates a romance, and wins over the local *goonda*s who had begun to physically demolish the theatre. The topics that they deal with then are as heterogeneous as the films, which address social problems through theatrical forms that range from street theatre to proscenium stages in the style of Parsi theatres and through genres that encompass political satire (*Khosla ka Ghosla*), comedy and farce (*Maan Gaye Mughall-e-Azam*), or tragedy (*Halla Bol*) to challenge systems and modes of authority. What also makes them additionally distinctive is that unlike the trends in earlier social realist cinema that drew a sharp dichotomy of village/city and rural/urban, in which the former was victimized, in these films everyone across class and gender living in rural, semi-rural, or the metropoles is subjected to systemic violence and abuse. The villains are more specifically local politicians, builders, and loan sharks.

Hindi Cinema and Theatre

While the separate histories of cinema and theatre cannot be collapsed, they are inevitably related and intertwined, the relationship between theatre and cinema being as old as the emergence of cinema itself. During the early days of cinema, mythological dramas derived from the epics and performed by Parsi theatres supplied and inspired mythological films including the first silent film, D.G. Phalke's *Raja Harishchandra* (1913). The fact that the play on which the film was based was performed 4,000 times at different venues across the subcontinent (Trivedi 2008: 201) attests to the popularity of theatre in the decades preceding cinema and demonstrates the faith that directors exhibited in the subject matter and techniques of theatre in generating interest in cinema. The influence of theatre also permeated cinema through the work of actors, artistes, and directors who entered and ultimately made their careers in cinema. Many of the early actresses—Naaz, Meena Kumari, and Madhubala, for example—were theatre actresses who joined cinema. In the decades immediately preceding Independence and after 1947, actors and directors involved in the Indian People's Theatre Association (IPTA), which was formed on an all-India basis to disseminate anti-colonial and anti-fascist messages in 1943, went on to make films and found successful careers in commercial and independent cinema, prominent among them being Balraj Sahni and Khwaja Ahmad Abbas.[8] Those involved with theatre also wrote scripts and songs for cinema.

Other influences of theatre included plots from the plays of Shakespeare, which became the subject matter of earlier films such as Udavadia's *Dil Farosh* (1927, a silent film inspired by *The Merchant of Venice*), *Zalim Saudagar* (1941, derived from *The Merchant of Venice*), J.J. Madan's *Hathili Dulhan* (1932, based on *The Taming of the Shrew*), and Rustom Modi's *Pak Daman* or *Shaeed-e-Naaz* (1940, from *Measure for Measure*). The tragedies included Dada Athawale's silent film *Khoon-e-Nahak* (1928, derived from *Hamlet*), Sohrab Modi's *Khoon-ka-Khoon* (1935, based on *Hamlet*), *Zan Mureed* (1936, based on *Antony and Cleopatra*), and *Romeo and Juliet* (1948) (Verma 2005: 270–1). Most of these films were inspired by the Parsi theatres' adaptations of Shakespearean plays and the 'dialogue and songs showed the continuing influence of the Parsi theatre' (Verma 2005: 271).[9] In postcolonial India, films such as *Angoor* (1982, adapted from *A Comedy of Errors*), *Shakespeare Wallah* (1965), Vishal Bharadwaj's *Maqbool* (2003, based on *Macbeth*) and *Omkara* (2006, based on *Othello*), and Rituparno Ghosh's *The Last Lear* (2007) have continued to seek inspiration from Shakespeare. Additionally, cinema also dealt with stories about actresses in films such as *Bhumika*; *nautanki* dancers, for instance in *Teesri Kasam* (adapted from Phanishwarnath Renu's short story 'Maare Gaye Gulfam') and courtesans and *devadasis* and their performance traditions. Stylistically, cinema borrowed from the aesthetic conventions of both folk and urban proscenium theatres in terms of dialogue delivery, the use of stage sets, curtains, scenery, images, and songs. Since its earliest formations, cinema has remained an important site for storing, documenting, and preserving numerous stories about theatre and its various dimensions mentioned above.

That cinema played an important role in documenting the importance of theatre is evident in the following evaluation by the London magazine *Bioscope* in the early twentieth century, when D.G. Phalke began making his mythological films such as *Raja Harishchandra, Mohini Bhasmasur,* and *Savitri Satyavan*:

> Since one of the greatest and most valuable possibilities of the cinematography is the circulation throughout the world of plays dealing with national life and characteristics, acted by native players amidst local scenes, it is with no small interest that one awaits the appearance in this country of Mr D.G. Phalke (cited in Chakravarty 1994: 37).[10]

In the 1920s, when film production rose to '172 by the end of the decade' (Chakravarty 1994: 40), films often derived plots and other elements from plays. Thus, a social farce titled *Tehmuras and Tehmuljee,* developed from a Gujarati play against the backdrop of Parsi life and produced in 1921 'introduced another perennial in Bombay filmmaking, an actor playing the dual role of twin brothers' (Chakravarty 1994: 40). According to J.B.H. Wadia,

> When the Parsee Natak Mandli of Appoo Brothers had staged the play in Bombay at Victoria Theatre, the producers resorted to an ingenious interlude. They projected a film sequence on the legitimate stage in which both the characters were shown together in camera frames by means of what is known in the film trade as 'masked shots'. This was the first time, at least in Bombay, that the stage and the film had combined to provide entertainment to the audience. (Cited in Chakravarty 1994: 40)

Overall, points out Booth, Hindi films 'represent a continuation of their culture's pre-cinematic forms and stories, transformed by the capitalist economy of scale and the power of the mass media' (1995: 172). In addition to stories from the Ramayana and Mahabharata that contributed to the source materials for popular theatres such as nautanki, the aesthetic and thematic range of Hindi cinema derives from popular traditions of the Marathi *tamasha,* the musical Marathi *natyasangit,* Bengali music-drama *jatra,* and Central Asian, Persian, and Punjabi myths and legends such as Rustom Sohrab, Laila Majnu, Shirin Farhad, Heer Ranjha, Sohni Mahival. One can also see the ongoing influence and presence of classical dance traditions in film songs and the importance of local places such as Bareilly in songs such as '*Nayi Dilli mein, Bareilly jaisa saiyaan*' from *U, Me, Aur Hum* (2008). As well, actors, such as Naseeruddin Shah, Amol Palekar, Seema Biswas, Shree Ram Lagoo, among others, from the Hindi and Marathi stages also continue to work in films.

Despite these historical and ongoing connections, scholarship on the relationship between cinema and theatre presents polarized viewpoints from the perspectives of film critics on the one hand and theatre critics on the other. Most film scholars see the influence of theatre on early cinema as a mark of its autonomous identity and its refusal to subscribe to Western influences. Priya Jaikumar, for example, argues that 'pre-cinematic as well as modern Indian art forms' cast a 'formative influence on film aesthetics in the later colonial era' and helped galvanize Indian cinema industry's goal of 'asserting a cultural identity' that was 'crucial to the industry's survival as a trade' (p. 195). Trivedi (2008: 201) views the influence of theatre as evidence that,

> ... filmmaking in India was from the start conceived of ... as a nationalist, spe-cifically 'Swadeshi enterprise' ... 'Swadeshi' signifying not only homegrown and indigenous, which is what the word means, but also a nationwide anti-British movement against the Partition of Bengal that began in 1905 and culminated successfully in the Partition being annulled in 1911.

Other critics, as Madhav Prasad points out, view the presence of the-atre and its influences such as melodrama, songs, and stage layout 'as evidence of the unbroken continuity of Indian culture and its tenacity in the face of the onset of modernity' (Prasad 2000: 15). While they note the aesthetic influences of theatre on cinema and its ability to maximize the entertaining appeal and pleasure of cinema, underlying such conclu-sions is the post-colonial need to reinforce the 'Indianness' of cinema and its autonomy from its Western counterpart—Hollywood—in the early years of Indian filmmaking.[11]

> Theatre critics, playwrights, and directors, on the other hand, examine this relationship primarily in terms of evaluating its consequences for theatre and provide a largely pessimistic outlook. Presenting cinema and theatre as separate, they view cinema as a threat to the popularity of theatre and the primary cause of dwindling theatre audiences. Such arguments are most sharply reflected in the following quotes by two important theatre personalities—J.C. Mathur and Sheila Bhatia—both of whom have been involved in some capacity with the National School of Drama, New Delhi. According to Mathur (1977: 9–10):
>
> > Unfortunately for drama, the first result of the introduction of the cinema in India was that as popular entertainment, it lost its hold on audiences, particularly in the vast Hindi-speaking region—in towns and later even in several rural areas. Several factors accounted for this situation. These are the exotic appeal of the

film, the low tariff, and its unlimited capacity to show any place or situations, realistic to the most convincing details and as fantastic as the wildest imagination. That is why the first to go down was the spectacular drama of the Parsi theatre, because its revolving stage and its trick scenes were no match for the marvels of trick-photography.

That in itself was not so much of a loss. But with it also seemed to go the core of the theatre—the power of speech, the beauty of the turn of phrase, the dialogue that illumines a situation in a flash, and brings out the clangors of the human soul in conflict. Gone was the gradual build-up of climax and the cathartic effect of passion in the throes of struggle. For some time it seemed that the theatre would not survive in the Indian situation where, unlike in the West, there had been a long break in the availability of state-patronage to the theatre during British rule.

And Sheila Bhatia, an important theatre personality known for her work on Punjabi drama, has regretfully said the following in an interview (cited in Kaushal 2000: 141–2; translation author's):

> When theatre is fighting a losing battle with cinema and television, when the government has not come up with any cultural norms and the media is out to ruin the interests of the viewers ... when increasing expenses prevent adequate rehearsal and staging, when viewers only want to spend money on cheap entertainment rather than on good theatre, when actors want to elevate themselves rather than their acting, and when everything has become so commercial that channels too are being sold, then what plans can one make [for theatre]?

The harshest critique comes from Deepti Priya Mehrotra, who, in her biography of Gulab Bai, suggests that even though the story of this famous nautanki dancer from Kanpur inspired *Teesri Kasam*, the film industry appropriated Gulab Bai's songs, which she had sung for HMV records, in particular '*Nadi nare na jao*' sung by Waheeda Rahman in *Mujhe Jeene Do* (1963) and '*Paan khaye saiyan hamaro*' in *Teesri Kasam*. Mehrotra (2006: 157) observes:

> Bollywood ... simply stole, brazenly and with impunity. Bollywood film directors, music directors, and singers heard Gulab Bai's records and picked up the words and tunes. They made a fortune. Their growing popularity was partly based on the use of music people already identified with. But this glamorous industry failed to acknowledge the debt it owed to the simple folk in remote villages, or to a professional stage artiste named Gulab Bai.

Yet cinema, as Indologist and literary critic Lutze (2009) points out, has been crucial for highlighting the importance of many of the regional theatrical forms such as *Ramlila*.[12] This has taken place not just through the theatrical influences that film critics often allude to but through a conscious presence accorded to different theatrical traditions. The distinct function of each—the influence of theatrical traditions as a natural outcome for cinema, on the one hand, and the incorporation within cinema of distinct theatre forms as independent genres on the other, should, therefore, not be collapsed. It is the latter that concerns this chapter. The aim is to examine the social function of cinema in consciously bringing in theatre and the implications of documenting and retrieving stories about theatre's role in the cultural life of the nation.

That there is an ideological and political purpose in showcasing and integrating theatrical forms in cinema became evident in the immediate post-Independence period when institutional bodies such as the National School of Drama and the three national academies were set up in 1953 and 1954: the Sangeet Natak Akademi (Academy of, Dance, Drama, and Music), the Sahitya Akademi (Academy of Letters), and the Lalit Kala Akademi (Academy of Fine Arts). These academies 'encouraged the study of the various arts under the auspices of the Ministry of Scientific Research and Cultural Affairs, established in 1958' (Chakravarty 1994: 63) and initiated the revival of traditional and folk theatres through theatre festivals, workshops, and conferences, providing cinema the opportunity to become a site for such preservation. For example, the Film Enquiry Committee, set up in 1950, 'to examine what measures should be adopted to "enable films in India to develop into an effective instrument for the promotion of national culture, education and healthy entertainment"' as one of its three aims (ibid.: 66), also set up cinema as an agent of nation-building. Thus, one saw in the 1960s significant attention given to folk forms such as nautanki in Basu Bhattacharya's *Teesri Kasam*. Coinciding with the 1960s revival of folk theatre as integral to the assertion of a cultural nationalism that reclaimed the nation's indigenous forms as 'authentic' (forms that were deemed to have been obscured because of the dominance of European theatres under colonial rule), *Teesri Kasam* focuses centrally on the nautanki dancer Hira Bai (played by Waheeda Rahman) and accords a legitimate space to nautanki as an important part of India's cultural heritage. The film reinforces its nationalistic affinity through the name of the company for which Hira Bai works—'The Great Bharat Nautanki Company'—and showcases a number of nautanki songs (many of which have acquired the status of classics), familiarizes the film's viewers with the form through speech patterns that encapsulate the simplicity of village life, and provides the audience with a glimpse of the sociological workings of nautanki, its importance at *melas*, its spatial flexibility as a mobile theatre form, and generic parameters regarding the stage, actors and audiences.

Even though ironically, 'the film industry was not integrated into the mainstream of nationalist planning' by the postcolonial Indian state before 1950 because 'as a culture industry, its products did not enhance or embody the prestige of the new nation' (Chakravarty 1994: 66), by the 1960s, films such as *Teesri Kasam*, which did exhibit a radical potential by showcasing the social exclusions faced by the nautanki dancer, were apparently participating in the nation's cultural investment in mobilizing, acknowledging, and reviving 'Indian' forms. So strong was the nationalist sentiment at this time that even a film like *Shakespeare Wallah*, which resulted from the transnational partnership between Ismael Merchant and James Ivory and was produced in English for a primarily Western or Westernized Indian audience, was deeply invested with a nationalistic message. Its nationalism was evident in Merchant's motivating impulse behind the film, which was to highlight the fact that the empire had ended. Aesthetically, this sentiment was conveyed in the film's representation of the dying influence of Shakespeare in post-Independence India as a metaphor for the end of the Raj. Located within such a nationalistic framework, *Shakespeare Wallah* nonetheless complicated the relationship of Shakespearean theatre to Hindi cinema, especially through the disruptive presence of the Hindi film actress Manjula in a performance of *Othello* and the emphasis on local traditions through a rehearsal of Manjula's song-and-dance sequence under a tree, for a film.[13]

This quest to reclaim indigenous traditions (that were seen as being marginalized during colonization) as an important part of India's national past emerged in response to the practices of colonialism, whose hierarchical privileging of English language, literatures, the arts, urban proscenium theatres, along with classical Sanskritic traditions were seen to have reduced popular cultural forms to a 'low' status and pushed them to the margins of mainstream cultural productions. However, the current return to theatre in cinema can be seen as an oppositional gesture to such earlier cultural attempts at nation-building. It emerges from cinema's need to address the social, economic, and cultural ramifications of the operations of power and the nexus of national and multinational forces under globalization, unlawful seizures of land through the nexus of private capital, builders, and politicians that result in the nation's failure to protect the rights of its citizen, and the vulnerable position of women and dalits, as in the case *Halla Bol*, referenced through a play on the theme of the rape of a dalit girl and through the interrogation of systemic roadblocks in the investigation of a young middle-class woman's murder. In doing so, this cinema speaks to the work undertaken by theatre activists. Having remained a powerful forum of protest since the days on the IPTA, activist theatre acquired a renewed political energy in the 1970s. The betrayals of the political Emergency (1975–7), the escalating dowry murders with little state intervention to alleviate the position of women, the increased reporting of rape in prisons and police custody, and the ongoing oppression of dalits, led to the formation of a number of women's groups, NGOs, and other organizations that turned to theatre as a form of social intervention. Examples include Theatre Union, formed by Anuradha Kapur, Rati Bartholomew, and Maya Rao who presented plays such as *Om Swaha* (Unholy Offering, on dowry deaths) and *Dafa 180* (Legislation 180, on the problem of custodial rape) in parks, neighbourhoods, side-walks, and college campuses.[14] In keeping with this trend, the satirical film *Jaane Bhi Do Yaaro* (1983) made use of theatre to comment on corruption. Yet largely speaking, the dominance of mainstream cinema overshadowed such interventions. The resurgence of political action-oriented theatre in the films discussed in this chapter serves as a reminder of the actual work being undertaken by theatre groups at grassroots levels for mobilizing action and for creating alternative possibilities that involve a range of classes and masses—from students to reformed criminals—for getting involved in struggles against oppressive forces. Thus theatre, in these films, becomes a viable medium for speaking out and as possessing the ability to include a multiplicity of voices. If, as Mishra (2002: 238) argues, Hindi cinema is an ideological apparatus that creates an imagined community in the diaspora with 'shared "structures of feeling" about the "homeland" and produces a transnational sense of communal solidarity', then these films, which traverse diasporic spaces, suggest that forms of theatre that call for an all-encompassing level of popular participation are inclusive of the widest possible political community. In doing so, these films expose viewers to acts of social protest that have the potential to render visible the underbelly of global capitalism, its effects on the displacement of people and their livelihood when their lands are seized under the rubric of 'development' and the corrupt practices of politicians sustained by systemic abuse. On another level, perhaps films such as *Halla Bol* are Bombay cinema's belated tribute to Safdar Hashmi, both through its title, which is evocative of Safdar's Hashmi's play *Halla Bol*, and through its representation of street theatre. Hashmi, a journalist and writer, who ran the theatre group *Janam* was killed on 1 January 1989 during the performance of play outside a factory in Sahibabad, East of Delhi (van Erven 1989: 45). If the latter is the case, then *Halla Bol* (the film) acknowledges the inspirational lessons to be learnt from theatre.

If, as Jaikumar, contends, the 'allusive commentary on the anti-colonial nationalist project and on British imperialism through visualizations of a new civil society' was an important influence on 'Indian film aesthetics in the late colonial era' (p. 196), the commentary on the nation provided through the deployment of theatre in these twenty-first-century films highlights the ways in which the intersections and even compatibility of contemporary national and global forces shape cinema's aesthetic and political meanings. The films introduce spectators to the performances as well as to the interactions between performers and viewers who are exposed to both proscenium style and street theatre through their cinematic apparatus. In *Welcome to Sajjanpur* and *Halla Bol*, the plays directly confront spectators, interact with them, and solicit their participation. In *Aaja Nachle* and *Maan Gaye Mughall-e-Azam*, the invisible fourth wall of the theatre distances the audience from the performance. In doing so, the films provide a window on theatre practices governed by different sets of conventions and the level of spectatorial involvement each is able to achieve as a consequence. These moments in the films are significant mediations and offer an aesthetic of recognition that proposes the social and agentive power of theatre. Here it may be useful to engage with Mishra's discussion of Bollywood cinema that emphasizes the 'transformative political potential' (2002: 20) of theatre. Building on Anuradha Kapur's argument about the formal mediation of Parsi theatre into cinema, Mishra identifies two framing devices that theatre supplied to cinema, both of which are linked to the 'spatial conditions' of the proscenium arch theatres. The first involved the relationship between spectators and the stage, which changed because 'the stage relations set in the proscenium arch were radically different from those of open staging that had existed in "pre-colonial and early colonial India"' (ibid.: 9).

According to Kapur, the 'frontality of the performer vis-à-vis the spectator' (cited in Mishra 2002: 9) generated a voyeuristic and erotic relationship and precluded the action from being seen from other angles as opposed to the multiple viewing angles that a street performance enables. Mishra complicates Kapur's argument by suggesting that the performances in Parsi theatre 'broke the laws of frontality' on two counts. One such device was the 'use of the twice tale, where events happen outside the frame of the theatre' (2002: 9). Use of 'direct communication with the audience in a self-conscious display of the self as well as departures from the letter of the script were other devices,' posits Mishra (2002: 9). Mishra's observations about theatre are astute, yet he affirms that the 'economy of the look and counterlook' enabled by the frontal vision of the proscenium theatre and which forges a complicit bond between spectators and performers, 'continues to govern Bombay Cinema' (2002: 9).

But what happens when actual theatrical performances enter the aesthetic frames of the cinema as opposed to the mere integration of theatrical elements. In the films mentioned in this chapter, we see a breakdown of this complicity as the camera in the proscenium style theatre in *Aaja Nachle* and *Maan Gaye Mughall-e-Azam* brings the stage and the spectators into one space and focuses on the spectators' identification with the efficacy of theatre and the solidarity experienced across the auditorium and between spectators and characters on stage. In so doing, the technology of the film, while breaking down the sanctity of the rules of the proscenium theatre, also exposes the film's audience to the spectators' engagement with the plays. In *Mughall-e-Azam* the theatre viewers' response is reinforced for the cinematic audience when the spectators locate the pleasures of the play (even though the same play is being performed over and over again), in its alteration of the predictable script of the story that introduces new surprises and meanings with each performance. And in *Aaja Nachle*, the camera is carefully manipulated to focus on the reactions of the MP, the opposition, and others members of the community who had initially favoured the tearing down of the theatre and opposed the planned performance.

Reconstructing the Local

It may be concluded with Armand Mattelart's suggestion about approaching the transnational perspective with caution as it bears a colonizing perspective/impulse that reframes local subjects as 'passive receptacles' of the 'norms, values, and signs of transnational power' (cited in Desai 2004: 6). The films discussed in this chapter suggest that far from being 'passive receptacles', locals, through alternative methods of organization, continue to oppose and interrogate corruption, and question policies and practices that are detrimental to the interests and well-being of citizens. To this end, this genre of commercial Hindi cinema becomes a productive site for restoring the importance of local theatrical practices within 'global culture', especially at a time when theatre continues to suffer from shrinking patronage, reduced funding, and spectatorship. Thus even though critics such as Madhava Prasad (2000) see Bollywood cinema as an ideological tool with a hegemonizing impulse, it may be argued that this cinema also functions as an agent of social change with the aid of genres such as theatre, as evident in the films under discussion here.

But as to whether such experimentation absorbs theatre within cinema and makes it invisible for viewers whose expectations have been shaped in the last couple of decades by representations where expensive cars, holidays abroad, cross-border mobility, and anglicized speech patterns are the norm, if the reviews of the films are any indication, then the answer seems to be in the affirmative. The reviews cited below are notable for eliding any substantial commentary on the role and significance of cinema's use of theatre. One review of *Aaja Nachle* remarks:

> *Aaja Nachle* is below the mediocre mark and doesn't meet the humungous expectations that you associate with the Yashraj—Madhuri combo. What's the problem? Without a doubt, the script! What starts off as a story that seems real and identifiable becomes a fairy tale in the latter hour. Also, with a title like *Aaja Nachle* and the story harping on music, the songs had to be chartbusters. That's just not the case here![15]

Another review praises 'the 20-minute grand finale in the form of a play' for the 'spectacle' it provides through its 'lyrics, the music, the performances, the costumes, the colours, the choreography' all of which inspired the 'audience in the theatre' to clap 'after the play'. Yet this praise overlooks the social significance of theatre, and marvels instead at the film's ability to make 'the who's who of the Indian "parallel" cinema' sing and dance and wonders if this is 'becoming a formula at Yash Raj Films'.[16] A review of *Welcome to Sajjanpur* recognizes the political satire in the film but faults it for its 'Dehati accent' which, in the reviewer's opinion, makes it 'sometimes difficult to figure out the jokes'. Instead, it commends the opening song for its 'nice fusion of American country music with Indian classical Instruments'. For these reasons, the reviewer gives the film a low recommendation.[17] Another review, while picking up on the contexts that vary 'from industrialization versus farmers, a well-connected housewife running for election against a quick-witted eunuch (Ravi Jhankal), a superstitious mother (Ila Arun) trying to ward off her tomboyish daughter's (Divya Dutta) manglik status by tying her knot to a manglik mongrel' that are carefully woven into the main storyline, entirely eschews any reference to the theatre scene.[18] A review of *Khosla ka Ghosla*, which applauds the film, asserts that,

> the narrative dips when the middle-class family takes the help of stage actors to free the land. The modus operandi of planting an actor as a Dubai-based entrepreneur holds your attention at the start (Navin Nischol's first scene with Boman Irani is remarkable), but isn't believable in latter portions. In fact, the film gets formulaic in the latter reels as the middle-class family successfully cons the scamster.

Seeing the insertion of theatre as an intrusion, the reviewer, Taran Adarsh, suggests that *Khosla ka Ghosla* 'gets filmy in the latter half, [and] you do feel that writer Jaideep Sahni and director Dibakar Banerjee could've stuck to realism. In fact, the film loses the sparkle towards the middle of the second hour.'[19] And a review of *Maan Gaye Mughall-e-Azam*, which berates the filmmaker Sanjay Chhel for lifting the plot from a Hollywood comedy *To Be or Not to Be* (1942, remade 1983), has the following to offer:

> *Maan Gaye Mughall-e-Azam* offers nothing more than heaps of juvenile humour, some tortuous songs and, most of all, lousy performances by almost everyone in the cast. Rahul Bose looks awkward speaking Hindi and doesn't do much else than fondle Mallika or persuade Paresh throughout the film. Paresh Rawal is not in form this time round. Mallika Sherawat does what she's known for—flash her cleavage, kiss her co-star, and do some booty shakin'. Kay Kay Menon (as the ghazal singer and a double agent) does hold your interest for a while, but his character is soon bumped off.[20]

Such lukewarm responses perhaps stem from a kind of genre-mixing that does not sit well with reviewers trained in Bollywood conventions of realism where the songs, dances, music, and melodramatic displays are predictably incorporated and carefully crafted in a coherent narrative to fulfil viewers' expectations. The insertion of theatre, as a distinct genre, violates such expectations and introduces an innovative framework that enables what Mishra, drawing on Benjamin's notion of a politicized art, calls cinema's 'radical possibilities' (2002: 33). It must be noted that the rhetoric of the performances at times overlaps with dominant nationalist ideas. In *Mughall-e-Azam*, for example, the terrorists are unambiguously Muslim and in *Aaja Nachle*, the case of reviving theatre is made through a vocabulary that evokes an 'authentic' cultural heritage. So the need for a theatre for social change in these two films takes place through a thematic apparatus that resorts to mainstream cultural and communal constructions. Yet the force of performance, especially in *Halla Bol*, *Welcome to Sajjanpur*, and *Khosla ka Ghosla* does draw attention to the work undertaken, for example, by theatre activists in the last two decades, by visionaries such as Hashmi, women's theatre groups such as Theatre Union, Tripurari Sharma's Alirippu, and by the Denotified Tribes in Gujarat through Budhan theatre. In that case, if cinema, as Madhava Prasad points out offers a 'ground for transformative struggles' (2000: 9) and 'contestations *over* the state form' (ibid.), the films under discussion in this chapter suggest that peripheral forms such as theatre are sites where such contestations can take place. And in doing so, they also pose a challenge to what Bhaskar Sarkar identifies as 'Bollywood's hankering for an Oscar nod [which] is couched in terms of its emergent technical sophistication, its overhaul in response to the demands of global capital' through stories that 'produce visions of India that are eminently marketable to western and diasporic audiences' (2008: 39). Most importantly, while demonstrating that theatre and film are mutually constituted and informed, these films become repositories of information about neglected theatrical traditions for transnational audiences, and in so doing, highlight the importance of Hindi cinema in storing information about 'other' cultural traditions that remain undocumented or whose knowledge continues to escape popular attention.

Notes

1. The name of the film is probably inspired by Sarjanpur, near Azamgarh, Uttar Pradesh or Shahajanpur.

2. Harish Trivedi (2008: 206), for example, asserts that 'Given the wide disparity in exchange rates between the Indian rupee and the British pound or the US dollar, even a small audience abroad is as lucrative as a large one at home; a ticket for *Monsoon Wedding* at a theatre in Leicester Square in London sold for 12 pounds sterling, which converted to approximately 1,000 rupees, whereas the most expensive

seat in the poshest Delhi cinema hall sells for 150 rupees. The current calculation is that the rights for foreign distribution of such Hindi films are sold for an amount that equals that for two out of the five 'territories' into which all of India is divided for the purpose of film distribution.'

3. Neelakantan 2006: http://www.himalmag.com/2006/october/special_report. htm; accessed on 20 April 2008.

4. Ibid.

5. On the basis of Sumita S. Chakravarty's ideas about 'commercial' cinema as that which incorporates a range of pleasures (stars, songs, dances) for wider popular appeal.

6. Formed in 1970 by Yash Chopra, Yash Raj Films is considered to be India's biggest film production company since 2006. It also markets its own music label called Yash Raj Music and under Yash Raj Films Home Entertainment produces DVDs, videos, and VCDs. According to a report on http://en.wikipedia.org/wiki/ Yash_Raj_Films, in May 2007, the company tied up with Walt Disney to co-produce animation movies in India. In a 2004 survey of the Biggest Film Distribution companies conducted by the *Hollywood Reporter*, Yash Raj Films was ranked twenty-seven.

7. Jessica Lal was a model who was shot dead in New Delhi at a celebrity party on 29 April 1999. The chief murder suspect, Manu Sharma, was initially acquitted but under intense media and public pressure, the Delhi High Court re-examined the case, found Sharma guilty, and sentenced him to life on 20 December 2006.

8. For details on the IPTA, see Bhatia (2004).

9. I am relying on Rajiv Verma (2005), for this information. The article provides an excellent discussion on the subject.

10. This interest in getting a glimpse of theatre could have been motivated on the one hand by Orientalist curiosity in Indian traditions, On the other hand, it could have been generated by the buzz that theatre was created as an anti-colonial tool since the circulation and banning of *Nil Darpan* (The Indigo Mirror) in 1861. An anti-colonial play against indigo planters in Bengal, *Nil Darpan* attracted the attention of the Press and Parliament in India and in England and was followed by the Dramatic Performances Act in 1876. The censorship legislation was routinely applied across Britain's Indian colony and continued to be implemented in post-colonial times.

11. Priya Jaikumar, however, also counters those arguments that rescue Indian cinema as 'Indian' and says instead that, 'We must abandon the rubric of national cinemas if we are to consider the multiple, conjunctural pressures applied by decolonization on the political entities of an imperial state and its colonies.'

12. If there are any neutral discussions, they are expressed in terms of a comparative aesthetic for theatre and cinema, as in Schulze's reference to Mrs Gokhale, a famous actress of the south Indian stage and one of the first few actresses of Indian cinema, who recalls the following comparison 'between acting on stage in front of an audience with acting in front of a camera' (Schulze 2003: 60)—'Theatre acting is done within norms of restraint. It is symbolic, particularly in love scenes. On the stage you can keep your distance, decide your limit and say that I would go

no further than holding hands (...) But, in a love scene in a film, you have to embrace—really embrace—the other fellow in front of the camera. Otherwise, it would make no sense' (ibid.).

13. Interestingly, many of the films of the 1960s were shown in a realistic idiom as they continued the legacy of filmmakers such as Khwaja Ahmad Abbas, Bimal Roy, and Nitin Bose. Abbas's film *Dharti ke Lal* (1953?) and Bimal Roy's *Do Bigha Zamin*, were both award-winning films (which flopped at the box office) and have become exemplary of Hindi-film realism of the 1950s (Chakravarty 1994: 89). Both Abbas and Roy also came from theatre backgrounds, with Abbas writing and organizing plays such as *Roar China, Four Comrades*, and *Yeh Kiska Khun Hai*, for the IPTA and Roy 'employed and trained by the New Theatres of Calcutta with its tradition of "socially conscious" cinema' (ibid.: 88).

14. For details, see Bhatia (2004).

15. Taran Adarsh, http://entertainment.oneindia.in/bollywood/reviews/2007/aaja-nachle-review-301107.html; accessed on 31 December 2008.

16. 30 November 2007. http://withoutgivingthemovieaway.com/main/review-aaja-nachle/; accessed on 31 December 2008.

17. Welcome to Sajjanpur: http://www.chakpak.com/movie/welcome-to-sajjanpur/19264; accessed on 8 January 2009.

18. Sukanya Verma, 'Worth a trip', http://in.rediff.com/movies/2008/sep/19saj.htm; accessed on 8 January 2009.

19. Taran Adarsh, '*Khosla Ka Ghosla*—Movie Review', http://entertainment.oneindia.in/bollywood/reviews/2006/khosla-ka-ghosla-220906.html; accessed on 8 January 2009.

20. Nikhil Kumar, *Maan Gaye Mughall-E-Azam*: Movie Review, http://www.apunkachoice.com/scoop/bollywood/20080822-4.html; accessed on 8 January 2009.

References

Bhatia, Nandi. 2004. *Acts of Authority/Acts of Resistance: Theatre and Politics in Colonial and Postcolonial India*, Ann Arbor: University of Michigan Press,

Booth, Gregory D. 'Traditional Content and Narrative Structure in the Hindi Commercial Cinema', *Asian Folklore Studies*, vol. 54.

Chakravarty, Sumita S. 1994. *National Identity in Indian Popular Cinema 1947–1987*, Austin: University of Texas Press.

Desai, Jigna. 2004. *Beyond Bollywood: The Cultural Politics of South Asian Film*, New York and London: Routledge.

Gokulsing, K. Moti and Wimal Dissanayake. 2004. *Indian Popular Cinema: A Narrative of Cultural Change*. Stoke-on-Trent, UK: Trentham Books.

Jaikumar, Priya. 2006. *Cinema at the End of Empire: A Politics of Transition in Britain and India*, Durham: Duke University Press.

Kaushal, J.N. 2000. *Sheila Bhatia*. Nai Dilli: Rashtriya Natya Vidyalay (New Delhi: National School of Drama).

Lutze, Lothar. 2009. 'Enacting the Life of Rama. Classical Traditions in Contemporary Religious Folk Theatre of Northern India,' in Nandi Bhatia (ed.), *Modern Indian Theatre. A Reader*, New Delhi: Oxford University Press.

Mathur, J.C. 1977. 'Encounter of the Performing Arts and Modern Mass Media', *Sangeet Natak*, vol. 46.

Mehrotra, Deepti Priya. 2006. *Gulab Bai: The Queen of Nautanki Theatre*. Delhi: Penguin.

Mishra, Vijay. 2002. *Bollywood Cinema: Temples of Desire*, London and New York: Routledge.

Prasad, M. Madhava. 2000. *Ideology of the Hindi Film. A Historical Reconstruction*, New Delhi: Oxford University Press.

Renu, Phanishwar. 'Teesri Kasam, Arthat Maare Gaye Gulfam', *Phanishwar Renu ki Shreshth Kahaniyan*, India: National Book Trust.

Sarkar, Bhaskar. 2008. 'The Melodramas of Globalization', *Cultural Dynamics*, vol. 20, no. 1.

Schulze, Brigitte. 2003. 'The First Cinematic Pauranik Kathanak', in Vasudha Dalmia and Theo Damsteegt (eds), *Narrative Strategies. Essays on South Asian Literature and Film*, New Delhi: Oxford University Press.

Trivedi, Harish. 2008. 'From Bollywood to Hollywood: the Globalization of Hindi Cinema', in Revathi Krishnaswamy and John C. Hawley (eds), *The Postcolonial and the Global*, Minneapolis: University of Minnesota Press.

van Erven, Eugene. 1989. 'Plays, Applause, and Bullets: Safdar Hashmi's Street Theatre', *TDR*, vol. 33, no. 4.

Verma, Rajiva. 2005. 'Shakespeare in Hindi Cinema', in Poonam Trivedi and Dennis Bartholomeusz (eds), *India's Shakespeare: Translation, Interpretation, and Performance*, Newark: University of Delaware Press.

Vohra, P. 2008. 'Astronomical Figures', *Outlook*, 13 May.

FILMS

Banerjee, Dibakar (Director). *Khosla ka Ghosla*, India, 2006.

Bhattacharya, Basu (Director). *Teesri Kasam*, India, 1966.

Benegal, Shyam (Director), *Welcome to Sajjanpur*, India, 2008.

Chhel, Sanjay (Director). *Maan Gaye Mughall-e-Azam*, India, 2008.

Devgan, Ajay (Director). *U, Me Aur Hum*, India, 2008.

Ivory, James and Ismael Merchant (Director-Producer). *Shakespeare Wallah*, UK, 1965.

Mehta, Anil (Director). *Aaja Nachle*, India, 2007.

Santoshi, Rajkumar, (Director). *Halla Bol*, India, 2008.

Shah, Kundar (Director). *Jaane Bhi Do Yaaro*, India, 1983.

Part 5

13 Diasporic Bollywood

In the Tracks of a Twice-displaced Community

MANAS RAY

The chapter examines the process of imagining into existence a sense of nationhood by a specific diaspora of Indian origin (namely, the Fiji Indians) in Australia and the role that Bollywood—in its different manifestations—plays in this.[1] The focus of the chapter is to understand how mass images of India can be made to speak and/or represent history far outside the geographical limits of India and the place of viewers in that history. For this, two separate but related journeys are brought together: one, the cultural trajectory of this twice-displaced people—from indenture to subsistence farming to their participation in urbanization of Fiji, and finally, the coup of 1987 that resulted in a big exodus to Western cities and placed the struggle for cultural identity in a new vortex of power; two, this journey is interlaced with another, that of the images of Bollywood over the decades and how it impacted lives far beyond the shores of India. Here we celebrate not so much the ontological condition of the diasporic imagination but focus on the contingent course of historical subjectivity of this twice-displaced community, a course that has vital links to the changing political economy of Bollywood, its images and image-making over the years. The diasporic media needs to be seen in the context of the politics of its production and dissemination. This is particularly so with Bollywood, which from its inception has situated itself in the locus of contending definitions of 'Indianness' (Rajadhyaksha and Willemen 1999: 10).

Different Diasporic Indias

By no means does the chapter seek to analyse the media use of *the* 'Indian' diaspora seen as one monolithic whole. In fact, it is the globality of such a concept that needs be contested and read as a sign of ahistoricity and ethnocentrism that so often underwrites the perception of postcolonial societies. This is not to deny that the different Indian diasporas do deploy their notions of 'India' as the broad symbolic horizon for constructing their respective identities. Neither is it to underestimate the crucial role that such pan-'Indianness' (largely derived from Orientalist discourse about India) played in imagining a nation into existence during the course of struggle against colonial rule and continues to do so long after the Raj. It is however to highlight the fact that for Indians (both inside India and outside) such 'Indianness'—like any other identity concept—is always already fissured. As a matter of *positioning* and not essence, this 'Indianness', which varies with different communities, is used at times for contradictory purposes and quite often gives rise to unintended consequences. It may be argued that the different empirical factors like language, region, or religion do not by themselves hold the key to cultural difference. It is the positioning of communities in postcolonial space that underpins the cultural lives of different Indian diasporas and sets the course for possible futures.

In an era of global spread of corporate capital and great demographic shifts, one of the key projects of political modernity is faced with serious crisis: instead of the 'nationalization of the ethnic' that Western nation-states banked their hopes on, we now face the opposite scenario, 'the ethnicization of the nation' (Žižek 1997). As a result, the notion of shared public space is increasingly challenged by a crisscross of different primordias tied together by the universal function of the market—what has been termed 'public sphericules' (Cunningham and Sinclair 2000).

For the Fiji Indians, if it was legislated racial discrimination that compelled them to leave Fiji, in Australia they find themselves in the middle of a new entanglement of different, contesting imaginings of 'roots'. In

Australia, they met with Indians from the mainland en masse for the first time. Over a century in Fiji, their romantic construction of India (and Indians) was derived initially from the different folk renderings of the Ramayana and then most significantly from the movies. This construction faced the rude shock of caste discrimination in their interactions with 'compatriot' Indians. Migration to Australia from mainland India has mostly been of the professional category. The social composition of India being what it is, this also means that the Indian representation in Australia is largely from the upper castes, many of whom are unwilling to give up their historical memory of unquestioned superiority vis-à-vis the lower castes. This has resulted in a change of focus of cultural antagonism of Fiji-Indians. Mainland Indians now constitute an *other* for this community, just as the ethnic Fijians did back in Fiji.

One of the results of this process is that Bollywood is taking new significance in their lives. Historically, the bond between them and India has been one of imagination. With time as memory of 'roots'—the *real* India—was fading away, films took over the responsibility of constructing an empty, many-coloured space through its never-ending web of images, songs, 'dialogues', and stars. In the new political context of Australia, this empty space would be shorn of even the pretence of a referent—it is space unto itself, a *pure* space so to say. Bollywood reciprocates this gesture by placing the diasporic *imaginaire* at the very heart of its new aesthetics.

Indenture and Beyond

The Fiji Islands was declared a British colony in 1874 when a group of indigenous 'chiefs' signed a Deed of Cession with the British. Five years later, the first Indian-indentured labourers arrived in the coolie ships from India, the labour for the sugar plantations and other enterprises that would make the new colony pay without exposing the indigenous population to the harmful consequences of an industrial economy (Kelly 1991; Jayawardena 1980). From 1903, they would be joined by new recruits from south India, who came through the *kangani* system—that is, the village-head corralled his village people and took them to the colony. By the end of indenture in 1919, about 60,965 Indians came to Fiji as indentured labourers, of which 23 per cent were from the south (see Mishra 1979 and Lal 1983). They called themselves *girmitiya*s (from the English word 'agreement', a reference to the labour contract). The British called them 'coolies', so did the indigenous Fijians (the word has an interesting twist, since the word for dog in Fijian language is similar: *kuli*). The lingua franca that developed among Fiji Indians (known as Fiji Hindi or Fiji Buli) reflects many different dialects of north India, though mostly Bhojpuri, with occasional European and Fijian words. In their new destination, the south Indians were moved around and scattered in different plantations and as such they had to adjust to the lingua franca. The Gujaratis first came in large numbers in 1920s and 1930s as shopkeepers, moneylenders, artisans, *sonars* (goldsmiths), and in numerous other trades and services. There were occupational as well as residential differentiations. Mostly they lived in urban areas with little social interaction with the rest of the Indian community. Utilizing the discipline of the 'lines', the Indians in Fiji, in course of time, have made much of what today's Fiji is—economically speaking—with their labour and management. This is a huge achievement given the way they began their journey. By 1986, the Indian population was in majority in Fiji (3,48,704 as against 3,29,305 ethnic Fijians) (Lal 1992: 337) and the country's economy was based on Indian management and labour.[2]

Unlike mainland India, Fiji was governed by British Common Law with no room for separate laws for different religious communities. However, this did not mean that for Fiji Indians the social system of Indian villages which reinforces compliance with accepted rituals gave way to the impersonality of a secular order. This could not have happened, given the built-in conditions of inequality of a plantation regime. For the indentured population, re-creating 'motherland' in its social, cultural, and religious manifestations became part of their wider political struggle. The culture that evolved, the fashioning of 'little India' as it is called, was not so much an expression of the desire to return, or idle nostalgia, nor a docile willingness to replay on a minor scale a mammoth original. Rather it was as an active attempt to yoke an identity in the face of little or no recognition as cultural or political beings.

Jayawardena observes that the complete proletarianization of Indians in Guyana meant near total loss of home traditions while the Fiji Indians could maintain cultural traditions because of isolated subsistence farming post-indenture (1980: 436). With time, the population become more scattered and professions diversified. This re-emphasized the need to preserve their culture and religion in order to provide support and solidarity among themselves. Culturally speaking, the passage from indenture to post-indenture can be seen as one of 'amnesiac recollection' to an active bid to construct a 'national memory' (Kelly 1998: 880). And what initially had provided fodder to the construction of national memory (in spite of its many divides like north Indians versus those who came from the south, Hindus versus Muslims, Gujratis vis-à-vis the rest) were the folk traditions of north India and particularly, the ancient epic Ramayana (or better, the popular version composed by Tulsi Das in the sixteenth-century *Ramcharitmanas*). This epic, along with other cultural expressions of the Bhakti movement, not only provided the cultural and moral sustenance to the community, in the very process of doing so, it also paved the way for the overwhelming popularity of Hindi popular cinema amongst Fiji Indians.

From the Ramayana to Bollywood

Unlike India, in indenture Fiji, there was no class of gentry to put through a nationalist sieve the various cultural forms that emerged in the encounter with colonial modernity and selectively adopt and combine the reconstituted elements of the supposedly indigenous tradition.[3] In the absence of any philosophical tradition, what prevailed at the beginning was the reminiscences of numerous local cultural traditions of the villages of India. The traditions of village India that survived were basically derived from bhakti; the bhajans (devotional songs) of such composers like Kabir, Mira, and Sur Das. But over and above anything else, what inspired their imagination was Tulsi *Ramcharitmanas*. Very early on, reciting, singing and enactment of the Ramayana was revived amongst the Indians of Fiji. This bound together a *cultural* community to brave the chains of bondage in the fissiparous environment of plantation capitalism where every one was an individual unit of production and daily existence was measured by work hours.

The Ramayana was shorn of deeper philosophical meanings. Its primary function was to serve emotional satisfaction and not individual spiritual enlightenment. The reasons for an overwhelming emotional identification with the epic is directly related to the predicament of an indentured diaspora. Ram was banished for fourteen years. For Fiji Indians, it was for at least five years. Ram's banishment was for no fault of his; similarly, it was not the fault of the Indians that they were extracted from their homeland and subjected to inhuman physical labour in this remote island (Lal 1998). The triumphant ending of all ordeals provided a kind of moral strength to withstand the brutalities of indenture. If Ram could survive for fourteen years, surely the Fiji Indians could do so for five years. The Ramayana thus was used to heal the wounds of indenture and provide a cultural and moral texture in the new settlement.

There is another reason for this strong identification and this involves the question of woman and sexual virtue. Throughout the phase of indenture and even later, the paucity of women vis-à-vis men was one of the primary social concerns among the girmitiyas. In a situation where many men lived without wives of their own, women were expected to serve two contradictory functions: they were at times forced by circumstances and even by violence to leave one man for another while the pressure was on them to comply with the standards of a good, chaste woman (Kelly 1991: chapter 9).

Hence, one of the central moral thematic of Hindi cinema, namely, the image of the devoted wife, the heroine struggling to be chaste, had a special appeal to the Fiji Indians, given the peculiar existential circumstances of indenture. A strong emotional identification with the Ramayana and other expressions of the Bhakti movement, a constrained cultural environment, continued degradation at the hands of the racist white regime, a disdain for the culture of the ethnic Fijians, a less hard-pressed post-indenture life, and finally, a deep-rooted need of a dynamic, discursive site for the imaginative re-construction of motherland: all of these factors together ensured the popularity of Hindi films once they began reaching the shores of Fiji. This was because Hindi film deployed the Ramayana extensively, providing the right pragmatics for 'continual mythification' of home.

The two Indian epics—Ramayana and Mahabharata—helped Bollywood fuse the history of the nation and the history of the family. In the Indian narrative tradition, family history is not strictly demarcated from social history. In the Mahabharata, the battle between the Kauravas and the Pandavas, two branches of the same family, engages vast social, political, and cosmic forces, all of which are then sought to be compressed within a single philosophical framework; in the Ramayana, Ram's relationship with Sita is largely determined by his obligation to his family and, more importantly, his social dharma.

Of the two epics, the Ramayana is again privileged because of its elaborations of the familial self and the focus on the duties and sufferings of *sati*—the chaste wife. Also to be taken into account is the fact that in north India, Ramayana's popularity far exceeds that of Mahabharata. The usual character stereotypes of Hindi films—the suffering but faithful wife (Sita) who is also a loving and somewhat indulgent sister-in-law; courageous, dutiful, and detached husband (Ram); the faithful brother (Lakshman) and the vengeful, evil villain (Ravan)—are mostly drawn from the Ramayana. Bollywood would experiment with these role models, bring in other stereotypes (like that of the frolicsome Krishna of the Radha-Krishna bhakti motif, popular in eastern India; or that of *dosti*—the friendship between two adult males which will be posited against heterosexual love for creating emotionally charged moments in the narrative). But never would Bollywood transgress the moral limits of the Ramayana.

Vijay Mishra (1985; 1992) points to the various underlying drives structuring the epics, invoking mythic figures from the epics as the substratum from which various Bollywood character-types emerge. The traffic between the epics and Bollywood is, however, complicated by the role of music and romance. Music functions to transform the epic narratives by foregrounding a romantic repertoire. Romance is absolutely crucial for Bollywood; it is defined by romance. Here Bollywood draws more from the Radha-Krishna trope (of love, desire, and erotica) of bhakti than it does from the epics. Bollywood, operating within the moral and social limits of the epics, extends its narrative scope by negotiating with other folk and emerging popular traditions.

Hindi cinema established its traffic to Fiji in the late 1930s. By then the period of indenture was over, the Indian community as independent cultivators had lost the solidarity that characterized life on 'the lines' of indenture and linguistic and religious identities were differentiating. Hindi cinema's primary impact in Fiji was to bond through meta-narratives with which all the different groups of Fiji Indians could identify. In this cinema, the Fiji Indians found the liveliest expression of their yearning for roots and bid to reconstruct an imagined homeland culture in an alien surrounding—at once simplified, quotidian, and concrete, but with a long tradition. And since in Hindi films 'nation' is imagined in familial terms, the physical distance between mainland India and Fiji did not interrupt this 'work of imagination'. Evidently, the folk traditions borrowed from the villages of India did not come in the way of Hindi cinema's popularity; on the contrary, by simplifying these traditions in a remote island with very little scope for other kinds of cultural traffic, the folk culture actually prepared the way for the unprecedented popularity of this quasi-globalizing mass culture.

As Fiji started urbanizing, the local Indian village cultures began to recede in influence, at least in the public cultural spaces of the cities. Once in place, Bollywood created its own public and psychic platform for people to interact.[4] The gossip columns, the twenty-four-hour Hindi service, the occasional visits of singers and stars from the then Bombay—all this went into constituting the culture of a community which harboured no illusion of return but for reasons of identity and cultural make-up, yearned for a romanticized version of India that Bollywood amply provided. The genealogy of unprecedented popularity of the mass cultural tradition of Bollywood in Fiji thus lies in the diasporic rediscovery of 'little' traditions that the girmitiyas brought with them and preserved over a century.

The cult of Bollywood that the Fiji Indians *re-produced* in Fiji is not a case of mimicry, since *repetition* is inscribed in the very being of Bollywood (Appadurai 1998). Once Bollywood is made the mainstay of cultural life (which to a very large extent is the case with Fiji Indians), it of necessity repeats its entire cultural ecology—its 'insiderism' (Rajadhyaksha and Willemen 1999: 10). This 'insiderism' constructs a sense of mythological nationhood with very tenuous links with the *actual* geography of a nation. Hence, living in the realities of Fiji and participating in the life of Bollywood is not a case of split existence, since such a split is postulated on a divide between the real and the imagined, something that Bollywood disavows.

Fiji Indian Cultural Ecology in Australia

Despite the recency of their arrival in Australia and the structural deficits they face in employment, the Fiji Indians have re-established themselves with a cultural dynamism that is out of all proportion to their numbers and which can be sourced to their embrace of the cultural repertoire proffered by Bollywood.

In Sydney, the professional Fiji Indians are scattered all over the city while those in blue collar jobs tend to concentrate in one or two regions.

In the immediate years after the coup, they concentrated in the Campsie region of Sydney. Latterly, Liverpool and to some extent Bankstown are the two suburbs where a majority of the working class Fiji Indians have moved. All these suburbs, with a number of big Indo-Fijian grocery shops, garment houses, movie hall, auditoriums, and night clubs, have emerged as different nodes of Fiji Indian cultural life, complete with beauty contests (where participants come from all over Australia, New Zealand, and Fiji), bands specializing in Hindi film music, music schools for 'filmy' songs, DJs, karaoke singers, film magazines, and community radio programmes. A number of Fiji Indian singers of Sydney have brought out several CDs in India. These are mostly popular Hindi movie songs and a couple of ghazals (light classical north Indian music that had its roots in the Mughal courts).

Brisbane's Bollywood cultural life, very much like in Sydney, is mostly a Fiji Indian affair. It has one regular band, Sargam, but relies on Sydney bands for major occasions. There are no night clubs and no established tradition of karaoke. Public performances, far less in number compared to Sydney, are hosted in rented auditoria. Like other Indian communities, for the Fiji Indians of Brisbane the relation to Bollywood is mostly restricted to renting Hindi videos, though as a community they are undoubtedly the highest consumers. The reason for Brisbane's lack of a public face for Bollywood culture is partly due to the composition of the Indian community with a preponderance of the professional class. But primarily it is a factor of size. With a population of less than 10,000, the Fiji Indian community does not have the resources to support an ongoing Bollywood cultural economy, that is, the required cultural mass. And, with migration having dwindled to barely a few hundred every year, there is no sign that the Fiji Indian presence in Brisbane will increase substantially.

Intercommunal Discord and Cultural Assertion

The ethnic, caste, and class differences between mainland Indians and Fiji Indians have given rise to intracommunal tensions and rivalries which are neither new nor restricted only to Australia.[5] Many mainland Indians exhibit deeply entrenched casteist attitudes and view the indentured past of the Fiji Indians as a non-negotiable barrier. On the other side, Fiji Indians often characterize mainland Indians with the same kind of negative attributes that they were wont to use for ethnic Fijians. Both realize the need for a united front to deal with Australian racism but both view each other as an obstacle to better acceptance by the 'white nation'.

Such rivalry between the two communities has seen the re-assertion of culture and ethnicity by Fiji Indians. This involves a positive mobilization of indenture history and an emphasis on a Hindu way of life in a Western context that bears similarities to Gillespie's account of self-construction of identity through the positive assertion of ethnicity (1995: 8–11). The dominant racism of white Australia, the ostracization by mainland Indians, the need of the older generation for a platform to socialize and to reflect (which will also function as a moral regime for younger people) have together fed in to a resurgence of religion and revival of folk traditions, neglected in today's urban Fiji.

One of the most creative methods of adaptation is the assertive construction of a cultural community around Ramayana *katha* and *bhajan mandalis* (small gatherings for devotional songs), which paved the way for Bollywood's popularity. For the last couple of decades, these traditions were mostly on the decline in urban Fiji. Once in Australia, these have regained their popularity as a platform to unite the community and act as a moral regime for young people.

Significantly enough, in Hindu religious traditions, devotion and erotica are rarely separate departments of life and one very often evokes the other. This is particularly so with the bhakti tradition from which Tulsi Das's *Ramcharitmanas* emanates. In the bhakti taxonomy, shringar—the erotic bond between the devotee (a woman) and the deity (a man)—is the highest form of devotion. In one of the forms of shringar, the female denies herself, her family, all bonds and social constrictions, and pursues the love of Krishna. Radha is the epitome of this love and devotion. The trope of Radha and Krishna puts together social transgression, erotica, and devotion. As the supreme expression of desire and pathos, it has for centuries provided inspiration for bhajans. It has also served Bollywood as a source of much of its music, narrative, and allegory. This means that cultural and religious assertion of tradition has not been in opposition to Bollywood; in fact, in a Western diasporic context, it provides young Fiji Indians with the cultural capital to really appreciate Bollywood.

The Fiji Indians, with a long tradition of attachment to bhajan and other devotional songs, have been influenced by the boom in classically-oriented devotional music market in India. For more than a century, Fiji Indians were used to singing the Bhojpuri style of bhajan called *tambura* bhajan. Now this is changing. Coming in contact with mainland Indians has not only meant digging up casteist and indenture memories; it has, more positively, opened new possibilities for creative expressions by exposing the community to the wider world of Indian music and dance. There are many more Indian dance and music (especially, classical) schools in Sydney than was the case in Fiji. The result has been quick to materialize: from receivers of Indian cultural artifacts, the community has become a producer.

Fiji Indian Youth Culture and Post-Zee Bollywood

The most dynamic aspect of Fiji Indian youth culture centres on the use of Bollywood to negotiate a kind of parallel cultural platform to the dominant Western pop culture. This can be understood through grasping the enormous changes that Bollywood itself has undergone in recent years, especially since the early 1990s. D.J. Akash of Sydney explains the implication of such music for young diasporic Indians in following terms:

> Fifteen or twenty years back a young Indian would listen to his music in a very low volume. He would consider his music to be very 'tacky' and would have felt awkward to play it publicly in a Western context. The contemporary Bollywood music, by blending Indian melody with Western beats, has changed all this. Nowadays if you go down the streets of Sydney very often you will hear Indian music blasting. Young people no longer consider Bollywood songs as curry music. It no longer sounds strange to the average Westerner.

Arguably because of this hybridization of Bollywood music, it manages to signify something special to the diasporic young Indians. Asked about the continued influence of Bollywood music, a young Fiji Indian performed this analysis:

> Bollywood has got the potential. It has got feeling. When you are happy you have something to sing, in love you sing, when you are sad you sing. You can relate to it. Consider the recent hit, *Dil To Pagaal Hai* (My Heart Has Gone Wild). It is about love and affection with which a young person can immediately identify. All those who are in love would buy the CD for their girlfriends; they would send requests to the radio channel for the song to be played. We relate to it in two ways: (i) visual part, that is, what the main guy and main girl did in the movie, and (ii) the meaning of the lyric. Compared to this, Hollywood music

hardly has any message that we can relate to. Take *Men in Black* for instance. We could barely identify with the hit score. The messages of Bollywood with which we are brought up hardly get conveyed to us there. There is nothing of our own in such music.

Fiji Indian young people use a wholly hybridized genre like the re-mixes to fashion a discourse of authenticity. On the one hand, they will deploy the re-mixes as part of syncretic metropolitan culture and thus break out of the cartography that views their culture as *ethnic*. On the other hand, they perceive these re-mixes (for them, an essentially diasporic phenomenon) as part of their attempt to promote Indian popular music by making it contemporary; this they will compare to the Indian night-club crowd which, according to them, is hooked on unadulterated Western hard rock and heavy metal. A Fiji Indian enthusiast of 'Indi-pop' describes her experience in terms that converge being 'Western' and being 'Indian': as a Westerner, she prefers Indi-pop to traditional Indian popular music (which for her is 'a bit too romantic and at times unacceptably melodramatic'); she is also 'far more of an Eastern person' vis-à-vis her Mumbai counterpart:

> When I went to India, I found that kids are not thrilled with re-mixes. To be honest, I got the impression that they are quite wary of this kind of experiments; they think that it is corrupting the original music scores. On the other hand, I found night clubs in Bombay (*sic*) are more influenced by Hollywood than Bollywood. I was shocked to find many Indian girls dancing to heavy metal and hard rock. This is pretty aggressive by Indian standards. I haven't seen any girl of Indian origin doing that sort of dance in Sydney .... Kids in Bombay go to night clubs to become Western. Here we go to assert our Eastern identity. The basic difference lies there.

Apart from re-mixes of popular scores, *bhangra* as a dance beat serves an important role in the deployment of Indian popular music for the purpose of being 'agreeably different' in a Western context. Fiji Indians were not exposed to bhangra in Fiji. But in the last fifteen years, it has gained great popularity amongst the young Fiji Indians of Australia. In recent years, on every Wednesday night, Sydney community radio 2 SER plays bhangra-pop. Bhangra did not come to Australia from India; rather, it came from London. In fact, it can be well argued that the popularity of bhangra-pop in India with the rise of such stars as Daler Mehendi is very much a case of the diaspora reworking the homeland.

Diasporizing Bollywood

Bollywood has not only coped with the challenges of globalization but taken advantage of the new situation by enlarging its terrain. This it has achieved by creating a spectatorship aware of the specific requirements of the diasporas, as well as those living in India. A globalizing world of communication and capital flow, instead of imposing a hegemonic cultural world order, has triggered a politics of space whereby the diasporas of a particular community dispersed over the world are networked to the homeland culture to such an extent that the traditional divide of outside/inside loses much of its analytical purchase. In contemporary Bollywood, it is interesting to see how the inscription of the citizen consumer, its ideal contemporary spectator, has offered spaces for assertion of identity for Bollywood's diasporic clientele vis-à-vis the host culture and in the case of Fiji Indians, with the mainland Indian communities as well.

Since the emergence of the super genre of the 'social' (see Prasad 1998: chapter 2) in the 1960s, Bollywood underwent its next major change in the late 1980s to early 1990s coping with the tides of globalization. Earlier, Bollywood was not governed by consideration of community 'out there'; community was securely at home. Hence, representations of abroad could only take the form of the travelogue. For instance, towards the latter part of the super-hit *Sangam* (1964), the couple go on an exotic tourist album honeymoon trip to the West. The exotic locales of such narratives provided not only visual pleasure but constructed a site for marking self's absolute difference from the *other* (one that lies outside the imagined boundaries of home). As compared to this, the diasporic Indian (popularly known as the non-resident Indian [NRI]) is now very much part of contemporary Bollywood address. In the new troping of the home and the world, those who are brought up outside India have *India* inside them very much as the *West* is inscribed in the heart of India. This enmeshing of identities has enabled Bollywood to address the moral and cultural alienation that diasporic youth feel with Hindi films made on 'standard formula', while it also offers them the difference they want vis-à-vis Hollywood.

With consumption acquiring a different inscription, recent Bollywood has offered for its diasporic youth clientele a trajectory of 'Western-style' glamour, wealth, and liberty, but on its own terms. Bollywood manages the ensuing alienation with the mass audience of

India by the sheer strength of its vast repertoire, which even now has a large space for films of the earlier eras. For the new Bollywood too, it is not as if though it merely mimics Hollywood. Rather, the semiotics of exchange with Hollywood has in recent years taken an interesting turn.[6] The biggest hit in recent years, *Kuch Kuch Hota Hai* (1998), for instance, completes this India/West circuit by not venturing to go abroad at all; instead, it creates a virtual 'West' within the bounds of India. In fact, in terms of mise-èn-scene, the film has internalized the West into India to the extent that it does not even have to announce that it is the West. Thematically, once the tomboy character of the heroine (played by the mega-star, Kajol) is established, the rest of the narrative concentrates on bringing to the fore her femininity. The framing of the woman as powerless, and above all a wife and a mother, and at the same time, allowing her a certain space, a freedom for the pleasure of her subsequent disciplining, has been the general narrative-ethical guideline since the early days of the 'social' in the 1950s. *Kuch Kuch Hota Hai* does not alter the terms of what one might call the 'Sita' trope, but pushes it to accommodate a decisively urbanized, globalized (basketball playing, baseball cap wearing) female prototype; neither is her subsequent realization of a more feminized 'Indian' self jarring to her earlier posturing. In fact, such realization will only act to make her a more holistic woman. In a similar vein, the other female protagonist of the film, the Oxford-returned, guitar-strumming girl (played by Rani Mukherjee), who can also quickly switch on to singing Hindu religious hymns—and to whom the hero gets married but who dies in childbirth—is not a 'vamp from the West' (as earlier films of similar narrative would almost certainly portray her to be) but a nice, pleasant woman who happens to wear Westernized clothes in a sexualized sense. This then would be internalized in the Indian imaginary as not someone who *represents* the West (since 'West' is very much in India) but simply as someone who has lived in the West.

Bollywood representation establishes 'India' community as a national but global community. To ritually assert, as Bollywood characters often do, that one is part of such an ideal community, it is important that one knows what one is part of. This involves returning to India and seeking sanctions from the original patriarchal order. *Dilwale Dulhania Le Jayenge* is a remarkable instance of such re-working of traditional patriarchal moral scheme. The film begins with the memorable montage of the heroine's father (acted by Amrish Puri) as a Punjabi farmer, straddling past the mustard fields of Punjab; then through dissolve, he is seen journeying past the Big Ben and Westminister (wearing his Punjabi *ajkan*), and finally feeding grains to the pigeons in the city square of London and remembering ancestral Punjab in a voice deeply laden with nostalgia. In the film, Puri is the epitome of a *darshanic* figure, bestowing sanction within the orbit of his *darshan*. The narrative then moves from the domestic space of the heroine in London to the continent with the couple, and finally reaches rural Punjab, where the heroine (acted by Kajol) is supposed to have an arranged marriage with a local boy. Once the couple reaches rural Punjab, the film changes gear and becomes unusually slow. The gaze is fixed on the nitty gritty of the marriage rituals, staged in a static, ornate fashion. The point of view is that of the hero, who witnesses the preparations but from a remove. It is important that the occasion is not contested since the pleasure lies in its staging. The spectatorship at this point is clearly diasporic.

The action takes place at the very end of the film, when the heroine's father throws the hero out of his house and the proposed son-in-law starts beating the hero in a typical vendetta fashion. The hero does nothing to defend himself but once his father is hit by one of the men of the heroine's father, plunges into action and manifests aggression to defend his father. It is at this point that the heroine's father gives sanction to the hero: defending the father means by logic of mirroring defending the future father-in-law, or in a broader sense, the father principle, being the originating source of authority. It is interesting for the elaborate carnival of identity where there is a kind of secret strategy to hold it at bay until one can actualize it on one's own terms, on terms of that freedom that the West has given but which needs to be ratified in the ancestral home. As a form, it has been clearly invented by contemporary Bollywood and has of late been repeatedly deployed as a major device to bring the West and the East in one place. It is also a ploy to re-inscribe the narrative space firmly within the darshanic orbit and very much like in old Bollywood, the climax comes in the form of defending the darshanic object.

Conclusion

This chapter shows how negotiation with the 'culture of the motherland' became for the Fiji Indian community part of a much broader question of negotiation with (post) indenture definition of the self. Needless to mention, this negotiation could not remain the same from the early days of 'extraction' and the physically arduous schedule of indenture through post-indenture life of subsistence agriculture, diversification of occupation, and differentiation of the community to enter into a Western context of late modern times with the option of 'multiplicity of forms of life and conscious adoption of lifestyles' (Dean 1996: 213).

The situation has been made more complex by the recent changes in the Western landscape of the 'social'. Here I go by the definition of the *social* provided by Nicholas Rose: a large abstract terrain of collective experience, the sum of bonds and relations between individuals and events within a more or less bounded territory governed by its own laws. Rose argues that ever since global capital attained prominence, the *social* in the West has been undergoing a transmutation in favour of the *community*—not one but a series of communities with different aims and constituencies but nonetheless basically constituted of self-monitoring, self-governing subjects (Rose 1996). However, the norms of such particularized communities of the contemporary West can barely negotiate with the religio-civilizational norms of the 'narrative communities' of a postcolonial formation. In the vortex of power and positionalities of the multicultural West, every ethnic community *owns* an identity (see Rouse, 1991, 1995). As an ethnic community, the Fiji Indians are attracted to new forms of association and intimacy of the West but written in this attraction also is the sign of resistance. Together, they feed a sense of imagined nationhood kept alive by continuously transforming and reconstructing its constitutive myths. Bollywood, as it caters to the changing market patterns of home and abroad, serves this dual purpose extraordinarily well.

The literature of transnationality is not known for its interest in investigating the different histories of postcolonial dynamics 'back home' as they manifest in the 'new imaginings and politics of community'. Rather, its main concern is to write diaspora as an enigmatic excess and privilege the aleatory nature of diasporic temporalities: the *true* people are the liminal people. It may be argued that what Bhabha does is to route the experience of the South Asian intellectual-in-exile through the discourse of black counter-hegemonic culture. This intellectual-in-exile syndrome, however, occupies only a minor part in the South Asian diaspora in general. This is not to say that the South Asians escape the problem of 'othering' in the West, nor it is to suggest that they would like to give up their own identities and become 'assimilated' in the dominant cultural order without a trace of difference. Perhaps a change of emphasis is in order here. Rather than celebrating the master narrative of diaspora as a 'slipzone' of indeterminacy and shifting positionalities, one focuses on the South Asian diaspora's widely agreed ability to *re-create* their cultures in diverse locations and locates the element of the liminal within the nitty gritty of this changing history. Scholars have often counterposed the reality of hybridity against the *illusion* of 'nameable groups' (see, for instance, Kelly 1998; Geschiere and Meyer 1998). This understanding may however somewhat be revised, and hybridity may be explained instead as the *nameable* held under the sign of erasure. The shift is one of emphasis.

Notes

1. Earlier and longer versions of this chapter came in *The Media of Diaspora*, Karim H. Karim (ed.) (Routledge, New York, 2003) and *City Flicks*, John Davis (ed.) (Seagull, Calcutta, 2004).

2. John Davies, a Canadian commentator on Fiji's latest crisis of 2000, describes it as a tragedy of 'separate solitudes'. Nothing could be more apt. He holds the Fiji Indians squarely responsible for this absence of cultural dialogue: their condescending attitude towards Fijians, their consumerist ways, economic domination, and media power. The culture of indigenous people needs to be safeguarded from the globally massive Indian culture, he warns. Towards this he advocates a series of positive discriminations, including the abolition of Hindi from the list of Fiji's official languages (Davies 2000). Davies' analysis is off track in crucial ways since the latest crisis is a fall out of disintegrating native Fijian social order and the rise of its middle-class leadership as has been argued by several scholars (Brij Lal 2000, Teresia Teaiwa 2000 among others). Some of the insights I derived from talking to Brij Lal have been incorporated in the chapter.

3. Partha Chatterjee discusses this process in detail in the context of nineteenth-century Bengal. See Chatterjee (1993).

4. For a very innovative discussion of the fantasy space that cinema and theatre creates in urban Nigeria, see Brian Larkin (1998).

5. For an early account of such communal discord Fiji Indians and mainland Indians in Vancouver, see Buchignani (1980).

6. I thank Ravi Vasudevan for an insightful discussion of textual strategies of what I call 'diasporic Bollywood'.

References

Appadurai, Arjun. 1998. 'The Politics of Repetition: Notes on the Reception of Indian Hit Films', Workshop on Media and Mediation in the Politics of Culture, Centre for Studies in Social Sciences, International Globalization Network, Calcutta, March, pp. 4–7.

Bhabha, Homi. 1994. *The Location of Culture*, London and New York: Routledge.

Buchignani, Norman. 1980. 'The Social and Self-identities of Fijian Indians in Vancouver', *Urban Anthropology*, vol. 9, no. 1.

Chatterjee, Partha. 1993. *The Nation and its Fragments: Colonial and Postcolonial Histories*, Princeton: Princeton University Press.

Cunningham, Stuart and John Sinclair (eds). 2000. *Floating Lives: The Media and Asian Diasporas*, St Lucia Queensland: University of Queensland Press.

Davis, John (ed.). 2004. *City Flicks*, Calcutta: Seagull.

Davis, John. 2000. 'On the sources of interethnic conflict in Fiji', *Peace Initiatives*, vol. VI, no. 1–3.

Dean, Michelle. 1996. 'Foucault, Government and the Enfolding of Authority' in Andrew Barry, Thomas Osborne, and Nikolas Rose (eds), *Foucault and Political Reason: Liberalism, Neo-Liberalism and Rationalities of Government*, Chicago: University of Chicago Press, pp. 209–29.

Geschiere, Peter and Birgit Meyer. 1998. 'Globalization and Identity: Dialectics of Flow and Closure', *Development and Change*, vol. 29, pp. 601–15.

Gillespie, M. 1995. *Television Ethnicity and Cultural Change*, London: Routledge.

Haq, Rupa. 1997. 'Asian Kool? Bhangra and beyond', in Sanjay Sharma and John Hutnyk (eds), *Dis-Orienting Rhythms: The Politics of the New South Asian Dance Music*, London: Zed Books.

Jayawardena, Chandra. 1980. 'Culture and Ethnicity in Guyana and Fiji', *Man*, no. 26.

Karim, Karim H. (ed.). 2003. *The Media of Diaspora*, New York: Routledge.

Kelly, John. 1991. *A Politics of Virtue: Hinduism, Sexuality, and Countercolonial Discourse in Fiji*, Chicago: University of Chicago Press.

—————. 1998. 'Time and the Global: against the Homogeneous, Empty Communities in Contemporary Social Theory', *Development and Change*, vol. 29, pp. 839–71.

Lal, Brij. 1983. *Girmitiyas: The Origins of the Fiji Indians*, Journal of Pacific History Monograph, Canberra: Australian National University.

—————. 1992. *Broken Waves: A History of the Fiji Islands in the Twentieth Century*, Pacific Islands Monograph Series No. 11, Centre for Pacific Islands Studies, School of Hawaiian, Asian, and Pacific Studies, University of Hawaii, Honolulu: University of Hawaii Press.

Lal, Brij. 1998. Another Way: *The Politics of Constitutional Reform in post- coup Fiji*, Canberra: Australian National University/Asia Pacific Press.

————. 2001. 'Fiji: A Damaged Democracy' in Brij Lal (ed), *Coup: Reflections on the Political Crisis in Fiji*, Canberra: Pandanus Books.

Larkin, Brian 1998. 'Theatres of the Profane: Cinema and Colonial Urbanism', *Visual Anthropology Review*, vol. 14, no. 2.

Mishra, Vijay (ed.). 1979. *Rama's Banishment: A Centenary Tribune to the Fiji Indians 1879–1979*, London: Heinemann Educational Books.

————. 1985. 'Towards a Theoretical Critique of Bombay Cinema', *Screen*, vol. 26, nos 3/4, May–August.

Mishra, Vijay. 1992. 'Decentring History: Some Versions of Bombay Cinema', *East-West Film Journal*, vol. 6, no. 1, January.

Naficy, Hamid. 1993. *The Making of Exile Cultures: Iranian Television in Los Angeles*, Minneapolis: University of Minnesota Press.

Prasad, Madhav. 1998. *Ideology of the Hindi Film: A Historical Construction*, Delhi: Oxford University Press.

Rajadhyaksha, Ashish and Willemen, Paul 1999. 'Introduction', *Encyclopaedia of Indian Cinema*, London: British Film Institute.

Rose, Nikolas. 1996. 'The Death of the Social? Re-figuring the Territory of Government', *Economy and Society*, vol. 25, no. 3, pp. 327–56.

Rouse, Roger. 1991. 'Mexican Migration and the Social Space of Postmodernism', *Diaspora*, vol. 1, no. 1, pp. 8–23.

————. 1995. 'Questions of Identity: Personhood and Collectivity in Transnational Migration to the United States', *Critique of Anthropology* 15(4).

Teaiwa, Teresia. 2000. 'An Analysis of the Current Political Crisis in Fiji: Online', at www.fijilive.com.

Žižek, Slavoj. 1997. *The Plague of Fantasie*, Verso: London.

14 Marketing, Hybridity, and Media Industries

Globalization and Expanding Audiences for Popular Hindi Cinema[1]

KAVITA KARAN AND DAVID J. SCHAEFER

Bollywood Studies in the New Millennium

As the biggest movie industry in the world in terms of the number of films produced, Bollywood's growing share in the global film industry 'signals [India's] determination to become a cultural as well as economic powerhouse' (Pillania 2008: 120). On an average 900 films are produced every year and are watched by more than 14 million or 1.4 per cent of the Indian population every day (Bollywood Charms 2010). Exported to over a 100 countries, these films are watched by the growing Indian diaspora across the world (Mishra 2002). For Ganti, Bollywood films are 'characterized by music, dance routines, melodramas, lavish production and an emphasis on stars and spectacle... [meeting] box office success and enthusiastic audiences around the world' (2004: i).

According to Kaur and Sinha (2005), it seems that the world is going mad about Bollywood, while film critics are now claiming it as 'the new cool in international cinema' (Banker, cited in Kaur and Sinha 2005: 17). Indian movies are becoming as internationally recognized as those from Hollywood. At the same time, Hollywood producers are turning to Bollywood to experiment with financial investments and co-productions. Lorenzen and Taeube note that in overseas markets where the 'Indian Diaspora ... is too geographically dispersed to fill cinemas, ... recent technological advances such as home video and internet streaming have made it possible for Bollywood to reach this huge and profitable export segment' (2008: 295). Moreover, auxiliary revenues from 'computer games, ring tones, and video clips' (Lorenzen and Taeube 2008: 290) for mobile phones can be gained by the film industry (Acharya 2004; Lorenzen and Taeube 2008). Given the evolution of Hindi films, this chapter examines how thematic shifts in content reflect the use of Indian and diasporic values to generate large box-office returns during the post-colonial period.

Greater intersections and crossovers are visible as Western media conglomerates are taking greater interest and investing in the production and distribution of Indian movies. Combining evolutionary perspectives with social network theory, Lorenzen and Taeube (2008) examined the recent growth and internationalization of Bollywood in an emergent economy through case studies and interviews. The authors noted that a handful of firms—utilizing economies of scales in marketing, distribution, financing, and digital technologies—released a range of Indian films across different territories and therefore positively influenced Bollywood's revenues and exports. Here the importance of marketing to the viability of film business can be seen in the functions that marketing performs. There are essentially two functions to marketing. The first is the gathering of information about what customers want through market research and then incorporating that market information into the design, production, packaging, and distribution of the product so as to satisfy customer wants (Marich 2005). Realizing the potential of global markets and gaining popularity of Indian films overseas, producers have leveraged on these factors in terms of investments, internal and external factors in production, financing, and the introduction of global themes, as well as the use of good marketing strategies in distribution and marketing overseas, which has resulted in boosting earnings and exports (Dudrah 2006; Lal and Nandy 2006; Kaarsholm 2007).

Though the bulk of revenues come from India, an important factor is the growing trend of internationalization of productions, story themes, and use of new technologies. Heavily influenced by Hollywood,

Bollywood producers have changed themes in order to attract wide audiences (Acharya 2004; Kaarlshom 2007), portraying feudal romances within Hindu patriarchal contexts in a much more stylized manner (for example, *Devdas* [Bhansali and Shah 2002]) than in the past (for example, *Devdas* [Roy 1955]). And some recent Hindi film socials (romance and family dramas) such as *Yeh Dillagi* (Malhotra, Chopra and Chopra 1994), *Judaii* (Kanwar and Kapoor 1997), *Chachi 420* (Hassan and Hassan 1998), and *Deewana Mastana* (Dhawan and Desai 1997) rework the Western films *Sabrina* (Wilder 1954), *Indecent Proposal* (Lyne and Lansing 1993), *Mrs Doubtfire* (Columbus, Radcliffe, Williams and Williams 1993), and *What about Bob* (Oz and Ziskin 1991) into ostensibly Indian ones (Nayar 2003). Additionally, Bollywood producers are experimenting with Hollywood formats, producing movies that are shorter in length, less dramatic, without songs and dances. All these are setting the trends in the production and marketing of films.

Second environmental factors—such as changes in audience demand and governmental support for the film industry—have propelled the globalization of Bollywood cinema (Acharya 2004; Lorenzen and Taeube 2008; Pillania 2008). The government gave filmmaking the official 'industry' status in 1998, allowing new types of private investments to enter into Bollywood. These forms included financial-institutional capital and corporate investments from other Indian industries, which required increased standardization. Acharya (2004) pointed out that in face of increased competition from cable TV and Internet, the Indian film industry has embraced new technologies and modes of distribution. For example, many theatres across India have been converted into multiplexes and digital cinema halls are being constructed across the country. Along with these, films are being distributed across countries with intensive marketing and advertising strategies, international releases, premiers, and merchandizing.

Unlike Hollywood, where mainstream films are produced, financed, and distributed by a handful of integrated media conglomerates [such as] News Corp, Walt Disney, Viacom, Time Warner, NBC Universal, and Sony, Bollywood films are mainly produced by hundreds of professional, specialized, and independent producers, 'each owning a small-scale production company' (Laurenzen and Taeube 2008: 290). These films are also being distributed and financed through the strategic alliances established between independent producers, distribution, and finance firms.

Moreover, the alliances are temporary rather than long-term (which is more typical in Hollywood; Lorenzen and Taeube 2008).

Though there currently appears to be more international interest in Indian movies, this attention is not necessarily new since Indian films and stars like Raj Kapoor and others have developed huge fan followings in various parts of the world since the 1950s. Pillania (2008) argued that the presence of Indian movies in the international market is by no means a recent phenomenon but has historical roots: India has experienced long-term international influence primarily by importing technological know-how, organizing international film festivals, screening overseas movies (especially Hollywood films), liberalizing local markets, and allowing the entry of foreign television channels.

The third contributing factor for the international popularity of Indian commercial cinema has been the huge spread of the Indian diaspora that has led to a growing global acceptance of Indian films abroad. The Indian diaspora is one of the fastest growing communities in the world. Most of the studies done on the Indian community point to the fact that Bollywood enables a religion-like nostalgia for Indians, or that it serves as an emotional and material link to the Indian homeland (Kaur 2005).

Therefore, given the importance of these emergent factors on the internationalizing influence of Indian cinema, one key area of inquiry is how film producers have deliberately drawn upon global trends in order to market filmic content for maximal box-office returns. In particular, what is the relationship between indigenous (India-focused) and exogenous (globally focused) content for attracting huge audiences? And how might this relationship have shifted between the 'Golden Era' of Indian cinema, defined as the period from 1947 through the 1950s, and the 'Global Era,' the period of increased liberalization and Bollywoodization (Rajadhyaksha 2003; Rao 2007) from the 1990s through the present?

Globalization Theory and Indian Cinema

The notion that planet-wide socio-politico-cultural processes are profoundly changing daily life for billions of people around the globe has gained increasing currency in the past fifteen years. Lechner defined *globalization* as 'the worldwide diffusion of practices, expansion of relations across continents, organization of social life on a global scale, and growth of a shared global consciousness' ((cited in Ritzer 2007: 4). While some scholars rejected the notion altogether (for example, Wallerstein 2000), Giddens (1999) defended the concept by pointing to the massive integration of the world's economic systems that occurred in the latter half of the twentieth century. For Giddens, 'Globalization, as we are experiencing it, is in many respects not only new, but also revolutionary' (1999: 28).

Likewise, Ritzer (2007) argued that globalization was characterized by a key socio-political-cultural struggle between two broad forces: *grobalization* and *glocalization*. Citing McDonalds restaurants and Starbucks coffee houses as examples, he defined grobalization as the diffusion of monocultural forces that promote '*nothing*'—social organizational forms that were 'centrally conceived, controlled, and comparatively devoid of distinctive substantive content' (Ritzer 2007: 36). On the other hand, glocalizational processes led to the expansion of *something*—organizational processes that were 'indigenously conceived, controlled, and comparatively rich in distinctive substantive content' (Ritzer 2007: 38), exemplified by art museums and stand-alone restaurants serving locally conceived cuisine. Put simply, *something* is complex, local, traditional, human-centered, and 'enchanted', while *nothing* is simplified, globally diffused, contemporary, automated, and banal.

As previously discussed in Schaefer (2006) and Schaefer and Karan (2008), producers of popular Hindi cinema often draw upon prevailing public debates defining the difference between Hindu-based Indian culture/traditions (that is, *something*) and Westernized cultures and practices (that is, *nothing*) in order to market their films to the widest possible audience. Gokulsing and Dissanayake (2004) and Mishra (2002) noted that distinctions between global-local, tradition-modernity, motherland-diaspora, and East-West appeared early on in Hindi cinema as D.G. Phalke, the director of India's first feature film *Raja Harischandra* in 1913, self-consciously 'Indianized' European film technology to create movies based on Hindu mythology as part of the anti-colonialist movement. Thomas (2005) noted that Australian actress Fearless Nadia deliberately used Western signifiers (modes of transportation, attire) to achieve fame as a modern, swashbuckling female persona. Gangoli (2005) agued that East-West tensions often materialized in characterizational or wardrobe choices for female characters, with Western-style clothing and social mannerisms equated with vampishness/moral weakness/sexual looseness/vulgarity, while saris, bindis (a red or coloured dot on a woman's forehead), salwar-kameezes (Indian dresses), and Hindu greetings served as codes for the devout and indigenous. In the 1990s, huge hits like *Dilwale Dulhania Le Jayenge* (Chopra 1995) and *Pardes* (Ghai 1997) also generated complex public spheres highlighting the 'struggles between modernity and tradition or between East and West in the context of uncertain globalization [that was] externalized and remapped onto the diasporic Indian' (Kaur 2005: 323). The dialectics also played themselves out in the debates over popular culture, with 1950s filmmakers like Satyajit Ray deliberately emulating European realist filmmaking modes (for example, neorealism, poetic realism) in films like *Pather Panchali* (Ray 1955) to promote an individualist-oriented cinema style in contrast to the collectivist song-and-dance style of popular cinema (Schaefer 2005; Vasudevan 2005).

The result was a uniquely Indian mode of filmmaking and marketing that utilized hybridized cultural markers to market films simultaneously to indigenous and exogenous audiences through four key thematic dialectics: East ←→ West, Local ←→ Global, Motherland ←→ Diaspora, and Traditional ←→ Modern (Schaefer 2006; Schaefer and Karan 2008). This resulted in complex cinematic products created by producers seeking to respond to shifts in audience demand from era-to-era. For example, filmmakers during the Golden Era, often utilized a thematic presentational style that compared colonialist culture to new nationalist possibilities in order to attract cinema audiences (for example, *Awaara* [Kapoor 1951], *Pyaasa* [Dutt 1957], *Mother India* [Khan 1957]). When liberalized government policy and new modes of distribution ushered in the Global Era, filmmakers adopted a 'global Indian' style of presentation that weaved India's indigenous cultural heritage into narratives set within global mediaspaces (for example, *Dilwale Dulhania Le Jayenge* [Chopra 1995]; *Hum Dil De Chuke Sanaam* [Bhansali 1999]; *Krrish* [Roshan 2006]) to attract a new, globalized audience.

Focusing in on the current Global Era, we identify three key emergent trends in producer-audience relations. First, the increased use of new technologies and investment approaches for the global distribution of Indian films, coupled with the rise of the middle classes and Western (globalized) audiences, led to changes in business practices and themes as a means of attracting global audiences (including increased adaptation of such themes from Hollywood productions [for example, the Western 'superhero' model used in *Krrish*]). Bollywood companies began the practice of world releases, simultaneously opening films in ten or more countries to maximize revenues. Indian companies opened offices in the US and UK; UTV and Eros Entertainment were listed on London's Alternative Investment market. These strategies also helped them control video piracy.[2] In 2007, the Indian government encouraged media firms to step up foreign markets by making overseas entertainment earnings tax free. Producers (for example, Yash Chopra and Karan Johar) started using in-house marketing and distribution networks. In the move towards corporatization, production houses like Mukta Arts and Pritish Nandy Communications went public, giving producers greater access to wider investments for experimenting and expanding the scope of Indian cinema. Producers used more sophisticated mixes of digital (satellites, subscriber lines, mobile telephones, Internet/web sites/blogs, VCDs/DVDs) and analog (broadcast [radio], print, and cassette) technologies to globally market and distribute Bollywood films (Bose 2006). Promotional tactics utilizing advertising, trailers, media coverage, ring tones, SMSs, and web downloads also raised public interest. Film stars became important brand ambassadors for Bollywood. International releases were also supported by award functions, musical nights, and star tours in many parts of the world that drew extensive media coverage. Assessing the popularity of Shah Rukh Khan, a top Indian actor, in Malaysia, the government conferred him with the title of 'Datuk', one of the highest honours given to people of exceptional calibre in public service. Indian films, subtitled or dubbed into local languages, were screened in cinemas or sold as VCD/DVDs. Merchandizing included non-film products like clothes, accessories, and jewellery.

Second, the worldwide growth of the Indian diaspora—which relied upon cable and satellite broadcasting of Indian television channels, videocassette, and VCD/DVD distribution to stay connected to home—fuelled international demand for Bollywood movies. Non-resident Indians (NRIs) were among the fastest growing Indian communities in the world, spread across America, the Middle East, South Africa, and Europe (Mishra 2002). The UK and US became the largest overseas markets, while numbers continued to grow in Southeast Asian countries like Singapore, Malaysia, Philippines, and Indonesia. *Om Shanti Om* (Khan, Khan, and Khan 2007), a blockbuster released in 2007 starring Shah Rukh Khan, was shown on more than 114 screens in the USA, collecting $1,764,131 ($15,475 per screen) during its opening weekend; in the UK, the film earned £518,845 on 52 screens during the same time period (imdb.com, 2008). Beginning in the 1990s, a number of NRI-related films adopted diasporic themes, with characters expressing their love for the motherland despite living in the Western world (for example, *Dilwale Dulhania Le Jayenge*, *Pardes*, and the USA-produced *Monsoon Wedding* (Nair and Baron 2001) (see Lal and Nandy 2006). Satellite channels like STAR, ZEE, and SONY were available to audiences in more than fifty countries, providing popular news, entertainment, film-based programmes, and soap operas, which often became points of conversation among Indians living overseas.

Third, the emergence of sophisticated indigenous-exogenous, in-tertextual thematic marketing strategies for the promotion of films at the national and global levels (for example, *Lagaan* [Gowariker 2001] and *Rang De Basanti* [Mehra 2006]) allowed producers to deliberately mix Eastern and Western narrative and character elements in their films to attract hybridized audiences. This was supported by international ad campaigns run by various media partners, sponsorships, film festivals, international releases, advertising, promotions and star launches (Kripalani 2006). Diasporic directors emulated similar tactics like Mira Nair (US) and Gurinder Chadha (UK), who targeted films to increasingly hybridized audiences (for example, *Monsoon Wedding* and *Bride and Prejudice* [Chadha and Nayar 2004]).

Thus, an open question is how producers exploit hybridized, globalized themes within the context of actual films to attract the attention of international audiences. How have these tactics changed between the Golden Era of Indian cinema—a period known for high quality and thought-providing films—and the current Global Era? Were films of the past more tied to indigenous, local Indian values—'something'—while the films of today are more thematically linked to exogenous, globalized, empty values? To address these questions, we posit the following hypotheses:

HYPOTHESES

H1) Films produced during the Global Era (1990s–2000s) will exhibit significantly more exogenous content than those produced during the Golden Era (1947–1950s).

H2) Indigenous content will be more directly related to box-office revenues for films produced during the Golden Era than those produced in the Global Era.

H3) Exogenous content will be more directly related to box-office revenues for films produced during the Global Era than those produced in the Golden Era.

METHODOLOGY

A content analysis technique was used to examine the relationship between content and globalization as filmmakers sought to market their films to broader international audiences. We compare thematic data to box-office revenues during these two periods in order to see how thematic shifts represent changes in the values being marketed to audiences.

In order to test the hypotheses, we utilized a systematic sampling framework for content analysis (Reinard 2006; Weber 1990) of twenty-five of the most popular Hindi films spanning a sixty-year period since Independence in 1947.[3] For the purpose of this analysis, there were three sets of variables: (a) indigenous, (b) exogenous, and (c) other globalizational influences. Drawing upon definitions used in previous work (see Schaefer 2006; Schaefer and Karan 2008), the variables were operationally defined as follows:

(1) Indigenous Predictors—thematic variables emphasizing Indian socio-cultural-political themes and traditional practices.

  (a) Local—visual or verbal references to India, Pakistan, Bangladesh, or Sri Lanka, or their cities, regions, or states.

  (b) East—visual or verbal references to Asian attire, social customs, religious practices, sports, or languages other than Hindi (the default language for all films).

  (c) Motherland—visual or verbal references to national symbols of the Indian subcontinent, particularly flags, famous leaders, official uniforms, or landmark building (for example, Red Fort).

  (d) Traditional—visual or verbal depictions of pre-modern (pre-Enlightenment) legal, technological, or social institutions.

(2) Exogenous Predictors—thematic variables emphasizing non-Indian socio-cultural-political themes and traditional practices.

(e) Global—visual or verbal references to countries other than India, Pakistan, Bangladesh, or Sri Lanka or their cities, regions, or states.

(f) West—visual or verbal references to European-American-Australian attire, social customs, religious practices, sports, or languages, particularly English.

(g) Diaspora—visual or verbal references to non-Indian national symbols, particularly flags, famous leaders, official uniforms, or landmark building (for example, Eiffel Tower).

(h) Modern—visual or verbal depictions of modern (post-Enlightenment) legal, technological, or social institutions.

(3) A final set of generalized thematic variables reflecting content likely to relate to glocalizing-globalizing forces:

(a) Popular—visual or verbal depictions of other films/songs, magazines, photography, vaudeville, and actors.

(b) Artistic—visual or verbal depictions of painting, books, classical musicians, classical dance, and other artists.

(c) Violence—visual or verbal references to non-peaceful means of communicating or imposing one character's will upon another character, including yelling, assaulting, raping, and murdering.

(d) Crime and social vice—visual or verbal references to other illegal or other anti-social behaviour, including theft, prostitution, swearing, drinking, smoking, or drug taking.

(e) Sexuality—visual or verbal depictions of sensually oriented physical behavior, dress, or situations, including kissing, fondling, nudity, live-in relationships, homosexuality, and wet sari scenes.

(f) Romance—visual or verbal references to respectful courting, innocent flirting, or related behaviour in relation to a developing or established long-term, couple-style relationship.

(g) Lower-class dwelling—visual or verbal depictions of huts, shacks, or slums.

(h) Middle-class dwelling—visual or verbal depictions of small or medium-sized houses with basic amenities.

(i) Upper-class dwelling—visual or verbal depictions of *havelis* or bungalows.

The criterion variable was box-office revenue, defined as total box-office collection information provided by publicly available sources.[4] The DVD chapters were selected as the unit of analysis. Five coders at a large university in Singapore both authors and three graduate students who were trained over a five-week period in 2008—attained very high levels of reliability using the Scotts Pi correction for multiple coders (Reinard 2006; Shoemaker 2003), with values ranging from 95.6 per cent to 99.6 per cent (see appendix). All statistical calculations were performed using the SPSS 16 statistical package, while LOTUS DOMINO was used for storing and sorting the data.

RESULTS

The first hypothesis predicted that films produced during the Global Era would exhibit significantly more exogenous content than those produced during the Golden Era. This hypothesis was supported. Figure 14.1 compares the percentages of the globalization predictors for the Golden Era (n = 149) and Global Era (n = 223) DVD chapters.

Interestingly, during the Golden Era, Eastern content was present in the largest percentage of DVD chapters (90.6per cent [n = 135]); however, during the Global Era, Western content accounted for the largest percentage (88.8 per cent [n = 198]) of chapters, providing solid evidence of an overall exogenous shift in filmic content. Looking only at indigenous variables, only Local content significantly increased and Traditional content exhibited a significant decrease. For exogenous variables, Global, West, and Modern contents demonstrated significant increases. Among the additional content variables, there were significant increases between the two periods for depictions of Sexuality and Middle-Class Dwellings. Conversely, several variables significantly decreased, including Artistic depictions, Violence, Romance, and depictions of Lower-Class and Upper-Class Dwellings.

The second hypothesis predicted that indigenous content would more significantly predict box office revenue during the Golden Era than during the Global Era. This hypothesis was supported. As illustrated in Table 14.1, when all predictors were regressed on to box-office revenues (in thousands) for films produced during the Golden Era, the model was highly significant (F [16, 132] = 2.78, p < .001), accounting for R^2 = 25.2 per cent of the variance, a large effect according to Cohen (Leech, Barrett, and Morgan 2008).

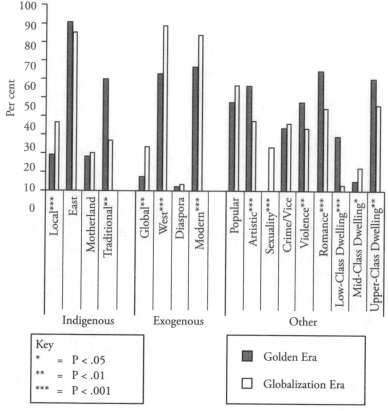

FIGURE 14.1 Comparing the Percentages of Globalizational Predictors for all DVD Chapters from Golden Era (1947–1950s) and Globalization Era (1990s–2000s) Films (n = 372)

Only one indigenous variable, Traditional, was a positive predictor of box-office revenue and none of the exogenous variables were significant predictors. Additionally, two additional content variables were negative predictors of box-office revenue—Middle-Class Dwelling and Artistic content.

The third hypothesis predicted that exogenous content would be more directly related to box-office revenues for films produced during the Global Era than those produced in the Golden Era. This hypothesis was supported. As illustrated in Table 14.1, when the predictors were regressed on to box office revenues for the Globalization Era, this model, too, was highly significant (F [17, 205] = 11.71, p < .001)

TABLE 14.1: Significant Positive and Negative Predictors when Regressing All Variables on to Box-office Revenues for the Golden Era and Global Eras, Categorized by Variable Type

Era	Positive Predictors			Negative Predictors		
	Indigenous	Exogenous	Other	Indigenous	Exogenous	Other
Golden Era (1947–1950s)	Traditional (Beta = 49.75; p<.05)					*Middle-Class Dwelling (-97.42; p<.05) *Artistic (Beta = -73.25; p=.001)
Global Era (1990s–2000s)	*Motherland [Beta = 1,352.84; p<.05]),	*Diaspora [Beta = 2,589.51; p<.05] *Modern [Beta = 1,693.03; p<.05]	*Crime [Beta = 2,027.40; p<.001], *Upper-Class Dwelling [Beta = 1,931.07; p<.001], *Middle-Class Dwelling [Beta = 1,869.39; p=.01])	*East [Beta = -5,597.16; p<.001] and *Traditional [Beta = -1,849.29; p=.001]		*Artistic [Beta = -2,075.05; p<.001])

accounting for R^2=49.3 per cent of the variance, a very large effect according to Cohen (Leech, Barrett, and Morgan 2008). For the Global Era, more exogenous variables significantly predicted box-office revenue than indigenous variables. The two positive exogenous variables were Diaspora and Modern, while only one indigenous variable, Motherland, was significant. Additionally, three additional content variables; Crime, Upper-Class Dwelling, and Middle-Class Dwelling were significant. The negative predictors included two indigenous variables; East and Traditional and one generalized content variable, Artistic.

Discussion and Conclusions

In this chapter, we have discussed some of the important issues affecting the internationalization of Hindi films. Many factors—from content to aggressive and professional marketing techniques to international releases—are all contributing to the demand and popularity of Bollywood films. One of the most significant impacts of globalization has been in the content and themes chosen by filmmakers when comparing films from the Golden Era to those produced in the Global Era.

We conducted a content analysis of twenty-five randomly selected popular Hindi films to examine the relationship between content and box-office receipts during the Golden Era and the Global Era as filmmakers sought to market their films to broader international audiences. We posited three hypotheses predicting that highly successful Golden Era films were more likely to emphasize indigenous (Indian) content, while highly successful Global Era films were more likely to emphasize exogenous (non-Indian/global) content. All the hypotheses were supported. Perhaps most interesting, the only positive predictor that regressed on to box-office receipts during the Golden Era was Traditional content (depictions of pre-modern legal, technological, or social institutions). During the Global Era, however, there were six positive predictors. However, only one—Motherland (that is, references to national symbols of the Indian subcontinent, particularly flags, famous leaders, official uniforms, or landmark buildings)—related to indigenous content. The other positive predictors included two exogenous variables—Diaspora and Modern—and three additional predictors: Crime, Upper-Class Dwellings, and Middle-Class Dwellings.

This provides clear evidence of the importance that filmmakers are giving to the marketing of hybridized content to attract contemporary audiences. What is even more surprising is that Artistic content; visual or verbal depictions of classical musicians, classical dance, paintings, books, or other artistic pursuits was negatively related to box-office receipts during both the Golden and Global Eras.

Thus, in terms of utilizing content as a marketing hook to lure audiences into cinema halls across the globe, we identified three key Hindi filmmaking trends from the findings:

1. Increasing complexity and hybridization: The most financially successful Indian films in the current, Global Era provided complex, hybridized narratives and visuals that mixed exogenous and indigenous content in order to attract the largest audiences. These highly successful films were not dominated by Indianized/ traditional content, despite the presence of such content in the narratives, but exhibited significant increases in Western, Modern, and Global content that freely combined with Eastern content.

2. Negative impact of classical/folk content on box-office returns: Despite conventional wisdom that suggests that Bollywood films *must* include classical or folk music and dance scenes (typically a song-and-dance sequence set during a wedding or festival), the findings indicate a negative relation between this type of Artistic content and box-office returns—interestingly, for both the Golden and Global Eras.

3. Significant rise in on-screen sexuality: Although sexuality did not emerge as a significant predictor of box office returns, there was a significant increase in the frequency of on-screen sexuality portrayed when comparing the Golden Era to the Global Era. In the Golden Era, there was no on-screen sexuality in the chapters that were analysed; however, in the Global Era, 23.8 per cent of 223 DVD chapters featured on-screen sexuality.

Given these findings, several areas of additional research should be explored. First, shaping content to market films to audiences is only one part of the filmmaking process in the Global Era. Researchers need to also examine how audiences enter into relations with films and filmmakers through new media, particularly in the online space now known as Bollyweb, which includes blogs, informational web sites, online fanzines, and the like (Mitra 2008). Does participation in these forums improve producer revenues? Can online sales of films and downloadable clips contribute to revenues through a 'long tail' effect? How does the availability of online content for highly successful films from previous periods in Indian cinema (for example, Golden Era, Angry Young Man phase, and so on) generate new revenue streams? What indigenous and exogenous forms of content attract the largest audiences in online environments? Future research can be undertaken to explore interactions among the subcomponents of these processes or to apply time-series analysis to identify shifts in these associations for specific time periods. Researchers should also seek to replicate the major findings reported here within other contexts—including the cinemas of other major film-producing countries (for example, China/Hong Kong, US/UK, France, Italy). Finally, given the recent surge in sexual violence against women in urban centres like Delhi and Mumbai, researchers should examine the relationship between cinematic depictions of sexuality and crime trends. For example, what is the impact when sexually charged scenes (for example, the *Jumma Chumma* song-and-dance scene from *Hum* [Anand and Sharma 1991]) are ripped from DVDs and uploaded as free-floating performative displays in online public spheres accessible to all age groups? Clearly, there are many more interesting areas to be explored.

Of course, these findings have their own limitations. First, our analysis has focused on significant relationships between the variables but do not indicate causality. Second, although a systematic random sample was used to select the analysed films, enlarging the sample size will help to overcome statistical limitations when using regression with a large number of predictor variables. Despite these limitations, this chapter provides strong empirical evidence that filmmakers have utilized hybridized indigenous/glocalized and exogenous/grobalized content in Hindi films to positively impact box-office returns and that this trend is accelerating in the Global Era.

Notes

1. A previous version of this chapter was presented as a keynote speech at the 5th International Conference on Internationalization of Business in Changed Environment, Rajiv Academy of Technology and Management, Mathura, UP, India, 12–14 February 2009. Funding for this project was supplemented by research grants awarded by Nanyang Technological University, Singapore and Franciscan University of Steubenville, Ohio, USA. Also, special thanks is given to graduate students Amarnath Donepudi, Divya Anujan, and Namrata Bansal for assistance with the film coding and Feng Yang for assistance with the literature review.

2. One of the good examples of marketing was the superhit *Hum Aapke Hai Kaun...!* (Barjatya, Barjatya, Barjatya, and Barjatya, 1994). The technique used by director Sooraj Barjatiya was the policy of 'video holdback'. Initially, he released only 100 prints at a high rate as a form of test marketing to arouse the curiosity and buzz for the movie. And gradually, the film was released when demand exceeded supply.

3. Publicly available Indian box office data was consulted to create a sampling frame of 120 films released between 1947 and 2007, consisting of the two highest-grossing films for each year. From this list, a random sample of 20 per cent of the films was drawn, yielding an initial list of 24 films for coding. The sample had to be modified because two of the titles were unavailable; thus, two additional titles were randomly drawn from the list. It was then discovered that only one film representing the 1980s had been included in the random sample ; in order to provide more robust data relevant to this decade, one additional title from the 1980s was included in the sample, bringing the total number of films analysed to 25, or 20.8 per cent of the corpus. Additionally, to compensate for the lack of chapter divisions on one title that could only be obtained in the VCD format, we implemented a five minutes rule that required the coders to insert chapter divisions at the end of scenes that fell at five minute intervals. The average length of a DVD chapter was 5.64 minutes. The sample yielded 683 chapters for analysis. The 25 films selected for analysis were *Mela* (1948), *Andaz* (1949), *Babul* (1950), *Anarkali* (1953), *CID* (1956), *Naya Daur* (1957), *Kohinoor* (1960), *Hariyali aur Raasta* (1962), *Aayee Milan Ki Bela* (1964), *Guide* (1965), *Aradhana* (1969), *Johnny Mera Naam* (1970), *Sachcha Jhutha* (1970), *Pakeezah* (1972), *Bobby* (1973), *Deewar* (1975), *Qurbani* (1980), *Mard* (1985), *Raja Hindustani* (1996), *Hum Dil De Chuke Sanam* (1999), *Mohabbatein* (2000), *Kabhi Khushi Kabhie Gham* (2001), *Devdas* (2002), *Bunty aur Babli* (2005), and *Dhoom 2* (2006).

4. Source: IBOS network (http://www.ibosnetwork.com/, all data recorded on 9 February 2007).

References

Acharya, S. 2004. 'Bollywood and Globalization', Unpublished master's thesis. San Francisco: San Francisco State University.

Bollywood Charms. 2010. Available at http://www.shubhyatra.com/maharash-tra/bollywood.html retrieved on 12 March.

Bose, D. 2006. *Brand Bollywood: A New Global Entertainment Order*, New Delhi: Sage.

Dudrah, R. 2006. *Sociology Goes to Movies*. New Delhi: Sage.

Gangoli, G. 2005. 'Sexuality, Sensuality, and Belonging: Representations of the "Anglo-Indian" and the "Western" Woman in Hindi Cinema', in R. Kaur and A.J. Sinha (eds), *Bollyworld: Popular Indian Cinema through a Transnational Lens*, New Dehli: Sage.

Ganti, T. 2004. *Bollywood: A Guidebook to Popular Hindi Cinema*. New York: Rotldge.

Giddens, A. 1999. *Runaway World.* New York: Routledge.

Gokulsing, K. and W. Dissanayake. 2004. *Indian Popular Cinema: A Narrative of Cultural Change,* UK: Trentham.

Internet movie database (IMDB). List of Highest Grossing Bollywood films. Retrieved November 2008 from http://www.imdb.com/.

Kaarsholm, P. 2007.'Unreal City: Cinematic Representation, Globalization and the Ambiguities of Metropolitan Life, in City flicks', in P. Kaarsholm (ed.), *Indian Cinema and the Urban Experience,* New York: Seagull.

Kaur, R. 2005. 'Cruising on the Vilayeti Bandwagon: Disaporic Representations and Reception of Popular Indian Movies', in R. Kaur and A. Sinha (eds), *Bollyworld: Popular Indian Cinema through a Transnational Lens,* New Delhi: Sage.

Kaur, R. and Sinha, A. 2005. 'Bollyworld: An Introduction to Popular Indian Cinema through a Transnational Lens', in R. Kaur and A. Sinha (eds), *Bollyworld: Popular Indian Cinema through a Transnational Lens,* New Delhi: Sage.

Kripalani, C. 2006. 'Trendsetting and Product Placement in Bollywood Film: Consumerism through Consumption', *New Cinemas: Journal of Contemporary Film,* vol. 4, no. 3.

Lal, V. and Nandy A. 2006. 'Introduction', in V. Lal, and A. Nandy (eds), *Fingerprinting Popular Culture: The Mythic and the Iconic in Indian Cinema,* New Delhi: Oxford University Press.

Leech, N., K. Barrett, and G. Morgan. 2008. *SPSS for Intermediate Statistics.* New York: Erlbaum.

Lorenzen, M. and F.A. Taeube. 2008. 'Breakout from Bollywood? The Roles of Social Networks and Regulation in the Evolution of Indian Film Industry', *Journal of International Management,* vol. 14.

Marich, R. 2005. *Marketing to Moviegoers,* Boston: Focal Press.

Mishra, V. 2002. *Bollywood Cinema: Temples of Desire,* New York: Routledge.

Mitra, A. 2008. 'Bollyweb: Search for Bollywood on the Web and See What Happens!', in A. Kavoori and A. Punathambekar (eds), *Global Bollywood,* New York: New York University Press.

Nayar, S J. 2003. 'Dreams, Dharma, and Mrs. Doubtfire', *Journal of Popular Film and Television,* vol. 31, no. 2.

Pillania, R.K. 2008. 'The Globalization of Indian Hindi Movie Industry', *Management,* vol. 3, no. 2.

Prasad, M. Madhava 1998. *Ideology of the Hindi Film,* New Delhi: Oxford University Press.

Rajadhyaksha, A. 2003. '"The 'Bollywoodization" of the Indian Cinema: Cultural Nationalism in a Global Arena', *Inter-Asia Cultural Studies,* vol. 4, no. 1.

Rao, S. 2007. 'The Globalization of Bollywood: An Ethnography of Non-Elite Audiences in India', *The Communication Review,* vol. 10.

Reinard, J. 2006. *Communication Research Statistics,* Thousand Oaks: Sage.

Ritzer, G. 2007. *The Globalization of Nothing 2*, Thousand Oaks, CA: Pine Forge.

Schaefer, D. 2005. 'Tales of Transitions: The Dialectics of Change in Indian Film and Television', *Asian Journal of Communication*, vol. 15, no. 3.

————. 2006. 'Popular Indian Cinema, Structural Fault Lines, and Dialectics of Control: Setting the Agenda for Hindi Film Research in the Era of Globalization', Paper presented at Dresden, Germany, International Communication Association Annual Conference, June.

Schaefer, D. and K. Karan. 2008. 'Bollywood Cinema at the Crossroads: Tracking the Dialectics of Globalization in Post-colonial Indian cinema'. Paper presented at Montréal, Canada, International Communication Association Annual Conference, May.

Shoemaker, P. 2003. *Intercoder Reliability*, Self-published monograph, Retrieved 26 May 2008. from http://web.syr.edu/~snowshoe/content_analysis/Intercoder_reliability.doc.

Thomas, R. 2005. 'Not quite (Pearl) White: Fearless Nadia, Queen of the Stunts', in R. Kaur and A. Sinha (eds), *Bollyworld: Popular Indian Cinema through a Transnational Lens*, New Dehli: Sage.

Vasudevan, R. 2005. 'An Imperfect Public: Cinema and Citizenship in the Third World, in Civil Society, Public Sphere and Citizenship', in R. Bhargava and H. Reifeld (eds), New Delhi: Sage.

Wallerstein, I. 2000. 'Globalization or the Age of Transition?' *International Sociology*, vol. 15, no. 2.

Weber, R.P. 1990. *Basic Content Analysis*, Newbury Park, CA: Sage.

FILMS

Anand, M. (Director) and R. Sharma (Producer), *Hum* (Motion Picture), India, 1991.

Barjatya, S. (Director), A. Barjatya (Producer), R. Barjatya (Producer), and R. Barjatya (Producer), *Hum Aapke Hain Kaun ...!* (Motion Picture), India: Rajashri, 1994.

Bhansali, S. (Producer-Director), *Hum Dil De Chuke Sanam* (Motion Picture), India: Bhansali Films, 1999.

Bhansali, S. (Director) and B. Shah (Producer), *Devdas* (Motion Picture), India: Mega Bolloywood Films, 2002.

Chadha, G. (Producer-Director) and D. Nayar (Producer), *Bride and Prejudice* (Motion Picture), UK: Pathe, 2004.

Chopra, A. (Director) and Y. Chopra (Producer). *Dilwale Dulhania Le Jayenge* (Motion Picture), India: Yash Raj Films, 1995.

Columbus, C. (Director), M. Radcliffe (Producer), M. Williams (Producer), and R. Williams (Producer), *Mrs. Doubtfire* (Motion Picture), Twentieth Century-Fox Film Corporation, 1993.

Dhawan, D. (Director) and K. Desai (Producer), *Deewana Mastana* (Motion Picture), India: MKD Films Combine, 1997.

Dutt, G. (Producer-Director), *Pyaasa* (Motion Picture), India: Guru Dutt Films, 1957.

Ghai, S. (Producer-Director), *Pardes* (Motion Picture), India: Mukta Arts, 1997.

Gowariker, A. (Director) and A. Khan (Producer), *Lagaan* (Motion Picture), India: Aamir Khan Productions and Ashutosh Gowariker Productions, 2001.

Hassan, K. (Producer-Director) and C. Hassan (Producer), *Chachi 420* (Motion Picture), India: Digital Entertainment, 1998.

Kanwar, R. (Director) and S. Kapoor (Producer), *Judaii* (Motion Picture), India: S.K. Films, 1997.

Kapoor, R. (Producer-Director), *Awara* (Motion Picture), India: RK Films, 1951.

Khan, F. (Director), G. Khan (Producer), and S. Khan (Producer). *Om Shanti Om* (Motion Picture), India: Red Chillies Entertainment, 2007.

Khan, M. (Producer-Director), *Mother India* (Motion Picture), India: Mehboob Productions, 1957.

Lyne, A. (Director) and S. Lansing (Producer), *Indecent Proposal* (Motion Picture), USA: Paramount.

Malhotra, N. (Director), U. Chopra (Producer), and Y. Chopra (Producer), *Yeh Dillagi* (Motion Picture), India: Aditya Films, 1994.

Mehra, R. (Director), *Rang De Basanti* (Motion Picture), India: UTV, 2006.

Nair, M. (Producer-Director) and C. Baron (Producer), *Monsoon Wedding* (Motion Picture), USA: IFC Productions, 2001.

Oz, F. (Director), *What About Bob?* (Motion Picture), USA: Touchstone Pictures, 1991.

Phalke, D. (Producer-Director), *Raja Harischandra* (Motion Picture), India: Phalke Films, 1913.

Wilder, B. (Producer-Director), *Sabrina* (Motion Picture), USA: Paramount, 1954.

Ray, S. (Producer-Director), *Pather Panchali* (Motion Picture), India: Government of West Bengal, 1955.

Roy, B. (Producer-Director), *Devdas* (Motion Picture), India: Bimal Roy Productions, 1955.

Roshan, R. (Producer-Director), *Krrish* (Motion Picture), India: Film Kraft, 2006.

APPENDIX A

Intercoder Reliability Agreement Percentages Among All 5 Project
Coders, by Variable, as Calculated on 10% of the Data and
Adjusted Using Scott's *PI* Correction

Variables	Agreement Percentage
Local	99.6
Global	98.6
East	99.6
West	99.3
Motherland	98.3
Diaspora	99.5
Traditional	96.2
Modern	98.3
Artistic	96.4
Popular	97.3
Violence	97.1
Crime	97.6
Sexuality	97.9
Romance	95.6
Lower-class Dwelling	98.4
Middle-class Dwelling	96.9
Upper-vlass Dwelling	96.5

APPENDIX B

Random Sample Films List

Title	Year Released
Mela	1948
Andaz	1949
Babul	1950
Anarkali	1953
CID	1956
Naya Daur	1957
Kohinoor	1960
Hariyali aur Raasta	1962
Aayee Milan Ki Bela	1964
Guide	1965
Aradhana	1969
Johnny Mera Naam	1970
Sachcha Jhutha	1970
Pakeezah	1972
Bobby	1973
Deewar	1975
Qurbani	1980
Mard	1985
Raja Hindustani	1996
Hum Dil De Chuke Sanam	1999
Mohabbatein	2000
Kabhi Khushi Kabhie Gham	2001
Devdas	2002
Bunty aur Babli	2005
Dhoom 2	2006

15 'It Was Filmed in My Home Town'

Diasporic Audiences and Foreign Locations in Indian Popular Cinema

ANDREW HASSAM

The defining feature of Hindi cinema for commentators in the West is the 'interruption' of the narrative, as Gopalan (2002) terms it, by the visualization of songs through dance. Headlines such as 'India's New Cinema has a Global Script' (Pfanner 2006) have, for the past decade, been proclaiming the birth of a globalized Bollywood, but the Bollywood that is 'globalizing' the UK and North America is the Bollywood culture industry of transcultural *bhangra*, dance fitness classes, and the celebrity world of Aishwarya Rai rather than Hindi cinema, notwithstanding the Oscar nomination of *Lagaan* (2001) for Best Foreign Language Film in 2002. For the groups of youngsters and young families who comprise the cinema audiences of the UK and North America avoid subtitled ('foreign language') movies, and outside of art film or Indian film festivals, Indian cinema is epitomized by its dance sequences.

Non-Indian critics have understandably, if rarely convincingly, read these dance sequences in terms of the Hollywood musical (Kao and Do Rozario 2008). Newcomers to Indian popular cinema lack the cultural competence to recognize references to earlier non-Western texts and conventions, such as the character types of the Sanskrit epics, the

Mahabharata and the Ramayana (Mishra 2001: 4), or the song sequences of earlier films, such as Shah Rukh Khan's homage to Rishi Kapoor in *Om Shanti Om* (2007), with their hidden intertextual meanings. More importantly, newcomers to Indian popular cinema fail to notice the importance of the playback singers and composers and the ways in which songs and song sequences circulate separately from the films: the sound track of *Lagaan*, for example, featuring the music of the revered A.R. Rahman, was released on CD two months before the opening of the film. In 2005, film music comprised 60–70 per cent of music sales in India (Kohli-Khandekar 2006: 143), and the sale of the soundtrack rights can considerably offset a film's production costs, with Aamir Khan selling the music and song rights of *Lagaan* to Sony for a reported Rs 60 million (ibid.: 157). In this context, the Indian phrase 'song picturization' to describe the visualization of the songs aptly reflects the primacy of music over the visual image, the song over the dance (Tyrrell and Dudrah 2006: 196).

Despite key differences between Hindi popular cinema and the Hollywood musical in terms of their production, distribution, and reception, Western audiences new to Hindi popular cinema come to it through a knowledge of the Hollywood musical and there is some sense in using the musical as a starting point for an analysis of Indian song picturizations, providing Hindi film is not forced to fit an outdated Western film genre and the emphasis is placed on difference rather than similarity. In an influential study of the Hollywood musical, Jane Feuer has probed the role of the on-screen audience of song and dance numbers. Feuer (1993: 26) distinguishes between the audience *in* the film (what she terms the *internal* or *theatrical audience*) and the audience *of* the film (the *spectator* or *film audience*), and she employs this distinction to argue that the role of the internal audience is to compensate the film audience for the loss of a live performance. Thus, when Fred Astaire and Ginger Rogers dance to a live audience on screen, the film audience shares in the live performance through the reactions of the on-screen audience, with the camera typically positioned behind an applauding audience at the close of the dance. As Feuer puts it: 'the internal audience serves a symbolic not a realistic purpose; they are the celluloid embodiment of the film audience's subjectivity' (ibid.: 27). Feuer notes that not all dances in a musical are performed in a theatre or on a dance floor and where the dance sequence is set outdoors, as in many of Gene Kelly's routines, the film audience is represented by an apparently impromptu gathering of non-elite bystanders, some of whom participate in the performance itself (ibid.: 31–4). Nonetheless, such scenes may incorporate a natural proscenium arch and once again, 'We, the spectators, are encouraged to identify with a spontaneous audience which has actually participated in the performance' (ibid.: 34).

Other scholars writing on the musical have assumed a similar correspondence between audiences *in* films and audiences *of* films. Susan Hayward in her explanation of diegesis as the fictional reality of a film, uses the musical to explain the difference between diegetic and extra-diegetic audiences: 'Musicals very commonly use diegetic audiences, dancing and singing around the main protagonist(s)—usually a couple—just to show off how brilliant they are in performing their song and dance' (1996: 68), And on the basis of this distinction, Hayward defines the role of the on-screen audience in much the same terms as Feuer: 'diegetic audiences also serve to draw us, the extra-diegetic audience, into the screen and thereby into the illusion that we too are part of the diegetic audience' (ibid.). Rachel Dwyer draws on this assumed identification between film audiences and internal audiences when she speaks of the song sequence in Hindi film, 'refracting the exchange of looks between the performer and the audience through the presence of an on-screen audience, onto whom the feeling of voyeurism may be transferred' (Dwyer and Patel: 2002: 38). Disappointingly, the only evidence offered for such readings is an implicit nod towards Freud's psychoanalytic theories of identification and voyeurism.

For others, however, the Indian concept of *darshan* ('seeing/looking'), integral to the practice of Hinduism and Sikhism, produces a very different cinematic effect in Indian audiences. Dwyer herself usefully defines *darshan* as, 'a two-way look between the devotee and the deity that establishes religious authority' (ibid.: 45)and notes that, according to Ravi Vasudevan, the *darshanic* may (contra Freud), 'deploy and subordinate modern methods of subject construction modelled on Hollywood narration' (ibid.: 46). Philip Lutgendorf makes the interactive nature of darshanic practice clearer:

> In a crowded Hindu temple, one can observe worshipers positioning themselves so that their eyes have a clear line of contact with those of the god. Their explanations emphasize that they do not merely want to *see* the deity, but to *be*

seen by him or her so that the deity's powerful and unwavering gaze may *enter into* them'. (2006: 233)

An interactive darshanic relationship between the on-screen performer and the film audience is held, therefore, to disrupt the voyeurism regarded as characteristic of Western audiences:

Unlike the 'gaze' of Western film theory, *darśan* [*darshan*] is a two-way street; a visual interaction between players who, though not equal, are certainly both in the same theatre of activity and capable of influencing each other, especially in the vital realm of emotion. (Ibid.: 234)

Accordingly, the subjectivity of Indian audience members is relational and reciprocal rather than individual and autonomous, as in the West.

For M. Madhava Prasad, this difference in the construction of subjectivity is paralleled by a difference in the mode of address adopted by Indian cinema and Hollywood. Feuer, in her study of the Hollywood musical, distinguishes between a first person and third person form of address: whereas the narrative of the musical occurs in the third person without a consciousness of the audience, the songs, with their live performances to on-screen audiences, adopt a direct or first-person form of address (1993: 23). Prasad employs a similar dichotomy to contrast the realist narrative of Hollywood with the self-consciousness of the 'frontal spectacle' that is characteristic of Indian cinema, 'frontality' as a cinematic mode of address precluding the voyeurism of Western audiences: 'The frontal orientation of the screen image, especially in the song-and-dance sequences, makes the erotic spectacle less capable of functioning as a device of male-to-male identification' (1998: 77). As a result, female eroticism (that is, 'skin show') is mostly confined to the more self-conscious, less voyeuristic performance space of the dance sequences.

It would be misleading to suggest that critics agree on the nature of Indian cinema, but there does emerge something of a consensus concerning an opposition between darshan and voyeurism in terms of a consciousness of the audience in the song picturizations in Indian cinema and the concealment of the audience in Hollywood realism. Yet such an opposition collapses any difference in address between on-screen audiences in Indian song picturizations and Hollywood musicals; in other words, the presence of an audience results in both Indian and Hollywood song sequences adopting a first person or darshanic form of address. The critic best placed to contrast the song sequences of the two cinemas, Rachel Dwyer, argues that the presence of an on-screen audience invites a transfer of voyeurism, while also accepting that darshan operates as 'a two-way look' between film star and audience and her argument sidesteps any need to reconcile this contradiction between a one-way voyeurism and a two-way look by dismissing the Hollywood musical as dead and of no consequence (Dwyer and Patel 2002: 36). In sum, critical treatment of the songs in Indian and Hollywood movies tells us little, if anything, about the differences between them.

The most visually attractive difference is the vibrancy of colour and movement, particularly in the wedding festivities, of Indian cinema, though there are numerous less obvious differences, especially the masala of languages, dialects, and linguistic registers found in any one film's lyrics. In her comparison of Hindi cinema with Hollywood movies, Dwyer draws attention to the shifts in location, time, and costume that occur in a single song sequence, breaking with the Hollywood convention of continuity of time and place (ibid.: 38). One of the most celebrated examples occurs in the Tamil film, *Jeans* (1998), and in the course of one song, '*Poovukul*', Aishwarya Rai dances in front of the Great Wall of China, the Eiffel Tower, the Empire State Building, the Taj Mahal, the Pyramids, the Colosseum, and the Leaning Tower of Pisa. To the degree that audiences make sense of such shifts in continuity as an expression of the dreams or fantasies of the protagonists, then similar shifts can occur within dream sequences in European or Hollywood realist movies, but ever since the first appearance of overseas locations in films like *Sangam* (1964) and *An Evening in Paris* (1967), song picturizations have come to include a foreign background as almost mandatory, at least in Hindi cinema. Indeed, according to Lakshmi Srinivas, viewing such sequences may contribute to the high level of repeat viewings of Indian films, with some viewers claiming that their sole reason for having repeatedly watched *Indian* (1996; Hindi title *Hindustani*) was a song picturization filmed in Australia featuring kangaroos (2002: 165).

The reasons for the increase in foreign locations are manifold and the inclusion of exotic locales reflects economic, technical, and aesthetic shifts within the Indian film industry. Today, as Gopalan has noted, song picturizations are related especially to tourism and consumerism: 'Not unlike the commercial imperative towards product placement in contemporary American cinema, song and dance sequences draw in a whole host of adjacent economies such as tourism and consumerism that are not so easily compartmentalized in Indian cinema (2002: 19). In other words, while audiences in South Asia may pay money to see their favourite stars singing in exotic locales and while they may especially enjoy images of a consumer lifestyle on display in the shopping malls of overseas cities, the film-maker's choice of locale has become heavily influenced by the production incentives offered by governments aiming to promote tourism, inward investment, and business migration from among the growing Indian middle-classes. The mountains of Kashmir as a romantic destination for the hero and heroine were replaced by the Swiss Alps in the 1980s, which were themselves supplemented by the mountains of New Zealand and Scotland in the 1990s; but the increase in overseas locations has also seen an increase in urban settings, with New York and London the pre-eminent choice due to a combination of their iconicity, blatant consumerism, and financial incentives. Sydney, Toronto and, more recently, Cape Town, are the other major cities outside of Asia that regularly attract Indian film-makers, though Rome and Paris have remained popular due to their romantic connotations, and Dubai is steadily building up its profile in Indian films. But the newest development has been the growth among the global cities of Asia, such as Seoul, Singapore, and especially, Bangkok.

The main cities appearing in Indian cinema—New York, London, Sydney, Toronto, Cape Town, Dubai, and Bangkok—have significant South Asian populations. While critics have recognized that such cities constitute strong overseas markets for Indian cinema, no one has attempted to examine what part of the diasporic family and business networks may play in the choice of overseas filming location, though given the size and spread of the Indian diaspora, the relationship is possibly no more than a coincidence. There is, however, a necessary high correlation between these cities and those Indian films that explore the lives of Indians overseas, marked in its most recent phase by the release of *Dilwale Dulhania Le Jayenge* (*DDLJ*) (1995). Like earlier Yash Chopra productions (*Faasle* 1985, *Chandni* 1989, *Darr* 1993), *DDLJ* sets the awakening of love between hero and heroine against the mountains of Switzerland, but the everyday life to which they return is that of London rather than Mumbai. Both hero and heroine have been brought up in Britain, one being born there and the other being taken there as a young child, and while not all non-resident Indian (NRI) heroes and heroines that have followed *DDLJ* have been born overseas, they have become increasingly comfortable with living their everyday lives outside India. Major Hindi productions, such as *Kal Ho Naa Ho* (2003), *Neal 'N' Nikki* (2005), *Salaam Namaste* (2005), *Kabhi Alvida Naa Kehna* (2006), *Heyy Babyy* (Sajid Khan, 2007), *Jhoom Barabar Jhoom* (2007), *Race* (2008), and *Crook* (2010) are set entirely overseas, whilst Tamil cinema (for example, *Nala Damayanthi* 2003, *London* 2005, *Unnale Unnale* 2007, *Aridhu Aridhu* 2010), Telugu cinema (for example, *Vamsi* 2000, *Mr. Errababu* 2005, *Chintakayala Ravi* 2008, *Orange* 2010) and, now, Punjabi cinema (*Virsa* 2010) have contributed to this trend by setting substantial parts of their stories overseas.

A number of studies have attempted to describe and explain these changes, assessing the shifts in the representation of NRIs in Indian cinema from the perspective of either Indian or diasporic audiences. Recent Indian interest in its diaspora was marked by the Report of the High Level Committee on the Indian Diaspora presented to the Indian prime minister in 2002, behind which lay those wealthy NRIs and Persons of Indian Origin (PIO) whom the Indian Government is trying to attract (back) to India, with recognition of NRIs and PIOs now being marked each January by Pravasi Bharatiya Divas, a special programme of events in partnership with the Ministry of Overseas Indian Affairs. In terms of popular culture, Sujata Moorti has looked not at the effect of India on the diaspora but at 'the effect of the diaspora on the Indian imagination'(2005: 50), in particular, at how the diaspora has produced a globalized Indian identity within India, while at the same time helping to reassert traditional Indian values. There has also been good work on Indian audiences, such as Shakuntala Rao's interviews with students in Patiala in Punjab that reveal how the lives of NRI yuppies as portrayed in Hindi cinema can alienate non-elite, rural Indian audiences; as one interviewee puts it: 'Only Punjabi films show what NRIs are really doing[,] like working in gas stations or working in a restaurant like in *Des Hoya[a] Pardes*. Hindi films don't show how Indians abroad are living' (2007: 68). This is not strictly true, and the petrol station in *Des Hoyaa Pardes* (2004) is prefigured in *DDLJ*, while the New York taxi drivers in *Aa Ab Laut Chalein* (1999) and *Ta Ra Rum Pum* (2007) also come to mind; but the sentiment nevertheless attests to an alienation of rural audiences from films featuring wealthy NRIs. Conversely, as Srinivas has observed in terms of Kannada cinema, where Indian middle-class audiences have been wooed away from India's regional cinemas towards Hindi movies, those cinemas have been forced to cater more exclusively for rural audiences, which is becoming their main market (2005: 107).

Rao's reference to Punjabi films is a rare acknowledgement of Indian cinemas in languages other than Hindi and scant critical attention has been paid to Tamil or Telugu cinema outside of India, despite each producing annually the same number of films as Hindi cinema (Kasbekar 2006: 181). Aswin Punathambekar has noted:

> While Bollywood may affect to speak for and about Indianness, we need to keep in mind our lack of understanding of how different linguistic groups in diverse settings in the Indian diaspora (Tamil, Telugu, Kannada, Bengali, and so on in Malaysia, Fiji, Norway, South Africa, etc.) engage with different regional cinemas and how the politics and pleasures in those cases intersect with Bollywood's 'national' narratives. (2005: 166)

In addition, studies of the reception of Indian films within the diaspora have concentrated on the USA or the UK, with the notable exception of the study of South Asian audiences in Germany by Christiane Brosius (2006). The least convincing of these studies make no reference to actual audiences, instead extrapolate from the films an ideal 'diasporic spectator' (Hu 2006) or 'imagined space' occupied by a diasporic audience (Kao and Rozario 2008). Happily, there are a growing number of studies based on surveys and interviews that, as in Rao and Brosius, draw attention to the complex, diverse, and frequently contradictory reactions of real people to these films. Drawing on her sociological study of cinema viewing in Bangalore, Srinivas writes:

> Through selective viewing [,] habituees do not consume a narrative with its own sequence and coherence. Their practices enable them to cobble together fragments to reconstruct an entertainment to suit their taste and needs. Cinema becomes a group construction, one which is particular to a local setting, rather than a mass media product which is universal. Consequently, the 'film' that emerges is the result of audience interaction rather than a construction of the film-maker's [sic] which audiences passively consume. In this context, cinema does not provide a homogenizing effect, rather, plural audiences construct differentiated experiences. (2002: 166)

We need, therefore, to be wary of extrapolating an ideal 'diasporic spectator' from the films as texts, and as Shakuntala Banaji notes of her study of young people in London of Indian, Pakistani, and Bangladeshi background: 'Rather than discovering a single, coherent "diasporic response" to the act of Hindi film viewing, I found major differences between the film viewing contexts and experiences of young British-Asian people from different communities in London' (2006: 48–9).

Despite the mantra of a globalized Bollywood, the study of the reception of Indian cinema outside of India has to date been narrow in scope, ignoring global diversity in favour of the globalizing 'diasporic response' to be found in the US. Putting to one side the dominance of inward-looking studies of either the US or the UK, the focus on Hindi cinema has not only marginalized other Indian cinemas, which most writers choose to ignore or are ignorant of, it has also been largely preoccupied with the role of cinema in the maintenance, negotiation, or creation of an Indian identity among the diaspora. Jigna Desai, for example, argues that, unlike in the darshanic relationship which depends on a recognition of difference between image and spectator, 'the diasporic spectator desires and aspires to be like and imitate the original upon which it gazes' (2004: 117). Such studies, therefore, tell us little about how, say, a Tamil movie like *Nala Damayanthi* which features a Sri Lankan Tamil Australian living in Melbourne may, as well as maintaining, negotiating, or creating a Tamilian identity (in all its political and cultural complexity), maintains, negotiates, or creates identification with an Australian host land within the Sri Lankan Tamil community in Melbourne. These may be considered as opposite sides of the same coin, but if Bollywood is truly globalized, then conclusions about British Asian identities drawn from, say, the reception in London of *Ramji Londonwaley* (2005) need to be compared not with the film's reception in Mumbai, which is implicit in studies of the 'diasporic' spectator or audience, but with the reception in Melbourne of *Nala Damayanthi*, the Tamil film of which *Ramji Londonwaley* was the Hindi remake.

Manu Madan has written of a screening of Rishi Kapoor's *Aa Ab Laut Chalein* in Perth, Western Australia, which attracted a much larger than usual Indian audience due to the appearance of Perth in a song picturization. Shots of Kings Park produced laughter, clapping, and cheers, and Madan suggests that the film helped its audience to articulate an Australian aspect of its diasporic identity: 'Bollywood's interest in Australia has made the diaspora take note of the specificities of their location (city, landscape, culture) and become conscious of both the Australian nuances that inform their identity and the disaporic aspect of their Indian identity' (2000: 29) With the growth in the number of Indian films featuring overseas locations, studies of the role of Hindi cinema in maintaining, negotiating, and creating an Indian identity among the diaspora need to be counter-balanced by studies of the role of Indian cinema in maintaining, negotiating, and creating an identification with the host land. To be sure, not many filmmakers in India would be able to explore diasporic lives in the way they have been explored by diasporic film-makers like Mira Nair and Gurinder Chadha, notwithstanding attempts such as Puneet Sira's *I... Proud to be an Indian* (2004) or Jag Mundhra's two films, *Provoked: A True Story* (2006) and *Shoot on Sight* (2007). Nonetheless, Madan's account of the celebration of brief glimpses of Kings Park appearing in a song sequence in a movie set in the US suggests an almost parochial desire by Indian communities overseas for their host land to be recognized by Indian cinema.

Raminder Kaur in her analysis of British Asian responses to Bollywood has sought to explore not only identification with India but the processes of self-identification involved in viewing representations of one's own diasporic community on-screen; that is, 'the idea that ingredients designed with the so-called NRI/"diasporan" in mind do not necessarily lead to a concerted series of identifications from British Asians' (2006: 315). Through interviewing second-generation British (South) Asians about their experiences of watching *DDLJ*, Kaur identified a 'disidentification' that co-existed with an emotional engagement with Indian cinema, a momentary and contingent resistance to attempts by Indian filmmakers and their corporate financiers to persuade them to maintain emotional and financial links with India; as one interviewee put it: 'The hero and heroine—they might have been born in England but they're like those in *Goodness Gracious Me* when the Indian students go on an outing to England' (ibid.: 319). Of particular interest, in terms of the song picturizations, is Kaur's finding that her interviewees were more critical of the realist (third-person) narrative sections of the film than of the fantasy (first-person) song sequences:

> The disposition to have a willing suspension of disbelief is less so for the familiar, the mundane, particularly if it pertains to an area that the spectators recognise and is firmly implanted as part of the narrative, rather than couched as a backdrop for a song routine. (Ibid.: 320)

In other words, while British Asian spectators may be prepared to immerse themselves in the romance of Shah Rukh singing to Kajol on an open-top London tourist bus, they find it improbable that Amrish Puri should, after feeding the pigeons in Trafalgar Square, walk past Buckingham Palace on his way to work.

Here we might return to the orthodoxy that film audiences identify with the on-screen audiences of musical sequences. If, as Feuer puts it, 'We, the spectators, are encouraged to identify with a spontaneous audience which has actually participated in the performance' (1993: 34), then Kaur's findings suggest that diasporic Indian audiences would find the representation of themselves as an on-screen audience unproblematic. Whilst couples in Indian films might dance romantically alone in the mountains of Switzerland, Scotland, or New Zealand, there is little chance of not drawing a crowd when dancing in the streets of New York or London, especially when news of the filming can be so rapidly circulated within diasporic communities via the internet and mobile phones. We need, of course, to be wary of the degree to which 'impromptu' audiences are spontaneous, and those discussed by Feuer are, as she admits, film extras, and the streets are studio sets. Indian cinema is more flexible, and film-makers regularly break the conventions of Hollywood realism by including in shot crowds who have gathered to watch the filming of fight scenes or dance sequences. One of the reasons given for filming overseas is to simplify the security arrangements required to prevent the film location being overrun by fans (Verma 2000) and it would be impossible to shoot street scenes in India without crowds quickly gathering. For similar reasons, impromptu crowds may appear more frequently in smaller budget films, especially Tamil and Telugu movies, which lack the resources for security and location fees required for street closures; indeed, lower budget films may dispense with professional dancers and co-opt bystanders into short routines, as in *Preetse* (2000), the songs of which were shot in Australia 'for the first time in the history of Kannada cinema' (Nagendrappa n.d.). Indian film-makers, therefore, seem to have made a virtue out of necessity by including casual bystanders in shot and, in so doing, mark the difference in cinematic culture between Indian cinema and Hollywood. Acknowledgement of the camera and film crew, obsessively hidden in Hollywood, disrupts the realist illusion and is consistent with the opposition between an interactive darshanic or first-person relationship between performer and audience and a Hollywood voyeuristic or third-person mode. In sum, we could posit that the difference between the Hollywood musical and the Indian song picturization is the possibility of including the casual bystander (in some cases, as in *Nala Damayanthi*, captured filming the filming), a difference that interestingly would situate in the Hollywood camp a major Hindi production like *Kabhi Alvida Naa Kehna*, which excludes the casual bystander by a combination of camera angle and restricting public access to outdoor public locations.

As Gopalan reminds us, song picturizations are now entangled with the adjacent economies of tourism and consumerism, with heroes and heroines dancing alternately in front of, say, Piccadilly Circus or the Brooklyn Bridge and an outlet for McDonald's or Starbucks (Emraan Hashmi, in fact, plays a UK tour guide in *Dil Diya Hai* 2006). To the degree that such sequences are to be read as romantic fantasies, enhanced by the fantasies of tourism and consumer marketing, then it may well be that diasporic audiences are disposed to suspend their disbelief and identify with the impromptu audiences that gather to watch the filming. Yet each of the various treatments of the supposedly symbolic process of audience identification assume a correlation in the composition of audiences *of* the film and *in* the film and such discussions tells us nothing about cases where there are differences in culture, skin colour, and location between film and on-screen audiences. At what level, for example, is there identification between Rao's Punjabi interviewees, who were critical of the representation of American NRIs in *Swades* (2004), and South Asian bystanders in Trafalgar Square in *Speed* (2007) Or between a Sikh spectator in Toronto and the Afro-American internal New York audience in *Jaan-e-Mann* (2006) Or between an Australian Tamil spectator and the white Australian on-screen audience in *Pokkiri* (2007) Or, indeed, between an Italian-Australian spectator and the Italian bystanders in Venice in *Bachna ae Haseeno* (2008)? And with some films set in one country yet filmed in another, there are almost countless possible permutations.

It would be absurd to suggest that sufficient audience research could produce an algorithm for processing data, such as the cultural background of the spectator and their degree of familiarity with the song locations, which would reveal the level of identification with the on-screen audience. Nonetheless, it seems equally unlikely that the cultural background of the spectator and their degree of familiarity with the locations of the song do not play a part in how song picturizations set outside of India are received by individual spectators. This is not to dismiss the idea that commercial cinemas address what Srinivas terms a 'habituated' audience, 'audiences who have developed a relationship with the films based on long acquaintance with them' (2002: 157). Cinema-going in India is generally a collective experience and, according to Srinivas, film-makers, 'attentive to the expectations of habituees, construct the films as a dialogue with such viewers' (ibid.). Yet it is also apparent that there are similar collective and habituated audiences for Indian films outside of India, audiences which can identify with their host land as well as their homeland, as Madan's example of the laughing, clapping, and cheering Indian audience in Perth demonstrates.

Possibly the willing suspension of disbelief, by which Kaur accounted for the less critical attitude of British Asians to the song sequences set in London, is related to a desire to see their city projected well overseas, especially in India. The shots of Kings Park in Perth that appear in the song in *Aa Ab Laut Chalein* project a romantic retreat of spring flowers and glimpses of the Swan River, the kind of image that makes Kings Park a popular location for local wedding photographers. Yet observations of cinema audiences undertaken by Srinivas suggest that fantasy song sequences nonetheless permit identification with the location as a real place that is knowable to a local audience. Audience members adopt a selective viewing style and have different levels of emotional engagement with what is happening on screen:

> Viewers may hum along with a tune or tap their fingers to the music even when it is background for a tense or tragic scene. Such aesthetic appreciation extends as viewers look beyond the film to the reality which contributed to it, in what may be termed a documentary mode of viewing (Sobchack, 1999), as they remark on scenery 'See it's [Melkote, where the film was shot] so beautiful! We can go there on a picnic all of us!'. (2002: 166)

Such a viewing style is not inconsistent with Kaur's findings, but it reveals identification with place as the result of a disruption of the 'first-person' fantasy by a documentary 'third-person' viewing mode. In other words, where spectators accept the idealization of a known location in a fantasy song sequence, their parochialism results in both a belief in the fantasy projected and a negation of the exotic nature of its location. While there may indeed be a desire on the part of members of a diasporic audience to believe in the touristic projection of their host land in India, spectators may *at the same time* adopt a documentary mode of viewing.

With studies of diasporic audiences so preoccupied with Indianness and with identification with the homeland, the data for an analysis of any documentary identification with the host land does not exist. However, a certain parochialism, or loyalty to one's city, comes into play when Indian films are discussed on internet forums. On the Internet Movie Database, a dispersed South Asian membership dominates discussions of major Hindi films. One contributor established a 'Torontonian' identity by pointing out that parts of *Kal Ho Naa Ho*, which was set in New York, were filmed in Toronto:

> In the very beginning when Pretti Zinta is talking about New York there is a scene where they are showing an intersection with traffic moving. At the red light you can clearly see many TTC (Toronto Transit Commission) buses go by which are unmistakable by any Torontonian. Just thought I'd point that out, found it to be rather interesting.[1]

Another contributor, who admitted watching *Salaam Namaste* largely, 'because it was filmed in my hometown, Melbourne',[2] provoked others into defending the film's depiction of life in Melbourne by commenting: 'I had no idea that the story would be about a couple having a "live-in" relationship. This is considered as taboo in our culture. Our parents would kill us or disown us. Come on think about it all you Indians out there.'[3] Although the main discussion was about cultural values within Indian overseas communities—'i live in canada (I'm indian) ... have lived here all my life, and u know what, its ok to cohabitate here'[4]—another contributor from Melbourne felt able to defend the film on the grounds of realism, of the film's depiction of life in Melbourne: 'i'm from melbourne as well and i have a lot of friends (desi and non-desi) who have found themselves in similar situations, be it live-in relationships, or unplanned pregnancies.'[5] Being a member of the Indian diaspora does not prevent spectators outside of south India from identifying with an 'exotic' locale as documentary where the overseas locale is their hometown.

While there is no data relating specifically to spectator identification with the on-screen audience in song picturizations, recognition of a familiar locale triggers a parochialism that we might anticipate would also be triggered by familiarity with the on-screen bystanders. In other words, a documentary mode of viewing song sequences does not lead to the kind of 'disidentification' with London as noted by Kaur in the comments by British Asians sceptical of the verisimilitude of the narrative, or third-person, sections of the film; rather, the overlaying of the fantasy of the song sequences by familiarity increases identification with the locale. Internet forums not only distribute information about the exact location in which film crews are filming, they also record the experience of watching the filming and, on occasion, the possibility of appearing on screen. In November 2006, notices were sent out inviting locals to participate as hockey spectators in the filming of *Chak De! India* in Melbourne: 'Crowds are desperately needed!! If you would like to meet Shah Rukh Khan, attend the state netball hockey centre in Melbourne on the 24th November, to be part of the crowd of this feature film. Wear your brightest colours—the more you stand out, the more likely you will be featured.'[6] Inevitably, the reality of the occasion did not match the expectation of meeting Shah Rukh, but even a glimpse of him made the waiting worthwhile:

> I was There!!! Yeah i only got to see a little of him when he got out of the car, then nothing happened for the rest of the night (that i saw). He came out of this white sedan (a holden i think) out of a tunnel and waved to the crowd. I think he might have had a bit of a beard and his hair kinda long and shaggy. Yeah, alot of people wore traditional indian costume and they split us into either 'Australian' or 'Indian' depending on what we were wearing. Yeah and they filmed us 'cheering' as they camera panned past us, so Yay! im in the movie!!![7]

When *Chak De! India* was released in Melbourne, many among the audiences were looking for glimpses of themselves among the crowd at the hockey match between India and Australia. Yet whilst, globally, such viewers comprise an insignificant proportion of a movie's total overseas box office, their mode of viewing is much the same as those who, like the contributor who provoked the discussion of morality in *Salaam Namaste*, watch a film 'because it was filmed in my home town'.[8]

Familiar places and faces are important in the kind of documentary mode of viewing which seeks them out. It plays to a parochialism that looks for similarity rather than difference, particularly among audiences more used to seeing Mumbai or Delhi on-screen than their hometown. And while, for first generation migrants, Mumbai or Delhi might be familiar as known places, images of Perth or Toronto or Cape Town appearing in Indian cinema break with the generic norms that create expectations of the places and faces most likely to appear on screen. The kind of audience reactions that Kaur noted, that at once criticize the verisimilitude of the narrative sections while relishing the tourism fantasy of the song sequences, depend on a parochialism induced by a documentary mode of viewing. This parochialism may in part reflect a desire for the host land to gain a certain status from recognition by Indian cinema and cinema audiences in Mumbai and Delhi. But it may also in part reflect a parochialism shared with non-South Asian spectators who are part of a non-ethnically defined viewing community, one which includes anyone who watches Indian popular cinema and which is defined by Adrian Athique as, 'the audience constructed by participation in the consumption of Indian movies, which are perceived as enacting diverse cultural dialogues across a wide and variegated social space' (2005: 119). The social space of the consumption of Indian cinema also includes non-South Asian film festival audiences and films like *Salaam Namaste* or *Kal Ho Naa Ho* have the potential to promote cross-cultural communication and a greater awareness of South Asian cultural values within Melbourne or New York.

In conclusion, Jane Feuer's argument that 'the internal audience serves a symbolic not a realistic purpose; they are the celluloid embodiment of the film audience's subjectivity' (1993: 27) is inadequate as an explanation of the role of internal audiences in Indian cinema. This is not only because the presence of casual bystanders taking photos of the stars and looking into the camera breaks the realist convention of concealing the presence of camera and film crew, a repudiation of Hollywood's practice that makes possible, in Lutgendorf's word, 'a visual interaction between players who, though not equal, are certainly both in the same theater of activity and capable of influencing each other'(2006: 234). Feuer's explanation is also inadequate because the increase in the number of overseas cities appearing in Indian cinema has resulted in more and more diasporic South Asian spectators seeing their home towns represented on screen in Indian movies, with the documentary mode of viewing familiar places and faces countering any purely symbolic identification with the casual bystanders.

Without data against which to test the interpretation of informal remarks posted on internet forums, how spectators view their home-towns in Indian cinema remains largely speculation. However, it is clear that studies of the representation of the diaspora in Indian cinema have mostly accepted the representation in those films and consequently focussed on the ways in which subjects negotiate the strength or precise configuration of their *Indian* identity. It is a commonplace among such studies that Indian films no longer set up an opposition between a Western lifestyle and a traditional Indian lifestyle and that the films depict a modern Indian lifestyle; as Punathambekar, quoting Arvind Rajagopal, puts it: 'NRIs are acutely conscious of their position as "an apotheosis of the Indian middle class, exemplifying what 'Indians' could achieve if they were not hampered by an underdeveloped society and an inefficient government"' (2005: 157). The conferring of identity by the film-makers on the locals who volunteered to play the hockey crowd in *Chak De! India* is, in this sense, retrogressive: 'alot of people wore traditional indian costume and they split us into either "Australian" or "Indian" depending on what we were wearing.'⁹ To be Indian, is to wear Indian costume (at least for women). Yet, even if scholars, like the film-makers, tell us that modern Indians who dress in a globalized Western style can still hold traditional values, they have lacked appreciation of the ways in which members of the diaspora can be Australian or British or American. What is missing from such studies is recognition of the ways in which Australians of Indian descent can barrack for the Australian hockey team in *Chak De! India* or cheer when a shot of Perth comes on screen in *Aa Ab Laut Chalein*. This is not to deny that others will not share such parochialism, or that parochialism is not part of a more complex 'hyphenated' identification, though it is also salutary to remember that not all among the Indian diaspora watch Indian films. We know little about how the representation of, say, Jaggu Yadav (Javed Jaffrey), the Australianized Indian in *Salaam Namaste*, is viewed among audiences in Australia in terms of 'Australianness'; or how, in *Thiruttu Payale* (2006), a Tamil film also shot in Australia, an advertisement for Jayco camper trailers is received by a local Tamil audience in Dandenong, where the trailers are manufactured. What is missing from most accounts of the 'globalization' of Indian popular cinema are the reactions of local audiences to the documentary depiction of familiar places and faces on screen.

Notes

1. For details see: hassan-sulaiman, 'Toronto', Internet Movie Database, 17 September 2008, http://uk.imdb.com/title/tt0347304/board/nest/117969381, accessed 17 February 2009.

2. bio_girl, 'Far fetched + against the indian culture!', Internet Movie Database, 16 September 2005, http://uk.imdb.com/title/tt0456165/board/thread/26366611?d=26366611&p=1#26366611, accessed 24 March 2010.

3. Ibid.

4. masudream, 'Re: Far fetched + against the indian culture!', Internet Movie Database, 18 October 2005, http://uk.imdb.com/title/tt0456165/board/nest/26366611?d=28157365&p=2#28157365, accessed 24 March 2010.

5. sonia-rhea33, 'Re: Far fetched + against the indian culture!' Internet Movie Database, 29 October 2005, http://uk.imdb.com/title/tt0456165/board/nest/26366611?d=28741462&p=1#28741462, accessed 24 March 2010.

6. DiMa_8, 'australians, look here!', Internet Movie Database, 21 November 2006, http://uk.imdb.com/title/tt0871510/board/thread/59258973, accessed 17 February 2009.

7. queen_kimbo, 'Re: Did anyone take part as an extra at the velodrome for this one?', Internet Movie Database, 8 January 2007 (05:54:19), http://uk.imdb.com/title/tt0871510/board/thread/62239867? d=63338336&p=1#63338336, accessed 17 February 2009.

8. bio_girl, 'Far fetched.'

9. queen_kimbo, 'Re: Did anyone take part.'

References

Athique, Adrian. 2005. 'Watching Indian Movies in Australia: Media, Community and Consumption', *South Asian Popular Culture*, vol. 3, no. 2.

Banaji, Shakuntala. 2006. *Reading 'Bollywood': The Young Audience and Hindi Films*, Basingstoke, Hants: Palgrave Macmillan.

Brosius, Christiane. 2006. 'The Scattered Homelands of the Migrant: Bollyworld through the Diasporic Lens', in Raminder Kaur and Ajay J. Sinha (eds), *Bollyworld: Popular Indian Cinema through a Transnational Lens*, New Delhi: Sage.

Desai, Jigna. 2004. *Beyond Bollywood: The Cultural Politics of South Asian Diasporic Film*, New York: Routledge.

Dwyer, Rachel and Divia Patel. 2002. *Cinema India: The Visual Culture of Hindi Film*, London: Reaktion.

Feuer, Jane. 1993. *The Hollywood Musical*, Bloomington and Indianapolis: Indiana University Press.

Gopalan, Lalitha. 2002. *Cinema of Interruptions: Action Genres in Contemporary Indian Cinema*, London: BFI.

Hayward, Susan. 1996. *Key Concepts in Cinema Studies*, London: Routledge.

Hu, Brian. 2006. 'Bollywood Dreaming: *Kal Ho Naa Ho* and the Diasporic Spectator', *Post Script*, vol. 253.

Kao, Kai-Ti and Rebecca-Anne Do Rozario. 2008. 'Imagined Spaces: the Implications of Song and Dance for Bollywood's Diasporic Communities', *Continuum: Journal of Media and Cultural Studies*, vol. 22, no. 3.

Kasbekar, Asha. 2006. *Pop Culture India! Media, Arts, and Lifestyle*, Santa Barbara: ABC-CLIO.

Kaur, Raminder. 2006. 'Cruising on the *Vilayeti* Bandwagon: Diasporic Representations and the Reception of Popular Indian Movies', in Raminder Kaur and Ajay J. Sinha (eds), *Bollyworld: Popular Indian Cinema through a Transnational Lens*, New Delhi: Sage.

Kohli-Khandekar, Vanita. 2006. *The Indian Music Business*, New Delhi: Sage.

Lutgendorf, Philip. 2006. 'Is There an Indian Way of Filmmaking?', *International Journal of Hindu Studies*, vol. 10, no. 3.

Madan, Manu. 2000. 'Bollywood Down Under: Imagining New Neighbours', *South Asia*, vol. 23.

Mishra, Vijay. *Bollywood Cinema: Temples of Desire*, London: Routledge, 2001.

Moorti, Sujata. 2005. 'Uses of Diaspora: Indian Popular Culture and the NRI Dilemma', *South Asian Popular Culture* 3 (1), pp. 49–62.

Nagendrappa, Vani, 'Preetse', indiainfo.com, accessed 18 February 2009, http://movies.indiainfo.com/reviews/south/kannada/preetse.html.

Pfanner, Eric, 'India's New Cinema has a Global Script', *International Herald Tribune*, 22 May 2006; accessed 4 February 2009, http://www.iht.com/articles/2006/05/21/yourmoney/movies22.php.

Prasad, M. Madhava. 1998. *Ideology of the Hindi Film: A Historical Construction*, New Delhi: Oxford University Press.

Punathambekar, Aswin. 2005. 'Bollywood in the Indian-American Diaspora: Mediating a Transitive Logic of Cultural Citizenship', *International Journal of Cultural Studies*, 8 (2), pp. 151–73.

Rao, S. 2007. 'The Globalization of Bollywood: an Ethnography of Non-Elite Audiences in India', *Communication Review*, vol. 10.

Srinivas, Laksmi. 2005. 'Imaging the Audience', *South Asian Popular Culture*, vol. 3, no. 2.

—————. 2002. 'The Active Audience: Spectatorship, Social Relations and the Experience of Cinema in India', *Media, Culture and Society*, vol. 24.

Tyrrell, Heather and Rajinder Dudrah. 2006. 'Music in the Bollywood Film', in Ian Conrich and Estella Ticknell (eds), *Film's Musical Moments*, Edinburgh: Edinburgh University Press.

Verma, Sukanya. 2000. 'Haire Mai', rediff.com, 21 July; accessed on 11 February 2009; http://www.rediff.com/entertai/2000/jul/21kiwi.htm.

16 Yaari with Angrez

Whiteness for a New Bollywood Hero[1]

TERESA HUBEL

One of the things I've always appreciated about Indian films in general and Hindi ones in particular has been the relative insignificance of whiteness to their narratives. While white characters do turn up occasionally, they are most often peripheral figures who work to create the effect of historical accuracy, like the British soldiers in both *Umrao Jaan* movies (directed by Muzzaffar Ali, 1981; directed by J.P. Dutta, 2006), or, in a more recent trend, to increase the hero's masculine status by functioning as backup trophy dancers in, for instance, *Singh is Kinng* (directed by Anees Bazmee, 2008). When white characters play roles more central to the story's political aspirations, they tend to work as somewhat simplistic foils for nationalist heroes, for example, in *The Legend of Bhagat Singh* (directed by Rajkumar Santoshi, 2002), where they are shown to be unremittingly cruel and callous in order to highlight the protagonist's courageous resistance to them and the unjust system they represent.

I've appreciated the peripheral nature of whiteness in Hindi cinema because it has always suggested to me that Bollywood[2] has had other fish to fry, so to speak, issues other than India's colonial legacy to explore and debate. This is not to say that Bollywood films haven't been the site of a certain degree of fixation regarding India's relationship to the

West, but such fixation usually plays itself out through the interaction of Indian characters, one or more of whom are depicted as in some way Westernized, either in terms of their apparent racial heritage or their cultural choices. Gangoli (2005) argues that it is the female characters who are more likely than the male to be the markers of an implied battle between the dichotomously constructed values of the West and those of the Indian, since it is on their bodies (the clothes and jewellery they wear, how their hair is done) and in terms of their fates (whether they die or live, are triumphally happy or tragically miserable by the end of the movie) that the West/India divide is delineated. Historically, then, the dilemmas posed by the West have been dealt with primarily by means of Indian characters.

In Bollywood films, whiteness cannot be said to function, therefore, as it does in the West, where the legacy of imperialism has made it an un-marked category, the invisibility of which allows it to behave as a norm that measures the aberrance of racial/cultural others. Hence, whites in the West get to see themselves, not as privileged or as the historical, local winners in an international structure of domination, but as people whose advantages are the result of their individual efforts, whose successes are all entirely earned rather than hugely over-determined, and, even more important, whites get to set the standards of such social institutions as civility, virtue, intelligence, cleanliness, and so on, without having to be aware of how those standards ensure or at least increase the likeli-hood that non-white, Western others will fail to live up to them and consequently be called criminal, stupid, corrupt, or dirty. It is, largely, though not completely, the unmarked quality of whiteness in the West that allows for this kind of covert and usually unselfconscious exercise of power. As Dyer insists,

> As long as race is something only applied to non-white peoples, as long as white people are not racially seen and named, they/we function as a human norm. Other people are raced, we are just people.
> There is no more powerful position than that of being 'just' human. The claim to power is the claim to speak for the commonality of humanity. (1997: 1–2)

But in Indian films (in India generally), whiteness, in its still uncommon appearances, *is* marked: it is markedly white, noticeably there, to be resisted or desired or dismissed. It cannot hide its privilege beneath its ubiquity, since it has no such ubiquity. Far from speaking for humanity, whiteness is delineated most frequently in an oppositional negative, usually as inferior, though rarely as subordinate.

Without its invisibility, whiteness in Bollywood films cannot truly be said to function as a norm, certainly not in Foucault's conception of the norm as a product of modernity that disguises its own historical embeddedness in order to present itself as a timeless, transcendent moral code. In *Discipline and Punish*, Foucault describes a sequential carceral archipelago, which emerged in the early to mid-nineteenth century and which included schools for juvenile delinquents, workhouses, lunatic asylums, prisons, and finally, charitable homes for the sick and dying. This network trapped for life those who were believed to be liable to exhibit signs of social disorder or who 'resisted disciplinary normalization' and was the model for the 'art of punishing' (1979: 296) we have inherited. It also allowed for the surfacing of, in Foucault's words, 'a new form of "law": a mixture of legality and nature, prescription and constitution, the norm' (1979: 304). What is implicit in his analysis is that this punitive system was/is dependent on historically contingent values hidden beneath a veil of normativity. For the system to remain fully operative, the normative status of disciplinary norms cannot be questioned, since such questioning would reveal them to be provisional, culturally and historically specific beliefs that they indeed are and so render them unstable.[3]

Given that whiteness is not a norm in Bollywood film or in India, because it is not hidden and does not go unquestioned, the theoretical and political purpose of naming it cannot be the same as in the West. Here is Dyer's justification for his study on whiteness in mainstream Western representations:

> The point of seeing the racing of whites is to dislodge them/us from the position of power, with all the inequities, oppression, privileges and sufferings in its train, dislodging them/us by undercutting the authority with which they/we speak and act in and on the world. (1997: 2)

It seems to me that Indian cinema already has a long history of racing whiteness. As part of its ongoing affiliation with nationalism, it has named whiteness to undercut its authority. A number of pre-1990 films have demonstrated the inability of white characters to seamlessly or effectively wield modern modes of power/knowledge. For example, in Satyajit Ray's *Shatranj Ki Khilari* (1977) not only is the imperial ability of whiteness to propagate norms exposed in the relationship between

Wajid Ali Shah, the Nawab of Awadh, and General Outram, the British resident of Lucknow sent by the governor-general to depose him and annex his kingdom, but the failure of Orientalist discourse to comprehend the principles through which this Indian king rules is also made evident, for Wajid, in all his complexity, ultimately escapes Outram's conceptions. As a justification for empire, Orientalism disintegrates in the film, its efficacy lost, and Outram is left having to rely on treachery and the threat of military might. These are the tools of tyrants, not the hegemonic power of modern empires wielding Orientalist discourse.[4]

So it is not the naming of whiteness that matters in Hindi cinema. What matters is that, though not normative, whiteness retains a structural positioning as dominant. It would be difficult to argue otherwise; in those few films where white characters feature as something more than mere figures of colonial authority or the jiggling symbols of a male protagonist's heroic masculinity, they are fundamental in some way. But what is dominance when it is detached from normativity? What does it do? Which ends, or perhaps *whose* ends, does this dominant but *not* normative whiteness serve in Bollywood films?

To answer these questions, I will examine two films, produced since the turn of the millennium in which white characters play significant roles: *Lagaan: Once upon a Time in India* (directed by Ashutosh Gowariker, 2001) and *Mangal Pandey: The Rising* (directed by Ketan Mehta, 2005), will be examined in this chapter. Both are set during the British Empire, a period which, as Chakravarty states, is 'generally absent from films' generated by the Indian commercial industry (1993: 183);[5] the previous uncommonness of the colonial setting, coupled with its emergence in these two as well as in other recent films, would seem to suggest the advent of a new trend in Bollywood. I think that what we're seeing here is a shift in the more typical deployment of whiteness as a simple foil for the purposes of nationalist identity formation. While most white characters in these films retain their adversarial meaning, two significant ones—Captain William Gordon (Toby Stephens) in *Mangal Pandey* and Elizabeth (Rachel Shelley) in *Lagaan*—assist in the development of an Indian nationalism that comes to define and be defined by the male heroes of the film, both of whom are played by Aamir Khan, whose body itself signifies as an erotic spectacle. Neither of these white characters functions as a norm through which we are supposed to judge the heroes, though both provide a desiring perspective and represent a structural positioning that boosts the heroes' status. Significantly, it is the racial dominance of whiteness in a globalized world, in tune with their taken-for-granted middle-classness, that make Captain Gordon and Elizabeth especially well suited to their roles as consolidators of an elite Hindu masculinity in a post-liberalization India that, in the filmic reality of Bollywood at least, is trying to forget its poor.

What first roused my curiosity and made me wonder whether something new was afoot in Bollywood cinema was the character of Captain Gordon in *Mangal Pandey*. As a scholar of the British Empire and the nationalist movement in India and a longtime eavesdropper on Indian movies, I found *Mangal Pandey* was intriguing not only because it was one of the few Indian films that explores an event from the colonial era but also because it chose the Rebellion of 1857 as its subject, which, with rare exceptions, hasn't been of much interest to writers or filmmakers from the subcontinent. I've done a considerable amount of research into the various narratives engendered by the events of 1857, with a particular focus on those by or about poor whites who lived or served in colonial India, reveals that there is a recurrent myth in these narratives about white men who crossed the line and fought with the Indian forces.[6] In the character of Captain Gordon, *Mangal Pandey* draws on this myth. At the end of the film, after the hanging of Mangal, an act which in this version of the story provokes a massive resistance from ordinary Indians and so incites the Rebellion proper, the narrator tells us that 'An officer by the name of Captain William Gordon was recorded as having joined the rebel forces and fought against the Company Raj.' No such rebellious officer is named in the historical records, or in the official documents or even in the narratives of the revolt. The various white men who are said to have gone over to the other side are usually believed to have been soldiers from the lower ranks,[7] though one memoir describes among the rebels 'a handsome-looking man, well-built, fair, about twenty-five years of age, with light moustaches, wearing the undress uniform of a European cavalry officer, with a blue, gold-laced cap on his head' whom the writer, a Mr Rees, guesses to have been 'either a Russian or a renegade Christian' (qtd. in Forbes-Mitchell 1893: 279). That the makers of *Mangal Pandey* evoked this historical myth, making it central to the storyline, points to its meaningfulness in the film.

Whether based on a fiction or a fact, Captain William Gordon serves a two-fold purpose: much like Captain Weston in Ray's *Shatranj Ki*

Khilari, he is the compassionate *Angrez* whose empathy for the plight of the Indians under the Empire stands as a testament to its severity, which in turn, supports the implicit argument for nationalist resistance to the British; but, unlike the character of Weston, whose sympathy is confined to verbal and facial expression, he is the hero's best friend. He is rescued by him and then rescues him, hears his doubts about the East India Company, tries to talk him into compliance with the British, and eventually becomes an active supporter of Mangal's growing nationalism and, following Mangal's lead after the film ends, a nationalist himself. Their friendship propels all the action in the film, since it is in reaction to what he perceives as Gordon's lies about the fat used to grease the rifle cartridges—lies that he reads as the white man's betrayal of him—that Mangal decides to take drastic measures against the British, and this friendship also provides the film with its only fully articulated emotional storyline. Mangal's alliance with the courtesan Heera (Rani Mukerji) and Gordon's with the almost-sati Jwala (Amisha Patel) are both much less important to the politics or even the narrative of the film and, it could be argued, work mostly to provide it with the heterosexual romance necessary in virtually every Bollywood production and to deflect any possible questions about the compelling homoeroticism implied by such scenes as the wrestling match between Mangal and Gordon and the bhang-induced cuddling that happens afterwards when the two men wander past a palatial British residence with their arms draped over each other's shoulders. Mangal and Gordon, in fact, are distinguished as characters more by their passionate attachment to one another as well as their antagonism to other, more powerful men—namely the upper-middle class Protestant English officers who occupy the elite echelons of the company[8]—than they are by their connections to any women. Speaking about the US, David Mamet, the well-known playwright whose consistent theme is masculinity, is quoted as saying, 'Women have, in men's minds, such a low place on the social ladder of this country that it's useless to define yourself in terms of a woman .... What men need is men's approval' (qtd. in Kimmel 1994: 129).

Much the same could be said about the articulation of masculinity in *Mangal Pandey*, where, from very early on, it's made abundantly clear that the story will in large part be about Gordon's efforts to secure Mangal's approval. The wrestling scene begins, for example, with Gordon asking Mangal, 'Why didn't you come today?' obviously referring to a pre-arranged meeting that Mangal has avoided. Mangal answers, 'I was angry,' and then implies that he was disappointed Gordon did not intervene when, in the previous scene, another British officer, the bully Hewson, almost beat an Indian servant to death. It was Mangal who stepped in to stop Hewson from killing the innocent man. Gordon's explanation—'What was I supposed to do? Stand between a fellow officer and a, a ...' a sentence Mangal finishes with the words 'a black dog!' echoing Hewson's term for the servant—demonstrates that the approval of other men, in this case his fellow British officers, *does* matter in the establishment of Gordon's masculinity. When Gordon apologizes to Mangal and is forgiven, the two men resolve their quarrel. At this point, we are aware that Gordon has switched his masculine allegiance: it is Mangal's sanction, and no longer that of white men, he will now seek, though the seeking of it will cause him great inner turmoil and compel him to turn his back on his ruling racial community. That Mangal is engaged in this passionate camaraderie with a white man and is the recipient of his loyalty appreciably bolsters his masculinity because in the film's world of mid-nineteenth-century India as well as in the contemporary audience's eyes, whiteness is a signifier of dominance and power; Mangal must be some kind of man if Gordon, a white man and his superior in the East India Company's army, loves him that much.

Significantly, all of this emotional and sexual desire is being communicated while the two men are placing each other in the most spectacularly suggestive wrestling holds. And when Mangal laughingly concedes the match to Gordon and they fall back separately to the ground, the crowd of men watching them bursts into shouts of approbation and delight. *Mangal Pandey* is not exceptional in its rendition of men desiring the attention, affection, and approval of other men. According to a number of Hindi film critics, Bollywood movies generally are founded on a blatant eroticism between men that the standard heterosexual romance is meant to dampen and camouflage.

Editor of *Bombay Dost*, a gay news magazine based in Mumbai, Kavi argues that the Bollywood hero is being increasingly eroticized on the Hindi screen, to such an extent that the heroine is ceasing entirely to be an object of sexual desire. While films from the 1950s pursued some storylines that attended to women's lives and cast actresses in commanding roles, but then thereafter, they have been relegated to the sidelines, as 'appendages to this high drama of the eroticization of the male' (2000: 309). By the 1970s, the era of Amitabh Bachchan and the angry young man, the bonds between the hero and his *yaar* or best friend had so crowded out the female characters that Kavi insists the films could be read as misogynistic in their 'focus on men to the utter exclusion of women' (ibid.: 310).

Amitabh, described by Kavi as 'only apparently the most heterosexual of Hindi film heroes' (ibid.), is also the subject of an essay by Rao, in which, recalling his own experience watching Amitabh Bachchan films in Bombay movie halls in the late 1970s, he theorizes the implications of these narratives as well as of the song lyrics that subtly endorsed the expression of men's love for one another: 'The bond that Amitabh Bachchan formed with other male actors on the screen, complemented by the presence of an all-male audience that had gathered to watch him, engendered a sort of homoeroticism in the dark of the movie hall' (2000: 303). The homoeroticism on the screen sometimes found a physical expression in the hall itself, where, Rao claims, the darkness provided a cover for sexual acts between men.

Deshpande contends that the eroticization of the Bollywood hero has taken a more intense turn since the 1990s and is indicative of a larger shift in the middle-class imagination that drives the mainstream film industry in India. The camera that lingers lovingly on the more muscled bodies of current male stars is a sign that Bollywood has learned how to fashion what he calls a 'consumable hero' (2005: 197), a masculine figure whose body itself, rather than his person or even his story, is an object of consumption. *Jodhaa Akbar* (directed by Ashutosh Gowariker, 2008) exemplifies Deshpande's argument perfectly; like *Mangal Pandey* and *Lagaan*, this film fixates on the hero's sexual desirability. Though ostensibly about Jodhaa, the wife (Aishwarya Rai Bachchan) of the Mughul Emperor Akbar (Hrithik Roshan), *Jodhaa Akbar* would be more appropriately titled merely 'Akbar,' since it is his agonies, his decisions, and, more important, his body that the film loves. One scene in particular stands out as an emblem of this shift in interest that the camera makes apparent: before their marriage has been consummated, when Jodhaa has not yet learned to adore her emperor, she surreptitiously watches him as, naked from the waist up, he practices his swordplay. Our gaze follows hers as her eyes travel down his almost impossibly superb masculine body to his appealingly sweat-strewn waist, then up again and along his strong sword arm, and finally, up further to his handsome profile where the camera stops and we find in Akbar's half-smile the sign that he knows she/we have been watching him and that he enjoys our sexualization of him. This kind of travelling body shot has traditionally been reserved for female bodies; that it is now being used in the pursuit of male sexuality and beauty would seem to suggest the validity of Deshpande's designation of the Bollywood hero's body as a new commodity in India.

This commodification of the male body at the expense of the female body, I would further argue, distinguishes contemporary Bollywood cinema from classic Hollywood film, where, as Mulvey has famously asserted, the female body is the object of consumption by a heterosexual masculinized look that structures the filmic text and determines how and with whom all spectators, male and female, can identify. In Mulvey's Lacanian analysis, the female body is vulnerable, subject as it is to a 'controlling male gaze' (2004: 845), and its exposure on the screen as a passive spectacle is a performance of its oppression within a patriarchal scopophilic regime. Mulvey describes woman as 'the ultimate fetish ... a perfect product whose body, stylized and fragmented by close-ups, is the content of the film, and the direct recipient of the spectator's look' (ibid.: 844–5). This look is always masculine; further, the male hero cannot be subject to the same sexual objectification because he functions as the ego ideal in the film, the character with whom we—that is, all of us in the audience, male and female—are supposed to identify. In mainstream Hollywood cinema even today, as Chaudhuri points out, 'One is unlikely to find similar sorts of shots of the male hero, unless the shots concern narrative events ... .' (2006: 37), or as Tasker has argued, unless that usually brawny male body is engaged in some kind of action that legitimizes its exhibition: 'it is perhaps inevitable that it is the *action* cinema which provides a showcase for the display of the muscular male body' (2000: 118).

The Bollywood male body, on the other hand, is emerging as an erotic spectacle in all kinds of movies: in historical epics, action films, and even the traditional masala film. A link to the action genre appears not to be absolutely necessary to justify the display of this body or to distinguish it from the female body, which in both the West and India, is habitually depicted as the passive receiver of an objectifying gaze that marks the feminine as powerless. This new type of male body is an intensely powerful one (capable even, in *Jodhaa Akbar*, of taming wild elephants!)

that frequently and purposefully looks back at us in such a way as to convey a command over our watching. The close-ups of his muscled torso insinuate not only that this man is beautiful and sexually desirable but that he is strong, authoritative, and potent. The ambivalence associated with the exhibition of the male body in the West for the purposes of sexual pleasure—an exhibition which signals both 'an assertion of male dominance' and 'an hysterical and unstable image of manhood' (Tasker 2000: 80)—seems to be absent in Hindi cinema. The lack of this ambivalence, I would argue, points to the existence of traditions of viewing on which Hollywood films cannot draw, Bollywood, however, can take them for granted.

Evoking the ritual of *darshana*, M. Madhava Prasad calls 'darshanic' (2008: 76) the gaze that makes the Indian viewing of Indian films different from anything to be found in the West. Describing it as a 'relation of perception within the public traditions of Hindu worship, especially in the temples, but also in public appearances of monarchs and other elevated figures' (ibid.: 75), darshana refers to the practice of going to a temple to view a divine image and to, in turn, be blessed by the divine gaze that looks back, thereby pulling the devotee into the god or goddess's orbit of protection and affection. Prasad argues that this pre-capitalist 'set of protocols of perception' (ibid.: 75) distinguishes the conventions of spectatorship that structure most (but not all) Indian film from the more voyeuristic politics of identification that solely govern the viewing of Western realist film and which Mulvey's (2004) theory of the masculine gaze has uncovered. Unlike in the mainstream Western performance tradition, where the imaginary fourth wall convention positions the viewer as an eavesdropper whose role is to identify with the protagonist in order to pull together the elements of the narrative into a coherent meaning, the Indian performance is informed by the principle of frontality, which assumes a reciprocity between the actor and the viewer, often evident in a look that moves from one to the other and back again, and more importantly, for our purposes, accords the actor a symbolic and transcendent authority: 'contrary to the voyeuristic relation, in the darshanic relation the object gives itself to be seen and in so doing confers a privilege on the spectator. The object of the darshanic gaze is a superior, a divine figure or a king who presents himself as a spectacle of dazzling splendour to his subjects, the *'praja'* or people' (Prasad 2008: 75–6). Prasad's theory certainly explains why the actors who play the heroes in Bollywood film are often so revered and influential in Indian society, but what it cannot account for is how their authority can be maintained in spite of the eroticization of their bodies in more recent films. For that, it seems to me, we need to turn to the aesthetics of *rasa* in the performance traditions of South Asia, specifically the rasa of *sringara* or erotic love.

The theatrical and dance traditions of India, out of which film arose, identify sringara as one of the eight rasas or expressions of human emotion that are evoked by an actor and simultaneously experienced by a spectator.[9] Most commonly enacted by a female performer, and in some cases by a male playing a female, sringara rasa is the expression of her sexual desire for an absent male figure who is often a man but just as likely to be a god. Although there are any number of possible sringara roles, Radha is the quintessential sringara heroine; in classical Indian dance her desire for her beloved is manifested as an acutely physical state of arousal, through the tingling of the skin when it is touched by a breeze, for instance, or the erection of nipples. Radha's beloved is always Krishna, the mischievous and playful god whose sexual desirability is one of the themes of the famous Sanskrit poem, *Gitagovinda*. In fact, it could be argued that the prevalence of the Radha/Krishna story in all forms of Indian performance—dance, music, drama, television, film, theatre, and so on—has made Krishna's status as a sexually attractive god fundamental in mainstream Indian culture: it's something that virtually all Indians would know about, whether or not they were actually Hindu, and so valued Krishna as a deity and the Radha/Krishna story as an emblem of the relationship between devotees and gods. If Radha is the quintessential sringara heroine who can be performed by either women or men, then Krishna is the male erotic spectacle par excellence. In him is combined power and sexual appeal. Linking sringara rasa to Prasad's theory of the darshanic gaze reveals a protocol of perception or convention of spectatorship that allows the male body to be displayed in recent Bollywood movies as an erotic spectacle that, unlike the muscled body of the Hollywood hero, is unambivalent, even assured, in its articulation of masculine authority.

But while Prasad identifies darshana as one of the foundational ideologies that structures Hindi film, he acknowledges that Bollywood is simultaneously invested in the realist paradigm more common to Western cinema, and this paradigm, as I've noted above, relies on the politics of viewer voyeurism and identification to make sense of narratives. Bollywood's new hero might be confident in his newly muscular body that is additionally a sign of his commodification, but, drawing on the homosocial mores of India, which allow, as Rao asserts, an easy expression of same-sex affection,[10] he is also, to quote Deshpande, 'the projection of the fantasies of a new spectator' (2005: 187). And I would add that what this new spectator wants to see on the screen through the depiction of the Bollywood hero is an exhibition of his own desire for control of his world and the resolution of his fear.

Kimmel contends that 'If masculinity is a homosocial enactment, its overriding emotion is fear ... [the] nightmare from which we never seem to awaken is that those other men will see [our] sense of inadequacy, they will see that in our own eyes we are not who we are pretending to be' (1994: 129–30). For Kimmel, 'the great secret of American manhood' (1994: 131) is that American men are afraid of other men, specifically that they are afraid of being seen by other men as feminine, and therefore, being assumed homosexual. I see his point and even grant that American popular culture, with its penchant for the uber-masculine type who almost never touches other men except violently—a type which includes every Clint Eastwood character and most of Schwarzenegger's, not to mention countless other male roles—would seem to attest to the existence of this style of homophobia. I'm not convinced, however, that it exists so definitively in Indian public society, where, as Kavi and Rao have testified, same sex relationships are accorded a freer rein than in the US. The 'great secret' of Indian manhood is not that it desires the masculine but that *it fears it cannot protect or control the feminine*, which in India's popular culture is sometimes imaged as actual girls and women and sometimes as typically feminine spheres, such as the home or, even, the nation: *Bharat Mata* or Mother India. The repeated invocations in the mainstream media of *izzat* or masculine honour, housed, as it always seems to be, in female bodies, would seem to point to this fear.

Indian male fear is everywhere in Bollywood cinema: in the rock hard abs of the heroes as well as in the sidelining of the heroines. It is especially evident in what is perhaps the most iconic storyline in Hindi movies, the one in which the feminine—imaged either as an actual female or females, the feminized domestic space of a home and family, or India itself—is threatened and so must be defended, usually violently, by the male hero.[11] *Mangal Pandey* certainly follows along these lines, with the motherland representing the vulnerable feminine that must be protected and the British that which must be purged, but so too does *Lagaan*. Similar to *Mangal Pandey*, in *Lagaan* the threat is figured as the British Empire, even more specifically a tax or *lagaan* that this empire requires from its princes who take it in the form of agricultural produce from an already overburdened peasantry. Unable to pay the tax because of poor rains, the peasants of Champaner, a village in central India, are forced at the whim of a malicious white officer to engage in a cricket match against British players who are likely to win since no one on the village team knows how to play cricket. Given the us-against-them, Indians-against-the-British configuration of the plot, it is no wonder that the film has been read, in mostly positive ways, as an anti-colonial/nationalist narrative.[12] Like so many nationalist films made before and after it, *Lagaan* constructs a simple dichotomous relationship between the corrupt external Western forces, represented here by white men, and Mother India's virtuous children, in this case her most authentic virtuous children, the villagers, whom some contemporary forms of nationalism continue to recognize as the 'real' India.

This 'real' India, as Chatterjee (1989) has argued, also has long-standing associations with the feminine sphere of domesticity. Nationalist ideology of late nineteenth century created a series of what Chatterjee calls 'false essentialisms of home/world, spiritual/material, feminine/masculine' (1989: 252), essentialisms that produced a new patriarchal subordination for women who became the bearers of a transcendent Indian culture correlated primarily with the Hindu home. The task of men, consequently, was to prevent any incursions into this sphere that nationalism had sanctified as fundamentally Indian. This lodging of national identity in the feminine, indeed in females themselves, left men free to engage in the world that, because of the system of dichotomies that structured nationalist ideology, came to be conceived of as masculine, and hence, as their natural place. So men could adopt Western values, don Western clothes, go to Western schools, and fight the colonizer in public spaces without losing their essential Indianness because this Indianness was being sustained by women, who, in their turn, embodied it in their Indian style of dress, their maintenance of Indian domestic customs, and their modest modes of behaviour. In Hindi cinema, this nationalist assumption about the feminine essence of Indian culture and the sanctity of the Hindu/Indian home and family[13] has been translated into the narrative I mentioned above. The typical plot sees these essentialized sites endangered by outside forces of evil, which seek either to destroy them or contaminate them beyond recognition. The hero must, therefore, confront the danger and dismantle it, usually by means of masculine rage and violence.

One of the things that makes *Lagaan* unusual is that the threat is not dispelled by violence, but through sport, specifically through cricket. But the displacement of the violent narrative of masculine nationalism on to a seemingly harmless game does not, however, dispel its nationalist nor its violent thrust, for, as Appadurai has argued,

> ... the bodily pleasure that is at the core of the male viewing experience is simultaneously part of the erotics of nationhood. This erotics ... is connected deeply to violence ... because the divisive demands of class, of ethnicity, of language, and of region in fact make the nation a profoundly contested community. The erotic pleasure of watching cricket, for Indian male subjects, is the *pleasure of agency* in an imagined community that in many other arenas is violently contested'. (Italics in original 1995: 44–5)

Numerous scholars have pointed out that a certain sort of Indianness coalesces around a cricket game, for cricket provides a safe place for men, even those from minority communities, to be Indian. *Lagaan* conjures up this convention when it pits a diverse band of Indian villagers, led by Bhuvan (Aamir Khan), against an all-white team of British officers. It is so easy in this film to root for the villagers and thus affirm the anti-colonialist nationalism that they are producing by defending the 'real' India, the village, against outside forces that would destroy it through excessive taxation and the careless exercise of imperial power. That the village is feminized and meant to stand in metonymically for the motherland is apparent in the film's depiction of Bhuvan's mother as the wise, all-suffering woman who perseveres even in the face of extreme adversity. Indeed, her character calls up another famous peasant woman, Radha in *Mother India* (directed by Mehboob Khan, 1957), which has long been analysed as the prototype of nationalist films, and about which Chakravarty writes, 'The chronicle of one woman's struggle against the oppressions of both man and nature becomes an unconscious encapsulation of India's long history of domination by foreign powers and its struggle to maintain the integrity of its soil' (1993: 151). This conflation of women and the nation, though appearing to imply a heightened valuing of the feminine, works predominantly for the constitution of the masculine hero as the saviour of India, a hero whose actions in defense of the feminized nation confirm his right to control its/her destiny. In *Lagaan*, Bhuvan's characterization as a playful Krishna figure with a youthful sense of fun and righteous indignation at injustice belies his repeated authoritarian behaviour, as he struts about the village berating others, even his elders, for their cowardice and their flawed traditions. And, although he is a young, still unmarried man, these others ultimately and with little resistance bow to his decrees about how the nation/the village should think and act. For, as his mother says, 'You talk just like your father, He was so spirited, And he spoke the truth.' This is a mother India identifying her son as the true patrilineal heir to a male, nationalist legacy that, following such exemplars as Gandhi, includes the right to determine and even dictate the morals and values that are appropriate to a national Indianness.

Lagaan has repeatedly been read as a subaltern narrative: Stadtler remarks that the film could be identified as 'form of subaltern history' (2005: 520); Rajan insists that it provides 'a subaltern corrective' to history (2006: 1113); and Chakraborty argues that its theme is 'the subalterns' destabilizing of the history of colonial cricket' (2004: 551). But unless the term 'subaltern' denotes a middle-class fantasy about poor people (and, for some post-colonial scholars, it does appear to mean this), then I cannot comprehend how *Lagaan* can be telling us anything about subalterns. I concur with Mannathukkaren (2007) in seeing the film as one in which subaltern agency is nowhere to be found.[14] Instead, what *Lagaan* offers us is a form of middle-class nationalism that uses the idea of the subaltern to justify itself, and in so doing silencing historical subalterns with their legitimate grievances, many of them against the ruling bourgeoisie, by speaking for them.[15] I do not need to rehearse this argument, since Mannathukkaren has presented it so well in his two essays, but I would like to add to it.

Referring back to Chatterjee's theory about middle-class nationalism's response to feminist and imperialist demands for female emancipation by linking the feminine to the nation, I find that its most salient implication is the idea that this correlation was a clever patriarchal move that left Indian men free to interact with the West—whether in pursuit of anti-colonial resistance to it or in imitation of it—without fearing that they might lose their Indianness, since this cultural identity had been lodged in the feminine. After the late nineteenth century, it therefore became particularly middle-class Indian women's responsibility to embody it. Because the feminine was something already controlled by patriarchal hegemonic masculinity, Indian men could be rest assured that they retained possession of an authentic Indianness by possessing the feminine in the form of women and girls.

In the realm of class relations, *Lagaan* works in a similar fashion to assuage the fear of middle-class viewers, both those in the various diasporas, the NRIs (non-resident Indians) and in India itself, each of which has a particular cause for fear: NRIs because of their residence in the West, where they must raise their children in unIndian lands and so run the risk that their traditions and even their bodies might be diluted by the traditions and bodies of Westerners; bourgeois Indians because of their increased interactions with the West as the result of the liberalization legislation of the early 1990s. What *Lagaan* does with its romanticized image of the villagers and their village is that it reassures middle-class Indians at home and abroad that a 'real' India did and does exist and, more important, that this India is resistant to foreign control: hence, the victorious outcome of the cricket game, which is followed by a truly fantastic scene that seems to re-enact on a small scale the transfer of power in 1947 when the villagers watch in triumph as all the whites desert their cantonment because, we are told, the British government was 'unable to bear this humiliation'. This association of anti-colonial resistance with village India, coupled with the delineation of the village as authentically Indian, works to release elite viewers, particularly male viewers, from having to be actively anti-colonial themselves or even resistant to the West. Instead, because villagers can be imagined to essentially personify an Indianness that defies the West, middle-class spectators are free, like the men in Chatterjee's theory, to interact with the West—whether by living in it, trading with it, or adopting its values, customs, and youth culture—knowing that in India villagers continue to exist and to behave in these predictable ways. What Chatterjee does not say about the feminine but what is certainly required by it if this correlation is to continue to work for men is that women must consent or be made to consent to it. Male control of the feminine becomes, consequently, the lynchpin in the theory. So too with the villagers in this middle-class conception of an authentic Indianness lodged in village India; villagers must remain unthreatening and willing to protect the borders of Indianness. The ending of *Lagaan* thus comforts the middle-class Indian community, both in India and the West, because it represents these villagers as compliant and willing to act their parts in this bourgeois dream drama and it shows the West being pushed outside of the 'real' India, the village. Mannathukkaren argues that the final effect of bourgeois nationalism generally is 'not only that the 'nation' becomes the legitimate community, but also that the imagined 'nation' becomes the mask worn by the ruling classes to cover their face of exploitation' 2001: 4582). *Lagaan* functions to do exactly this: it appeals to a well-to-do Indian audience in various global South Asian diasporas and in India itself, in its evocation of these various nationalist myths because it does not threaten to expose any undesirable truths about modern India, such as the appalling conditions under which rural dalits actually live now and their historical poverty which nationalism did not alleviate, nor does it reveal the collaboration of Indian elites with the West.

But though the film does not reveal this collaboration, it does hint at it in the relationship between the villagers, Bhuvan especially, and Elizabeth Russell, the sister of the tyrannical Captain Russell (Paul Blackthorne) who initiates the cricket match. In her efforts to teach the village team the game of cricket, she helps them defeat the British players, and so she is like Gordon in *Mangal Pandey* in that she goes beyond the role of the sympathetic white person only occasionally found in Hindi movies and actively contributes to nationalism by assisting nationalist characters to achieve their goals and oust the colonizer. Considering that this is not the usual role for a white character, I find it surprising that despite the copious amount of scholarship on *Lagaan*, very little of it addresses the ramifications of Elizabeth in terms of the film's nationalist politics; in fact, she is usually just barely mentioned and sometimes not mentioned at all.

But Elizabeth is crucial in the reading of the film not only for her potential to normalize an alliance between the West and India, but also because, again like Gordon, she works to eroticize the hero for the audience, who get to share with her the visual pleasure of seeing him frequently naked from the waist up and this eroticization tremendously enhances his masculinity, originating as it does in the gaze of a white woman whose racial dominance in a globalized world makes her desire that much more valuable than that of Bhuvan's Indian beloved, Gauri (Gracy Singh). Gauri's desire cannot destabilize '[c]olonial stereotypes of effete, weak, and passive Indian men' (Rajan 2006: 1115), as Elizabeth's can. The hero's ability to evoke the sexual interest of a white woman also suggests an even more consequential outcome: the taming of the West by the Indian male, a West that has been feminized in Elizabeth and so made tamable. And, again, this is not something that Gauri's passion for Bhuvan can do.

But Gauri is still vital in the love triangle that involves the Hindu lovers and Elizabeth because the Indian woman is the safe, sustaining option that Bhuvan ultimately must choose in order to avoid the possibility of miscegenation, with all its metaphorical implications about the porousness of the borders that separate Indianness/Hinduness from Westernness. And he has no trouble choosing it since throughout the film he remains indifferent or even oblivious to the white woman's desire. Bhuvan's choice plays to the NRI as well as the elite audience in India. By making the Indian hero sexually attractive to the Western woman but not sexually available to her, *Lagaan* shuts down the possibility of mixed-race children who would threaten to blur the boundaries between whiteness and Indianness. It also dismisses Elizabeth's desire, enacting a sort of reverse psychology that works to assuage the fear of both these groups that their own desire for the West, indicated by their interactions with it, need not undermine their Indianness. They can be in it, trade with it, or adopt its customs—even desire the West and be desired by it—without being polluted by it. Indeed, quite the opposite is suggested by two of the final lines of the film. Taking her leave from the villagers, Elizabeth goes first to Bhuvan's mother, who draws her into the Hindu/Indian family when she blesses her with the words, 'Be happy, my daughter, Live long.' And after we see the pale face of the pining white woman for the last time, the male narrator tells us, 'Elizabeth returned to England, holding Bhuvan in her heart. She did not marry and remained Bhuvan's Radha all her life.' Constructing the now-Hindi-speaking Elizabeth as a Radha, the eternally infatuated lover of the Hindu god Krishna, reassures *Lagaan*'s audiences around the world that it is the Westerner and not the Indian who has been and will be altered by their cross-cultural encounter. This implicit moral of the story could perhaps go part of the way towards explaining the popularity of *Lagaan* both in and outside of India.

That Bollywood films in the post-liberalization age are made for and by the Indian elite at home and abroad has been argued by a number of scholars. Athique, for example, writes that Hindi cinema today is,

... defined by the high-budget, saccharine, upper middle-class melodrama which represents a tongue-in-cheek repackaging of the masala movie within an affluent, nostalgic and highly exclusive view of Indian culture and society. These productions are consciously transnational.... Indian politicians have recently become keen to emphasize the worldwide popularity of these films and, in particular, their success as 'ambassadors' for India's growing global ambitions. (2008: 301)

It is to this affluent Indian audience, far more than to any other, that films like *Mangal Pandey* and *Lagaan* speak. By defining whiteness conventionally in the joint depiction of a larger white and simplistically adversarial group of colonizers while introducing this new and more complex character of an active white nationalist, these films allow for the possibility that whiteness/the West can be dichotomously and safely severed into enemy and friend. This splitting of the West into two groups endorses a post-liberalization form of a Hindu bourgeois nationalism that is founded on general contemptuous sentiments towards British colonialism, the enemy outside the nation that draws attention away from the enemies within,[16] but that also espouses a willingness to consort with friendly white others who, far from threatening Indianness, consolidate it through their desire for the masculine hero, whose authority over the feminized nation allows him to represent an authentic India.

It is important to note that only a certain kind of white person can secure the borders and confirm the value of this new nationalist Indian man. Working-class whites, whose presence in the colonial India that these films remember was as much a historical fact as the presence of ruling whites, are entirely absent from *Lagaan* and figure in *Mangal Pandey* only as the British soldiers who rush in to stop Mangal from successfully starting his revolution. They are, in fact, missing from Bollywood representations generally. In *Mangal Pandey*, this absence is particularly revealing, since it is far more likely that an ordinary soldier like Mangal Pandey, if he had a white best friend, rather than finding him in the officers' mess, would have chanced upon him among ordinary British soldiers, with whom he would have had something in common, namely, the subordinate status of another ranker. But in the perpetual state of national crisis that traverses Bollywood films, poor whites are insufficiently white; though white, they are subordinate in the West, even to the many communities of diasporic South Asians that enjoy middle-class status. Their whiteness, which is normed in the West, is not now dominant on the world stage, nor has it ever been, and therefore, they don't have the capacity to consolidate an elite nationalist Hindu/Indian masculinity or to soothe its apprehension about the dangers of that globalizing economy, being themselves among the losers in that economy. But they were the other side of whiteness in colonial India; that they've gone missing in the contemporary mythologies that structure Bollywood films in this era of open borders and supposedly free markets is a testament to the class alliances that covertly opened those borders and freed those markets.

Notes

1. I would like to thank Brian Patton, Nandi Bhatia, and Emily Campbell for their valuable assistance with the writing of this essay as well as all the participants, from whom I learned so much, in the 'From Bombay to LA,' workshop at the Asian Research Institute at the National University of Singapore, and especially Chua Beng Huat, Anjali Roy, and the student organizers who made that workshop possible.

2. For the purposes of this essay, I use Raminder Kaur and Ajay J. Sinha's definition of Bollywood as 'India's commercial Hindi film industry, based primarily, but not exclusively, in the city of Bombay, now officially designated as Mumbai since 1995' (2005: 16).

3. See Foucault (1979: 293–308).

4. I'm grateful to Darius Cooper's essay for this interpretation of *Shatranj ki Khilari*.

5. Sharmistha Gooptu observes in her essay that 'the East-West binary, as seen in *Lagaan*, has been less noticeable in popular cinema in recent years' (2004: 541–42), arguing further that the kind of 'jingoistic nationalism' (ibid.: 541) that requires such a binary has, since the 1990s, constructed the Pakistani rather than the white colonizer as the other.

6. I call this narrative a myth, first, because I've not been able to verify it as a historical fact, and, second, because its factuality interests me less than its multiple iterations, which suggest its significance as a signifier of some kind of psychological reality for those British people who survived the Rebellion.

7. See, for example, William Forbes-Mitchell's *Reminiscences*, where he describes having himself heard an English voice among the rebels taunting the soldiers of his company 'in unmistakable barrack-room English' (1893: 280). He also claims to have spoken to a rebel many years later who repeatedly identified the man as a former sergeant-major (ibid.: 282).

8. Gordon is Scottish and Catholic and, in one scene, makes it clear that he comes from a lower middle-class background.

9. Trying to explain the conventional understanding of rasa as a flavour or a taste, Schechner describes it in the following way:

> The *sthayi bhava*s are the 'permanent' or 'abiding' or indwelling emotions that are accessed and evoked by good acting, called *abhinaya*. *Rasa* is experiencing the *sthayi bhava*s. To put

it another way, the sweetness 'in' a ripe plum is its *sthayi bhava*, the experience of 'tasting the sweet' is *rasa*. The means of getting the taste across—preparing it, presenting it—is *abhinaya*. Every emotion is a *sthayi bhava*. Acting is the art of presenting the *sthayi bhavas* so that *both* the performer and the partaker [or spectator] can 'taste' the emotion, the *rasa*. (2001: 31)

10. Rao writes, 'same sex closeness exists in every walk of Indian life, especially among the lower-middle classes: in bedrooms and public transport, on the street. India is like that only. What conspires to give this a sexual coloration is that social mores in India do not permit men and women to be demonstrative until marriage, and even then never in public places. Sex is only for procreation, not entertainment. Also, sex has nothing to do with love. Every Indian thus grows up with a certain degree of sexual repression. Even if one is not born gay, it is so easy to become gay in India' (2000: 303–4).

11. I am indebted to Rai's essay (2006) for his description of this classic Bollywood narrative.

12. For largely or entirely affirmative interpretations of the film, see Chakraborty (2004), Rajan (2006), and Majumdar (2001).

13. The conflation of the Indian with the Hindu, particularly in Hindi cinema of the last fifteen or so years has been noticed by many scholars, including Mishra, who acknowledges that, although the Bollywood industry retains its traditional cultural syncretism, there is today 'an implicit directive to work within the formal determinants of Hindu culture' (2002: 63).

14. See both his earlier argument to this effect in *Economic and Political Weekly* (2001) and his analysis of the film in terms of the contemporary material reality of the cricket industry in India and of dalit politics and life in *The International Journal of the History of Sport* (2007).

15. Though I don't believe that this film can be read as one that promotes the interests of the subaltern, it's still refreshing to see a recent Bollywood film that presents rural poor people in a positive light, as Deshpande states (2005: 195–6), and that depicts cricket being played by non-elite players, since this is a reality in India today, where I have seen boys, whose ragged clothes suggest their poverty, commandeer the open space even in a graveyard to play a game they were so obviously passionate about.

16. See Mannathukkaren's essays for an elaboration of this theory.

References

Appardurai, Arjun. 1995. 'Playing with Modernity: The Decolonization of Indian Cricket', in Carol A. Breckenridge (ed.), *Consuming Modernity: Public Culture in a South Asian World*, Minneapolis and London: University of Minnesota Press.

P. Athique, Adrian M. 2008. 'The "Crossover" Audience: Mediated Multiculturalism and the Indian Film', *Continuum: Journal of Media & Cultural Studies*, vol. 22, no. 3.

Chakraborty, Chandrima. 2004. 'Bollywood Motifs: Cricket Fiction and Fictional Cricket', *The International Journal of the History of Sport*, vol. 21, nos 3/4.

Chakravarty, Sumita S. 1993. *National Identity in Indian Popular Cinema, 1947–1987*, Austin: University of Texas Press.

Chatterjee, Partha. 1989. 'The Nationalist Resolution to the Women's Question', in Kunkum Sangari and Sudesh Vaid (eds), *Recasting Women: Essays in Colonial History*, New Delhi: Kali for Women.

Chaudhuri, Shohini. 2006. *Feminist Film Theorists: Laura Mulvey, Kaja Silverman, Teresa De Lauretis, and Barbara Creed*, London and New York: Routledge.

Cooper, Darius. 1994. 'The Representation of Colonialism in Satyajit Ray's *The Chess Players*', in Wimal Dissanayake (ed.), *Colonialism and Nationalism in Asian Cinema*, Bloomington and Indianapolis: Indiana University Press.

Deshpande, Sudhanva. 2005. 'The Consumable Hero of Globalized India', in Raminder Kaur and Ajay J. Sinha (eds), *Popular Indian Cinema through a Transnational Lens*, New Delhi and London: Sage.

Dyer, Richard. 1997. *White*, London and New York: Routledge.

Forbes-Mitchell.1893. *Reminiscences of the Great Mutiny, 1857–59*, London: Macmillan.

Foucault, Michel. 1979. *Discipline and Punish, the Birth of the Prison* (trans. from French by Alan Sheridan), New York: Vintage.

Gangoli, Geetanjali. 2005. 'Sexuality, Sensuality and Belonging: Representations of the "Anglo-Indian" and the "Western" Woman in Hindi Cinema', in Raminder Kaur and Ajay J. Sinha (eds), *Popular Indian Cinema through a Transnational Lens*, New Delhi and London: Sage.

Gooptu, Sharmistha. 2004. 'Cricket or Cricket Spectacle? Looking Beyond Cricket to Understand *Lagaan*', *The International Journal of the History of Sport*, vol. 21, nos. 3/4.

Kaur, Raminder and Ajay J. Sinha. 2005. 'Introduction', in Raminder Kaur and Ajay J. Sinha (eds), *Popular Indian Cinema through a Transnational Lens*, New Delhi and London: Sage.

Kavi, Ashok Row. 2000. 'The Changing Image of the Hero in Hindi Films', *Journal of Homosexuality*, vol. 39, nos 3/4.

Kimmel, Michael S. 1994. 'Masculinity as Homophobia: Fear, Shame, and Silence in the Construction of Gender Identity', in Harry Brod and Michael Kaufman (eds), *Theorizing Masculinities*, London, Delhi: Thousand Oaks, Sage.

Majumdar, Boria. 2001. 'Politics of Leisure in Colonial India: *"Lagaan"*: Invocation of a Lost history?' *Economic and Political Weekly*, vol. 36, no. 35.

Mannathukkaren, Nissim. 2001. 'Subalterns, Cricket and the 'Nation': The Silences of "Lagaan," in *Economic and Political Weekly*, vol. 36, no. 49, pp. 4580–8.

Mannathukkaren, Nissim. 2007. 'Reading Cricket Fiction in the Times of Hindu Nationalism and Farmer Suicides: Fallacies of Textual Interpretation', *The International Journal of the History of Sport*, vol. 24, no. 9.

Mishra, Vijay. 2002. *Bollywood Cinema: Temples of Desire*, New York and London: Routledge.

Mulvey, Laura. 2004 (1975). 'Visual Pleasure and Narrative Cinema', in Leo Braudy and Marshall Cohen (eds), *Film Theory and Criticism: Introductory Readings*, New York and Oxford: Oxford University Press.

Prasad, M Madhava. 2008. *Ideology of the Hindi Film: a Historical Construction*, New Delhi: Oxford University Press.

Rai, Amit S. 2006. '"Every Citizen is a Cop without the Uniform": the Populist Outsider in Bollywood's New Angry Young Man Genre', *Interventions*, vol. 8, no. 2.

Rajan, Gita. 2006. 'Constructing-Contesting Masculinities: Trends in South Asian Cinema', *Signs: Journal of Women in Culture and Society*, vol. 31, no. 4.

Rao, R. Raj. 2000. 'Memories Pierce the Heart: Homoeroticism, Bollywood-Style', *Journal of Homosexuality*, vol. 39, nos 3/4.

Schechner, Richard. 2001. 'Rasaesthetics', *The Drama Review*, vol. 45, no. 3.

Stadtler, Florian. 2005. 'Cultural Connections: *Lagaan* and Its Audience Responses', *Third World Quarterly*, vol. 26, no. 3.

Tasker, Yvonne. 2000. *Spectacular Bodies: Gender, Genre and the Action Cinema*, London and New York: Routledge.

17   Bollywood Films and African Audiences

GWENDA VANDER STEENE

India has been exporting films to Southeast Asia, the Middle East, Turkey, Africa, the Soviet Union, Eastern Europe, and Colombia, as well as to Europe and North America, since the 1950s where they were mainly watched by an Indian expatriate community (Pendakur and Subramanyam 1996; Abdazi n.d.; Kaur 2002: 200; Larkin 1997: 172, Fuglesang 1994: 166). Unlike the UK, the Middle East, and the US that constitute the three key export markets for Indian cinema in the present (Pendakur and Subramanyam 1996: 77), Africa has traditionally served as an important distribution territory for Indian films (Pendakur and Subramanyam 1996).[1] In contrast to Bollywood's popularity in other African countries like Kenya, Nigeria, and South Africa that have a large Indian expatriate community, Senegal does not have an Indian expatriate population.[2] In this chapter, this gap will be filled in by looking at a francophone country without an Indian expatriate community. Focusing on the concept of Indophilie, Indophie associations, and Bollywood dance groups performing at *soirées indous* (Indian evenings), the reasons for Bollywood's appeal for a Senegalese audience will be examined to argue that the Indophiles' discourse on similarities can be related to globalization theories on 'parallel modernities' (Larkin 1997, 2000, 2003) and 'cultural proximity' (Straubhaar 1991a).

Bollywood: A Successful Export Commodity for African Audiences and the Senegalese Example

Research on Indophile and the popularity of Bollywood films in Africa is a rich and emerging area. Being a francophone country, Senegal lies out of the English influence sphere, which is much stronger in Anglophone Africa. The research devoted to the concept of Indophile in Africa has exclusively concentrated on Anglophone Africa. Similarly, although the import of Bollywood films to Africa began in the 1950s, it has attracted academic attention only during the last decade. While Fuglesang has researched the popularity of Bollywood films among female Kenyan youth in her book *Veils and Videos* (1994: 7, 163–70, 302–3), Behrend has worked on the influence of Bollywood on Kenyan photography (1998). Larkin (1997, 2000, 2003), Furniss (2003), and Adamu (2002) have examined the popularity and influence of Bollywood films on Hausa culture in Nigeria. Amkpa (2004) has conducted research on the influence of Bollywood on Ghanaian cinema and religion respectively and Rush (1999) has explored the incorporation of imported Hindu chromolithographic imagery in Benin vodun.

In his essay 'Itineraries of Indian cinema', Larkin attempts to answer the question why Indian films have travelled across the world. He attributes the popularity of this genre throughout the world to the understanding that it offers a way of being modern without being Western (Larkin 2003, 1997: 407). In northern Nigeria (Hausa region), on which his own research is focussed, it is also a means through which Hausa distinguish themselves from the south, which is oriented towards the 'West'. He argues that these transnational cultural flows become 'a foil against which post-colonial identity can be fashioned, critiqued, and debated. They allow an alterity to Hollywood domination' (2003: 178).

According to Fuglesang, Bollywood offers female Kenyan audiences a 'reassuring familiarity', which means that the audience knows what to expect (1994: 169).[3] Similarly, a number of Hausas state that 'Indian culture' (as presented in the films) is 'just like Hausa culture'.[4] According to Larkin, the popularity of Indian films among Hausa rests, in part, on the dialectic of sameness ('just like') and difference (id.). Characters in Indian films struggle over whether they should speak Hindi or borrow from English, whether they should marry the person they love or the one their parents choose, elements which are very relevant for Hausa viewers (1997: 410). But the popularity of Bollywood goes beyond people going to the cinema or watching videos. In Nigeria, for example, Bollywood has an important influence on local (especially Hausa) video production (called 'Nollywood'), literature, and music (Larkin 1997, 2000, 2003; Haynes 2000). In Senegal, too, Bollywood's popularity has catalysed the development of several Indophile associations and dance groups.

While recent studies have focussed on the Bollywood influence in Anglophone Africa, little work has been done on the francophone parts of Africa, such as Senegal. Scheld (2003) came across Bollywood when examining the 'style *indou*' (dress style) in her dissertation on clothing consumption among youth in Dakar. Other than her cursory discussion of this dress style, Augis refers to a Hindi music store in Dakar in her research on youth creating new subcultures with transnational 'cultural artefacts' in Dakar (personal communication). Apart from these passing references, no research has been done on the Indophile scene in Senegal.

A COMMUNIST TOUCH

According to the first Indophile generation, *Aan* (or *Mangala*, 'daughter of India') was the first Indian film released in Senegal in 1953 and created a furore. Prior to that, one could only watch French or American films. *Aan*, a film about the power-struggle between rich and poor, good and evil, was produced by Mehboob Khan and released in India in 1952 but also in other parts of the world.[5] The plot deals with a Rajput prince who tries to kill his father in order to usurp the throne. A peasant, who wishes to prevent this, kidnaps the princess, who eventually ends up falling in love with him. In the end, the conspiracy is unmasked and the peasant is rewarded for his virtues.

Other films, such as *Mother India* (Mehboob Khan, 1957), were imported after *Aan* and enjoyed an immense success.[6] In *Mother India*, a film about a poor peasant woman's struggle to raise her children, the mother and her son successfully fight against a rich exploitative landowner. Mehboob Khan, the producer, was inspired by *The Mother* (Pudovkin, 1926), a Russian film on the Lenin revolution of 1917. Although Mehboob Khan was not formally a member of the Communist Party, the fact that he used the hammer and the sickle as the emblem for his production house, Mehboob Productions, reiterates his communist leanings. In his film *Mother India*, his tendency towards the communist ideology becomes evident in the theme of the film, class struggle and the usurpation of power by the poor.[7] Apart from Mehboob Khan, other film producers, such as Raj Kapoor in *Awaara* and *Sri 420*, made communist-inspired films (Pendakur and Subramanyam 1996: 72).

According to Tremblay (1996: 2), a strong reflection on political idealism is characteristic of the films of the 1950s and 1960s. A recurring trope in these films is the subordination of individual and family fulfilment to the welfare of the community. The first 'generation' of Bollywood movies imported in Senegal remains popular even now not only among the older generation but also among the youth. Most dances performed at the *soirées indous* ('Indian evenings') are from the older films (from the 1960s or 1970s).

In 1960, the Indian Government established the Film and Television Institute of India (FTII) in Poona, where students were trained in an environment that 'fostered social intellectual traditions' (Jaikumar 2003: 5). These films opened up another export market, that is, in Eastern Europe and the former USSR (Pendakur and Subramanyam 1996: 72), the 'communist world' during the Cold War period.

THE MIDDLE EAST

As in the rest of francophone Africa (Vieyra 1983: 18),[8] two French private import companies COMACICO and SECMA controlled the cinematic landscape in Senegal before independence (1960),with programming and import decisions made mainly in Europe (ibid.: 22). In 1974, both were merged in a single state-directed company called SIDEC[9] (ibid.: 26). The import companies did not deal directly with Indian distributors, but worked together with distributors from France and the Middle East to import films via the Middle East.

The Middle East seems to have had an important role in distributing and subtitling Indian films in Africa. As Larkin points out, Arabic and Indian films were first imported in Nigeria by Lebanese cinema owners in the 1950s, who had anticipated that Arabic films would become very popular in African Islamic countries (Larkin 2003: 181, 1997: 411). Contrary to Middle Eastern distributors' expectations, Indian films became much more popular than Arabic films in these countries. In

Senegal, too, Arabic and Indian films were imported simultaneously with Indian films proving to be the more popular of the two.

In the 1970s, Indian films outnumbered and surpassed Arabic films in their popularity.[10] Those belonging to the older generation, in particular perceived Arabic films as imitating Western films and as inclined towards the 'West'. This suggests that Indian films' popularity partly arises from the perception that they are not Western. A characteristic of the Hindi films of the 1950s and 1960s is that 'tradition' and 'modernity' are presented in dichotomous terms (Tremblay 1996: 304–5; Kaur 2002: 204). Apart from their emphasis on nationalist and/or religious themes, they address the dichotomies of urban/industrial (and often 'Western') versus rural. This aspect reflects the dichotomous views held by the older generation of Senegalese Indophiles. Their inclination towards films showing the 'rural' that they define as 'tradition' would explain the popularity of the films from the 1950s–1960s. Indeed, the themes of the films have changed from the 1970s onwards (cf. Kaur 2002: 204–5; Tremblay 1996: 305–6). The films of the last two decades offer an alternative view on modernity and the characteristic opposition between Indian and Western culture has disappeared as a major frame of reference (ibid.). Instead of seeking to reinforce traditional Indian culture, the films of the 1980s have examined the problems particular to Indian modernity (ibid.: 306). Although the films from the 1970s and 1980s were still popular among the older generation, more recent films (from 1990s onwards) appear to appeal only to a youth audience.

A final aspect often emphasized by Senegalese Indophiles is the fact that Arabic films have lesser song and dance sequences than Bollywood ones. Fuglesang also mentions this explanation was often given to account for the fact that Arabic or American films are less popular than Bollywood (1994: 165).

THE FOLLOWING DECADES

Indian films became increasingly popular and were imported massively in the 1970s. People often recalled that they had watched a number of Indian films as children, irrespective of whether they came to the cinema to watch a Hindi film or the Western or Chinese films shown afterwards. Even today, there are Indophiles who go to the cinema weekly, or even daily.

Most urban cinemas screened at least one Indian film every day. In addition to the big cinemas, many quarters in Dakar also had a small 'cinema' inside a house where films were shown. While only four out of the eleven cinemas in the city centre were dedicated to Bollywood, the number of screenings of Bollywood in cinemas in popular quarters in Dakar such as Médina, Colobane, or Grand Dakar was relatively higher. An extract from the journal *Le soleil* in Vieyra's book, reproduces the film programme of twenty-four cinemas in the region Dakar-Pikine and Rufisque for the week of 28 December 1979 (1983: 36) which illustrates the difference in programming between cinemas in the city centre and those in suburban areas.[12]

MEDIA

The media have played an important role in dispersing the phenomenon of Indophile. The first Indophile radio programme, broadcast by Radio Sénégal in 1967, was an immediate success. Today, almost every radio station has an Indophile programme consisting of Bollywood music, discussions on Indian news and Bollywood, and 'call in' that is often broadcast live. The radio programmes bring the Indophile community closer together through an anchorman who plays a lead role in many Indophile associations. It is the anchormen, one of the celebrity Indophiles, who often organize soirées indous for their fan clubs.

Since the end of 2004 onwards, there is also an Indophile TV programme, broadcast every Saturday and Sunday on RTS2S, from 6 p.m. to 7 p.m. in which Bollywood clips from old as well as new releases are shown and additional information about films and actors provided.

WINDING DOWN?

Between the 1960s to 1980s, Indian films apparently reached a wide audience, including many who would not strictly fall into the category of (or would not wish to) Indophiles as the term is understood today. Today, a smaller group of people, who identify themselves as Indophiles, account for the popularity of Bollywood films. Instead of looking at this as a 'winding down' of the Indophile movement, one can make a clear distinction between the widespread popularity of Indian films from the 1960s to the end of the 1980s on the one hand and the emergence of the new Indophile movement (with Bollywood dancing and soirées indous) on the other. The Indophile movement, originating in Indian cinema's popularity in the past, has existed simultaneously with it for a long time and may be viewed as a spin-off of Bollywood's new-found popularity. While the Indophile movement has continued in the present, the widespread popularity of Indian films has declined.

The Bollywood Appeal to a Senegalese Audience

In this section, the reasons for Indophiles' preference for Bollywood films will be examined. As an Indophile stated, a large part of the audience for Indian films between the 1960s and 1980s consisted of non-literate women, who 'would nevertheless tell you the story from A to Z afterwards', despite the films being subtitled in French. In most Bollywood films (especially the older ones), however, the story is usually not that difficult to follow even if one doesn't understand the dialogues, thanks to, for example, the use of visual symbols making a clear distinction between good and bad. Bollywood films have what Gillespie terms a 'language openness': Although the audience of the Hindi films comes from a myriad of cultures and countries, the language barrier can be overcome by the abundance of clear and simple codes and binary values which cannot easily be misinterpreted... (cited in Fuglesang 1994: 167). This 'language openness' facilitates transcultural transmission and cross-cultural understanding. According to Larkin, the same reason accounts for the transnational success of action films (1997: 435).

MUSIC AND DANCE

Many Indophiles claimed that they loved Bollywood because it was full of songs and dance sequences and compared the importance of music and dance in Bollywood to their importance in Senegalese 'culture'.

BEAUTY AND MELODRAMA: SENTIMENTAL TRASH OR NURTURE?

The aesthetic aspects, the 'beautiful women', the picturesque scenery, the marvellous clothes and make-up, are one of the first reasons why Indophiles love Bollywood. Second, the melodramic plot dealing with romance and sentimentality was mentioned by several Indophiles as a reason for their appeal.

Bollywood melodrama (which has many parallels with English soap-opera or Brazilian telenovelas) should, however, not be interpreted as 'sentimental trash' (Fuglesang 1994: 170, 180) or as an escapist means to keep the masses under control (Kaur 2002: 201, Tremblay 1996: 303). It is important to look at it from the point of view of the audience, who takes an active part in its (in this case cross-cultural) reception demonstrating that melodrama can become 'nurture' (ibid.). Fuglesang refers to the studies of Radway (1983, 1987) who has worked with American middle-class women reading romantic novels. Radway stipulates that the romances replenish women emotionally and function to promote psychological recovery. Fuglesang explains that Bollywood films function in a way that young Lamu women can connect the stories to their own lives or fantasize about their idols or become a place in which people can invest their fantasies (ibid.: 178–80). Bollywood is not merely 'passive' entertainment for people but has an empowering effect as a tool for reshaping one's own life.

DISCOURSE ON SIMILARITIES

For other Indophiles, Indian and Senegalese culture are connected in more than one way. Many claim that they love watching Bollywood because it makes them think of their own culture, country, or customs. Senegalese Indophiles have developed, what may be called, a discourse on similarities.[12] The similarities are perceived as a 'cultural approach' between 'Senegalese and Indian culture'.

The Senegalese tend to identify with 'Indian culture' more than other parts of Africa, partially due to the perceived similarities with the Fulani, the Fouta, or with the Sereer. Larkin has come across similar ideas on cultural approaches between Hausa and 'Indian culture'. Although the constituent aspects of the discourse of similarities of his research participants are very similar to those mentioned by Senegalese Indophiles (cf. infra), he does not refer to the Fulani, who are also found in northern Nigeria (Larkin, personal communication), nor to the Sereer, who are to be found in Senegal only.

In the following section, this discourse is elaborated further, explaining its different constituent aspects. Following this, these ideas will be put in a broader theoretical frame, drawing on the theory of cultural proximity in media studies and on the related ideas of parallel modernities as developed by Larkin.

'When I'm in India, It is as if I'm at Home': Two Approaching Cultures

CLOTHING—STYLE INDOU

Several Indophiles point to the similarities between Senegalese and Indian sartorial styles, especially between the grand *boubou* and the sari or with Fulani costumes. A grand boubou consists of a big, loosely fitting piece of cloth, which can fall down to the ankles. A wrap-around (sër) is also worn underneath, and usually this two-piece garment is completed with a *musoor* (from the French 'mouchoire'), a stiff scarf elegantly draped around one's head. Other Indophiles mention resemblances with the Mauritanian women's dress or the *melehvo* in particular. According to some, this can be explained by the large number of Fulani living in Mauritania. Mauritanian women drape a large, colourful, very light cloth around their body. The last part is used to cover their head, something Indian women also do with their pallu or the end of the sari hanging down from their shoulder when showing respect or modesty (Bannerjee and Miller 2003: 36). Many Indophiles possess saris, which they flaunt at soirées indous. Saris are even said to have become popular outside the soirées indous in the early 1990s.

Apart from direct similarities between Senegalese and Indian dress styles, the style indou is also extremely popular among Indophiles. The style indou can be described as a kind of mixed style. It uses either Senegalese or imported Indian cloth and the patterns are often Senegalese interpretations of Bollywood inspired costumes.

Clothing is a way to express one's identity and dressing up in the style indou is a statement by Indophile women to articulate their Indophile 'identity' or self illustrating Bourdieu's notion of the sartorial production of the self. '...The way we clothe the body can be regarded as an active process and a technical means by which we construct and present a bodily "self" ...' (Bourdieu 1977: 20). Being an Indophile encompasses more than the love for Bollywood films. It is nearly a lifestyle: the way one dresses, the venues one goes to, the music one listens to, the people one hangs out with. All these aspects contribute to the dynamic process of identity construction.

FAÇON DE VIVRE (WAY OF LIVING)

The term *façon de vivre* ('way of living') were used when talking about films of the 1950s and 1960s, such as *Mère indienne* (*Mother India*). The images of village life, horses and carts, women fetching water at the well, or carrying firewood on their heads 'really make you think you are in Senegal'. Some Indophiles especially stressed similarities with the Fouta (Fouta) or the Sereer. Some linked the 'animistic beliefs' of the Sereer or the importance of cows in the religious and cultural practices of the Fulani with 'animistic practices in Hinduism, such as the veneration of snakes or cows'. Indophiles, especially of the older generation, stressed these aspects of way of living and village activities.

VALUES

According to some Indophiles, values such as hospitality, respect for elders, marriage, piety and respect for women, and hospitality, that are highly regarded in Senegalese society reverberate with those extolled in Bollywood films. The importance of family networks and living in an extended family is also mentioned as a strong similarity. The appreciation of these values also relates to a preference for older films. As mentioned earlier, the subordination of personal happiness to the welfare of the extended family or community is a recurrent theme in the films from the 1950s and 1960s. The fact that Senegalese appreciate this aspect of Bollywood, demonstrates how their self-definition is projected on Bollywood films.

FULANI

Earlier, the link made by some Indophiles between Indians and Fulani was mentioned. It is remarkable that many Indophiles belonging to Indophile associations are of Fulani origin and their love for Bollywood is explained by the fact that they would like to have an

Indian connection. Many Indophiles talk about their physical resemblance to Indians, an idea related to the 'common origin' discourse and the idea of *peul indou* ('Hindu Fulani').

Apart from physical resemblances, Indophiles explain strong similarities by stressing that the similarities in values, clothing, or ways of life is pertinent to Fulani society in particular. This brings us to the myth about a common origin. Related to this discourse about common origin is the concept of peul indou used by several (mostly Fulani) Indophiles to refer to the south Indian Tamil population. As the origin of Fulani is, according to Indophiles, to be found in India, the Tamil groups in India are believed to be strongly related to the Fulani.

Tamils (even called 'black Indians', *les noirs indiens*) are referred to as the original inhabitants of India before the invasion of the (more pale skinned) Aryans from the north.[13] Although not stated explicitly by any Indophile, the fact that they use the term 'black Indians' shows that they could link their ideas about the Aryan invasion in India to their own colonial situation. It has, however, not made Tamil films more popular than Hindi ones, probably because Hindi films were more accessible.

LANGUAGE

According to Larkin, the argument that Hausa language and Hindi are similar is often used by people to stress the similarities between both cultures. The same holds true for Senegal. Wolof or Fulani are said to be 'very similar' to Hindi. Some Indophiles even claim that they speak Hindi fluently. Indophile informants often repeat the same words when asked to provide examples of similarities: *caabi* (key-Wolof) and *caabu* (Hindi), *asamaan* (heaven-Wolof and Hindi). Linguists reinforced my suspicion that most of these words are of Arabic origin (for example, asamaan). Why else would Hausa *and* Wolof *and* Fulani *and* Sereer be similar to a language like Hindi? Wolof, as well as Fulani and Sereer, are very mixed languages, with a strong Arabic influence of which people are often unaware.

OUTSIDE SENEGAL

With regard to the similarities discourse, Larkin's research among Hausa revealed more or less the same discourse of similarities: visual (dress) and linguistic similarities, ways of life (marriage celebrations, village life, and so on), and the importance of values such as family and kinship (1997: 412–13, 2003: 183). He also stresses the Hausa preference for older films and their belief that Indian films 'have culture' in a way that American films seem to lack. Thus, the 'West' is defined by them as the 'other' whereas Indian culture is perceived as similar, similar because American films are different. Similar views are expressed by Fuglesang's Kenyan research respondents, who perceive a strong familiarity or similarity with their own lives in Indian films (1994: 177).

Parallel Modernities and Cultural Proximity

In the following section, an attempt has been made to go beyond the case study of Indophile and consider it from a broader perspective of parallel modernities and constructions of difference and sameness on a transnational level. Central to this analysis will be the concept of presence linked to theories of cultural proximity.

PARALLEL MODERNITIES

The phenomenon of Indophile makes one think about Larkin's reflections on parallel modernities (1997: 407–10, 434): 'I use the term "parallel modernities" to refer to the coexistence in space and time of multiple economic, religious and cultural flows that are often subsumed within the term "modernity"' (ibid.: 407).

He makes a distinction between his ideas and the concept of alternative modernities as defined by Appadurai (1991), who links it with increased deterritorialization and the increasing movement of people. Larkin's point is that for the Hausa (especially the younger people), watching Bollywood films is a way of being modern without being Western, without being criticized for being 'Western decadent' (1997: 433, 2003: 172). Scheld (2004: 9–10) reinforces Larkin's ideas by arguing that modernities develop in tandem with and not as 'alternative' to 'dominant' discourses. Appadurai's term, on the other hand, implies an unequal relationship. Larkin's reservations about the use of the adjective alternative, that is, parallel instead of alternative modernities, thus appears to be more preferable.

An idea definitely applicable to the Senegalese case is that Bollywood films offer Hausa viewers a third space, mediating between the Hausa Islamic tradition and Western modernity, which disrupts the dichotomies between 'West' and non-'West' (Larkin 2003: 172; 1997: 414). Indian films are seen as being situated in a cultural space that stands outside the binary distinctions between tradition and modernity, Africa and West, resistance and domination (Larkin 1997: 433). According to Larkin, the Hausa engage with forms of tradition different from their own while at the same time conceiving of a modernity that comes without the political and ideological baggage of the 'West' (2003: 176, 183). Indian films work for Hausa because they rest on a dialectic of presence and absence culturally similar to Hausa society but at the same time reassuringly distant (ibid.: 188).

These politics of absence and presence, desire and imagination, proximity and distance, difference and sameness are also one of the constituting aspects of the Senegalese Indophile. Bollywood is 'just like', but at the same time different, 'exotic'.

SIMILAR BECAUSE THE WEST IS DIFFERENT

Moreover, the considerations mentioned above can also account for the reason why Bollywood might be conceived as 'just like', explaining the discourse on similarities (cf. supra): Indian culture is similar because Western is different. This aspect occurs frequently in Indophiles' discourse. The idea of 'the West is different' is a constituent aspect of the concept of parallel modernities. This idea of parallel modernities may be linked to the concept of cultural proximity.

CULTURAL PROXIMITY

Here, the concept of cultural proximity has been borrowed from the domain of communication and media studies, more specifically from Straubhaar, a sociologist working on the audience reception of telenovelas in different parts of Latin America (Straubhaar 1991a and b; 1997). The cultural proximity theory is based on the assumption that audiences actively make choices in their consumption of media products (Straubhaar 1991a: 39, 41). In their choices, audiences prefer media, which reflect their own culture regionally, as well as nationally (Straubhaar 1991a: 39; Burch 2002: 572). Straubhaar argues that cultural proximity plays an important role in understanding why viewers embrace or reject programmes.

The idea that audiences participate actively in their consumption of media products, implies a 'dialogical approach',[14] a concept used by Barker when discussing audience reception of comics (Barker, cited in Kaur 2002: 202). According to him, 'there exists a "contract" between the reader and the text, an *agreement that the text will talk to us in ways we recognize*' (ibid., emphasis author's). Kaur applies this idea to the relation between filmmakers and their audiences: 'film narratives emerge from a "minimal consensus" between filmmakers and the audience' (2002). The fact that the author of comics or the filmmaker talks to us in ways we recognize refers to Straubhaar's concept of cultural proximity: audiences prefer to experience similarities when consuming media products (whether they find it in local products or not), preferring those products which are recognizable, understandable, and therefore, more enjoyable.

Straubhaar developed his ideas to counterbalance theories on media imperialism and cultural dependency, which have dominated studies of popular culture since the late 1970s until recently. The cultural dependency theory is based on the assumption that audiences (not only 'Third World' audiences, but also audiences in Western and Eastern Europe) are dependent on other, more dominant regions for the consumption of media products, resulting in an asymmetrical interdependency between the two regions (1991a: 43–4, 1997: 284). Gramsci's concept of hegemony, in which elites compete to use media and other cultural structures to set a dominant ideology, was a central idea in these theories (Gramsci, cited in Straubhaar 1991a: 40). This way of thinking has to be placed in the context of globalization theories emphasizing homogenization and Westernization, saying that the world is becoming 'more uniform and standardized, through a technological, commercial and cultural synchronization emanating from the West' (Pieterse, cited in Straubhaar 1997: 284).

Straubhaar, along with others such as Ferguson, Robertson, or Featherstone, shows that this interpretation of reality is overly simplistic. In the Latin American context, the audience's preferences are not really prescribed by imported products that reflect the 'traditional' dependency theory of North-South unbalance, as demonstrated by theories of media imperialism. To the contrary, audiences, particularly those from the middle-class and down, prefer local cultural products when available (1991b: 191, 1991a: 39). Earlier, telenovelas were seen as an 'imposition of commercialization and consumption pressure by adapting United States soap opera models to Latin America' (1991b: 192). As he shows in his later article (1991b), the situation is far more complex.

It may be argued that the theory of cultural proximity is very applicable to the case of Senegalese Indophile. It should, however, be broadened and put in another light, as the cultural proximity in this case is not a proximity favouring national or regional products. The difference between geographical proximity (as implied in Straubhaar's ideas) and what we could call imagined proximity is, however, a non-existing one. Places can be geographically close but perceived as very distant, such as neighbouring quarters in the same city gathering a socially very different group of people. On the other hand, places which are geographically very distant can be perceived as close as illustrated through in the Senegalese example. Straubhaar used the theory of cultural proximity to illustrate how people prefer local or regional products in their consumption of media products. However, I would question the geographical implications of his use of proximity. The fact that Bollywood has also (been?) popular in some Latin American countries such as Colombia (Pendakur and Subramanyam 1996) could illustrate a gap in Straubhaar's theory. Cultural proximity in Straubhaar's sense implies a (colonial) view as it is restricted to its geographical contours, without taking into account the aspect of people's imagination, which is always present in any experience of proximity or distance.

Cultural proximity can be part of international flows. Indian culture is being perceived as close, although India is geographically very distant. In this way, we can broaden Straubhaar's concept of cultural proximity to embrace more than regional products. If we conceive Senegalese Indophile as such, the ideas of Straubhaar can be very useful. They provide us an alternative to the theories of cultural North-South dependency in media consumption, or, to put it in Larkin's words, a way towards parallel modernities, standing outside the dichotomy of West/modern and rest/traditional. Cultural proximity accounts for the creation of a third space, breaking through the asymmetrical chain North-South, provision-consumption, export-import, dominant-dependent, active-passive audience.

Notes

1· Nigeria, which gives Indian distributors an income of approximately 39,00,000 through the export of video tapes, significantly more than the income from Canada (21,00,000), Malaysia (25,00,000), or Kenya (12,40,000), is particularly interesting (1991–2).

2. The studies of Behrend (1998) and Fuglesang (1994), however, illustrate that Bollywood is also popular outside the Kenyan Indian community.

3. This idea will be developed in more detail further on and is also mentioned by Larkin (2003: 183, 1997: 414).

4. As we shall see, this 'discourse on similarities' is also found in Senegal.

5. Helen Abdazi (n.d.) mentions that it was also the first Bollywood movie seen in Greece. For details see: 'Hindi Films in the Fifties in Greece: the Latest Chapter of a Long Dialogue'. http://www.sangeetmahal.com/journal_hindi_films_greece.asp;

6. Larkin also mentions this film as being the most popular among Nigerian Hausa (1997: 433).

7. A dance scene in the film shows peasant women dancing in a row stretching out their arms with sickles in their hands. Even if the audience had not caught the communist message until then, this visual pun would offer them a very clear clue.

8. COMACICO was installed in 1926, after it has been installed in Morocco, which explains its name: *Compagnie Marocaine de Cinéma Commercial* (Moroccon Company of Commercial Cinema). SECMA (*Société d'exploitation cinématographique africaine*, Society for the Exploitation of African Cinema) was installed afterwards, in 36–37 (Vieyra 1983: 18).

9. *Société d'Importation, de Distribution et d'Exploitation Cinématographique*, Society for Cinematographic Import, Distribution, and Exploitation.

10. Vieyra mentions that in 1975, 65 per cent of the films imported were French films, the rest mainly consisting of Indian films, Egyptian films, and a few American and Italian films (1983: 28).

11. This is an interesting topic I have approached in my PhD but which I can unfortunately not develop here.

12. Foucault describes discourse as a group of acts of formulation or statements (2003: 120). These are context-specific, an individual or collective act, and are therefore always related to an author. They should be located in its spatio-temporal coordinates. In his article on the systems of exclusion and control in discourse, he states that discourse is everything which is said about something, without implying whether it is 'true' or not (1984: 118). Foucault's concept of discourse can be useful to talk about the group of statements heard from Indophiles on similarities between

India and Senegal. These statements are context-specific and related to an author. By calling the statements from Indophiles 'a discourse', one need not attach judgements on whether the statements are true or not. Furthermore, discourses are always produced inter-subjectively (Moore 1994: 54–5). According to Moore, discourses can be interpreted as a kind of 'situated knowledges'.

13. I will not go into this contested theory of Arian invasion. I am just focussing on Indophiles' discourses.

14. Cf. the remarks by Fuglesang and Radway on audience reception of melodrama earlier.

References

Adamu, Y M. 2002. 'Between the Word and the Screen: a Historical Perspective on the Hausa Literary Movement and the Home Video Invasion', *Journal of African Cultural Studies*, vol. 15, no. 2.

Amkpa, A. 2004. *Theatre and Postcolonial Desires*, London, New York: Routledge.

Appadurai, A. 1991. 'Global Ethnoscapes: Notes and Queries for a Transnational Anthropology', in R. Fox (ed.), *Recapturing Anthropology: Working in the Present*, Santa Fe, California: Sar Press.

————. 1996. *Modernity at Large: Cultural Dimensions of Globalization*, Minnesota: University of Minnesota Press.

Bannerjee, M. and D. Miller. 2003. *The Sari*, New York: Berg.

Behrend, H. 1998. 'Love a la Hollywood and Bombay in Kenyan Studio Photography', *Paideuma*, vol. 44.

Bourdieu, P. 1977. *Distinction: a Social Critique of the Jugement of Taste*, Cambridge, MA: Harvard University Press.

————. 1980. *Le Sens Pratique*, Paris: Les Editions de Minuit.

Burch, E. 2002. 'Media Literacy, Cultural Proximity and TV Aesthetics: Why Indian Soap Operas Work in Nepal and the Hindu Diaspora', *Media, Culture and Society*, vol. 24.

Chakravarty, S.S. 1989. 'National Identity and the Realist Aesthetic: Indian Cinema of the Fifties', *Quarterly Review of Film and Video*, vol. 11, no. 3.

————. 1993. *National Identity in Indian Popular Cinema, 1947–1987*, Austin, Texas: University of Texas Press.

Das Dasgupta, S. 1996. 'Feminist Consciousness in Woman-Centered Hindi Films', *Journal of Popular Culture*, vol. 30, no. 1.

Foucault, M. 1984. 'The Order of Discourse', in M. Shapiro (ed.), *Language and Politics*, Oxford: Blackwell.

————. 2003. *The Archaeology of Knowledge*, London and New York: Routledge.

Fuglesang, M. 1994. 'Veils and Videos. Female Youth Culture on the Kenyan Coast', *Stockholm Studies in Social Anthropology*, vol. 32, Department of Anthropology, Stockholm University.

Furniss, G. 2003. 'Hausa Popular Literature and Video Film: the Rapid Rise of Cultural Production in Times of Economic Decline', Working Papers, no. 27, Mainz: Department of Anthropology and African Studies.

Gillespie, M. 1989. 'Technology and Tradition—Audio-Visual Culture among South Asian Families in West London', *Cultural Studies*, vol. 3, no. 2.

Haynes, J. 2000. 'Introduction', in J. Haynes (ed.), *Nigerian Video Films*, Athens: Ohio University Center for International Studies.

Jaikumar, P. 2003. 'Bollywood Spectaculars', *World Literature Today*, vol. 77, no. 3/4.

Kaur, R. 2002. 'Viewing the West Through Bollywood: a Celluloid Occident in the Making', *Contemporary South Asia*, vol. 11, no. 2.

Larkin, B. 1997. 'Indian Films and Nigerian Lovers: Media and the Creation of Parallel Modernities', *Africa*, vol. 67, no. 3.

—————. 2000. 'Hausa Dramas and the Rise of Video Culture in Nigeria', in J. Haynes (ed.), *Nigerian Video Films*, Ohio: Ohio University Centre for International Studies.

—————. 2003. 'Itineraries of Indian Cinema: African Videos, Bollywood and Global Media', in E. Shohat and R. Stam (eds), *Multiculturalism, Postcoloniality, and Transnational Media*, New Brunswick, New Jersey, and London: Rutgers University Press.

Moore, H. 1994. *A Passion for Difference: Essays in Anthropology and Gender*. Cambridge: Polity Press.

Pendakur, M. and R. Subramanyam. 1996. 'India. Part I: Indian Cinema Beyond National Borders', J. Sinclair, E. Jacka, and S. Cunningham (eds), *New Patterns in Global Television, Peripheral Vision*, Oxford: Oxford University Press.

Radway, J. 1983. 'Women Read the Romance: the Interaction of Text and Context', *Feminist Studies*, vol. 9, no. 1.

—————. 1987. *Reading the Romance*, London: Verso.

Rush, D. 1999. 'Eternal Potential. Chromolithographs in *Vodunland*', *African Arts*, vol. 32, no. 4.

Scheld, S. 2003. 'Clothes Talk: Youth Modernities and Commodity Consumption in Dakar, Senegal', PhD dissertation, City University of New York.

Straubhaar, J.D. 1991a. 'Beyond Media Imperialism: Asymmetrical Interdependence and Cultural Proximity', *Critical Studies in Mass Communication*, vol. 8.

—————. 1991b. 'The Reception of Telenovelas and Other Latin American Genres in The Regional Market: the Case of the Dominican Republic', *Studies in Latin American Popular Culture*, vol. 10.

Straubhaar, J.D. 1997. 'Distinguishing the Global, Regional and National Levels of World Television', in A. Sreberny-Mohammadi, D. Winseck, J. Mckenna, and O. Boyd-barrett (eds), *Media in Global Context. A Reader*, London, New York: Arnold.

Tremblay, R.C. 1996. 'Representation and Reflection of Self and Society in the Bombay Cinema', *Contemporary South Asia*, vol. 5, no. 3.

Vieyra, P. 1983. *Le Cinema Au Senegal. Collection Cinémedia. Cinémas d'Afrique Noire*, Bruxelles: Editions Ocic, L'Harmattan.

to number about 25 million spread among 110 countries (*Overview*, 2007; p. 3).[1] Jigna Desai (2004: 40) notes that 'South Asian diasporas are one of the largest sites of consumption of Bollywood films and are considered a distribution territory by the Indian film industry [*sic*].' It is estimated that the sale of overseas distribution rights for a big-budget Bollywood film now rakes in twice the revenues brought in via the largest domestic market, namely, Mumbai (Deshpande 2005: 190–91). Brosius and Yazgi (2007: 358fn) note that 'NRIs account for approximately 65 per cent of Bollywood's earnings'.[2]

However, Bollywood's appeal outside of the Indian subcontinent is not limited to the Indian *diasporic* populations (that is, NRIs) in the US, Canada, UK, Middle East, southern and East Africa, the Caribbean and elsewhere. Bollywood's presence in many African countries is not only a long-established one, as media anthropologist, Brian Larkin (2002; 2003), has documented in his studies of film audiences in northern Nigeria, where we see the importation of Indian film styles into Nigerian Hausa 'video films', but its popularity there has been consolidated in the *absence* of an Indian diasporic population.[3] Rajagopalan (2005) has documented a 'taste' for Indian cinema in post-Stalinist Soviet society and Bollywood is said to have something of a cult status in Japan. In October 2006, the North American journal, *South Asian Popular Culture*, dedicated an issue to the study of Indian cinema's global reach. Seeking to de-centre Hollywood in debates on cinema and globalization, it includes articles and anecdotal accounts of Indian cinema in countries as diverse as Spain, Romania, Bulgaria, Egypt, Greece, Israel, the former Yugoslavia, Italy, and Turkey, among others—by non-NRIs.

South Africa, however, does have a diasporic Indian population, numbering about 1 million. Most South African-Indians are descendants of either indentured labourers or passenger Indians (that is, traders, artisans, teachers, and so on, who paid their own way), who arrived in South Africa in the mid-nineteenth to early twentieth century. Consequently, in South Africa, Indian cinema exhibition has an established history, beginning with screenings of Indian films in the 1930s. In 1939, the Avalon Cinema was opened by A.B. Moosa, Snr., in Durban, and by the 1940s, Moosa had become one of the pioneer importers of Indian films to South Africa.[4] Other South African Indian-owned cinemas followed. The Naaz group of cinemas imported films from India via London and circulated them among several cinemas in both the city centre and surrounding Indian-occupied areas of Merebank, Chatsworth, and Verulam.[5]

In Durban, the city with the largest Indian-descent population in South Africa, Indian films were screened in large, grand cinemas with names like Shah Jehan (a 2,000 seater), Isfahan, Raj, and Shiraz, some quite luxurious in decor. Jagarnath (2004: 218) describes the success of these films from the 1950s to the mid-1970s as 'quite phenomenal'. In referring to the migration of Bollywood from the ghetto to the mainstream in South Africa, the term 'ghetto' is used ironically; it reflects an ethnically-bounded cultural space and practice, but cinema-going by Indian South Africans saw patrons dressing up in their Saturday evening best and the cinemas becoming 'palaces of excess and enjoyment'. Both in name and décor, they 'aimed at linking themselves with an Indian past of royal dynasties, and Mughal extravagance' (ibid.: 215).

From about the mid-1980s onwards, however, Durban saw its once thriving Indian film scene begin to decline with the advent of video and India's boycott of South Africa's apartheid policies. Pirated videos abounded, and many of Durban's once luxurious Indian cinemas were shut down.[6] Independent (Indian) distributors fought to revive the industry, with mainstream exhibition chains like Ster-Kinekor only coming in once the revival was already well under way. Screening the film *Kuch Kuch Hota Hai* in 1998,[7] Ster-Kinekor was surprised when it grossed more than some of the Western films against which it was competing. The country's biggest distribution and exhibition chain woke up and took notice. In 2002, Ster-Kinekor launched its Bollywood circuit with the Oscar-nominated film *Lagaan* (Tax, 2001), and hosted a Bollywood film festival in the cities of Durban, Cape Town and Johannesburg.

Ster-Kinekor's decision in 2002 to include Indian films on its screens not only testified to the substantial market for Bollywood films in South Africa, but also heralded a shift from the 'ghetto' to the mainstream. The term 'mainstream cinema complexes' refers here to the previously so-called 'white' areas where many of the popular shopping malls are situated, and in which the larger multiplexes are housed, as opposed to residential and/or commercial areas in which people of Indian descent predominate (a legacy of the spatial/racial segregation policies of the apartheid era). A year later, the other major film distributor, Nu-Metro, began exhibiting ten to twelve Bollywood films per year.

Ster-Kinekor's initiatives could be seen as a major development in the trajectory towards what has been referred in this chapter as the 'mainstreaming' of Bollywood in South Africa. While Ster-Kinekor's statements to the media acknowledged the crucial role of independent Indian film distributors in the survival of Indian films in the South African market, the company's public relations strategy was careful to present Indian films as entertainment for *all* ethnic groups. The expansion of the market for Bollywood films to 'crossover audiences' involved several strategies, including (a) expansion to mainstream cinema venues, (b) the screening of subtitled versions of Hindi films—both for Indian-descent audiences no longer familiar with Indian vernaculars, and for non-Indian audiences, (c) the marketing of Bollywood through festivals, and the hosting of both the Second IIFA Awards (2002, Sun City) and the Fourth (2004, Dome at Northgate) in South Africa, (d) expansion of distribution and exhibition to cinemas in small towns across the country, and (e) the stocking of Indian diaspora films, such as *East is East, Fire, Bend it Like Beckham,* and *Monsoon Wedding,* and later (much less profitably) Bollywood films, by video stores.[8]

In April 2004, all of the film distributors' efforts to appeal to a crossover audience and to expand the market for Bollywood were eclipsed by an independent decision by the national public broadcaster, SABC, to begin screening—often in direct competition with theatre distributors—a series of Bollywood films on SABC 3, South Africa's 'public commercial' television service on Saturday nights, a move that catapulted Bollywood into the South African mainstream. Bearing in mind that most of the South African population has access only to a few free-to-air television channels—although more affluent viewers can subscribe to the pay-TV satellite network, DSTV—and that South African television channels have national coverage, exhibition on the national broadcaster epitomizes mainstream exhibition.

Although a mixture of condescension and scepticism met the then commissioning editor's initial proposal to screen Indian films and de-spite being given the channel's 'dead slot', namely, the 10 p.m. slot on Saturday nights, the audience ratings surprised the sceptics at the SABC. The screening of the first ten films reflected a substantial increase in the channel's viewership in this time slot including a 700 per cent increase in Indian-descent audiences, a 115 per cent increase in English-speaking audiences, and a 20 per cent increase in Afrikaans-speaking audiences,

30 per cent in the category called All Adults, with a 35 per cent increase in All Adults in the LSM[9] 8–10 category, and finally, a 70 per cent increase in coloured audiences. The huge increase in Indian descent audiences is not as unsurprising as it may seem—Indian audiences have a notably high rate of VCR/DVD ownership and access to low-cost rentals or purchases of Indian films; in addition, many subscribe to the Indian bouquets on the DSTV pay-TV service which include Indian channels such as ZEE TV, B4U, and Sony.[10] SABC's 'dead slot', previously lacking advertiser support, began to attract substantial advertising, primarily mainstream advertising (cellphones, fast food, and so on).[11]

Public demand resulted in repeat screenings, which started in August 2004, on Saturday afternoons (2 pm). This became the primary screening time for Indian films, with SABC 3 creating a marketing brand called 'Bollywood on 3' which, in fact, increasingly included non-Bollywood Indian films, especially those in the south Indian languages of Telugu and Tamil.

Also in 2004, the pay TV/subscription channel, Saffron TV, began a broadcast service targeted to Indians in South Africa. In 2008, it became part of DSTV's north and south Indian bouquets. Primarily a lifestyle and entertainment channel, most of Saffron's content is international in origin, although the station does produce about 20 per cent of its content locally.[12] Much of the international content, as well as some of the local content, is focused on Bollywood films and news, celebrity gossip, and so on.

Although it is difficult to obtain verification from the distributors/exhibitors, there is anecdotal evidence that exposure to Bollywood films via television has motivated some non-Indian viewers to attend theatrical screenings and even—according to some DVD retailers—to buy Bollywood titles. Such retailers mention, additionally, that a number of their customers are West and East Africans, such as Somali and Nigerian immigrants.

In the late 1990s and into the 2000s, the commercial potential of Bollywood was increasingly acknowledged by players other than film distributors, with segments of the leisure and entertainment industry, including film producers, bankrolling local tours by Bollywood actors, musicians, and so on. Rajadhyaksha (2003: 27) argues that the diffused nature of Bollywood as a cultural industry leaves many producers of its filmic narratives bemused, unable to identify how to best exploit or consolidate what appears to be a lucrative marketing opportunity. How-ever, other players in the entertainment and publication industries have increasingly exploited the entire 'Bollywood phenomenon', frequently using the term 'Bollywood' to label anything Indian and glamourous, colourful, or extravagant. The past five years has seen an expansion of the commercial exploitation of Indian cinema and, more generally, of Indian culture, as a number of live performances, including both locally and Indian-produced stage shows, beauty pageants, fairs and exhibitions, musical extravaganzas, and so on, have increasingly utilized the brand appeal of Bollywood by attaching the label 'Bollywood' to anything reflecting any connection to India.

In April-May 2009, the IPL cricket tournament was held in South Africa. The tournament was closely linked to Bollywood with media coverage, including television coverage of the actual matches, highlight-ing (co)ownership of several teams by Bollywood stars such as Shah Rukh Khan, Preity Zinta, and Shilpa Shetty. The Bollywood link was strengthened by the launch of a Miss Bollywood IPL South Africa beau-ty pageant, in which contestants were cricket fans and selected during each match. Prizes included a guided trip through Bollywood and a role in a Bollywood film.[13] The pageant included contestants from different race groups, but the pageant came under heavy criticism when, in a practice reminiscent of apartheid South Africa, all the finalists selected were white and the winner admitted to never even having seen a single Bollywood film!

Lifestyle magazines focusing on Indian South Africans have also emerged in recent years. Publications such as *SAINDIA* and its accom-panying website, SAIndia.com and *SUTRA* include news and gossip about Bollywood.

Bollywood-South Africa: Co-operation and Connections

Both the Indian film industry's and Bollywood's global profile extends beyond its market penetration of overseas markets to its production locations in an increasing number of countries worldwide, to the growing international fame of its stars, to its increased co-production (including animation) and co-distribution agreements with media giants like the Disney and Sony Corporations. The Disney film, *Cheetah Girls: One World*, for example, is targeted to the lucrative tween market (ages 8–12) and portrays the Cheetah Girls travelling to India to star in a Bollywood film. It also includes a dance-off between Indian and American dancers. Additionally, the global visibility of Bollywood is both reflected in and promoted by its acknowledgement in Western academia. Academic publishing on Indian cinemas (especially on Bollywood) outside of India has mushroomed in the past decade.

> Indian co-operation with South Africa in relation to film production invites further examination with regard to two aspects: (a) South African—Indian film industry co-operation; and (b) Bollywood's use of South Africa for location shooting.

Eddie Mbalo, CEO of the National Film and Video Foundation (NFVF), stated in an address to a workshop[14]: 'The Indian industry has two important lessons for South Africa: the first is how to build a film industry in a developing country: and the second, how to enable commercially viable films to be produced in a multilingual, culturally diverse society.'[15]

Soon afterwards, Mbalo and other senior staff from the NFVF visited India to solidify relationships with the Indian production community and to establish an agreement with a film school in India that offered placements to South African students. Subsequently, a number of visits and events have solidified South Africa's links with the Indian film industry. These include the signing of a Memorandum of Understanding (MOU) which makes provision for Indian-South African co-operation in film in the areas of *co-production and distribution*, that is, the joint funding of development, production, and distribution of films from both countries; *festivals and cultural programmes*, that is, exchanging film-related information about cultural programmes in the respective countries and information exchange.

In 2004, an entire day of the three-day-long India International Film Convention, held in New Delhi, was dedicated to South Africa, and South Africa has also begun entering some films in Indian film festivals. In 2005, a Bollywood delegation was received in South Africa to discuss Bollywood-South African Film industry co-operation. While no co-operative film production appears to have taken place under the aegis of the MOU, private arrangements with local entrepreneurs and industry players such as Avalon Productions have been established, with the past few years seeing a number of Bollywood productions using South African locations. However, there is little evidence of actual co-production between parties in South Africa and in Mumbai. It is worth remarking that official statements from local government and NFVF executives tend to focus more on the potential benefits of Bollywood to the local tourist and film industries through their use of South African locations rather than to issues of co-production. The discourse around such co-operation is often couched in terms that make for easy slippage between use of the local film industry as a support service and co-production. For example, a report commissioned by the Western Cape Department of Economic Development and Tourism on the film industry argues:

> Developing the Indian Memorandum of Understanding into a full co-production treaty would also provide substantial returns. Although Indian budgets tend to be a great deal smaller than those of European and American origin, the tourism spin-offs are substantial. Indian tourists are renowned for travelling to locations showcased in Indian films. Furthermore, a co-production treaty could 'work both ways'. (Tuomi 2005b: 6)

While plans to shoot part of the sequel to the hit comedy 'Mr Bones' on location in India in 2007 as a co-production with Indian production partners were abandoned, the potential access to a massive Indian market for films was clearly an incentive.

> Mr Bones was very popular with Indian audiences, both in theatres and on TV, and it was dubbed into Hindi and other local languages .... It makes perfect sense for Mr Bones, a white African sangoma, to end up in India to continue his journey in an exotic location and to generate his unique brand of chaos .... The sequel to Mr Bones is scheduled to be shot in India later this year [2007] and marks the first time that a SA/India co-production will be shot in both SA and India. This production is an extension of the significant economic and cultural ties that the two countries have developed.[16]

However, a mutual sense of the other's exoticism appears to inform much of the Indian-South African film co-operation agreements. For example, the Sun City sequences in the Bollywood film *Hera Pheri* fully exploits the iconography of colonial nostalgia (a hallmark of much of South Africa's tourist appeal), of African exoticism, and so on.

Bollywood's use of South Africa for location shooting

Before expanding on Bollywood's use of South Africa for location shooting, a brief contextualization is in order regarding the use of unfamiliar or exotic locations, especially in the song and dance sequences. Song and dance, involving the lover-protagonists against a scenic backdrop, is a long-established tradition or convention in Bollywood films. Perhaps originating in the romantic idea rooted in Urdu poetry (which had, for a long time, constituted the basis of the song lyrics of Hindi cinema) of the longed for earthly paradise to which lovers can escape, the song and dance sequences frequently utilized the beautiful scenery of the state of Kashmir as a romantic backdrop, which was substituted later with the Swiss countryside and the Alps, as political developments made Kashmir inaccessible. If contemporary Bollywood includes, as part of its menu of spectatorial pleasures, a form of cinematic sightseeing, countries like South Africa are poised to exploit the opportunities Bollywood offers to promote tourism to its shores by the increasingly globally mobile Indian population. In the past decade, a number of Bollywood films have been shot in South Africa, including *Cash, Race, Hera Pheri, Filhaal, Aankhen, Dil Ka Rishta, Armaan, Ishq Vishq, Andaaz, Khel,* and *Dhoom 2.*

The city of Cape Town and the province of Gauteng remain in the forefront as preferred locations for film productions. While local film-makers utilize Gauteng locations extensively for both feature films and commercials, it is Cape Town which has established itself as the premier location of choice for international films. The use of the city as a film location pumps in hundreds of millions of rand into the local economy. On any day, there are as many as forty shoots in and around Cape Town (including commercials, Indian films, and Hollywood films). The city and its environs are particularly popular with Bollywood producers. For example, in 2001, only one Bollywood film (*Rehnaa Hai Terre Dil Mein*) was shot in Durban, while seven Bollywood films were shot in Cape Town.

More recently, however, Bollywood has begun utilizing Durban and other KwaZulu-Natal locations. One film shot in Durban as well as the Sun City holiday resort is *Hera Pheri*, a comedy revolving around three working-class, unemployed heroes with the thinnest of romantic sub-plots, and a set of rather gritty, even grimy, locations—elements unusual for a contemporary Bollywood film.[17] Bollywood song and dance sequences are already famously global and *Hera Pheri* simply uses locations around Durban as a backdrop for a song and dance sequence, without any explicit acknowledgement of the geographical location, nor reference to it in the narrative, which is set in Mumbai. However, some of the scenes do include signs on vehicles or buildings that indicate the location is Durban, and of course, those familiar with Durban's Pavilion shopping mall and beachfront will recognize the rickshaws and the landmarks around which a female character tries to seduce one of our hapless heroes. The film also includes a song-and-dance sequence shot at Sun City.

The film, *Andaaz*, however, uses South African locations in the song and dance sequences and in some of the narrative sequences. Scenes shot in the outskirts of Cape Town stand variously for 'somewhere in Europe'. Reportedly, South African authorities were upset to discover this geographical substitution—which deprives South Africa of the beneficial spin-offs for tourism when locations are passed off as being elsewhere—and particularly after the Minister of Defence agreed to allow the South African Air Force to do a flypass for the film.[18] Similarly, the blockbuster *Dhoom 2* (2006), a stylish action thriller, passes off its locations in Oribi Gorge on the KwaZulu Natal South Coast and parts of Durban as parts of Brazil, substituting Durban for Rio and parts of Mumbai. The spectacular opening sequence, however, is shot in the Namib Desert and is acknowledged as such.

The use of South African locations by international film productions benefits the country in several ways. Film production units are often thought of as 'super tourists' because of their extensive use of resources such as airlines, vehicle rental (not just car hire, but truck, bus, fire engine, and ambulance rentals), accommodation, restaurant and catering services, electrical and other equipment, and so on—all of which benefit a large number of auxiliary industries. In addition, there are spin-offs in terms of marketing the country or city as a tourist attraction, and the employment of local technical and creative crew as well as extras. Domestic and international commercial and feature film production in South Africa currently generates about R7 billion annually, and revenues were expected to rise substantially as a result of the government's launch of a rebate scheme for the film and television industries in 2007. Additionally, some Bollywood film producers have reportedly moved productions from the UK to South Africa as a result of a new, less favourable tax system introduced there, including a 'cultural test' for Britishness.[19]

A challenge for South Africa is that its reliance on a Hollywood model of production hinders its ability to adapt to the needs of industries that utilize an alternative mode of production. Both the Cape Film Commission (CFC) and the Durban Film Office expresses frustrations about their interactions with Indian film producers resulting from the more informal/unstructured mode of production as compared to that of American and European filmmakers.[20] In arguing for a higher degree of reciprocity in the relationship between the production and the country of production, local film offices demand greater use of local production and auxiliary industry resources in return for (free) use of locations by international film producers. Both offices expressed dissatisfaction in this regard with Indian film productions, noting that Indian filmmakers simply do not make sufficient use of local production crew because they generally bring with them their own designers, script editors, make-up artists, catering crews, and so on. Both expressed a desire to maintain a hospitable environment for Indian film productions, but clearly perceived the Indian mode of film production as less than beneficial for South Africa.

It is apparent, however, that systems put in place for the facilitation of film productions in South Africa are structured on a Hollywood model of film production in which the process of film production is based on a script, storyboard, and so on. The Bollywood (and more generally, Indian popular cinema) mode of film production is far less structured in that Indian filmmakers frequently proceed without a finalized script in place. Clearly, South African film offices are unable (and unwilling?) to comprehend modes of production that do not adhere to the highly specialized, well-resourced, and highly structured production practices (feature film and commercials) of North American and European producers.

Notable too, is that while requesting that more use be made of local production crew, both offices acknowledged that they are not always able to cater to the needs of Indian film producers. It was acknowledged that local film training institutions do not train students in techniques of costume and set design, make-up, and so on, that meet the particular (and sometimes culturally-specific) needs of Indian film productions. It is not unsurprising then that Indian film producers and directors bring their own make-up artists, designers, choreographers, and so on. Arguably, even Indian culinary needs require specialized knowledge of Indian cuisine.

In August 2009, the CFC, somewhat belatedly announced its recognition of the lucrative Bollywood industry's almost insatiable appetite for new shooting locations and announced that it will undertake a mission to India later in the year to cement its relationship with Bollywood and to market the Western Cape and its film industry's services to the huge Indian film industry. At the time of writing, in August 2009, the CFC noted that the Bollywood production of *No Problem*, a police action thriller which was being shot in Cape Town, had already shown significant spin-offs in the city's tourism sector and had contributed to 2000 bed nights, as well as employment for a number of local residents as crew and cast members.[21] The CFC's CEO, Laurence Mitchell, further added that the CFC is already conducting discussions with the Department of Trade and Industry to look at a restructured film rebate system that would make it much easier to enter into co-production treaties with a specific focus on markets such as India.

After a visit to the set of the production, the province's Minister of Finance, Economic Development and Tourism, noted the potentially lucrative market that both the Indian tourism and the Indian film industries offer the Western Cape via the use of the Cape's locations in Bollywood films.[22] Not yet acknowledged is the exposure to the country offered to Bollywood audiences outside India and the undermining of this potential for tourism if the practice of geographical anonymity or geographical substitution persists.

South Africans of Indian origin who are key players in the film industry include Anant Singh, a film producer known both for producing some of South Africa's best known anti-apartheid films, as well as the country's biggest locally produced commercial (if not critical!) success, *Mr Bones*. Singh's Videovision Entertainment has been involved in the local productions of Bollywood-style stage musicals, such as *Bombay Crush*. Videovision Entertainment is also a partner in the construction of the Cape Town Film Studios, described by Singh as 'the first custom-built, Bollywood-style studio complex of its kind in Africa'.[23] A.B. Moosa Jnr., the grandson of A.B. Moosa, Snr. has, in addition to establishing Avalon Productions, acted as line producer for the record-breaking Bollywood blockbuster *Dhoom 2*.

There are, additionally, the beginnings of a South African Indian filmmaking practice influenced by Bollywood. The first film focusing on South African Indian characters was Kumaran Naidu's domestic drama—*Broken Promises* (2005)—and its sequel—*Broken Promises 2*. However, it is show promoter, Pinky Mothie, whose forays into film production reflect a Bollywood consciousness. Her first production, with her daughter as screenwriter and her son in the starring role was *Hip Hop 2 Bollywood* (2007). Shot in Durban and Mumbai, the film tells the tale of a South African Indian dancer/student from Durban who is discovered as a fresh new talent for a stage show. He travels to Mumbai where he falls in love and finds himself torn between returning to South Africa and staying in India with the woman he loves (Thangavelo 2007). Mothie's second production is *Bollywood Campus* (2009). The cast is entirely South African and the dialogue is in English (Pillay 2009).

Kaur (2002) notes that 'the factors of demand, supply and profitability guide the actual production of cultural products'. It is the recent wave of emigration to the First World nations and the consequent establishment of diasporas with significantly high disposable incomes that has asserted the primacy of diasporic markets. Desai (2004) notes that until recently, '… diasporas hardly registered in the national filmic imaginary; in other words, diasporic lives and experiences rarely were the subject of films. This is clearly not the case any more, because Indian film industries have "discovered" the diasporas (as lucrative markets).'

Until recently, despite (very) occasional use made of South African actors, South Africans of Indian descent did not appear as *characters* in Bollywood films, not even as minor or secondary characters with speaking parts.[24] While Bollywood obviously relies on the star power of its leading *actors*, Bollywood films usually *characterize* diasporic pro-tagonists as NRIs from the US, Canada, Australia, or the UK. This lack of acknowledgement of Indian diasporas in Fiji, Mauritius, Guyana, Trinidad, Surinam, Malaysia, South Africa, Sri Lanka, and the Middle East reflects the class bias of Bollywood which tends to focus on the lives of high-caste Hindus belonging to the upper-middle or professional classes, many of whose emigration to the West is of relatively recent vin-tage. Indians in the Caribbean or South Africa, for example, left during British colonial rule and the majority emigrated as indentured labourers, while many Indians in the Middle East whose emigration is more recent appear to be included in some other regional cinemas such as Malayalam cinema.

South Africa's relative invisibility as a source of diasporic narratives and characters is reproduced in scholarly analyses of Indian cinema's international markets. Despite Bollywood's own recognition of South Africa as an important overseas market—the International Indian Film Awards have already been twice hosted by South Africa—Pendakur and Subramanyam (1996), for example, exclude South Africa from their discussion of Indian cinema's major diasporic markets; they do acknowledge two other African countries, Kenya and Nigeria (although the latter hardly counts as 'diasporic'). Additionally, scholarly analyses of Bollywood in the diaspora reveals a tendency to give lip service to the existence of Indian diasporas in many parts of the world, before proceeding with analyses that assume all Indian diasporic subjects reside in the first world nations of the US, Canada, England, and sometimes, Australia.

One scholarly analysis that does focus on South Africa is by Hansen, who argues that the Bollywood film *Kuch Kuch Hota Hai* (1998) gave South Africans—'a glimpse of being a modern "diasporic Indian" in contemporary South Africa' (2005: 257) by providing, it seems, 'a fantasy India widely held among Indians in South Africa' (ibid.: 256)—one devoid of squalor and poverty. This reflects a similar view to that of Kaur (2002) who argues that the shift seen in Bollywood's themes and protagonists reflect the emergence of a globalized Indian middle-class resulting from the economic liberalization policies of India in the 1990s. Kaur suggests that their conspicuous consumption allows diasporic Indians 'to feel neither shame of their motherland's poverty nor guilt about their own comparative riches', and that the Indian diaspora is 'particularly prone to lap up rosy pictures of Indian society'. Kaur also argues that

> ... [b]oth privileged Indians at home and the diaspora abroad who had grown tired of routine stories of callous deaths, mishaps, drought, or famine in India as reported in the international media are keen to devour a cultural product that brings them no shame. Indeed, they can claim moral superiority over their Western counterparts by emphasizing family values, commitment, and traditional oriental warmth.

Although not in the scope of this chapter, it could be argued that spectatorial pleasure and consumption of Bollywood films by diasporic audiences may in fact reflect a rather more complex pattern/negotiation of identification and disdain than either Kaur or Hansen recognize.

Also arguable is the assumption made by Hansen that 'Bollywood films have for a long time been a type of "mega-signifier" of Indianness in South Africa (and elsewhere).' Although Hansen also pays little attention to class, religious, and generational differences in the reception of Bollywood films, or in relation to South African Indian subjectivities, reading sources such as the newspaper, *The Post*, as representing the views of a homogenous and monolithic 'Indian community', it would be interesting to further interrogate Hansen's argument that, in fact, for most South Africans, 'India is nowhere in the picture as an object of identification and even less as a destination of emigration' (2005: 258).

Anecdotal evidence emerging from this author's teaching of an introductory undergraduate course on Bollywood at the University of the Witwatersrand suggests that many young South Africans—*of all races*, including those of Indian-descent—draw on Bollywood as just one of many global cultural references which support their perceptions of themselves as cosmopolitan, sophisticated, and media-savvy. A colleague who approached a number of Indian South Africans students at Wits about whether they perceived Indian-targeted media as a way of returning to their cultural roots to find their identities in a post-apartheid South Africa, has argued that '... to most of the students, the cultural worth of Bollywood movies was no different from MTV, markers of fashion trends that one might emulate at a family wedding, just like replicating a popular Western culture fashion trend on campus' (Mistry 2004: 34).

In the light of recurring questions of multiple and shifting identities, a valuable arena of research would be to conduct ethnographic audience studies in order to ascertain the role of Bollywood not only in the South African Indian imaginary, but also in relation to identity construction among South Africans of different races. Ethnographic studies among diasporic Indians may elicit little insights beyond reproducing existing perceptions that the consumption of Bollywood films signifies a desire for the idea of either an authentic or a romanticized homeland to con-fused diasporans—a narrative favoured by Bollywood itself it seems. Ethnographic research is necessary to provide verification of, and insights into, anecdotal accounts of the popularity of Bollywood among many African/black domestic workers and nurses, and some white teenagers among others. Such research may uncover practices and perceptions that challenge Hansen's concluding argument that '... the deep running racialization of cultural practices in South Africa mean that there are few signs of Indian cinema becoming a ... medium of entertainment and visceral engagement between the city's Indian and African worlds' (2005: 259).

Notes

1. For details see: 'Overview: Ministry of Overseas Indian Affairs', *Pravasi Bharatiya: Connecting India with its Diaspora*, vol. 2, no. 2 (February), http://www.overseasindian.in/pdf/2007/feb/ENGLISH_PAGES.pdf.; accessed on 24 March 2007.

2. The term 'non-resident Indian'—commonly abbreviated as NRI—is a term referring to Indian nationals living outside India, but is commonly used to refer to the diasporic Indians in general (regardless of nationality).

3. Additionally, in interviews with this author, several West African filmmakers from countries such as Senegal and Burkina Faso have attested to exposure to Indian films in their youth; neither country has any Indian diaspora population of any note. Despite the immense popularity of Indian films among African audiences, their prevalence on African screens (together with Hollywood movies and Kung fu fare) has long been a bone of contention among those filmmakers and film scholars committed to expanding African audiences for African films. The only home-grown African 'industry' to have achieved substantial popular/commercial appeal in Africa is Nollywood.

4. For details see: 'Avalon Group—70 years and Beyond', NFVF (National Film and Video Foundation), http://www.nfvf.co.za/article/avalon-group-70-years-and-beyond; accessed on 27 August 2009.

5. For details see: 'The Warwick Precinct: *The Currie's Fountain and Grey Street Areas*', Durban, 2007, http://www.sahistory.org.za/pages/places/villages/kwazuluNatal/grey-street/cinemas.htm; accessed on 27 August 2009.

6. For a discussion of the early history of Indian cinema exhibition in Durban, including the impact of the apartheid laws of racial/spatial segregation, see Jagarnath (2004).

7. 'Popcorn Seller Now Cinema Boss', *The Tribune, Online Edition*, 2001, http://www.tribuneindia.com/2001/20010922/biz.htm; accessed on 28 August 2009.

8. Bollywood films are available for purchase at relatively low cost. Additionally, most DVDs contain more than one title and fans generally engage in repeated viewings of the popular song-and-dance sequences, making the rental of such films less cost-effective than their purchase.

9. LSM refers to the Living Standards Measure, a marketing research tool that segments the South African market according to their living standards, using criteria such as degree of urbanization and ownership of cars and major appliances. It divides the population into ten LSM groups, 10 (highest) to 1 (lowest).

10. There are two such bouquets: 'DSTV North Indian' includes Zee TV, Sony, B4U and NDTV 24×7 as well as the Arabic Islamic channel IQRAA; 'DSTV South Indian' focuses on Tamil-language entertainment and includes the Indian channels, Sun TV and KTV.

11. Statistics cited here were obtained from Anu Nepal, then a commissioning editor at the SABC, who procured Indian films for the SABC.

12. 'Saffron TV Goes Out from Historic Broadcast House', 2008, http://www.gfo.co.za/live/content.php?Item_ID=586; accessed on 28 August 2009.

13. 'Gauteng's first hopeful in the search for Miss Bollywood SA', 2009; http://www.bizcommunity.com/Article/196/440/35404.html; accessed on 3 September 2009.

14. 'Towards a KZN Film Office', Address to the 22nd Durban International Film Festival, September 2002.

15. Although looking to Bollywood may provide some lessons for the development of a local film industry in South Africa, it would perhaps be more productive for us to look closer to home—to Nollywood and the Ghanaian video film industry—for models. South Africa does not share with India a large domestic market, a crucial factor in the success of the Indian film industries. Film ticket sales in India average 12 million per day; in South Africa the figure is 26–30 million per year!

16. For more details see: 'Mr Bones' sequel to be co-produced in India', *Screen Africa*, 14 March 2007, http://www.screenafrica.com/news/stop_press/687510.htm; accessed on 20 March 2007.

17. In recent years, Bollywood films have increasingly focused on the lives and loves of the affluent classes or the 'transnational Indian' with opulent sets, designer clothes, and so on.

18. The supposedly European plane clearly displays the colours of the South African flag!

19. For details see: 'Bollywood prefers South Africa to UK', *The Hindu*, 25 December 2006.

20. Both offices simply categorize productions as 'Indian' and do not distinguish among the different cinema industries of India. Interviews were conducted by the author in December 2007.

21. 'Cape Town Film Industry Set to Experience Influx of Bollywood Film Productions', http://www.capefilmcommission.co.za/.; accessed on 28 August 2009.

22. Ibid.

23. 'Anant Singh and Marcel Golding Debut Cape Town Film Studios to International Film Community', NFVF, 2009, http://www.nfvf.co.za/article/anant-singh-marcel-golding-debuts-cape-town-film-studios-international-film-community; accessed on 28 August 2009.

24. The white South African actress, Shannon Ezra, plays a Canadian in *Salaam-e-Ishq* (2007). More recently, the film *Just Married*, included a South African actress of Indian-descent, Tarina Patel, in a secondary role.

References

Brosius, C. and N. Yazgi. 2007. '"Is There No Place Like Home?": Contesting Cinematographic Constructions of Indian Diasporic Experiences', *Contributions to Indian Sociology*, vol. 41, no. 3, pp. 355–86.

Desai, J. 2004. *Beyond Bollywood: The Cultural Politics of South Asian Diasporic Film*, New York: Routledge.

Deshpande, S. 2005. 'The Consumable Hero of Globalised India, in Raminder Kaur and Ajay J. Sinha (eds), *Bollyworld: Popular Indian Cinema through a Transnational Lens*, New Delhi: Sage.

Ganti, T. 2004. *Bollywood: A Guidebook to Popular Hindi Cinema*, New York and London: Routledge.

Hansen, T.B. 2005. 'In Search of the Diasporic Self: Bollywood in South Africa', in Raminder Kaur and Ajay J. Sinha (eds), *Bollyworld: Popular Indian Cinema through a Transnational Lens*, New Delhi: Sage.

Iordanova, Dina. 2006. 'Indian Cinema's Global Reach', *South Asian Popular Culture*, vol. 4, no. 2.

Jagarnath, V. 2004. 'The Politics of Urban Segregation and Indian Cinema in Durban', in Preben Kaarsholm (ed.), *City Flicks: Indian Cinema and the Urban Experience*, Calcutta: Seagull Books.

Kaur, R. 2002. 'Viewing the West through Bollywood: a Celluloid Occident in the Making', *Contemporary South Asia*, vol. 11, no. 2.

Kaur, R. and A.J. Sinha (eds). 2005. *Bollyworld: Popular Indian Cinema through a Transnational Lens*, New Delhi: Sage.

Larkin, B. 2002. 'Indian Films and Nigerian Lovers: Media and the Creation of Parallel Modernities', in Jonathan Xavier Inda and Renato Rosaldo (eds), *The Anthropology of Globalization: A Reader*, Malden: Blackwell Publishing.

—————. 2003. 'Itineraries of Indian Cinema: African Videos, Bollywood, and Global Media', in Ella Shohat and Robert Stam (eds), *Multiculturalism, Postcoloniality, and Transnational Media*, New Brunswick: Rutgers University Press.

Ministry of Overseas Indian Affairs. 2007. Overview. *Pravasi Bharatiya: Connecting India with its Diaspora*. vol. 2, no. 2 (February), http://www.overseasindian.in/pdf/2007/feb/ENGLISH_PAGES.pdf; accessed March 24, 2007.

Mishra, V. 2002. *Bollywood Cinema: Temples of Desire*, New York: Routledge.

Mistry, J. 2004. 'Beyond Homeland Nostalgia', *The Media*. September.

Pillay, S. 2009. 'SA Show Promoter's Second Bollywood Film Set to Hit Screen', *The Times*, 22 March, http://www.thetimes.co.za/PrintEdition/News/Article.aspx?id=963766;accessed on 31 August.

Pendakur, M. and Subramanyam, R. 1996. 'Indian Cinema beyond National Borders', in J. Sinclair, E. Jacka, and S.C. Cunningham (eds), *New Patterns in Global Television Peripheral Vision*, Oxford: Oxford University Press.

Rajadhyaksha, A. 2003. 'The "Bollywoodization" of the Indian Cinema: Cultural Nationalism in a Global Arena', *Inter-Asia Cultural Studies*, vol. 4, no. 1.

Rajagopalan, S. 2005. 'A Taste for Indian Films: Negotiating Cultural Boundaries in Post-Stalinist Soviet Society', PhD dissertation, Indiana University.

Ram, A. 2002. 'Framing the Feminine: Diasporic Readings of Gender in Popular Indian Cinema', *Women's Studies in Communication*, vol. 25, no. 1.

Thangavelo, D. 2007. 'Word's Out: Hip Hop's Going Bhangra', *IOLTechnology. co.za*, 11 January, http://www.ioltechnology.co.za/article_page.php?iArticleId =3621243; accessed on 31 January 2009.

Tuomi, K. 2005a. 'Micro Economic Development Strategy (MEDS) Western Cape Department of Economic Development and Tourism: Film Sector: Paper One', www.capefilmcommission.co.za/documents/ Western%20Cape%20Report-%20K%20Tuomi.doc.; accessed on December 2006.

————. 2005b. 'Micro Economic Development Strategy (MEDS) Western Cape Department of Economic Development and Tourism: Film Sector: Second Paper, Policy Recommendations and Interventions', http://www. capegateway.gov.za/other/2005/11/final_second_paper_film_printing.pdf; accessed on 21 March 2007.

Lal, P. 2004. 'Bollywood Ain't World Cinema', http://www.greencine.com/ article?action=view&articleID=125; accessed 5 November 2004.

Contributors

ISHTIAQ AHMED was born in Lahore on 24 February 1947. He secured a PhD in Political Science from Stockholm University in 1986, taught at Stockholm University from 1987 to 2007, and was then invited as Senior Research Fellow and Visiting Research Professor by the Institute of South Asian Studies (ISAS), National University of Singapore (NUS) during 2007–10. He is now Professor Emeritus of Political Science, Stockholm University, and Honorary Senior Fellow, ISAS, NUS. He has published extensively on Pakistani and South Asian politics.

BILL ASHCROFT is an Australian Professorial Fellow at the University of New South Wales (UNSW). A founding exponent of postcolonial theory, he is the co-author of *The Empire Writes Back*, the first text to systematically examine the field of postcolonial studies. He is author and co-author of sixteen books, variously translated into five languages, including *Post-colonial Transformation* (Routledge 2001), *On Post-colonial Futures* (Continuum 2001), *Caliban's Voice* (Routledge 2008), and over 150 chapters and papers.

NANDI BHATIA is Professor in the Department of English at the University of Western Ontario (UWO). She works on film, theatre, and literatures of India and the British Empire. She is the author of *Performing Women/Performing Womanhood: Theatre, Politics and Dissent in North India* (OUP 2010) and *Acts of Authority/Acts of Resistance: Theater and Politics in Colonial and Postcolonial India* (University of Michigan Press and OUP 2004). She has also edited a collection of essays titled *Modern Indian Theatre* (OUP 2004) and has co-edited, with Anjali Gera Roy, *Partitioned Lives: Narratives of Home, Displacement and Resettlement* (Pearson-Longman 2008).

VIJAY DEVADAS is Senior Lecturer in the Department of Media, Film and Communication at University of Otago, New Zealand. He is the co-editor of *Cultural Transformations: Perspectives on Translocation in a Global Age* (2010) and the special issue of *Continuum: Journal of Media & Cultural Studies* themed 'Postcolonial and Popular Cultures' (2011). He is co-editor of the international journal *Borderlands* and was recently Visiting Senior Research Fellow at the Asia Research Institute, National University of Singapore (NUS).

HASEENAH EBRAHIM teaches Film and Television Studies in the Wits School of Arts, University of the Witwatersrand, Johannesburg. Her current areas of research and teaching interests includes questions of spectacle and narrative in cinema, ideology, and narrative strategies in children's films, and debates relating to media culture and consumption. Her current research explores the textual and marketing strategies of commercial cinemas, specifically Hollywood, Bollywood, and Nollywood, both globally and in the South African context.

ANURADHA GHOSH teaches in the Department of English at Jamia Millia Islamia (JMI), New Delhi. She completed her doctoral thesis on Indian cinema from Jawaharlal Nehru University (JNU) in 2000. She has several articles and research papers in the area of literature, film and culture studies, literary theory, and criticism, as well as Indian philosophy published in journals of national and international repute. She has a volume of essays, *Imperialism and Counter Strategies*, co-edited with Ravi Kumar and Pratyush Chandra (Aakar Books 2004).

ANDREW HASSAM is Visiting Fellow in the School of English Literatures and Philosophy at the University of Wollongong (UOW). He is currently researching Indian film production in Australia and the use of Bollywood in Australian cultural diplomacy. His most recent writing has appeared in *Food, Culture and Society* (2009) and *Studies in South Asian Film and Media* (2009), and he is editor of *Bollywood in Australia: Transnationalism and Cultural Production* (2010).

TERESA HUBEL is an Associate Professor of English at Huron University College, University of Western Ontario (UWO), Canada. She has written numerous essays on a variety of subjects, most of which have arisen out of her continuing captivation by the literature, dance, film, and history of India. Duke University Press published her book, *Whose India? The Independence Struggle in British and Indian Fiction and History* in 1996. These days she is working on a series of essays on early Indian women writers in English, while also finishing her new book about the white working classes of colonial India.

KAVITA KARAN is an Associate Professor at the School of Journalism at the Southern Illinois University (SIU), Carbondale, Illinois. She has extensively investigated issues related to advertising, women's magazines, political communication, Indian cinema, health communication, new media technologies, and rural communities in Asia. She teaches courses in research methods, marketing, and advertising. She has presented papers at various international conferences and contributed several papers for journals and chapters for books. Her edited and co-edited books include *Cyber Communities in Rural Asia: A Study of Seven Asian Countries, Commercializing Women: Images of Asian Women in the Media*, and *Singapore General Elections 2001: Study of the Media, Politics and Public*.

NICOLA MOONEY is author of *Rural Nostalgias and Transnational Dreams: Identity and Modernity among Jat Sikhs* (University of Toronto Press 2011). Her work broadly concerns ethnicity, urbanization, migration, and what it is to be modern among Jat Sikhs, along with the impacts of the transitions from rural to urban and diasporic life on class, gender, religion, memory, identity, and popular culture. She teaches anthropology in the department of Social, Cultural and Media Studies at the University of the Fraser Valley (UFV), where she is Senior Associate of the Centre for Indo-Canadian Studies.

MADHUJA MUKHERJEE teaches Film Studies at Jadavpur University, India. She is the author of *New Theatres Ltd., The Emblem of Art, The Picture of Success* (NFAI 2009). Recently, she received the Golden Jubilee Fellowship from Film and Television Institute of India (FTII), Pune, to 'write histories of regional cinemas'. Mukherjee has published articles on history of Indian cinema, urban studies, sound cultures, gender, and media. She is a cross-media artist making films, doing graphic essays, and media installations.

MAKARAND PARANJAPE is Professor of English at Jawaharlal Nehru University (JNU), New Delhi. His recent publications include the two monographs, *Altered Destinations: Self, Society, and Nation in*

India (Anthem Press 2009) and *Another Canon: Indian Texts and Traditions in English* (Anthem Press 2009*)*, in addition to two edited volumes, *Indian English and Vernacular India* (Pearson-Longman 2010), co-edited with G.J.V. Prasad, and *Bollywood in Australia: Transnationalism and Culture* (University of Western Australia Press 2010), co-edited with Andrew Hassam.

D. PARTHASARATHY is Professor of Sociology at the Indian Institute of Technology (IIT), Bombay. He has earlier worked at International Crops Research Institute for the Semi-Arid Tropics (ICRISAT), was a Visiting Fellow at the Australian National University (ANU), and a Visiting Senior Research Fellow, Asia Research Institute, National University of Singapore (NUS). He is the author of *Collective Violence in a Provincial City* (OUP 1997), co-editor of *Women's Self-Help Groups: Restructuring Socio-Economic Development* (Dominant Publishers 2011), and has authored articles in journals and edited books in the areas of development, risk and vulnerability, urban studies, and governance.

MEENA T. PILLAI is the Director of Centre for Comparative Literature and Associate Professor at the Institute of English at University of Kerala, Trivandrum. Her publications include *Modern American Fiction: The Novel of Terror* (Creative Books 2005), *Rohinton Mistry: An Anthology of Recent Criticism*, co-edited with Anjali Gera Roy (Pencraft 2007), and an edited volume, *Women in Malayalam Cinema: Naturalising Gender Hierarchies* (Orient Blackswan 2010). Her areas of interest include gender and film studies in which she has published extensively.

M.K. RAGHAVENDRA is a film critic and scholar living in Bangalore, India. He was one of the founder editors of *Deep Focus* and is a winner of the 'National Award for the Best Film Critic—The Swarna Kamal'. He is the author of the critically acclaimed *Seduced by the Familiar: Narration and Meaning in Indian Cinema* (OUP 2008), included by The International Federation of Film Critics (FIPRESCI) in its list of the best books on film (3rd edition).

ZAKIR HOSSAIN RAJU is Associate Professor of Film and Media Studies at Independent University, Bangladesh (IUB). He obtained a PhD in cinema studies from La Trobe University, Melbourne in 2005. Raju taught at Monash University campuses in Malaysia and Australia for five years. He also taught at La Trobe University in Australia and

University of Dhaka in Bangladesh. He served as a Visiting Scholar at Australian National University, Canberra in 1999, and at University of Malaya, Kuala Lumpur, in 2007. His research focuses on media and cultural translation in postcolonial Asia. He is the author of *Bangladesh Cinema and National Identity: In Search of the Modern?* (Routledge, forthcoming). He has published many articles on Asian cinemas in various journals and anthologies.

MANAS RAY is a Fellow in Cultural Studies at the Centre for Studies in Social Sciences (CSSS), Kolkata. He has published on a wide range of areas, including Frankfurt School Marxism, liberalism and critique, postmodernism, New German Cinema, Bollywood, Foucault, governmentality and law, cultural lives of Indian diasporas, post-partition Kolkata, and politics of memory. He has also done ethnographic accounts of ordinary lives. He is working on two anthologies of his essays: *Postcolonial Journeys: Indenture, Diaspora and Indenture and The Caring, Terminating State: Essays on Biopolitics*. He is currently the editor of *Studies in Humanities and Social Sciences*, the journal of Indian Institute of Advanced Study (IIAS), Shimla.

DAVID J. SCHAEFER is Professor and Chair of the Department of Communication Arts at Franciscan University of Steubenville in Ohio, USA. His research and teaching interests include global/intercultural communication, international cinema, media competency/literacy, and Internet-multimedia production, and has published journal articles and book chapters on many of these topics. He serves on the Board of Directors for Urban Mission Ministries. He also served as a Fulbright Scholar (2004–05) and Visiting Senior Research Fellow (2008–09) at the Wee Kim Wee School of Communication and Information, Nanyang Technological University (NTU), Singapore.

GWENDA VANDER STEENE is a PhD candidate at the Department of Comparative Cultural Sciences, Ghent University. She did her fieldwork in Senegal (Dakar) for a total span of one year. Apart from being a researcher, she is also a dancer and teaches Bharata Natyam and Bollywood dance. She has published 'Processes of Cultural Translation as a Post-Colonial Dynamic in Senegalese "Hindu" dances', in John Hawley (ed.), *Africa in India, India in Africa* (Indiana University Press 2007).

Sᴇʟᴠᴀʀᴀᴊ Vᴇʟᴀʏᴜᴛʜᴀᴍ is a Senior Lecturer in the Department of Sociology at Macquarie University, Australia. He is the editor of *Tamil Cinema: The Cultural Politics of India's Other Film Industry* (2008), co-editor of *Dissent and Resistance in Asia's Cities* (2009) and *Everyday Multiculturalism* (2009), and has also published on south Indian migration and transnationalism and the sociology of everyday life.

Index